ADVANCED AND MULTIVARIATE STATISTICAL METHODS FOR SOCIAL SCIENCE RESEARCH

Also Available from Lyceum Books, Inc.

Advisory Editor: Thomas M. Meenaghan, *New York University*

USING STATISTICAL METHODS IN SOCIAL WORK PRACTICE:
A COMPLETE SPSS GUIDE
by Soleman H. Abu-Bader

RESEARCH METHODS FOR SOCIAL WORKERS:
A PRACTICE-BASED APPROACH
by Cynthia A. Faulker and Samuel S. Faulkner

SOCIAL WORK EVALUATION: ENHANCING WHAT WE DO
by James R. Dudley

CLINICAL ASSESSMENT FOR SOCIAL WORKERS:
QUALITATIVE AND QUANTITATIVE METHODS, 3rd Edition
edited by Catheleen Jordan and Cynthia Franklin

COMPLEX SYSTEMS AND HUMAN BEHAVIOR
by Christopher G. Hudson

A PRACTICAL GUIDE TO SOCIAL SERVICE EVALUATION
by Carl F. Brun

ESSENTIAL SKILLS OF SOCIAL WORK PRACTICE
by Thomas O'Hare

PRACTICAL TIPS FOR PUBLISHING SCHOLARLY ARTICLES:
WRITING AND PUBLISHING IN THE HELPING PROFESSIONS
by Rich Furman

TOWARD EVIDENCE-BASED PRACTICE: VARIATIONS ON A THEME
by Joel Fischer

ADVANCED AND MULTIVARIATE STATISTICAL METHODS FOR SOCIAL SCIENCE RESEARCH WITH A COMPLETE SPSS GUIDE

Soleman Hassan Abu-Bader
Howard University

LYCEUM
BOOKS, INC.

Chicago, Illinois

© 2010 by Lyceum Books, Inc.

Published by

LYCEUM BOOKS, INC.
5758 S. Blackstone Avenue
Chicago, Illinois 60637
773-643-1903 fax
773-643-1902 phone
lyceum@lyceumbooks.com
www.lyceumbooks.com

6 5 4 3 2 1   10 11 12 13

ISBN 978-1-933478-82-1

Printed in the United States of America.

Library of Congress Cataloging-in-Publication Data

Abu-Bader, Soleman H., 1965–
  Advanced and multivariate statistical methods for social science research
with a complete SPSS guide / Soleman H. Abu-Bader.
     p. cm.
  Includes bibliographical references and index.
  ISBN 978-1-933478-82-1 (pbk. : alk. paper)
  1. Social sciences—Statistical methods. 2. SPSS (Computer file) I. Title.
II. Title: Advanced and multivariate statistical methods for social science
research.
  HA29.A29   2010
  519.5—dc22
                                                              2009040076

Contents

Preface

Since I began teaching advanced statistical courses for social science graduate students four years ago, I have searched for a simple step-by-step advanced statistical textbook that teaches students not only the different advanced statistical techniques but also when to apply them, how to run them, and how to read and report their results. My search, however, produced no results, which encouraged me to write this book.

In addition, the encouragement of numerous graduate students and social science research faculty who have utilized my previous book, *Using Statistical Methods in Social Work Practice: A Complete SPSS Guide*, also inspired me to write a similar textbook on advanced and multivariate statistics that integrates both theory and practice and provides real examples. *Advanced and Multivariate Statistical Methods for Social Science Research* is the result of my teaching experience, the success of the first book, the encouragement of many students and faculty, and my confidence that there is a need for such a book.

I am aware that there are many great statistical textbooks on advanced and multivariate techniques that social science research faculty and students may utilize. However, most of these books are written from a mathematical perspective and focus on various mathematical formulas. Some present only theoretical background, and some use only hypothetical examples to illustrate the techniques. Moreover, users of these books often acquire additional books to guide them on the utilization of SPSS or other computer programs to compute the statistical tests.

Unlike those textbooks, *Advanced and Multivariate Statistical Methods for Social Science Research* integrates both theory and practice in one simple step-by-step book. It uses real social science examples and data files and describes in detail the utilization of the SPSS program in conducting the analysis. Furthermore, it fully explains how to read the SPSS output and how to write and present the results in academic tables and graphs. Most of all, it stays away from mathematical formulas, especially complex ones, and thus reduces students' anxiety about statistics.

This book is written as a primary textbook for social and health science graduate students who enroll in advanced and/or multivariate statistics courses. It can also be used as a guidebook for graduate students as well as research faculty conducting advanced and multivariate statistics and writing the results for their theses, dissertations, or peer-reviewed research publications.

The book has ten chapters, each with two main parts. The first part discusses the purpose, theoretical background, and assumptions underlying each advanced or multivariate statistical technique and defines main terms and statistics associated with each test. The second part presents practical examples using real social science data and details the step-by-step methods for examining research questions and hypotheses under study. It explains how to select the appropriate statistical techniques, examine their assumptions, conduct the analyses, and interpret and write the results. In addition, each chapter includes a step-by-step guide to using SPSS to compute the statistics.

DATA FILES

This book uses the Statistical Package for the Social Sciences (SPSS) for Windows, Version 18.0 to evaluate, summarize, and run the analyses for each statistical test. The book describes the step-by-step use of SPSS 18.0 to compute each analysis, and fortunately these steps are the same in previous SPSS versions, especially 17.0 and 16.0. In addition, the book describes in detail all SPSS syntax files for each analysis, so these analyses still can be generated using earlier SPSS versions that may have different menus.

Moreover, although this book uses SPSS as the primary computer software to conduct the analyses, users of other statistical computer software, such as SAS or Stata, can also greatly benefit from the book, as it integrates the theory and the application for each test statistic, uses real social science data files and examples, and discusses in detail how to interpret, write, and present the results of each test statistic.

This book utilizes six data files to demonstrate the use of advanced and multivariate statistical techniques. These files include Anxiety (N = 50), Health Control (N = 60), Job Satisfaction (N = 218), Mental Health (N = 155), PTSD (N = 230), and Well-Being (N = 182). These files are available in SPSS, Excel, and SAS v9+ Windows files and can be downloaded from www.lyceumbooks.com (see appendix for detailed descriptions of the files).

Finally, we hope you find this book helpful and that it meets your statistical needs. We welcome your feedback and suggestions so that we can incorporate them in and improve our future edition.

ACKNOWLEDGMENTS

I would like to thank the faculty of Howard University School of Social Work for their support and encouragement. I am especially grateful to Dr. Sandra Edmonds Crewe, Dr. Fariyal Ross-Sheriff, Dr. Jacqueline Smith, and Dr. Cudore L. Snell for their tremendous support, review of the book, and feedback. I also would like to thank my graduate assistant, Heather Edwards, and my doctoral students for their assistance with the review of literature, checking the SPSS screens, and editing the manuscript.

I would like to extend my special thanks to the reviewers, Thomas O'Hare of Boston College and John McNutt of the University of Delaware, whose feedback was helpful in improving the quality of the book. My special thank-you also goes to copy editor Jess Biscamp, whose in-depth edit helped fine-tune the book.

Lastly, I am profoundly thankful to my wife, children, and family abroad for their unconditional love and support. This book is done because of them.

CHAPTER 1

Review of Bivariate Statistical Tests

LEARNING OBJECTIVES

1. Understand the process of selecting a statistical test
2. Understand the purpose and assumptions of parametric bivariate tests
3. Understand the purpose and use of Pearson's correlation coefficient
4. Understand the purpose and use of the Student's *t*-tests (independent *t*-test and dependent *t*-test)
5. Understand the purpose and use of the one-way analysis of variance
6. Understand the purpose and use of the chi-square test of association

DATA SETS (APPENDIX)

Anxiety

Well-Being

INTRODUCTION

If you have been assigned this textbook, you probably already completed basic statistics courses. In those courses you likely learned about descriptive statistics, including data organization, graphs (bar graphs, pie charts, histograms, box-plots, stem-and-leaf plots, etc.), measures of central tendency (mean, median, and mode), and measures of variability (range, variance, standard deviation, and quartiles). It is also very likely that you learned some inferential statistical tests (Pearson's product-moment correlation coefficient, Student's *t*-tests, one-way analysis of variance, chi-square test of association, etc.) for testing the relationship between two variables, the independent and dependent variables.

As you may recall, these and other inferential statistics are divided into two groups, parametric and nonparametric tests. Because these tests are essential in the forthcoming chapters, it will be beneficial to briefly review their purpose and assumptions.[1]

---

[1]For a comprehensive discussion of these tests, see Abu-Bader (2006).

PARAMETRIC AND NONPARAMETRIC TESTS

The main purpose of any quantitative research study is to examine whether there are statistically significant relationships between constructs and whether these relationships can be generalized to the population from which the sample was drawn. In other words, a researcher's aim is to find out if there is statistical evidence to reject the null hypothesis and, in turn, support the alternative hypothesis.

However, in order for researchers to reach a conclusion, they must first decide which statistical test is most appropriate to analyze the data. This decision is a critical one, because choosing an inappropriate statistical test may result in making a false decision, an inaccurate interpretation, and an incorrect conclusion of the research findings. Therefore, careful data inspection and evaluation to ensure that certain conditions are met (e.g., normality of distributions) must precede any hypothesis testing.

Once data evaluation is completed, the next step is to decide which test(s) are most suitable to analyze the data. Researchers may choose from a large number of statistical tests. However, the purpose of the study and the type and size of the data to be analyzed have a great influence on the number of tests the researcher may have to choose from. These tests are grouped into two sets, *parametric* and *nonparametric* tests.

Factors Influencing Selection of a Statistical Test

There are four main factors that greatly influence selecting the appropriate test(s) to be utilized in examining the null hypotheses: (1) sampling methods, (2) levels of measurement, (3) normality of distributions, and (4) sample size.

Sampling methods.   Although each statistical test has one or more of its own assumptions or requirements, all parametric and nonparametric tests alike require that the data are collected from a *representative sample;* that is, the characteristics of the sample (gender, age, race, marital status, etc.) are similar to those of the population to which generalization of the results will be made. Generally, probability sampling methods (e.g., random samples) satisfy this assumption.

Levels of measurement.   To utilize parametric tests, the dependent variable must be continuous data and should be measured at the interval or ratio levels of measurement. However, parametric tests could be utilized to analyze ordinal dependent variables given that other assumptions, especially normality of distribution, are met.

Normality of distributions.   Parametric tests require that the shape of the distribution of the dependent variable approach the shape of a normal curve. In other words, the distribution should not be severely skewed. If severe skewness is evident, a transformation of the variable raw scores should be considered.

Sample size. Finally, the sample size should be large enough to select a parametric test. As you may recall from your basic statistics courses, the larger the sample size is, the smaller the standard error of the mean. Also, with a large sample size, the *central limit theorem* ensures that the distribution of the means approximates a normal distribution, which is an assumption for parametric tests. Ideally, a sample size of 30 subjects or more is sufficient for most bivariate parametric tests.

When one or more of these assumptions is violated, nonparametric tests, also known as *distribution-free tests,* can be used. In other words, nonparametric tests are appropriate when the dependent variables are measured at the ordinal or nominal levels of measurement, when the distribution of the dependent variables is severely skewed (free distribution), and/or when smaller sample sizes are used.

Although most bivariate parametric tests have their own corresponding, or alternative, nonparametric tests, parametric tests are more powerful than their alternative nonparametric tests. This is the case because parametric tests give a better chance of detecting significant results when, in fact, they exist. Thus if data violate, for example, the assumption of normality, it is highly recommended that a data transformation (e.g., transforming raw score into square root, log, or other functions) be conducted. This transformation will likely produce a normal distribution. However, if departure from normality cannot be adjusted, it is recommended that both parametric and nonparametric tests be conducted. If the results of both tests are consistent, report the results of the parametric test.

Table 1.1 summarizes a number of parametric tests, their alternative nonparametric tests, and their assumptions.

Table 1.1:   Bivariate Parametric and Nonparametric Tests

Test	Type[a]	Observation	Distribution	IV[b]	DV[c]	N	Symbol
Pearson	Par	Paired	Normal	Interval+	Interval+	30+	r
Spearman	Nonpar	Paired	Free	Ordinal+	Ordinal+	>30	ρ
Indep. *t*-test	Par	Paired	Normal	2 groups	Interval+	30+	t
MWU[d]	Nonpar	Paired	Free	2 groups	Ordinal+	>30	z
Dep. *t*-test	Par	Repeated	Normal	Interval+	Interval+	30+	t
Wilcoxon	Nonpar	Repeated	Free	Ordinal+	Ordinal+	>30	Z
ANOVA	Par	Paired	Normal	3+ groups	Interval+	30+	F
KWH[e]	Nonpar	Paired	Free	3+ groups	Ordinal+	>30	χ^2
Chi-square	Nonpar	Paired	N/A	2+ groups	2+ groups	20+	χ^2

[a]Par = parametric; Nonpar = nonparametric

[b]IV = independent variable

[c]DV = dependent variable

[d]MWU = Mann-Whitney *U* test

[e]KWH = Kruskal-Wallis *H* test

1. When both the independent and dependent variables are interval or higher and both are paired observation (measured at the same time), the Pearson *r* correlation may be used. If the dependent variable is ordinal, then the Spearman *rho* may be used.

2. When the independent variable is nominal with two groups (e.g., gender: male and female) and the dependent variable is interval or ratio, the independent *t*-test may be used. However, if the dependent variable is ordinal, then the alternative nonparametric Mann-Whitney *U* test may be used.

3. When the independent variable is nominal with three groups or more (e.g., race: Caucasians, African Americans, Native Americans, Hispanics, and others) and the dependent variable is interval or ratio, the one-way analysis of variance (one-way ANOVA) may be used. If the dependent variable is ordinal, then the alternative nonparametric Kruskal-Wallis *H* test may be used.

4. When both the independent and dependent variables are interval or higher and one is a repeated measure of the other (pretest and posttest), the dependent *t*-test may be used. If one or both variables are ordinal, then the Wilcoxon sign test may be used.

5. When both the independent and dependent variables are measured at the nominal level of measurement, the nonparametric chi-square test may be used. This test does not have a corresponding parametric test.

PEARSON'S PRODUCT-MOMENT CORRELATION COEFFICIENT

The purpose of Pearson's product-moment correlation coefficient, simply known as Pearson's *r* correlation or simple correlation, is to examine the strength and direction of a linear relationship between two continuous variables (independent and dependent). In other words, it examines whether an increase in the independent variable leads to a significant increase or decrease in the dependent variable. For example, Pearson's *r* correlation may be utilized to examine whether a decrease in an individual's physical health leads to an increase in his or her levels of depression.

Pearson's *r* correlation is a parametric test. Thus it requires that the parametric assumptions (representative sample, continuous and normally distributed dependent variable, and sample size of 30 subjects or more) are met. In addition, it requires that data for both dependent and independent variables are paired observations (collected simultaneously). Furthermore, it requires that the independent variable is continuous data, usually interval or higher, and is normally distributed.

Spearman's Rank Test

When data violate one or more of the assumptions of the Pearson's *r* correlation, the *nonparametric Spearman's rank correlation coefficient test,* simply called

Spearman's *rho,* can be utilized to test the relationship between the two variables. Whereas Pearson's correlation uses the raw scores of both variables to compute the correlation coefficient (*r*), the Spearman's *rho* uses the ranks to compute the correlation coefficient (ρ, read *rho*).

Both correlation coefficients (*r*, ρ) range between "−1" (perfect negative correlation) and "+1" (perfect positive correlation) and are interpreted in the same way. Squaring the correlation coefficient (*r*, ρ) produces the coefficient of determination, which refers to the percentage of the variance in the dependent variable that is due to the independent variable. Finally, the correlation between two variables is considered strong if the coefficient of determination is greater than or equal to .64, moderate if it is greater than .25 and less than .64, and weak if it is less than or equal to .25.

Example of Simple Correlation Analysis (Data File: Well-Being)

RESEARCH QUESTION: Is there a significant correlation between levels of self-perception of physical appearance and levels of depression among college students?

RESEARCH HYPOTHESIS: There is a significant negative correlation between levels of self-perception of physical appearance and levels of depression among college students.

In this example, the two variables are Self-Perception (independent variable) and Depression (dependent variable). Both are continuous data and are interval level of measurement.

Pearson's Correlation SPSS Syntax[1]

CORRELATIONS
/VARIABLES=Depression SelfPerception
/PRINT=ONETAIL NOSIG
/MISSING=PAIRWISE.

Spearman's *rho* Correlation SPSS Syntax

NONPAR CORR
/VARIABLES=Depression SelfPerception
/PRINT=SPEARMAN ONETAIL NOSIG
/MISSING=PAIRWISE.

---

[1]For more detail on how to use SPSS and run analyses, see Abu-Bader (2006).

Analysis: SPSS output.   Table 1.2 presents the results of Pearson's *r* correlation, and table 1.3 presents the results of Spearman's *rho* correlation.

The results of Pearson's *r* correlation show that there is a significant negative correlation between self-perception and depression ($r = -.426, p < .05$). Similarly, the results of Spearman's *rho* correlation show that there is a significant

Table 1.2:   SPSS Pearson's *r* Correlation Output

Correlations - Pearson's r Correlation

		Depression	Self Perception
Depression	Pearson Correlation	1	-.426**
	Sig. (1-tailed)		.000
	N	182	182
SelfPerception	Pearson Correlation	**-.426***	1
	Sig. (1-tailed)	.000	
	N	182	182

** Correlation is significant at the 0.01 level (1-tailed).

Table 1.3:   SPSS Spearman's *rho* Correlation Output

Correlations - Spearman rho Correlation

			Depression	Self Perception
Spearman's rho	Depression	Correlation Coefficient	1.000	-.410**
		Sig. (1-tailed)	.	.000
		N	182	182
	SelfPerception	Correlation Coefficient	**-.410***	1.000
		Sig. (1-tailed)	.000	.
		N	182	182

** Correlation is significant at the 0.01 level (1-tailed).

negative correlation between the two variables ($\rho = -.41, p < .05$). Thus the null hypothesis is rejected.

Recommendation: when both tests have similar results, report the results of the parametric test, in this case the results of Pearson's *r* correlation.

INDEPENDENT *t*-TEST

The purpose of the independent *t*-test, also known as *independent samples* t-test, is to examine the difference between two independent groups (independent variable) on one continuous variable (dependent variable) and determine whether this difference is statistically significant. For example, the independent *t*-test may be utilized to examine whether a significant difference exists between Democrat and Republican voters on their attitudes toward abortion. Here the two groups are Democrat and Republican voters, and the continuous variable is Attitudes toward Abortion.

Like Pearson's *r* correlation, the independent *t*-test is a parametric test and therefore requires that the parametric assumptions are met. Also, it requires that data for both dependent and independent variables are paired observations. However, unlike Pearson's *r* correlation, the independent *t*-test requires that the independent variable is measured at the nominal level of measurement and has only two groups (dichotomous). Furthermore, the independent *t*-test requires that variances of both groups on the dependent variable are equal (also known as the assumption of homogeneity of variances).

Mann-Whitney *U* Test

When data violate one or more of these assumptions, the *nonparametric Mann-Whitney* U *test,* can be utilized to examine the difference between the two groups on the dependent variable.

The independent *t*-test utilizes the raw score to compute the mean for each group on the dependent variable and then computes the test statistic *t*. This statistic measures how far apart the means are in standard error units. On the other hand, Mann-Whitney *U* ranks the scores for each group, computes the mean rank, and then computes the test statistic *z* (also known as *z* score).

Example of Two Independent Group Comparison (Data File: Well-Being)

RESEARCH QUESTION: Is there a significant difference between male and female college students with regard to their levels of self-esteem?

RESEARCH HYPOTHESIS: Female college students will have significantly higher levels of self-esteem than male college students.

In this example, the two variables are Gender (independent variable) and Self-Esteem (dependent variable). Gender is a categorical dichotomous variable (nominal level of measurement), and self-esteem is continuous data measured at the interval level of measurement.

Independent *t*-Test SPSS Syntax

```
T-TEST GROUPS=Gender(0 1)
/MISSING=ANALYSIS
/VARIABLES=SelfEsteem
/CRITERIA=CI(.9500).
```

Mann-Whitney *U* Test SPSS Syntax

```
NPAR TESTS
/M-W= SelfEsteem BY Gender(0 1)
/MISSING ANALYSIS.
```

Analysis: SPSS output.   Tables 1.4.A and 1.4.B present the results of the independent *t*-test, and tables 1.5.A and 1.5.B present the results of the Mann-Whitney *U* test.

Table 1.4.A: SPSS Independent *t*-Test Output—Group Statistics

Group Statistics

	Gender	N	Mean	Std. Deviation	Std. Error Mean
SelfEsteem	0 MALE	78	**31.282**	3.7759	.4275
	1 FEMALE	104	**32.452**	3.3901	.3324

Table 1.4.B: SPSS Independent *t*-Test Output—Independent Samples Test

Independent Samples Test

		Levene's Test for Equality of Variances		t-test for Equality of Means						95% Confidence Interval of the Difference	
		F	Sig.	t	df	Sig. (2-tailed)	Mean Difference	Std. Error Difference		Lower	Upper
SelfEsteem	Equal variances assumed	.852	.357	**-2.19**	**180**	**.030**	-1.1699	.5333		-2.222	-.1176
	Equal variances not assumed			-2.160	155.7	.032	-1.1699	.5416		-2.240	-.1001

The results of the independent *t*-test show a significant difference between male and female college students with regard to their levels of self-esteem (table 1.4.B: $t = -2.19$, $df = 180$, $p < .05$). Female students reported significantly higher levels of self-esteem than male students (table 1.4.A: mean = 32.45, mean = 31.28, respectively).

Table 1.5.A: SPSS Mann-Whitney *U* Output—Ranks Statistics

Ranks

	Gender	N	Mean Rank	Sum of Ranks
SelfEsteem	0 MALE	78	**81.99**	6395.00
	1 FEMALE	104	**98.63**	10258.00
	Total	182		

Table 1.5.B: SPSS Mann-Whitney *U* Output—Test Statistics

Test Statistics[a]

	SelfEsteem
Mann-Whitney U	3314.000
Wilcoxon W	6395.000
Z	**-2.118**
Asymp. Sig. (2-tailed)	**.034**

[a.] Grouping Variable: Gender

The results of the Mann-Whitney U nonparametric test show a significant difference between male and female college students with regard to their levels of self-esteem (table 1.5.B: $z = -2.12, p < .05$). Female students reported significantly higher levels of self-esteem than male students (table 1.5.A: mean rank = 98.63, mean rank = 81.99, respectively).

DEPENDENT *t*-TEST

The purpose of the dependent *t*-test, also known as *paired-samples* t-*test,* is to compare the difference between the mean scores of two repeated measures, two related topics of the same sample, or subjects under two different conditions. For example, the dependent *t*-test may be utilized to examine whether levels of self-esteem among sexually abused women significantly increase after they participate in a ten-week psychological intervention targeting their damaged self-esteem. Also, the dependent *t*-test would assist in analyzing whether a significant difference exists between English proficiency in reading and writing among a group of immigrants seeking social services benefits in one U.S. county.

Like the Pearson's *r* correlation, the dependent *t*-test is a parametric test, and therefore it follows the same assumptions of the parametric test (representative sample, continuous and normally distributed dependent variable, and sample size of 30 subjects or more). Unlike the Pearson's *r* correlation, the dependent *t*-test requires that both measures (pre and post) are repeated measures (not paired observation) or related variables measured at the same range of scores. Finally, the dependent *t*-test requires that data for both measures are continuous, usually interval or higher, and are normally distributed.

Wilcoxon Signed Ranks Test

When data violate one or more of these assumptions, the *nonparametric* Wilcoxon signed ranks test can be utilized to test the differences between the two measures. Similar to the Spearman's *rho* test, the Wilcoxon test uses the ranks of the two measures to compute the test statistic (z).

Example of Dependent *t*-Test Analysis (Data File: Anxiety)

RESEARCH QUESTION: Is there a significant decrease in the levels of anxiety among women exposed to interpersonal violence after they completed psychological therapy?

RESEARCH HYPOTHESIS: There is a significant decrease in the levels of anxiety among women exposed to interpersonal violence after they completed the therapy.

In this example, anxiety is measured twice, once before and once after intervention. Scores at both times are continuous data and are measured at the interval level.

Dependent *t*-Test SPSS Syntax

T-TEST PAIRS=Anxiety_Pre WITH Anxiety_Post (PAIRED)
/CRITERIA=CI(.9500)
/MISSING=ANALYSIS.

Wilcoxon Signed Ranks Test SPSS Syntax

NPAR TEST
/WILCOXON=Anxiety_Pre WITH Anxiety_Post (PAIRED)
/MISSING ANALYSIS.

Analysis: SPSS output.   Tables 1.6.A and 1.6.B present the results of the dependent *t*-test, and tables 1.7.A and 1.7.B present the results of the Wilcoxon signed ranks test.

Table 1.6.A: SPSS Dependent *t*-Test Output—Paired Samples Statistics

Paired Samples Statistics

		Mean	N	Std. Deviation	Std. Error Mean
Pair 1	Anxiety_Pre	78.86	50	11.763	1.664
	Anxiety_Post	72.36	50	9.542	1.349

Table 1.6.B: SPSS Dependent *t*-Test Output—Paired Samples Test

Paired Samples Test

		Paired Differences							
		Mean	Std. Deviation	Std. Error Mean	95% Confidence Interval of the Difference Lower	95% Confidence Interval of the Difference Upper	t	df	Sig. (2-tailed)
Pair 1	Anxiety_Pre - Anxiety_Post	6.50	7.223	1.022	4.447	8.553	6.4	49	.000

Table 1.7.A: SPSS Wilcoxon Signed Ranks Test—Ranks

Ranks

		N	Mean Rank	Sum of Ranks
Anxiety_Post - Anxiety_Pre	Negative Ranks	40[a]	24.85	994.00
	Positive Ranks	6[b]	14.50	87.00
	Ties	4[c]		
	Total	50		

[a.] Anxiety_Post < Anxiety_Pre

[b.] Anxiety_Post > Anxiety_Pre

[c.] Anxiety_Post = Anxiety_Pre

Table 1.7.B: SPSS Wilcoxon Signed Ranks Test—Test Statistics

Test Statistics[b]

	Anxiety_Post - Anxiety_Pre
Z	**-4.959**[a]
Asymp. Sig. (2-tailed)	**.000**

[a] Based on positive ranks.

[b] Wilcoxon Signed Ranks Test

The results of the dependent t-test show a significant change between pretest and posttest levels of anxiety (table 1.6.B: $t = 6.4$, $df = 49$, $p < .001$). Participants involved in the therapy program decreased their anxiety scores from 78.86 to 72.36 (see table 1.6.A). On average, participants decreased their levels of anxiety by 6.50 points on the scale that was utilized (see table 1.6.B). The results of the Wilcoxon signed ranks test confirm the results of the dependent t-test (table 1.7.B: $z = -4.96$, $p < .001$).

ONE-WAY ANALYSIS OF VARIANCE

Like the independent t-test, the purpose of the one-way analysis of variance, simply known as one-way ANOVA or ANOVA, is to examine the difference between groups with regard to one continuous dependent variable. In fact, one-way ANOVA is an extension of the independent t-test. It allows researchers to examine the mean differences among two or more independent groups (independent variable) and determine whether these differences are statistically significant.

For example, one-way ANOVA may be utilized to examine whether significant differences exist between social work, psychology, sociology, and nursing students on their final grades in statistics. Here there are four major groups (social work, psychology, sociology, and nursing students), and the continuous variable is Final Statistics Grades.

Because the one-way ANOVA is an extension of the independent t-test, it requires the same assumptions as the independent t-test. These assumptions include the main parametric assumptions (representative sample, continuous dependent variable, normal distribution, and sufficient sample size, i.e., $N \geq 30$). The assumptions also include paired observations, categorical independent variable (nominal level of measurement), and homogeneity of variances (also known as equality of variances). The only difference is that the independent variable in ANOVA can have any number of groups (recall that the independent t-test is limited to only two groups).

Kruskal-Wallis H Test

When data violate one or more of these assumptions, the *nonparametric Kruskal-Wallis* H *test* can be utilized to examine the difference between the groups with regard to the dependent variable.

Similar to the independent t-test, one-way ANOVA uses the raw score to compute the mean for all groups with regard to the dependent variable and then computes the test statistic F to measure how far apart these means are in standard error units (mathematically, $F = t^2$). On the other hand, the Kruskal-Wallis H test, like the Mann-Whitney U, ranks the scores for all groups, computes the mean rank, and then computes the test statistic, chi-square (χ^2).

Post Hoc Tests

Unlike the independent t-test and the Mann-Whitney U test, the one-way ANOVA and Kruskal-Wallis H test examine whether there is an overall significant difference between the groups with regard to the dependent variable. It does not examine what specific groups are different. Thus when significant results are detected, post hoc tests must be conducted to examine where the difference exists.

Post hoc tests statistically compare each pair of groups separately on the dependent variable. There are a large number of post hoc tests that can be calculated by SPSS. Some are used when the assumption of homogeneity of variances (equality of variances) is met, and others are used when the assumption is violated. The four most frequently reported post hoc tests when *equality of variances is assumed* include the *LSD* (least significant difference), *Bonferroni* (also known as *Bonferroni correction*), *Scheffe,* and *Tukey.* The *Tamhane's T2* is another post hoc test that is based on the independent t-test; however, it is most appropriate when *equality of variances is not assumed.*

Example of Multiple Independent Group Comparisons (Data File: Well-Being)

RESEARCH QUESTION: Are there significant life satisfaction differences based on college students' marital status (single, married, and other)?

RESEARCH HYPOTHESIS: There are significant life satisfaction differences based on college students' marital status.

In this example, the two variables are Marital Status (independent variable) and Life Satisfaction (dependent variable). Marital Status is a categorical variable (nominal level of measurement with three groups), and Life Satisfaction is continuous data measured at the interval level.

Analysis: SPSS output.   Tables 1.8.A, 1.8.B, 1.8.C, and 1.8.D present the results of the one-way ANOVA, and tables 1.9.A, 1.9.B, and 1.9.C present the results of the Kruskal-Wallis H test.

The results of the test of homogeneity of variances (see table 1.8.B) indicate that the variances of the three groups on life satisfaction are not significantly different ($p > .05$). In other words, the assumption of homogeneity (equality) of variances is met.

One-Way ANOVA SPSS Syntax

ONEWAY LifeSatisfaction BY MaritalStatus
/STATISTICS DESCRIPTIVES HOMOGENEITY
/MISSING ANALYSIS
/POSTHOC=BONFERRONI ALPHA(0.05).

Kruskal-Wallis H Test SPSS Syntax

NPAR TESTS
/K-W=LifeSatisfaction BY MaritalStatus(1 3)
/STATISTICS DESCRIPTIVES
/MISSING ANALYSIS.

Table 1.8.A: SPSS One-Way ANOVA Output—Descriptives

Descriptives

LifeSatisfaction

	N	Mean	Std. Deviation	Std. Error	95% Confidence Interval for Mean		Minimum	Maximum
					Lower Bound	Upper Bound		
1 SINGLE	127	**25.96**	4.988	.443	25.08	26.84	12	35
2 MARRIED	31	**27.77**	4.695	.843	26.05	29.50	15	35
3 OTHERS	24	**22.83**	6.625	1.352	20.04	25.63	8	31
Total	182	25.86	5.329	.395	25.08	26.64	8	35

Table 1.8.B: SPSS One-Way ANOVA Output—Test of Homogeneity of Variances

Test of Homogeneity of Variances

LifeSatisfaction

Levene Statistic	df1	df2	Sig.
2.522	2	179	**.083**

Table 1.8.C: SPSS One-Way ANOVA Output—ANOVA

ANOVA

LifeSatisfaction

	Sum of Squares	df	Mean Square	F	Sig.
Between Groups	334.730	**2**	167.365	**6.234**	**.002**
Within Groups	4805.556	**179**	26.847		
Total	5140.286	181			

Table 1.8.D: SPSS One-Way ANOVA Output—Post Hoc Test

Multiple Comparisons

Dependent Variable: LifeSatisfaction
Bonferroni

(I) MaritalStatus	(J) MaritalStatus	Mean Difference (I-J)	Std. Error	Sig.	95% Confidence Interval	
					Lower Bound	Upper Bound
1 SINGLE	2 MARRIED	-1.814	1.038	.247	-4.32	.69
	3 OTHERS	3.127*	1.153	**.022**	.34	5.91
2 MARRIED	1 SINGLE	1.814	1.038	.247	-.69	4.32
	3 OTHERS	4.941*	1.409	**.002**	1.54	8.35
3 OTHERS	1 SINGLE	-3.127*	1.153	.022	-5.91	-.34
	2 MARRIED	-4.941*	1.409	.002	-8.35	-1.54

*. The mean difference is significant at the .05 level.

The results of the one-way ANOVA show an overall significant difference between the three marital statuses with regard to their life satisfaction (table 1.8.C: $F = 6.23$; $df = 2$, 179; $p < .05$).

The results of the post hoc Bonferroni (see table 1.8.D) show significant life satisfaction differences between students who have other marital status and single students ($p = .022$ or $p < .05$). These results also show significant life satisfaction differences between students with other marital status and married students ($p = .002$ or $p < .05$). Students with other marital status reported the lowest levels of life satisfaction (table 1.8.A: mean = 22.83), followed by singles (mean = 25.96) and married students (mean = 27.77).

The results of the Kruskal-Wallis H nonparametric test show significant life satisfaction differences based on students' marital status (table 1.9.B: $\chi^2 = 8.899$, $df = 2$, $p < .05$).

The results of the post hoc Tamhane's T2 test (see table 1.9.C) show a significant life satisfaction difference between married students and students with other marital status ($p = .011$ or $p < .05$). Married students reported greater life satisfaction than those who self-identified as other in their marital status (table 1.9.A: mean rank = 110.81 and 68.25, respectively).

Table 1.9.A: SPSS Kruskal-Wallis H Test Output—Ranks

Ranks

	MaritalStatus	N	Mean Rank
LifeSatisfaction	1 SINGLE	127	91.18
	2 MARRIED	31	**110.81**
	3 OTHERS	24	**68.25**
	Total	182	

Table 1.9.B: SPSS Kruskal-Wallis H Test Output—Test Statistics

Test Statistics[a,b]

	Life Satisfaction
Chi-Square	**8.899**
df	**2**
Asymp. Sig.	**.012**

[a.] Kruskal Wallis Test

[b.] Grouping Variable: MaritalStatus

Table 1.9.C: SPSS Post Hoc Output—Tamhane's T2

Multiple Comparisons

Dependent Variable: LifeSatisfaction

Tamhane

(I) MaritalStatus	(J) MaritalStatus	Mean Difference (I-J)	Std. Error	Sig.	95% Confidence Interval Lower Bound	Upper Bound
1 SINGLE	2 MARRIED	-1.814	.952	.177	-4.17	.54
	3 OTHERS	3.127	1.423	**.105**	-.48	6.74
2 MARRIED	1 SINGLE	1.814	.952	.177	-.54	4.17
	3 OTHERS	4.941*	1.594	**.011**	.97	8.91
3 OTHERS	1 SINGLE	-3.127	1.423	.105	-6.74	.48
	2 MARRIED	-4.941*	1.594	.011	-8.91	-.97

*. The mean difference is significant at the .05 level.

However, unlike the results of the post hoc Bonferroni test (used when equality of variances is assumed), the Tamhane's T2 test shows no significant life satisfaction difference between single students and other students (p = .105 or p > .05). Keep in mind that this test is most suitable when the assumption of homogeneity of variances is not met (it is met in this example).

CHI-SQUARE TEST OF ASSOCIATION

Unlike the previous bivariate tests, the chi-square test of association, also known as *chi-square goodness-of-fit test,* is a nonparametric test and has no alternative parametric counterpart. It is used to examine the association between two categorical (nominal) variables. In other words, it examines whether the observed frequencies obtained from a sample are similar to those frequencies expected in the population, or how well the observed data *fit* the population. For example, the chi-square test may be utilized to examine if race affects individuals' political party affiliation (Democrat, Republican, Independent, others).

Because the chi-square test is a nonparametric test, it does not follow the same assumptions of the parametric test (mainly continuous data and normal distribution). On the other hand, it still requires that data are obtained from a representative sample. Both variables to be analyzed must be categorical variables (nominal level of measurement) with two or more groups. In addition, chi-square requires that no more than 20 percent of the joint cells have expected frequencies of less than five subjects. However, if both variables are dichotomous (each has two groups, that is, a 2x2 table), all cells must have five cases or more.

Measures of *Phi* and Cramer's *V*

Similar to the Pearson's *r* correlation, chi-square test produces symmetric measures that are interpreted in the same way as the correlation coefficient (*r*). They are *phi* and Cramer's *V*. The only difference between these two coefficients is that the *phi* is used when the two variables are dichotomous. Cramer's *V* is used with all other categorical variables. Squaring these coefficients is interpreted in the same way as the coefficient of determination (r^2), the proportion (%) of variance in the dependent variable that is accounted for by the independent variable.

Example of Chi-Square Analysis (Data File: Well-Being)

RESEARCH QUESTION: Is there a significant association between students' gender and their body mass index?

RESEARCH HYPOTHESIS: There is a significant association between students' gender and their body mass index.

The two variables under analysis in this example are Gender (male and female) and Body Mass Index (normal weight, overweight, and obese). Both variables are categorical and measured at the nominal level of measurement.

Chi-Square/Crosstabs Test SPSS Syntax

```
CROSSTABS
/TABLES=Gender BY Weight
/FORMAT=AVALUE TABLES
/STATISTICS=CHISQ PHI
/CELLS=COUNT EXPECTED TOTAL SRESID
/COUNT ROUND CELL.
```

Analysis: SPSS output.   Tables 1.10.A, 1.10.B, and 1.10.C present the results of the chi-square test of association.

The results of the chi-square test show a significant association between students' gender and their weight (table 1.10.B: chi-square = 13.64, *df* = 2, *p* <

Table 1.10.A: SPSS Chi-Square Output—Cross-Tabulation

Gender * Weight Crosstabulation

			Weight			
			Normal weight	Over weight	Obese	Total
MALE	Count		**28**	**37**	13	78
	Expected Count		**39.9**	**26.6**	11.6	78.0
	% of Total		15.4%	20.3%	7.1%	42.9%
	Std. Residual		**-1.9**	**2.0**	.4	
FEMALE	Count		65	25	14	104
	Expected Count		53.1	35.4	15.4	104.0
	% of Total		35.7%	13.7%	7.7%	57.1%
	Std. Residual		1.6	-1.8	-.4	
Total	Count		93	62	27	182
	Expected Count		93.0	62.0	27.0	182.0
	% of Total		51.1%	34.1%	14.8%	100.0%

Table 1.10.B: SPSS Chi-Square Output—Chi-Square Tests

Chi-Square Tests

	Value	df	Asymp. Sig. (2-sided)
Pearson Chi-Square	**13.644**[a]	**2**	**.001**
Likelihood Ratio	13.783	2	.001
Linear-by-Linear Association	7.461	1	.006
N of Valid Cases	182		

[a] 0 cells (.0%) have expected count less than 5. The minimum expected count is 11.57.

Table 1.10.C: SPSS Chi-Square Output—Symmetric Measures

Symmetric Measures

		Value	Approx. Sig.
Nominal by Nominal	Phi	.274	.001
	Cramer's V	**.274**	**.001**
N of Valid Cases		182	

.05). The results of the standardized residuals[2] (see table 1.10.A) show that the number of overweight males (37) is significantly higher than expected (26.6). In addition, the number of normal weight males (28) is significantly lower than what may be expected in this sample (39.9).

Finally, although the two variables are significantly associated, Cramer's *V* (table 1.10.C: .274) indicates that only 7.5 percent (Cramer's V^2) of the variance in weight can be explained by gender. This is a weak correlation.

SUMMARY

This chapter reviewed the common and major bivariate statistical techniques that are used either to test the relationship between the independent and dependent variables or to examine certain assumptions for advanced and multivariate tests.

The chapter began by discussing the process of selecting the most appropriate test to analyze the data. This process depends on a number of assumptions, including sample selection, level of measurement, normality of distribution, and sample size. The chapter then discussed the differences between parametric and nonparametric tests with regard to the previously mentioned assumptions.

Next the purpose and assumptions of four parametric tests and their alternative nonparametric tests were presented and discussed. An example for each test was also presented. These tests included Pearson's correlation and its alternative, Spearman's *rho* test; independent *t*-test and its alternative, Mann-Whitney *U* test; dependent *t*-test and its nonparametric, Wilcoxon signed ranks test; and the one-way analysis of variance and its nonparametric version, Kruskal-Wallis *H* test. Finally, the chapter discussed the chi-square nonparametric test.

Chapter 2 will discuss a prerequisite step in data analysis, data evaluation. The discussion will include the importance of data cleaning and inspecting variables, coding, and missing values and methods to overcome problems if they are presented. The chapter will also discuss both univariate and multivariate outlier cases. It will then deal with normality of distributions and types of data transformation. Also presented is a detailed discussion of the use of SPSS in evaluating each concern.

PRACTICAL EXERCISES

Part 1

A social work researcher was interested in the relationship between levels of burnout and several demographic and job-related variables among social and human services employees. For this purpose, the researcher collected data from 218 social services employees who completed the *Job Satisfaction* survey (see appendix, Data File 3).

---

[2]A cell with a standardized residual of 1.96 or more is considered a major contributor to the significant results.

In this study, the researcher was interested in examining the association between ethnicity (Ethnicity) and marital status (MStatus). In addition, the researcher was interested in examining the relationship between levels of burnout (Burnout) and employees' ethnicity, marital status, and opportunities for promotion (Promotion). (*Note:* capitalized words in parentheses are the SPSS variable names.)

For each analysis, answer the following questions:

1. State the null and alternative hypotheses.

2. What are the independent and dependent variables and their levels of measurement?

3. What statistical test(s) will you use to examine the null hypothesis? Why?

4. What will be the alternative test(s), if any?

5. Run the test statistics you selected in questions 3 and 4.

6. What is your decision with regard to the null hypothesis? Write your answer in detail.

7. Present the results for each question in a summary table.

Part 2

A psychologist conducted an eight-week group therapy session for thirty battered women with high levels of anxiety. All women completed a self-administered standardized anxiety measure at the beginning of the first session (Pretest) and then at the conclusion of the therapy (Posttest). The following are the raw scores of women's levels of anxiety at the pretest and posttest.

Case #	Pretest	Posttest	Case #	Pretest	Posttest
1	18	12	16	23	11
2	20	10	17	19	12
3	23	13	18	19	13
4	20	12	19	24	12
5	20	13	20	20	13
6	18	13	21	24	15
7	21	12	22	18	11
8	24	12	23	21	10
9	17	11	24	22	16
10	19	14	25	26	18
11	26	13	26	17	19
12	21	14	27	24	18
13	21	14	28	20	19
14	21	15	29	20	19
15	20	17	30	19	20

Enter the raw scores into an SPSS data file and answer the following questions:

1. State the null and alternative hypotheses.

2. What are the independent and dependent variables and their levels of measurement?

3. What statistical test(s) will you use to examine the null hypothesis? Why?

4. What will be the alternative test(s), if any?

5. Run the test statistics you selected in questions 3 and 4.

6. What is your decision with regard to the null hypothesis? Write your answer in detail.

7. Present the results in a summary table.

CHAPTER 2

Data Evaluation: Data Cleaning, Missing Values, Outlier Cases, Normality, and Data Transformation

LEARNING OBJECTIVES

1. Understand the purpose and importance of data evaluation
2. Understand how to clean data
3. Understand the importance of missing values and how to replace them
4. Understand the importance of outlying cases and how to inspect data for outlier cases
5. Understand normality of distributions
6. Understand methods of data transformation

DATA SETS (APPENDIX)

Mental Health

Job Satisfaction

INTRODUCTION

Many graduate students and inexperienced researchers believe that once they enter their data into a statistical program such as SPSS, they are ready to utilize the statistical procedures they have chosen to address their research hypotheses. In fact, because data are a collection of numerical values, any statistical program will run any statistical command researchers request and results will be obtained (e.g., frequency tables, means, standard deviations, statistical values, p values, etc.). The question is then, how accurate are these results? Do they reflect a true picture of the population's parameters? Can they be generalized to the population from which they were collected? How confident are the researchers of these results?

The answers to these and many other questions depend on how good the data are. To determine how good the data are one must address a number of critical questions. These questions include the following:

1. Are data correctly entered? Are categorical variables properly coded? Are dummy variables coded as "0" and "1"?

2. Are there any missing data? If so, what percentages of data are missing? What are the patterns of these missing data?

3. Are the data within the expected values? Are there any unexpected or extreme values?

4. Do the distributions approach the shape of a normal curve?

5. If not, how far are they from normality?

6. What can be done to "fix" these distributions?

Careful consideration and attention to these questions are a necessity and prerequisite for most advanced and multivariate statistical procedures. In the following sections, each one of these questions will be defined and discussed in detail. The Mental Health and Job Satisfaction SPSS data files will be used to clarify each step and demonstrate how to utilize SPSS in data evaluation.

DATA CLEANING AND CATEGORICAL CODING

As human beings, researchers are likely to make some type of error when entering data, especially when entering large amounts of data. Errors in data entry can significantly skew the distributions of the data and distort the results. This distortion, in turn, leads to ambiguous conclusions and inaccurate generalization.

Thus the first step after the data have been completely entered into an SPSS file, or any other statistical software, is to make sure that all values, whether categorical or numerical, are correctly entered. This step can be achieved by running and inspecting frequency tables for all variables in the data set. These frequency tables display the actual scores, from low to high, for continuous data (e.g., age) or actual categories for categorical data (e.g., gender). Given the prior knowledge about the study and its variables, all values that appear outside the possible range for each variable should be re-evaluated for errors.

Example

In the Mental Health SPSS data file, data were collected from people ages fifty years and older. The Iowa Self-Assessment Inventory was utilized to capture subjects' emotional balance (EB), physical health (PH), and cognitive status (CS). Total scores for each subscale range between 2 and 32. The Center for Epidemiologic Studies Depression Scale (CES-D) was used to measure participants' levels of depression. Possible scores for the CES-D range from 0 to 60.

Therefore, in this file any value that is less than 50 for age; less than 2 or greater than 32 for EB, PH, and CS; or less than 0 or greater than 60 for CES-D is considered an error. When an error occurs, researchers need to find out the case number associated with it, return to the original survey marked with this case number, check the actual value, and correct the error.

Using SPSS to Run Frequencies and Variable's Range

For this example, SPSS will be used to examine the frequency distributions and range of the age (Age), emotional balance (EB), physical health (PH), cognitive status (CS), and CES-D (CESD) variables. To begin, follow these steps:

1. Open the SPSS Mental Health data file.
2. Click on *Analyze, Descriptive Statistics,* and *Frequencies.*
3. Highlight all variables of interest (Age, EB, PH, CS, and CESD), and click on the middle arrow to move them into the *Variable(s)* box.
4. Make sure the *Display Frequency Tables* box is checked (this is SPSS default; see screen 2.1.A).
5. Click on *Statistics,* and check the boxes *Minimum* and *Maximum* under "Dispersion" (see screen 2.1.B).
6. Click on *Continue,* and click on *OK.*

Screen 2.1.A: SPSS Frequencies Tables Dialog Box

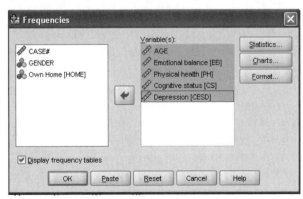

Screen 2.1.B: SPSS Frequencies Statistics Dialog Box

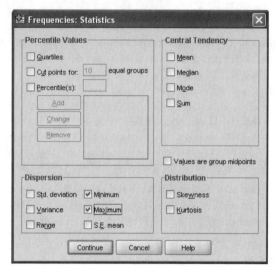

You also can request frequency tables and range using the SPSS syntax file:

1. Open the SPSS Mental Health data file.

2. Click on *File* in the main menu, then *New,* then *Syntax.*

3. Type the following syntax:

SPSS Syntax for Frequency Table

FREQUENCIES VARIABLES=**AGE EB PH CS CESD**
/STATISTICS=MINIMUM MAXIMUM
/ORDER=ANALYSIS.

---

4. Highlight the entire syntax, right-click on the mouse, and click *Run Current.*

Table 2.1.A displays the overall summary results for all variables. It displays the number of cases in each analysis, the number of subjects who have missing values in each variable, and the minimum and maximum scores.

Table 2.1.A shows that age ranges between 50 and 96. Emotional balance, physical health, and cognitive status range between 2 and 32, and CES-D ranges between 0 and 60. None of these values is outside the predetermined ranges, indicating no errors.

If, for some reason, there were values outside the pre-established ranges, the researcher would need to inspect the frequency table for the particular variable

Table 2.1.A: Summary—Statistics

Statistics

		AGE	Emotional balance	Physical health	Cognitive status	CES-D
N	Valid	144	153	154	152	148
	Missing	11	2	1	3	7
Minimum		**50**	**2**	**2**	**2**	**0**
Maximum		**96**	**32**	**32**	**32**	**60**

with such problem. He or she would then identify the number of subjects/cases outside of these ranges, return to the SPSS data file to identify the case number associated with the problem, and return to the original survey to determine the correct answer. Tables 2.1.B, 2.1.C, 2.1.D, 2.1.E, and 2.1.F display the frequency tables for all variables.

In general, a frequency table displays the following information:

1. Raw scores from lowest to highest

2. Frequency (number of subjects who reported a given score)

3. Percent (percentage of subjects who reported a given score, including missing cases)

4. Valid percent (percentage of subjects who reported a given score, excluding missing cases)

5. Cumulative percent (percentage of subjects who reported a given score or below)

For example, table 2.1.B shows that sixteen participants were sixty-five years old. They make up 10.3 percent of the total participants ($\frac{16}{155} \times 100\% = 10.3\%$). However, notice that eleven participants are missing, which makes the valid number of cases 144 (155 − 11 = 144). Thus the valid percent of participants who are sixty-five years old is 11.1 percent ($\frac{16}{144} \times 100\% = 11.1\%$).

During the process of data cleaning, researchers should inspect the codes for categorical values. Remember, these are numerical codes that are assigned for each level of a categorical variable. For example, in this study, Gender is classified as male or female. A male was coded as "0," and a female was coded as "1." The variable Home was measured with the following question: "Do you own a home?" An answer of no was coded as "0," and yes was coded as "1." These levels could be coded as "1" and "2," or any other numerical code; however, many statistical tests, such as multiple regression, logistic regression, and canonical regression, require that any categorical variable that will be entered in the statistical analysis be coded as a dummy variable, "0" or "1."

To inspect the coding for the variables Gender and Home in the Mental Health data file, follow the SPSS steps for frequency distributions and run fre-

Table 2.1.B: Frequency Table for Age

		Frequency	Percent	Valid Percent	Cumulative Percent
Valid	50	4	2.6	2.8	2.8
	51	4	2.6	2.8	5.6
	52	3	1.9	2.1	7.6
	53	3	1.9	2.1	9.7
	54	4	2.6	2.8	12.5
	55	4	2.6	2.8	15.3
	56	1	.6	.7	16.0
	57	2	1.3	1.4	17.4
	58	5	3.2	3.5	20.8
	59	5	3.2	3.5	24.3
	60	9	5.8	6.3	30.6
	61	7	4.5	4.9	35.4
	62	6	3.9	4.2	39.6
	63	7	4.5	4.9	44.4
	64	5	3.2	3.5	47.9
	65	**16**	**10.3**	**11.1**	**59.0**
	66	5	3.2	3.5	62.5
	67	7	4.5	4.9	67.4
	68	6	3.9	4.2	71.5
	69	2	1.3	1.4	72.9
	70	3	1.9	2.1	75.0
	71	1	.6	.7	75.7
	72	2	1.3	1.4	77.1
	73	3	1.9	2.1	79.2
	74	2	1.3	1.4	80.6
	75	**3**	**1.9**	**2.1**	**82.6**
	78	2	1.3	1.4	84.0
	79	1	.6	.7	84.7
	80	4	2.6	2.8	87.5
	82	3	1.9	2.1	89.6
	83	1	.6	.7	90.3
	84	1	.6	.7	91.0
	85	2	1.3	1.4	92.4
	86	1	.6	.7	93.1
	87	2	1.3	1.4	94.4
	88	1	.6	.7	95.1
	90	1	.6	.7	95.8
	92	2	1.3	1.4	97.2
	93	1	.6	.7	97.9
	94	1	.6	.7	98.6
	95	1	.6	.7	99.3
	96	1	.6	.7	100.0
	Total	**144**	**92.9**	**100.0**	
Missing	**System**	**11**	**7.1**		
	Total	**155**	100.0		

quency tables with minimum and maximum values for both categorical variables. Tables 2.2.A and 2.2.B display the frequency tables for these two variables.

Notice that the frequency tables show the values for males and females as well as for no and yes as "0" and "1." In other words, no other values were present. If, for any reason, these values were "1" and "2" or any other codes, they would need to be recoded into "0" and "1." This recoding can be achieved in SPSS through the *Transform* and *Recode into . . .* commands.[1]

---

[1] For more on using SPSS to run frequency tables and on recoding variables, see Abu-Bader (2006).

Table 2.1.C: Frequency Table for Emotional Balance

EB Emotional balance

		Frequency	Percent	Valid Percent	Cumulative Percent
Valid	2	3	1.9	2.0	2.0
	6	1	.6	.7	2.6
	8	3	1.9	2.0	4.6
	9	2	1.3	1.3	5.9
	10	1	.6	.7	6.5
	11	6	3.9	3.9	10.5
	12	6	3.9	3.9	14.4
	13	7	4.5	4.6	19.0
	14	5	3.2	3.3	22.2
	15	9	5.8	5.9	28.1
	16	6	3.9	3.9	32.0
	17	9	5.8	5.9	37.9
	18	10	6.5	6.5	44.4
	19	9	5.8	5.9	50.3
	20	7	4.5	4.6	54.9
	21	13	8.4	8.5	63.4
	22	13	8.4	8.5	71.9
	23	14	9.0	9.2	81.0
	24	4	2.6	2.6	83.7
	25	2	1.3	1.3	85.0
	26	2	1.3	1.3	86.3
	27	5	3.2	3.3	89.5
	28	4	2.6	2.6	92.2
	29	3	1.9	2.0	94.1
	30	4	2.6	2.6	96.7
	31	1	.6	.7	97.4
	32	4	2.6	2.6	100.0
	Total	153	98.7	100.0	
Missing	System	2	1.3		
Total		155	100.0		

Table 2.1.D: Frequency Table for Physical Health

PH Physical health

		Frequency	Percent	Valid Percent	Cumulative Percent
Valid	2	2	1.3	1.3	1.3
	3	1	.6	.6	1.9
	8	1	.6	.6	2.6
	9	4	2.6	2.6	5.2
	10	3	1.9	1.9	7.1
	11	7	4.5	4.5	11.7
	12	3	1.9	1.9	13.6
	13	5	3.2	3.2	16.9
	14	7	4.5	4.5	21.4
	15	8	5.2	5.2	26.6
	16	8	5.2	5.2	31.8
	17	10	6.5	6.5	38.3
	18	8	5.2	5.2	43.5
	19	13	8.4	8.4	51.9
	20	18	11.6	11.7	63.6
	21	8	5.2	5.2	68.8
	22	8	5.2	5.2	74.0
	23	5	3.2	3.2	77.3
	24	8	5.2	5.2	82.5
	25	5	3.2	3.2	85.7
	26	6	3.9	3.9	89.6
	27	6	3.9	3.9	93.5
	28	1	.6	.6	94.2
	29	4	2.6	2.6	96.8
	30	4	2.6	2.6	99.4
	32	1	.6	.6	100.0
	Total	154	99.4	100.0	
Missing	System	1	.6		
Total		155	100.0		

Table 2.1.E: Frequency Table for Cognitive Status

CS Cognitive status

		Frequency	Percent	Valid Percent	Cumulative Percent
Valid	2	1	.6	.7	.7
	8	1	.6	.7	1.3
	9	1	.6	.7	2.0
	11	3	1.9	2.0	3.9
	12	2	1.3	1.3	5.3
	13	1	.6	.7	5.9
	14	1	.6	.7	6.6
	15	5	3.2	3.3	9.9
	16	5	3.2	3.3	13.2
	17	5	3.2	3.3	16.4
	18	10	6.5	6.6	23.0
	19	5	3.2	3.3	26.3
	20	9	5.8	5.9	32.2
	21	13	8.4	8.6	40.8
	22	10	6.5	6.6	47.4
	23	13	8.4	8.6	55.9
	24	7	4.5	4.6	60.5
	25	5	3.2	3.3	63.8
	26	10	6.5	6.6	70.4
	27	11	7.1	7.2	77.6
	28	7	4.5	4.6	82.2
	29	10	6.5	6.6	88.8
	30	9	5.8	5.9	94.7
	31	6	3.9	3.9	98.7
	32	2	1.3	1.3	100.0
	Total	152	98.1	100.0	
Missing	System	3	1.9		
Total		155	100.0		

When data cleaning and value inspections have been completed, the next step is to answer these questions: Are there any cases with missing values? If so, how large is the problem? What is the pattern of these missing values?

MISSING DATA

Missing data may occur when subjects withdraw from the experiment, complete the pretest but not the posttest, or simply fail to answer one or more of the questionnaire's items for various reasons. Missing data could also occur for technical reasons during data entry, for example, when researchers accidentally fail to enter one or more values, the keyboard is not responding, or researchers strike the wrong key on the keyboard (e.g., *Tab* key instead of the *Caps Lock* key).

Whatever the reason, the problem of missing data must be addressed prior to moving forward to the next steps in data evaluation and definitely prior to hypothesis testing. There are two aspects to the problem of missing data: the number of cases with missing values and the pattern of missing values.

Pattern of Missing Data

Depending on the sample size, the pattern of missing values is more influential than the number of cases with missing values[2] and could significantly impact the results of the study and its generalizability.

---

[2]For more on missing data, see Tabachnick & Fidell (2007).

Table 2.1.F: Frequency Table for CESD

CESD Depression

		Frequency	Percent	Valid Percent	Cumulative Percent
Valid	0	4	2.6	2.7	2.7
	5	2	1.3	1.4	4.1
	6	2	1.3	1.4	5.4
	8	1	.6	.7	6.1
	9	2	1.3	1.4	7.4
	10	5	3.2	3.4	10.8
	11	2	1.3	1.4	12.2
	12	7	4.5	4.7	16.9
	13	3	1.9	2.0	18.9
	14	7	4.5	4.7	23.6
	15	8	5.2	5.4	29.1
	16	5	3.2	3.4	32.4
	17	7	4.5	4.7	37.2
	18	9	5.8	6.1	43.2
	19	4	2.6	2.7	45.9
	20	2	1.3	1.4	47.3
	21	6	3.9	4.1	51.4
	22	4	2.6	2.7	54.1
	23	3	1.9	2.0	56.1
	24	4	2.6	2.7	58.8
	25	7	4.5	4.7	63.5
	26	2	1.3	1.4	64.9
	27	1	.6	.7	65.5
	28	3	1.9	2.0	67.6
	29	2	1.3	1.4	68.9
	30	3	1.9	2.0	70.9
	31	5	3.2	3.4	74.3
	32	4	2.6	2.7	77.0
	33	3	1.9	2.0	79.1
	34	3	1.9	2.0	81.1
	35	2	1.3	1.4	82.4
	36	4	2.6	2.7	85.1
	37	2	1.3	1.4	86.5
	38	1	.6	.7	87.2
	39	3	1.9	2.0	89.2
	40	3	1.9	2.0	91.2
	41	1	.6	.7	91.9
	42	2	1.3	1.4	93.2
	45	1	.6	.7	93.9
	46	1	.6	.7	94.6
	48	1	.6	.7	95.3
	51	3	1.9	2.0	97.3
	52	1	.6	.7	98.0
	60	3	1.9	2.0	100.0
	Total	148	95.5	100.0	
Missing	System	7	4.5		
Total		155	100.0		

Data can be either randomly missing or not randomly missing. Randomly missing data occur when missing values are spread throughout the data set. For example, one subject did not report his or her age, another did not report his or her race, two more did not answer one of the CES-D items, and so on.

Table 2.2.A: Frequency Table for Gender

		Frequency	Percent	Valid Percent	Cumulative Percent
Valid	0 Male	75	48.4	48.4	48.4
	1 Female	80	51.6	51.6	100.0
	Total	155	100.0	100.0	

Table 2.2.B: Frequency Table for Home

HOME Own Home

		Frequency	Percent	Valid Percent	Cumulative Percent
Valid	0 No	75	48.4	49.3	49.3
	1 Yes	77	49.7	50.7	100.0
	Total	152	98.1	100.0	
Missing	System	3	1.9		
Total		155	100.0		

On the other hand, not randomly missing data occur when missing values are centered on one or a few questionnaire items. For example, a few subjects did not answer a question on sexuality, nine did not report their annual income, ten more did not report their immigration status, and so on. The question is then, what needs to be done with cases with missing values?

The decision on how to deal with missing data depends on, first, how many cases have missing values and, second, what the patterns of these missing values are.

Excluding Cases with Missing Values

With large sample sizes and few cases with values that are randomly missing, the decision is a simple one: exclude these cases from the analysis. As a general guideline, if only 5 percent (or less) of cases have missing values at random, then "almost any procedure for handling missing values yields similar results" (Tabachnick & Fidell, 2007, p. 63). Thus excluding these cases from the analysis is less likely to influence the results of the study.

Fortunately, researchers do not need to manually delete each case with missing values. SPSS provides two options for data analysis, *pairwise* and *listwise* deletion. When pairwise is selected, all cases that have missing values on one or both variables will be excluded from the specific analysis. On the other hand, when listwise is selected, any case with missing values will be excluded from all analyses.

For example, if the pairwise option is selected when conducting the Pearson correlation to examine the relationship between age and depression and between self-esteem and depression, cases with missing values on either age or depression will be excluded from the first analysis and cases with missing values on self-esteem or depression will be excluded from the second analysis. However, when the listwise option is selected, cases with missing values on all these variables will be dropped from the two analyses. Tables 2.3.A and 2.3.B display two different analyses for the same variables.

Recall that 155 subjects participated in the Mental Health study. Table 2.3.A, however, shows that 139 subjects have completed values on both age and self-esteem. Furthermore, 145 subjects have completed values on both self-esteem and depression. Notice that table 2.3.A shows that there are 144 valid

Table 2.3.A: Pearson Correlation Coefficients—Pairwise Analysis

Correlations

		AGE	Self-Esteem	Depression
AGE	Pearson Correlation	1	-.260**	.200*
	Sig. (2-tailed)		.002	.019
	N	144	139	137
Self-Esteem	Pearson Correlation	-.260**	1	-.339**
	Sig. (2-tailed)	.002		.000
	N	**139**	149	145
Depression	Pearson Correlation	.200*	-.339**	1
	Sig. (2-tailed)	.019	.000	
	N	**137**	**145**	148

**. Correlation is significant at the 0.01 level (2-tailed).

*. Correlation is significant at the 0.05 level (2-tailed).

Table 2.3.B: Pearson Correlation Coefficients—Listwise Analysis

Correlations[a]

		AGE	Self-Esteem	Depression
AGE	Pearson Correlation	1	-.271**	.192*
	Sig. (2-tailed)		.001	.026
Self-Esteem	Pearson Correlation	-.271**	1	-.346**
	Sig. (2-tailed)	.001		.000
Depression	Pearson Correlation	.192*	-.346**	1
	Sig. (2-tailed)	.026	.000	

**. Correlation is significant at the 0.01 level (2-tailed).

*. Correlation is significant at the 0.05 level (2-tailed).

a. Listwise N=135

ages (Age with Age), 149 valid self-esteem scores (Self-Esteem with Self-Esteem), and 148 valid depression scores (Depression with Depression).

Table 2.3.B, on the other hand, uses the listwise option to determine the correlation coefficients. Table 2.3.B shows that of the 155 subjects who participated in the study, 135 have completed values (valid cases) on all three variables, and therefore the correlation coefficients are based on only these cases.

Recommendation: Use the pairwise option when conducting a univariate (frequency tables, graphs, descriptive statistics, etc.) or bivariate (e.g., Pearson correlation, *t*-tests, ANOVA, chi-square, etc.) statistical technique. Pairwise is the default in SPSS for most bivariate tests.

Replacing Missing Values

When the number of cases with missing values is large (i.e., > 5%) and/or if they are not randomly missing, excluding these cases from the analysis could affect the study results and its conclusion. Thus when this situation occurs, it is important that researchers evaluate the likelihood that the missing values will affect the study results.

This evaluation can be done by creating a new dummy variable (0 and 1) comprised of all valid cases (1 = valid case) against all cases with missing values

(0 = missing case). For example, if many subjects did not report their ages, you may recode Age into a new variable (say, Missing_Age) where you recode all cases with missing ages into "0" and all other cases (valid cases) into "1." This can be done through the *Transform* and *Recode into Different Variables* commands in SPSS. You may use SPSS syntax to create a new variable.

Once a new variable (Missing_Age) has been created, you may examine whether there are significant differences between subjects with valid ages and subjects with missing ages with regard to other variables, usually the dependent variable(s). In this case, you may conduct an independent *t*-test to compare both groups with regard to their levels of self-esteem and depression. (*Note:* use the chi-square if the dependent variable(s) are categorical data.) If no significant differences exist between the two groups, then excluding these cases from the analysis will be less likely to affect the study's results. But what if the two groups are significantly different on the dependent variable(s)?

If a significant difference between the two groups is found, this difference may indicate that those who declined to answer the item(s) did so for one or more reasons, perhaps unknown to the researchers. Thus excluding these cases is most likely to affect the study's results and its conclusion.

As an alternative in such cases, researchers should consider replacing the missing values using some procedures that most likely produce values close to the actual values. Two methods are discussed here.

Replacement with the mean or median.   Replacement with the mean is perhaps the most used method to replace missing values. This method, however, is appropriate only if the variable with the missing data is continuous data (interval or higher). Replacement with the mean involves computing the mean score for the variable(s) with the missing values and then replacing all missing values with the mean. With this method, researchers rely on the assumption that the sample's mean (statistic) is the best measure of central tendency to represent the population's mean (parameter).

When variables with missing data are measured at the ordinal level of measurement, replacement with the median is more appropriate than the mean.

Replacement with the mean or median is an option that is available in SPSS through the *Transform* and *Replace Missing Values . . .* commands. This procedure will be discussed later in this chapter.

Replacement with a predicted value.   Another method for replacing missing values is replacement with predicted scores. This method requires the utilization of a regression analysis. The variable with missing data is treated as the dependent variable, and variables with completed data are treated as the independent variables.

Once these variables are identified, researchers then utilize a multiple regression analysis for continuous data (see chapter 4) or a logistic regression analysis for dichotomous data (see chapter 5) to develop a regression equation that best predicts the dependent variable. Next researchers use the equation to predict scores for all cases with missing data. These predicted scores are then used to replace the scores for all missing cases.

This method is available in SPSS through *Analyze, Regression, Linear,* or *Binary Logistic* commands. SPSS also computes predicted scores when this option is requested in regression analysis.

Example

We will use the Mental Health data file to identify cases with missing values and to demonstrate how to inspect their patterns and replace them with both the mean and the predicted scores.

Using SPSS to inspect missing values.   To begin, follow these SPSS steps:

1. Open the SPSS Mental Health data file.

2. Click on *Analyze, Descriptive Statistics,* and *Explore.*

3. Highlight all variables of interest, click on the upper arrow, and move them into the *Dependent List* box.

4. Click on *Statistics* under "Display" to request only statistics (*Both* will be used later in this chapter).

5. Click on *Options,* and click on *Exclude Cases Pairwise.*

6. Click on *Continue,* and click on *OK* (see screen 2.2).

Screen 2.2:   SPSS Explore Dialog Box

To use the SPSS syntax, type the following:

SPSS Syntax to Examine the Amount of Missing Data

EXAMINE VARIABLES=GENDER HOME AGE EB PH CS CESD
/PLOT NONE
/STATISTICS DESCRIPTIVES
/CINTERVAL 95
/MISSING PAIRWISE
/NOTOTAL.

SPSS will produce two tables: "Case Processing Summary" and "Descriptives." At this point, the researcher is interested in only the first table. The second table is returned to later in this chapter.

Table 2.4 displays the case processing summary statistics. It displays the number of valid cases, missing cases, and total cases (sample size) and their corresponding percents for each variable. Recall that a pairwise analysis was requested. Thus the total number of cases (sample size) for all variables is the same, but the number of valid and missing cases for each variable is different. If listwise is selected, these numbers will be equal for all variables.

Table 2.4 has six columns, two for valid cases, two for missing cases, and another two for total cases. The table shows that 155 subjects participated in the study. All participants reported their gender (Missing: N = 0, Percent = 0). Three participants (1.9%) did not answer the item regarding their home, eleven (7.1%) did not report their age, and seven (4.5%) did not have a total score for depression.

The amount of cases with missing values is less than 5 percent in all variables except Age, where 7.1 percent of cases (n = 11) failed to report their age. Thus using the 5 percent rule of thumb, it is beneficial to inspect this variable further to examine if there is a significant difference between those 11 cases and

Table 2.4: Summary of Valid and Missing Cases

Case Processing Summary

| | \multicolumn{6}{c}{Cases} | | | | | |
| | Valid | | Missing | | Total | |
	N	Percent	N	Percent	N	Percent
GENDER	155	100.0%	0	.0%	155	100.0%
HOME Own Home	152	98.1%	3	1.9%	155	100.0%
AGE	144	92.9%	**11**	**7.1%**	155	100.0%
EB Emotional balance	153	98.7%	2	1.3%	155	100.0%
PH Physical health	154	99.4%	1	.6%	155	100.0%
CS Cognitive status	152	98.1%	3	1.9%	155	100.0%
CESD Depression	148	95.5%	7	4.5%	155	100.0%

the remaining 144 cases with regard to other variables, such as Depression, the dependent variable.

Using SPSS, we will create a new variable called Missing_Age, which will consist of two groups: valid cases versus missing cases. We will recode all cases with missing values in Age, the original variable, into "0" and all cases with valid values into "1."

Using SPSS to create a new variable.   To begin, follow these SPSS steps:

1. Open the SPSS Mental Health data file.

2. Click on *Transform* and *Recode into Different Variables.*

3. Click on *Age,* the variable to recode, and click on the right arrow to move it into the *Numeric Variable . . . Output Variable* box.

4. Type the new variable's name, "Missing_Age," in the "Output Variable" *Name* box.

5. Click on *Change* to confirm you are recoding Age into Missing_Age (see screen 2.3).

6. Click on *Old and New Values.*

7. Select *System-missing* under "Old Value."

8. Type "0" in the *Value* box under "New Value" (to recode all missing values into 0).

9. If you have assigned numerical codes to identify missing values (e.g., 9, 99, 999), then select *System- or User-missing* instead of *System-missing.*

10. Click on *Add.*

11. Select *All Other Values* (which are the valid values) under "Old Value" and type "1" in the *Value* box under "New Value" (see screen 2.4).

Screen 2.3:   SPSS Recode into Different Variables Dialog Box

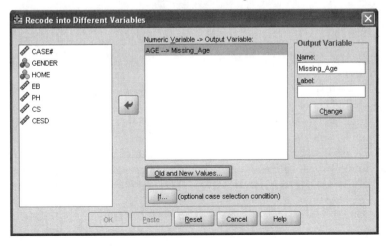

Screen 2.4:   SPSS Recode into Different Variables Old and New Values Dialog Box

12.   Click on *Add.*

13.   Click on *Continue,* and click on *OK.*

To use the SPSS syntax, type the following:

SPSS Syntax to Create a New Variable

RECODE
AGE (SYSMIS=0) (ELSE=1) INTO Missing_Age.
EXECUTE.

Once these commands are completed, SPSS creates a new variable called Missing_Age. It will be placed in the last column in the SPSS data view (see screen 2.5).

The next step is to examine whether a significant difference on the dependent variable exists between valid and missing cases. To examine this, we will utilize the independent *t*-test (the independent variable, Missing_Age, is dichotomous; the dependent variable is continuous).[3]

The results of the independent *t*-test are shown in table 2.5. The results show no significant difference between both groups with regard to their levels of

---

[3]For more information on the independent *t*-test, see Abu-Bader (2006).

Screen 2.5:   SPSS Data View

	CASE#	GENDER	HOME	AGE	EB	PH	CS	CESD	Missing_Age
1	1	1	0	66	20	10	29	10	1.00
2	2	1	1	66	15	12	18	20	1.00
3	3	1	1	66	14	13	24	21	1.00
4	4	0	0	66	32	14	25	11	1.00
5	5	1	1	66	14	18	13	28	1.00
6	6	0	1	66	11	19	27	14	1.00
7	7	0	0	66	30	19	28	20	1.00
8	8	0	1	66	15	22	22	34	1.00
9	9	1	1	66	12	23	16	34	1.00
10	10	0	0	66	16	26	17	6	1.00
11	11	0	0	66	23	30	31	13	1.00
12	12	1	0	50	17	9	27	10	1.00
13	13	0	0	50	31	24	28	15	1.00
14	14	0	0	50	23	25	22	18	1.00
15	15	0	0	50	32	29	31	12	1.00
16	16	1	0	51	27	24	28	12	1.00
17	17	1	0	51	18	24	26	27	1.00
18	18	1	0	51	19	26	29	19	1.00
19	19	1	0	51	28	30	31	18	1.00
20	20	1	0	52	11	15	23	52	1.00
21	21	1	1	52	17	21	22	22	1.00
22	22	1	0	52	22	32	32	8	1.00
23	23	1	1	53	17	9	17	33	1.00
24	24	0	0	53	28	27	30	5	1.00

depression ($t_{(df = 146)} = -1.23, p > .05$). Thus the exclusion of these 11 cases will not likely affect the study results and its conclusion. Remember, this study has 155 cases, only 11 cases with missing values. However, what if significant results have occurred? In this case, we will use one of the methods discussed above to replace the missing scores.

Table 2.5:   Results of the Independent t-Test

Independent Samples Test

		Levene's Test for Equality of Variances		t-test for Equality of Means					95% Confidence Interval of the Difference	
		F	Sig.	t	df	Sig. (2-tailed)	Mean Difference	Std. Error Difference	Lower	Upper
Depression	Equal variances assumed	1.169	.281	-1.23	146	.220	-4.818	3.909	-12.544	2.908
	Equal variances not assumed			-1.567	13.00	.141	-4.818	3.075	-11.462	1.826

Using SPSS to replace missing values with mean/median.   To replace missing values in Age with the mean or median, follow these steps:

1. Open the Mental Health SPSS data file.

2. Click on *Transform,* and click on *Replace Missing Values.*

3. Click on *Age,* and click on the arrow to move it into the *New Variable(s)* box.

4. SPSS automatically assigns a name for the new variable, usually the original name plus "_1" (i.e., Age_1). You could type a different name, if you chose to do so (see screen 2.6.A). This new variable includes all original scores and replaces all missing values with the mean.

5. Make sure the *Series Mean* appears in the *Method* box (SPSS default).

6. If you would like to replace the missing values with the median, click on the drop-down *Method*'s arrow and select *Median of Nearby Points,* select *All* under "Span of Nearby Points," and click on *Change* (see screen 2.6.B).

Screen 2.6.A: SPSS Replace Missing Values with Mean Dialog Box

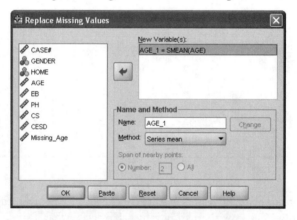

Screen 2.6.B: SPSS Replace Missing Values with Median Dialog Box

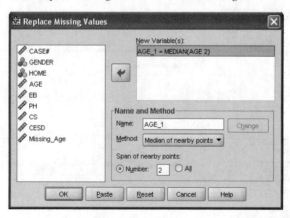

7. Click on *OK.*

8. A new variable, Age_1, will be created and placed in the last column in the SPSS data view.

To use SPSS syntax to replace missing values with the mean or median, use the following SPSS syntax:

SPSS Syntax for Replacing Missing Values with Mean

RMV
/AGE_1=SMEAN(AGE).

SPSS SYNTAX FOR REPLACING MISSING VALUES WITH MEDIAN:

RMV
/AGE_1=MEDIAN(AGE).

Once these commands are executed, a new variable, Age_1, will be added to the SPSS data file. It will be located in the last column in the data view. SPSS will produce a table showing some information about the new variable (see table 2.6).

Table 2.6 displays the name of the new variable, Age_1, the number of cases that have been replaced (11), the cases with no missing values (1 to 155), the total number of participants (155), and the method used for replacement (series mean of Age).

Using SPSS to replace missing values with predicted scores.   Recall that when replacing missing scores with predicted scores, the variable with the missing values is treated as the dependent variable and others are treated as independent variables. Also, if categorical variables are entered in the analysis as independent variables, they must be coded as dummy variables (0 and 1).

To replace missing values in age with predicted scores (ages), follow these steps:

1. Open the SPSS Mental Health data file.

2. Click on *Analyze, Regression,* and *Linear.*

3. Click on and move *Age* into the *Dependent* box.

Table 2.6:   Summary Results of Replacement of Missing Values

Result Variables

	Result Variable	N of Replaced Missing Values	Case Number of Non-Missing Values		N of Valid Cases	Creating Function
			First	Last		
1	AGE_1	11	1	155	155	SMEAN(AGE)

Screen 2.7.A: SPSS Linear Regression Dialog Box

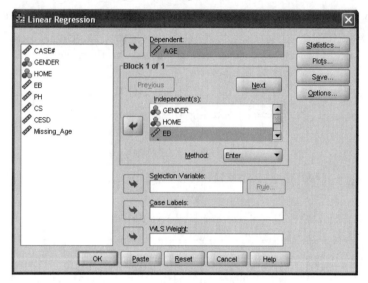

4.   Click on each independent variable and move it into the *Independent(s)* box (see screen 2.7.A).

5.   Click on *Save.*

6.   Check *Unstandardized* under "Predicted Values" (see screen 2.7.B).

7.   Click on *Continue,* and click on *OK.*

Screen 2.7.B: SPSS Linear Regression Save Dialog Box

To use SPSS syntax to generate predicted scores for Age, type the following syntax:

SPSS Syntax for Predicted Scores

REGRESSION
/MISSING LISTWISE
/DEPENDENT AGE
/METHOD=ENTER GENDER HOME EB PH CS CESD
/SAVE PRED.

These commands produce a new variable labeled as Pre_1 (unstandardized predicted values), which are the predicted scores for Age. This variable will be placed in the last column in the SPSS data file. If more predicted scores are computed for other variables, they will be labeled as Pre_2, Pre_3, Pre_4, and so on.

To replace missing values with the predicted scores, first sort the data from low to high using the variable Age. In SPSS:

1. Click on *Data,* then scroll down to and click on *Sort Cases.*

2. Move *Age* into the *Sort By* box; make sure that *Ascending* under "Sort Order" is checked (SPSS default).

3. Click on *OK* (see screen 2.8).

This command will sort the data by Age, from low to high, with missing values on Age first.

Next you may highlight and copy the first eleven values (equal the number of missing values) of the variable Pre_1 and paste them in the first eleven cases of Age. You may also manually type each value of the predicted values in the associated missing value (see screen 2.9).

After missing values have been replaced with the appropriate technique (mean, median, or predicted scores), it is recommended that you conduct two

Screen 2.8:   SPSS Sort Cases Dialog Box

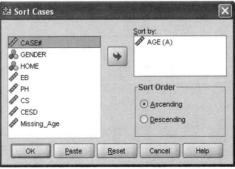

Screen 2.9:   SPSS Main Data View

	GENDER	HOME	AGE	EB	PH	CS	CESD	Missing_Age	AGE_1	PRE_1
1	1	0	.	20	10	29	10	.00	66.3	65.97874
2	1	1	.	15	12	18	20	.00	66.3	69.99492
3	1	1	.	14	13	24	21	.00	66.3	67.15827
4	0	0	.	32	14	25	11	.00	66.3	74.01085
5	1	1	.	14	18	13	28	.00	66.3	67.26080
6	0	1	.	11	19	27	14	.00	66.3	66.97066
7	0	0	.	30	19	28	20	.00	66.3	69.19359
8	0	1	.	15	22	22	34	.00	66.3	68.01795
9	1	1	.	12	23	16	34	.00	66.3	62.39134
10	0	0	.	16	26	17	6	.00	66.3	63.32748
11	0	0	.	23	30	31	13	.00	66.3	58.46277
12	1	0	50	17	9	27	10	1.00	50.0	66.38172
13	0	0	50	31	24	28	15	1.00	50.0	65.97103
14	0	0	50	23	25	22	18	1.00	50.0	64.78413
15	0	0	50	32	29	31	12	1.00	50.0	61.85101
16	1	0	51	27	24	28	12	1.00	51.0	58.81320
17	1	0	51	18	24	26	27	1.00	51.0	56.97759
18	1	0	51	19	26	29	19	1.00	51.0	54.83311
19	1	0	51	28	30	31	18	1.00	51.0	54.16227
20	1	0	52	11	15	23	52	1.00	52.0	62.41839
21	1	1	52	17	21	22	22	1.00	52.0	63.20311
22	1	0	52	22	32	32	8	1.00	52.0	50.49040
23	1	1	53	17	9	17	33	1.00	53.0	73.19846
24	0	0	53	28	27	30	5	1.00	53.0	62.20693
25	0	0	53	28	27	30	5	1.00	53.0	62.20693
26	1	0	54	18	17	23	22	1.00	54.0	62.63544

analyses: one with missing values replaced and one without missing values replaced. If both analyses produce similar results, it is highly recommended to report the results of the test using original data. Also indicate that replacement of missing values produced similar results.

Note that when missing values are replaced with predicted scores, you could conduct two analyses, one with the variable with the replaced scores (e.g., Age_1) and a second one with the predicted variable for Age (Pre_1).

Table 2.7 presents the correlation between depression (CESD) and three scores for Age: Age (raw scores with missing values), Age_1 (mean replacement), and Pre_1 (predicted age). Although the correlation between depression and these various Age data is significant, the correlation between depression and the predicted ages is somewhat stronger than the other two forms. Predicted scores tend to fit the population better than raw scores.

Table 2.7:   Correlation between Depression and Age

Correlations

		AGE	AGE_1	PRE_1
CESD	Pearson Correlation	.200	.195	.256
	Sig. (2-tailed)	.019	.018	.002
	N	137	148	144

Thus researchers should be cautious when replacing missing values with predicted scores. They need to be careful to select only variables that illustrate strong correlation with the predicted variable (in this case Age).

OUTLIERS

Univariate Outlier Scores

Univariate outliers occur when there is one or more extreme or unusual score at either end of a distribution of one variable. In other words, an outlier is a score in a distribution that is far from the remaining scores, at either the lower or upper end of the distribution. For example, ideally the age for undergraduate students ranges between eighteen and twenty-five. If in a study of 100 students, three were thirty years old and two were sixteen years old, then these scores, given no data entry errors, would be considered outlier scores.

Identifying univariate outliers.   There are a few simple ways to identify cases with outlier scores: computing standard z scores (z scores) and inspecting boxplots and stem-and-leaf plots.

The first way to identify outlier cases is to convert raw scores into z *scores.* As you may recall from basic statistics courses, z scores are raw scores converted into standard deviation units. They indicate how many standard deviation units a corresponding raw score is above or below the mean.

Raw scores are converted to z scores simply by subtracting the mean from each raw score and dividing it by the standard deviation.

$$\text{Formula: } Z_x = \frac{X - \overline{X}}{SD}$$

X = raw score
$\overline{X}$ = mean
SD = standard deviation

When converting raw scores into z scores, 99.74 percent of subjects will fall between a z score of 3 and a z score of -3. Thus as a general rule, a raw score that has a z score greater than 3 or smaller than -3 should be considered an outlier case. Other researchers suggest that raw scores greater than 2.5 or less than -2.5 should be considered outlier scores (Hair, Black, Babin, Anderson, & Tatham, 2006). However, it is recommended to use this rule (± 2.5) when sample sizes are too small ($N \leq 10$) (Mertler & Vannatta, 2005).

Raw scores can be converted into z scores in SPSS through the *Analyze, Descriptive Statistics,* and *Descriptives . . .* commands.

Another way to identify univariate outliers is to inspect *boxplots* of distributions. A boxplot is a graphical presentation that illustrates the median (50th percentile, or P_{50}), the range (minimum and maximum), the 25th percentile (P_{25}), and the 75th percentile (P_{75}).

The distance between the 25th percentile (Q1, Quartile 1) and the 75th percentile (Q3, Quartile 3), also known as quartiles, is referred to as the interquartile range (IQR). As a rule of thumb, any score that falls between 1.5 times the IQR and 3 times the IQR is considered a minor outlier. On the other hand, any score that is more than ±3 times the IQR is considered an extreme outlier and is subject for deletion.

Formula

IQR = Q3 - Q1

Q3 + 1.5 x (IQR) < Minor Outlier < Q3 + 3.0 x (IQR)
Q1 – 3.0 x (IQR) > Minor Outlier > Q1 – 1.5 x (IQR)

Extreme Outlier > Q3 + 3.0 x (IQR)
Q1 – 3.0 x (IQR) > Extreme Outlier

In SPSS boxplots, minor outliers are denoted with "O" and extreme outliers are denoted with "E" or "*" (see figure 2.1.B for clarification only). Figure 2.1.A displays a boxplot for levels of depression in the Mental Health data. As it appears in figure 2.1.A, there are three cases with scores greater than 1.5 (IQR)

Figure 2.1.A: Boxplot for Depression

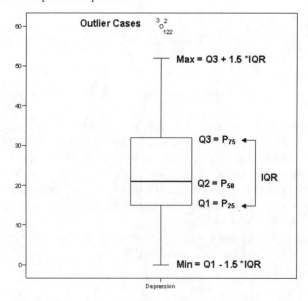

Figure 2.1.B: Boxplot for Variable *X* with Minor and Extreme Outliers

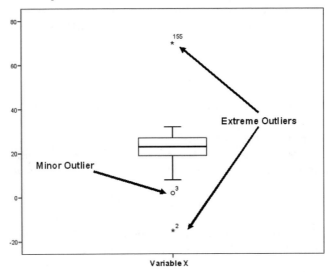

but less than 3 (IQR), thus indicating minor outlier scores. These are case numbers 2, 3, and 122.

Another way to visually display raw scores and identify univariate outlier scores is the *stem-and-leaf plot.* This plot displays the distribution of scores or values for a continuous variable. Each raw score is subdivided into two components, stem and leaf. The stem includes the leading digits, and the leaf includes the trailing digits. A stem-and-leaf plot displays each value, a group of values, frequency for each value, frequency for each group of values, and the total sample size. Unusual values will be marked at either end of the plot. Figure 2.2 displays a stem-and-leaf for depression.

Figure 2.2: A Stem-and-Leaf Plot for Depression

```
Depression Stem-and-Leaf Plot

  Frequency     Stem &  Leaf

      4.00         0 .  0000
      7.00         0 .  5566899
     24.00         1 .  000001122222222333 4 44444 4
     33.00         1 .  5555555566666777777788888888889999
     19.00         2 .  0011111122223334444
     15.00         2 .  555555566788899
     18.00         3 .  000111112222333444
     12.00         3 .  556666778999
      6.00         4 .  000122
      3.00         4 .  568
      4.00         5 .  1112
      3.00  Extremes    (>=60)

Stem width:       10
Each leaf:        1 case(s)                Outlier Cases
```

Like the boxplot display, the stem-and-leaf plot shows that there are three extreme outliers at the upper end of the distribution. Any case with a score of 60 or above is considered an outlier case. No cases with outlier values exist at the lower end of the distribution.

Multivariate Outlier Scores

A case is considered a multivariate outlier if it has extreme or unusual scores on two or more variables. For example, a participant in a study of welfare recipients in Prince George's County, Maryland, who is Caucasian, has twenty years of education, ten years of work experience, and no children will be considered a multivariate case. Another example is a participant in a study of job satisfaction among social services professionals where one subject is twenty-four years old, a medical doctor, and making $100,000 a year.

Identifying multivariate outliers.   Unlike univariate outlier cases, multivariate outliers are more difficult to identify and definitely cannot be identified using any of the previous methods. There are two ways to identify multivariate outlier cases: scatterplots and the Mahalanobis distance test.

A *scatterplot* may be used to identify cases with outliers, however, only in two variables. A scatterplot, as you may recall, is a graph that simultaneously displays scores for each case on two continuous variables, for example, participants' levels of Job Satisfaction and Burnout. Figure 2.3 displays a scatterplot for satisfaction and burnout.

Figure 2.3:   A Scatterplot for Satisfaction and Burnout

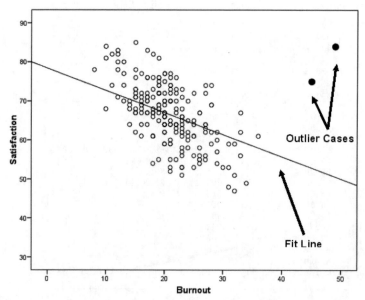

The scatterplot shows two scores that are somewhat far from the fit line, the line around which most scores are clustered. The plot represents the correlation between the two variables (Satisfaction and Burnout). It indicates that two participants have high scores in burnout *and,* at the same time, high scores in job satisfaction.

Mahalanobis distance is perhaps the most frequently used statistical technique to identify cases with extreme multivariate outliers. It was first introduced by P. C. Mahalanobis in 1936.

Mahalanobis distance, also known as Mahalanobis D^2, measures how far a given score is from the centroid, mean score of a combination of variables. Mahalanobis D^2 is similar to the z score, which measures how far each score is from the mean of the z scores distribution. As with z score, Mahalanobis D^2 is used with continuous data.

Mahalanobis distance uses the chi-square distribution for the statistic to examine the distance of each score from the centroid of the distribution. A score is considered a multivariate outlier if its Mahalanobis value (D^2) exceeds a chi-square critical value at alpha of .001. The degrees of freedom are equal to the number of variables in the analysis.

Finally, Mahalanobis distance can be computed in SPSS through the linear regression commands. All variables with continuous data serve as the independent variables, and an arbitrarily created variable (such as ID#, Case#, etc.) with *no missing values* serves as a dependent variable. If no such variable exists, you can create a new variable (e.g., ID) that ranges from 1 to N, where N is the number of cases in the sample (e.g., if $N = 150$, ID ranges between 1 and 150).

Using SPSS to Identify Univariate Outliers

Computing z scores.   We will begin this process to compute z scores for the variables Age (with mean replacement), Emotional Balance (EB), Physical Health (PH), Cognitive Status (CS), and Depression (CESD).

To use SPSS to compute z scores, follow these steps:

1. Click on *Analyze, Descriptive Statistics,* and *Descriptives.*
2. Click on *Age,* and click on the middle arrow to move it into the *Variable(s)* box.
3. Move the remaining variables, EB, PH, CS, and CESD into the *Variable(s)* box.
4. Check the *Save Standardized Values as Variables* box (see screen 2.10).
5. Click on *OK.*

To use SPSS syntax to compute z scores, type the following syntax in the syntax file:

Z Scores SPSS Syntax

DESCRIPTIVES VARIABLES=AGE EB PH CS CESD/SAVE.

Screen 2.10:   SPSS Descriptives *z* Scores Dialog Box

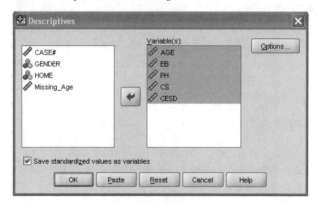

Five new variables that begin with the letter *Z,* for *z* scores, will be created and placed at the end of the SPSS data view file. These variables are ZAGE, ZEB, ZPH, ZCS, and ZCESD.

Next, use the SPSS *Analyze, Descriptive Statistics,* and *Frequencies* commands to run frequency tables and request *Minimum* and *Maximum* scores for these new variables under "Statistics."

Tables 2.8.A and 2.8.B display the SPSS output. Table 2.8.A shows that *z* scores for Age, EB, PH, and CESD are within the acceptable *z* score ranges (±3), thus indicating no univariate outliers. On the other hand, table 2.8.A shows that the lower end of the distribution of CS (-3.692) is outside the acceptable range, thus indicating one or more outlier cases.

The frequency table for CS (table 2.8.B) shows that only one subject has a *z* score of −3.692. All other subjects have *z* scores between −2.620 and 1.666. The data file shows that this *z* score (−3.692) is for case number 141. Thus this case is subject to deletion.

Boxplot and stem-and-leaf plots.   The second method to identify uni-variate outlier cases is through the inspection of distribution's graphs, boxplots, and stem-and-leaf plots. To generate these graphs in SPSS, follow these steps:

Table 2.8.A: *Z*-Score Statistics

Statistics

		ZAGE	ZEB	ZPH	ZCS	ZCESD
N	Valid	155	153	154	152	148
	Missing	0	2	1	3	7
Minimum		-1.572	-2.75	-2.91	**-3.692**	-1.8919
Maximum		2.860	2.064	2.243	1.66620	2.90945

Table 2.8.B: *Z* Scores Frequency Table for CS

ZCS Zscore: Cognitive status

		Frequency	Percent	Valid Percent	Cumulative Percent
Valid	**-3.692**	**1**	.6	.7	.7
	-2.62033	1	.6	.7	1.3
	-2.44173	1	.6	.7	2.0
	-2.08451	3	1.9	2.0	3.9
	-1.90591	2	1.3	1.3	5.3
	-1.72730	1	.6	.7	5.9
	-1.54870	1	.6	.7	6.6
	-1.37009	5	3.2	3.3	9.9
	-1.19149	5	3.2	3.3	13.2
	-1.01288	5	3.2	3.3	16.4
	-.83428	10	6.5	6.6	23.0
	-.65567	5	3.2	3.3	26.3
	-.47706	9	5.8	5.9	32.2
	-.29846	13	8.4	8.6	40.8
	-.11985	10	6.5	6.6	47.4
	.05875	13	8.4	8.6	55.9
	.23736	7	4.5	4.6	60.5
	.41596	5	3.2	3.3	63.8
	.59457	10	6.5	6.6	70.4
	.77317	11	7.1	7.2	77.6
	.95178	7	4.5	4.6	82.2
	1.13038	10	6.5	6.6	88.8
	1.30899	9	5.8	5.9	94.7
	1.48760	6	3.9	3.9	98.7
	1.66620	2	1.3	1.3	100.0
	Total	152	98.1	100.0	
Missing	System	3	1.9		
Total		155	100.0		

1. Click on *Analyze, Descriptive Statistics,* and *Explore.*

2. Click on *Age,* and click on the upper arrow to move it into the *Dependent List* box.

3. Repeat step 2 to move EB, PH, CS, and CESD into the *Dependent List* box (see screen 2.11.A).

4. Under "Display," select *Plots.*

Screen 2.11.A: SPSS Explore Dialog Box

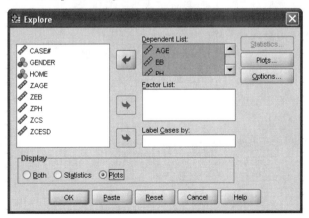

Screen 2.11.B: SPSS Explore Plots Dialog Box

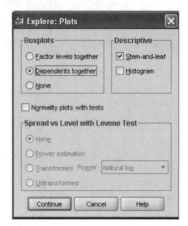

5.   You may check *Factor Levels Together* or *Dependents Together* under "Boxplots." The first option creates a boxplot for each variable separately, and the second creates all boxplots in one graph (which is easier to inspect).

6.   Check *Stem-and-Leaf* under "Descriptive" (SPSS default). You may also check *Histogram* to create histograms for all variables (see screen 2.11.B).

7.   Click on *Continue,* and click on *Options.*

8.   Click on *Exclude Cases Pairwise* to exclude missing cases only for each variable for a particular analysis. Check *Exclude Cases Listwise* (SPSS default) if you want to delete every case that has missing values.

9.   Click on *Continue,* and click on *OK.*

To use SPSS syntax to create boxplots, type the following syntax:

SPSS Syntax

1. All Variables Together:

   EXAMINE VARIABLES=AGE EB PH CS CESD
   /PLOT BOXPLOT STEMLEAF
   /COMPARE VARIABLES
   /MISSING PAIRWISE
   /NOTOTAL.

2. Variables not Together:

   EXAMINE VARIABLES=AGE EB PH CS CESD
   /PLOT BOXPLOT STEMLEAF
   /MISSING PAIRWISE
   /NOTOTAL.

Note: for Listwise, replace PAIRWISE with LISTWISE.

Figure 2.4: Boxplots for All Variables

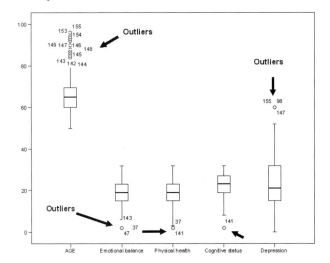

Figure 2.4 displays the boxplots for all variables in the analysis. The graph shows boxplots for Age, Emotional Balance, Physical Health, Cognitive Status, and Depression. The figure shows a number of outliers in all variables. However, none of these outlier cases is considered an extreme outlier. In this graph, all of the outliers are denoted with an "o." Extreme outliers would be denoted with an "x." This result is consistent with the results of z scores, except for Cognitive Status, where one case has a z score smaller than −3.

The stem-and-leaf plots also show that outlier values exist in all variables. The stem-and-leaf plot follows the boxplot's rule of thumb of 1.5 (IQR). However, unlike the boxplot, all cases that are greater than 1.5 (IQR) in a stem-and-leaf plot will be denoted with the word *extremes*.

Figure 2.5.A shows that fourteen cases are considered outliers. These are all cases with ages eighty-four or above.

Figure 2.5.B shows three outlier cases. These are all cases with a score of 2 or below in emotional balance.

Figure 2.5.C shows two outlier cases in physical health. These are all cases with a physical health score of 2 or below.

Figure 2.5.D shows only one outlier case in cognitive status. This is a case with a cognitive status score of 2 or below.

Figure 2.5.E shows three outlier cases in depression. These are cases with a depression score of 60 or above. Recall, 60 is the maximum score in depression.

Finally, it seems that all methods discussed to identify univariate outliers (z scores, boxplots, and stem-and-leaf plots) show that although there are a number of cases with minor outlier values, none, except one in cognitive status, is considered extreme. Thus it appears that the data are within the range for the population from which the data were collected. Next we should examine the data for multivariate outliers.

Figure 2.5.A: Stem-and-Leaf Plot for Age

```
AGE Stem-and-Leaf Plot

 Frequency     Stem &  Leaf

       8.00      5 .   00001111
       6.00      5 .   222333
       8.00      5 .   44445555
       3.00      5 .   677
      10.00      5 .   8888899999
      16.00      6 .   0000000001111111
      13.00      6 .   2222223333333
      21.00      6 .   444445555555555555555
      23.00      6 .   66666666666666667777777
       8.00      6 .   88888899
       4.00      7 .   0001
       5.00      7 .   22333
       5.00      7 .   44555
        .00      7 .
       3.00      7 .   889
       4.00      8 .   0000
       4.00      8 .   2223
      14.00 Extremes  (>=84)
```

Figure 2.5.B: Stem-and-Leaf Plot for Emotional Balance

```
Emotional balance Stem-and-Leaf Plot

 Frequency     Stem &  Leaf

       3.00 Extremes  (=<2)
        .00      0 .
       1.00      0 .   6
       5.00      0 .   88899
       7.00      1 .   0111111
      13.00      1 .   2222223333333
      14.00      1 .   44444555555555
      15.00      1 .   666666777777777
      19.00      1 .   8888888888999999999
      20.00      2 .   00000001111111111111
      27.00      2 .   222222222222233333333333333
       6.00      2 .   444455
       7.00      2 .   6677777
       7.00      2 .   8888999
       5.00      3 .   00001
       4.00      3 .   2222
```

Figure 2.5.C: Stem-and-Leaf Plot for Physical Health

```
Physical health Stem-and-Leaf Plot

 Frequency     Stem &  Leaf

     2.00 Extremes (=<2)
     1.00      0 .  3
     5.00      0 .  89999
    10.00      1 .  0001111111
     8.00      1 .  22233333
    15.00      1 .  444444455555555
    18.00      1 .  666666667777777777
    21.00      1 .  888888889999999999999
    26.00      2 .  00000000000000000011111111
    13.00      2 .  2222222233333
    13.00      2 .  4444444455555
    12.00      2 .  666666777777
     5.00      2 .  89999
     4.00      3 .  0000
     1.00      3 .  2
```

Figure 2.5.D: Stem-and-Leaf Plot for Cognitive Status

```
Cognitive status Stem-and-Leaf Plot

 Frequency     Stem &  Leaf

     1.00 Extremes (=<2)
      .00      0 .
     2.00      0 .  89
     3.00      1 .  111
     3.00      1 .  223
     6.00      1 .  455555
    10.00      1 .  6666677777
    15.00      1 .  888888888899999
    22.00      2 .  0000000001111111111111
    23.00      2 .  22222222223333333333333
    12.00      2 .  444444455555
    21.00      2 .  666666666677777777777
    17.00      2 .  88888889999999999
    15.00      3 .  000000000111111
     2.00      3 .  22
```

Figure 2.5.E: Stem-and-Leaf Plot for Depression

```
Depression Stem-and-Leaf Plot

 Frequency      Stem &  Leaf

      4.00         0 .  0000
      7.00         0 .  5566899
     24.00         1 .  000001122222223334444444
     33.00         1 .  555555556666677777778888888889999
     19.00         2 .  0011111122223334444
     15.00         2 .  555555566788899
     18.00         3 .  000111112222333444
     12.00         3 .  556666778999
      6.00         4 .  000122
      3.00         4 .  568
      4.00         5 .  1112
      3.00 Extremes (>=60)
```

Using SPSS to Identify Multivariate Outliers

Unlike with univariate outliers, when evaluating data for multivariate outliers, a listwise analysis must be conducted. In listwise analysis, all cases with at least one missing value will be excluded from the multivariate analysis. This rule applies to all advanced and multivariate tests that examine a number of variables in the same analysis.

Computing Mahalanobis distance statistics.   As discussed, we will examine the data for multivariate outliers using the Mahalanobis distance statistic. This test is available through the linear regression commands. To begin, follow these steps:

1. Click on *Analyze, Regression,* and *Linear.*

2. Click on *Case#* (remember, this is an arbitrarily created variable), and click on the upper arrow to move it into the *Dependent* box.

3. Move Age, EB, PH, CS, and CESD into the *Independent(s)* box by clicking on the *Independent(s)* arrow (see screen 2.12.A).

4. Click on *Save,* and check the *Mahalanobis* box under "Distances" (see screen 2.12.B).

5. Click on *Continue,* and click on *OK.*

You can also compute the Mahalanobis distance using the following SPSS syntax:

Mahalanobis Distance SPSS Syntax

REGRESSION
/DEPENDENT CASE#
/METHOD=ENTER AGE EB PH CS CESD
/SAVE MAHAL.

Screen 2.12.A: SPSS Linear Regression Dialog Box

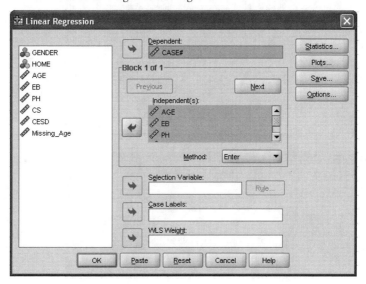

Once this command is executed, a new variable labeled Mah_1 will be created and added to the SPSS file and will be located in the last column in the data
view. The next step is to find what case(s), if any, have a probability of less than
1 percent (*alpha* = .001) of being far from the centroid point.

There are two ways to do this step. First, find the critical value for a chi-
square (in any chi-square table) given the number of degrees of freedom (*df* =
number of independent variables = 5) and alpha of .001. In this case, the critical value is 20.515. Then run a frequency table for the new variable, Mah_1. Any
value that exceeds the critical value is considered a multivariate outlier.

Another way is to utilize SPSS to compute the probability for the Mahalanobis D^2 (Mah_1). Any score with a probability of less than .001 will be considered a multivariate outlier. To do so, follow these steps:

1. Click on *Transform,* and click on *Compute Variable.*

2. Type in the *Target Variable* box "Prob_Mah_1" (probability of Mahalanobis
    distance).

Screen 2.12.B: SPSS Linear Regression Distance Dialog Box

3. Type in the *Numeric Expression* box "1-CDF.CHISQ (MAH_1, 5)" and click *OK*. The *Mah_1* is the Mahalanobis distance variable, and the 5 represents the number of degrees of freedom (see screen 2.13).

You may use the following syntax to compute the probability for the Mahalanobis distance:

Probability of Mahalanobis Distance SPSS Syntax

COMPUTE Prob_Mah_1 = 1-CDF.CHISQ (**MAH_1, 5**).
EXECUTE.

A new variable labeled as Prob_Mah_1 will be added to the data file and will be placed in the last column in the SPSS data view. Next sort the data file

Screen 2.13:   SPSS Compute Dialog Box Probability of Mahalanobis Distance

in ascending order by Prob_Mah_1, as done in screen 2.8 (*Data, Sort Cases,* and move Prob_Mah_1 into the *Sort By* box).

Screen 2.14 displays the SPSS data file sorted by Prob_Mah_1. Notice that only one case has a probability value that is less than .001. This is case number 38, which has a Mahalanobis value of 20.67197 (recall that the chi-square critical value with 5 degrees of freedom and alpha of .001 is 20.515).

To conclude, only one case has a multivariate outlier value. This case is number 38. Thus this case may be deleted.

Now that data have been evaluated for data entry errors, missing values, and univariate and multivariate outliers, the next step is to examine the normality of distributions of all continuous data.

Screen 2.14:   SPSS Data View Sorted by Prob_Mah_1

NORMALITY AND DATA TRANSFORMATION

Normality

Perhaps you are already familiar with the normal distribution and its characteristics. As you may recall, a normal distribution represents continuous data. It is unimodal (one mode), symmetric (both halves are mirror images), and bell shaped. It is also asymptotic to the X axis (the farther it goes from the mean, the closer it gets to the X axis; yet it never touches the X axis). Figure 2.6 displays a normal distribution. The X axis represents the raw scores for a given variable, and the Y axis represents the frequency for each score.

In real life, however, not all distributions follow the shape of a normal curve. A distribution may be positively skewed or negatively skewed. In a positively skewed distribution (see figure 2.7.A), most cases fall to the left of the distribution. In a negatively skewed distribution (see figure 2.7.B), on the other hand, most cases fall to the right of the distribution.

Figure 2.6:   Normal Distribution

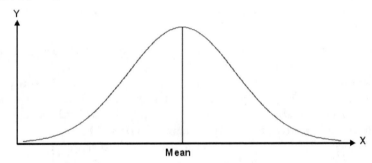

Figure 2.7:   Skewed Distributions

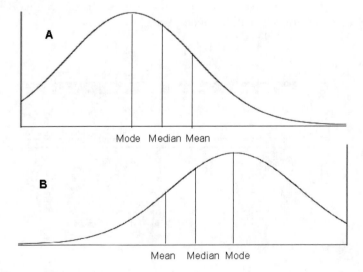

A distribution may also be slightly skewed or severely skewed. With slight skewness, positive or negative, the problem of normality can be ignored. However, if skewness is severe, the problem must be addressed prior to conducting any inferential statistics to ensure that test results can be generalized to the population from which data are collected.

There are two main methods to evaluate normality of distributions: graphs and statistical coefficients.

Graphs.   Traditionally, normality of distributions have been assessed through eyeballing the univariate histograms and the normal probability plots (also known as normal Q-Q plots) for each continuous variable in the study. These plots can be generated by most statistical programs. In SPSS, these plots can be generated through the *Analyze, Descriptive Statistics,* and *Explore* commands (this process will be discussed later in this chapter).

Statistics.   Normality can also be assessed using various statistical techniques and coefficients. The most common are the Fisher's skewness and kurtosis coefficients.[4] As a general rule, a distribution is said to be severely skewed if its skewness value (S) is more than twice its standard error (SES, standard error of skewness). Also, a distribution is said to be severely skewed if its kurtosis value (K) is more than twice its standard error (SEK, standard error of kurtosis). In other words, a distribution is considered normal if it meets these conditions:

$$\text{Skewness: } -1.96 < \frac{S}{\text{SES}} < 1.96$$

$$\text{Kurtosis: } -1.96 < \frac{K}{\text{SEK}} < 1.96$$

S: skewness coefficient
SES: standard error of skewness
K: kurtosis
SEK: standard error of kurtosis

Fisher's measures of skewness and kurtosis are extremely sensitive to outlier cases. Thus they should be examined after outlier cases have been evaluated and the appropriate measures have been taken. Still, the results of skewness and kurtosis should be interpreted with caution. It is highly recommended to also eyeball the distribution to evaluate its skewness and determine whether it is severe.

Recall from your previous classes that most statistical analyses, especially parametric techniques, require that the shape of all dependent variables follow the shape of a normal curve. The question is then, what if a distribution is severely skewed?

---

[4]For more on skewness and kurtosis, see Abu-Bader (2006).

Data Transformation

When data violate the assumption of normality, experienced researchers may consider conducting data transformation on the variable(s) that are severely skewed. Data transformation refers to converting the raw scores of a variable into another type of scores. This conversion could produce a distribution that approaches the shape of a normal curve without affecting the original meaning of the data. Data transformation can also assist in satisfying the assumptions of linearity and homoscedasticity (these assumptions will be discussed in chapter 4).

In order to transform raw data into another form of data, researchers must first examine (1) the direction of the skewness (positive vs. negative) and (2) the severity of the skewness.

With *negatively skewed distributions,* we first must reflect the raw scores so that the distribution becomes positively skewed. By reflecting raw scores, we reverse the interpretation of the scores. That is, if higher scores indicate greater values in the original raw data, then higher scores will indicate lower values in the reflected data. If the original distribution is *positively skewed,* there is no need to reflect the raw data.

To reverse raw scores, follow these three steps:

1. Find the maximum score for the raw data in a given variable.
2. Add one to the maximum score. This sum will serve as a constant.
3. Subtract each raw score from this constant.

Once a negatively skewed distribution is reversed to one that is positively skewed, you should inspect its severity by eyeballing its shape. This inspection will guide you to the appropriate transformation method.

Tabachnick and Fidell (2007) identify six types of skewed distributions and the appropriate method of data transformation. Tables 2.9.A and 2.9.B describe these distributions and their appropriate data transformation.

After the appropriate transformation is completed and a new variable is created, we then should evaluate the distribution of the new variable using both graphs and Fisher's coefficients. Sometimes, however, utilization of a specific method of transformation may not lead to the desired outcome (normal distribution). In such cases, we should try the other methods of transformation until the desired outcome is achieved. Once we achieve a normal distribution, we should use the new variable instead of the original raw data in our data analysis.

Practical Example

To demonstrate how to evaluate normality and conduct data transformation we will use the variable Supervision from the Job Satisfaction SPSS data file.

First we will use SPSS to run a histogram with a normal curve, minimum and maximum values, and measures of skewness and kurtosis coefficients for the variable Supervision. We will also generate normal probability plots.

Table 2.9.A: Positively Skewed Distributions and Type of Transformation

	Shape	Method of Transformation
1		Square root: Compute the square root for each raw score Formula: *TransX = SQRT (X)*
2		Logarithm: Compute the logarithm for each raw score Formula: $TransX = Lg_{10}(X)$
3		Inverse: Reverse each raw score (divide 1 by each score) Formula: *TransX = 1/X*

Notes: $TransX$ = the new variable; $SQRT$ = square root; X = raw score; Lg_{10} = logarithm

Rules: The smallest raw score must by greater than zero (or equal 1) when conducting Lg_{10} or *inverse*.[5] If this occurs, add a constant to each number so the smallest number can be greater than zero. For example, if the smallest number in a distribution is, say, −2, then add 3 (constant) to each number so the smallest number becomes 1. If the smallest number is, say, zero, then add 1 to each raw score.

Table 2.9.B: Negatively Skewed Distributions and Type of Transformation

#	Shape	Method of Transformation

1		1. Reflect each raw score:
		   RX = K − X
		2. Compute their square root:
		   TransX = SQRT (RX)

2		1. Reflect each raw score:
		   RX = K − X
		2. Compute their logarithm:
		   $TransX = Lg_{10}(RX)$

3		1. Reflect each raw score:
		   RX = K − X
		2. Inverse the reflected scores:
		   TransX = 1/RX

Notes: RX = reflect raw scores; K = highest score on the raw data + 1

To generate these graphs and statistics, follow these steps:

1.   Open the Job Satisfaction SPSS data file.

2.   Click on *Analyze, Descriptive Statistics,* and *Explore.*

3.   Scroll down on the variables list (left box), click on *Supervision,* and click on the upper arrow to move *Supervision* into the *Dependent List* box (see

---

[5]Remember, you cannot compute Lg_{10} for either a negative value or zero. In addition, you cannot divide 1 (or any number) by zero.

Screen 2.15: SPSS Explore Dialog Box

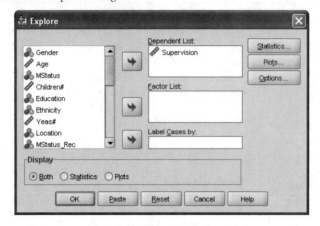

screen 2.15). (You can add more variables to be analyzed by repeating this step. If more than one variable is entered, click on *Options* and choose *Exclude Cases Pairwise,* and click on *Continue.*)

4.   Make sure that *Both* is checked under "Display" in the lower left corner.

5.   Click on the *Statistics* button in the upper right corner. A new dialog box called "Explore: Statistics" will open (see screen 2.16).

6.   Make sure that *Descriptives* is checked. This is the SPSS default.

7.   Click on *Continue* to return to the previous "Explore" dialog box (see screen 2.15).

8.   Click on the *Plots* button. An "Explore: Plots" dialog box will open (see screen 2.17).

9.   Check *None* under "Boxplots," check *Histogram* under "Descriptive," and check *Normality Plots with Tests* in the middle.

10.   Click *Continue,* and click *OK.*

Screen 2.16: SPSS Explore Statistics Dialog Box

To use an SPSS syntax file to generate these plots and statistics, open a new (or existing) syntax file and type the following syntax:

SPSS Explore Syntax

EXAMINE VARIABLES=Supervision
/PLOT HISTOGRAM NPPLOT
/STATISTICS DESCRIPTIVES
/CINTERVAL 95
/MISSING LISTWISE
/NOTOTAL.

Note: if more than one variable is used, change LISTWISE with PAIRWISE.

Screen 2.17:   SPSS Explore Plots Dialog Box

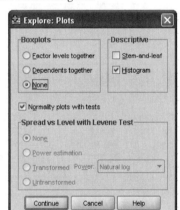

When these commands are executed, SPSS produces a number of tables and graphs. We will discuss only those that are appropriate to our current discussion, which are table 2.10 and figures 2.8 and 2.9.

Table 2.10 displays the measures of central tendency and variability for supervision. In addition, it displays the skewness and kurtosis coefficients and their standard errors. Although all of these descriptive values are important, we are interested in only the maximum, skewness, and kurtosis values.

Skewness.   As it appears, skewness has a value of −1.293. The "−" sign indicates a negative skewness. The question raised is, how severe is this skewness? To answer it, we should divide this skewness value by its standard error, which is .166.

$$\frac{S}{SES} = \frac{-1.293}{.166} = -7.789$$

Table 2.10:   SPSS Explore Output—Descriptives

Descriptives

			Statistic	Std. Error
Supervision	Mean		54.71	1.007
	95% Confidence Interval for Mean	Lower Bound	52.73	
		Upper Bound	56.70	
	5% Trimmed Mean		55.96	
	Median		58.00	
	Variance		217.050	
	Std. Deviation		14.733	
	Minimum		2	
	Maximum		79	
	Range		77	
	Interquartile Range		17	
	Skewness		*–1.293*	*.166*
	Kurtosis		*2.184*	*.331*

This value falls way outside the acceptable range of ±1.96, thus indicating *severe negative skewness.*

Kurtosis.   Kurtosis has a value of 2.184 and a standard error of .331. To examine the severity of kurtosis, we divide kurtosis by its standard error.

$$\frac{K}{SEK} = \frac{2.184}{.331} = 6.598$$

This value also falls way outside the acceptable range of ±1.96. This value indicates severe kurtosis, which is consistent with the results of skewness.[6]

Maximum.   We need this value only if we have a *negatively* skewed distribution that needs to be transformed. This value plus one will serve as a constant (K = Maximum + 1). In our case, the maximum value is 79. If we decide to transform the raw scores, then we will first subtract each supervision score from 80 (79 + 1 = 80) to reflect the shape of the distribution (from negative to positive) and then conduct the appropriate transformation.

However, before we make such a decision, we need to inspect both the histogram and the Q-Q plot.

---

[6]*Note:* Due to the complexity of the calculations of these coefficients, their results may not always be consistent. In addition, they may not be consistent with our own judgment when eyeballing the distribution.

Figure 2.8:   SPSS Explore Output—Histogram

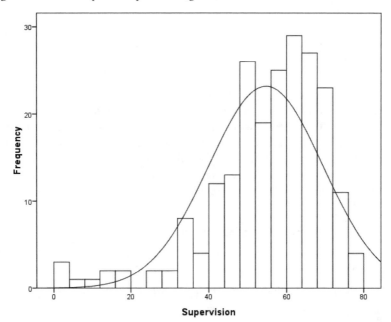

Figure 2.8 displays the histogram with a normal curve for the variable Supervision. As it appears in the graph, Supervision is skewed to the left (long tail to the left), thus indicating a negative skewness. This finding is consistent with both skewness and kurtosis coefficients.

Lastly, we will inspect the normal Q-Q plot displayed in figure 2.9. For a distribution to be considered normal, all scores should fall on a straight line. Figure 2.9, however, indicates that a few cases depart from this fit line on both ends, thus indicating a departure from normality (skewed distribution).

Figure 2.9:   SPSS Explore Output—Normal Q-Q Plot

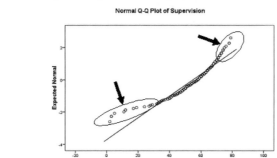

To conclude, both eyeballing the distribution of supervision and evaluating both skewness and kurtosis coefficients indicate a significantly skewed distribution to the left (negative skewness). Therefore, this distribution is eligible for data transformation, which may convert it into one that approaches the shape of a normal curve.

Transformation of supervision.   Recall that supervision has a negative skewness. As it appears in figure 2.8 (histogram), its shape may look like that in table 2.9.B, #2. To transform supervision into a normal distribution, we need to take two actions: (1) reflect the shape of supervision into positive skewness, and (2) compute the square root for the reflected scores.

To reflect supervision,[7] we need to subtract each supervision score from 80. Recall that 80 equals the highest score in supervision (79) plus one. Follow these steps in SPSS to reflect supervision:

1.   Open the Job Satisfaction SPSS data file.

2.   Click on *Transform* and *Compute Variable.* A new dialog box called "Compute Variable" will open.

3.   Type the new variable name in the *Target Variable* box, "R_Supervision."

4.   Type "80-" in the *Numeric Expression* box.

5.   Scroll down in the *Type & Label* box, click on *Supervision,* and click on the upper arrow to move it into the *Numeric Expression* box after "80-" so you have "80-Supervision" (see screen 2.18).

6.   Click on *OK.*

You can also use the following SPSS syntax to compute this variable:

SPSS Compute Variable Syntax

COMPUTE R_Supervision=80-Supervision.

Both the SPSS toolbar and syntax commands will add a new variable labeled R_Supervision in the last column in the SPSS data file.

Table 2.11 and the graphs in figure 2.10 compare both original supervision scores and the reflected scores. Notice that both variables still have the same skewness and kurtosis coefficients, except that the raw data have a negative value (−1.293) and the reflected data have a positive value (1.293), indicating a positively skewed distribution.

---

[7]Remember, you do not need this step if the variable of interest has positive skewness. Also, when scores are reflected, their meaning is reversed as well.

Screen 2.18:   SPSS Compute Variable Reverse Score Dialog Box

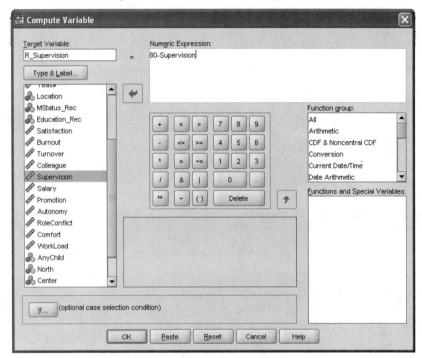

Table 2.11:   Comparison between Original and Reflected Supervision Scores

Statistics

		Supervision	R_Supervision
N	Valid	214	214
	Missing	4	4
	Skewness	−1.293	1.293
	Std. Error of Skewness	.166	.166
	Kurtosis	2.184	2.184
	Std. Error of Kurtosis	.331	.331

Transformation of (reflected) supervision.   We will begin by transforming supervision into the square root. If this transformation does not lead to a normal distribution, we should try other methods of transformation.

To compute the square root of R_Supervision, follow the same steps used to reflect supervision. Here, however, you should call the new variable SQRT_Supervision. Also, in the *Numeric Expression* box, type SQRT(R_Supervision) as it appears in screen 2.19.

Figure 2.10:   Histograms for Original and Reflected Supervision Scores

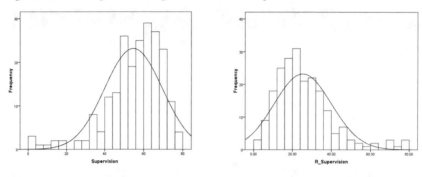

Screen 2.19:   SPSS Compute Variable Square Root Dialog Box

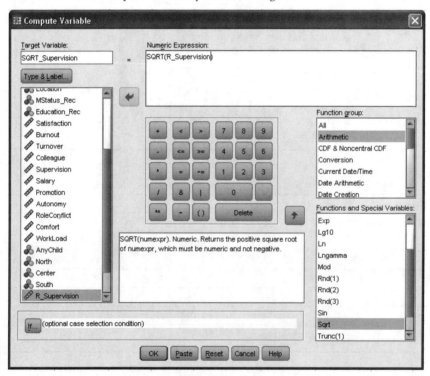

The following are the SPSS syntax commands to compute square root, logarithm, and inverse:

Square Root Syntax

COMPUTE SQRT_Supervision=SQRT(R_Supervision).

> Logarithm Syntax
>
> COMPUTE LOG_Supervision=LG10(R_Supervision).
>
> Inverse Syntax
>
> COMPUTE Inverse_Supervision=1/(R_Supervision).

Table 2.12:   Descriptive Statistics for SQRT_Supervision

Statistics

SQRT_Supervision

N	Valid	214.000
	Missing	4.000
	Skewness	.354
	Std. Error of Skewness	.166
	Kurtosis	.447
	Std. Error of Kurtosis	.331

After transformation is completed, we should evaluate the shape of the newly created variable SQRT_Supervision. You can use SPSS *Analyze, Descriptive Statistics,* and *Frequencies* commands to request the skewness, kurtosis, and histogram with a normal curve for SQRT_Supervision. Table 2.12 and figure 2.11 display the SPSS output.

The results presented in table 2.12 indicate that the skewness value is slightly greater than twice its standard error $\{\frac{S}{SES} = \frac{.354}{.166} = 2.13\}$ and kurtosis is actually smaller than twice its standard error $\{\frac{K}{SEK} = \frac{.447}{.331} = 1.35\}$. Thus, based on these results, we may conclude that the shape of the newly transformed distribution approaches the shape of a normal curve. This conclusion is also supported by the histogram in figure 2.11.

Finally, given these results, it is highly recommended to use this variable, SQRT_Supervision, instead of the original raw scores of Supervision in all analyses. Remember, however, that higher scores in this SQRT_Supervision variable indicate lower quality of supervision and lower scores indicate greater quality of supervision.

SUMMARY

This chapter presented the first and most important step in data analysis. No data analysis is complete or results accurate until data have been inspected for various concerns, if any, and the appropriate measures have been taken to address these concerns.

This chapter began by discussing methods of data cleaning and inspecting categorical data coding. The chapter then discussed evaluation of missing data

Figure 2.11:   Histogram for SQRT_Supervision

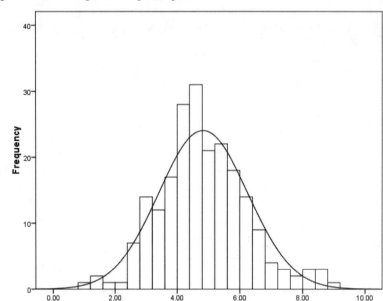

and their severity in data analysis. It presented methods for dealing with cases with missing values. These methods include excluding cases with missing values and replacing missing values. As a rule, cases with missing data could be excluded from analysis if they represent 5 percent or less of the total number of cases. Otherwise, replacement of missing values with the mean or median or replacement with a predicted value could be used.

The chapter then dealt with one of the most significant issues that may affect the results of the data. This issue relates to unusual scores known as outlier cases. Two types were discussed, univariate outliers and multivariate outliers. The first type can be evaluated by inspecting z scores, boxplots, and stem-and-leaf plots. The second can be evaluated by inspecting scatterplots and by computing and evaluating the Mahalanobis distance using the chi-square test.

Chapter 2 then discussed another major issue that could determine what statistical technique can be used to analyze the data. This issue relates to the shape of the distributions of continuous scores, known as normality of distributions. The chapter presented two methods used in evaluating the shape of distributions, graphs and measures of skewness and kurtosis.

Then the chapter presented methods of data transformation to "fix" the problem of normality. These methods depend on the severity and direction of the skewness (positive vs. negative).

Finally, the chapter presented a step-by-step guideline of how to use SPSS to examine missing data, outlier cases, and normality of distribution and how to conduct data transformation.

Chapter 3 will introduce the first advanced statistical technique in this book, simple linear regression. The chapter will present its objectives, purpose, regression equation, coefficients, and assumptions of simple linear regression. It will then present a real example, explaining in detail the utilization of the test from stating the hypotheses to writing and presenting the results in a summary table.

PRACTICAL EXERCISES

A clinical researcher working at the Office of Refugee Resettlement in the Washington, D.C., metropolitan area was interested in the post-traumatic stress disorder (PTSD) and health locus of control among refugees who were admitted into the United States in the past year. The researcher recruited 230 recently arrived refugees who then completed the *PTSD* survey (see appendix, Data File 5).

Access the PTSD SPSS data file and answer the following questions:

1. Check the data for possible data entry errors.
2. Check all variables for missing values. Are there any missing values? If yes, what variable appears to have the most missing values?
3. How would you deal with these missing values? Discuss your answer.
4. Recode the variable PTSD into a new variable (MissingPTSD), and code all missing cases as "0" and all valid cases as "1."
5. Compare the two groups you created in question 4 on levels of physical health. Is there a significant difference between the two groups? Discuss your answer in detail.
6. Based on your answer for question 5, how would you deal with these missing cases? Discuss your answer in detail.
7. Check the variables PTSD, IHLC, CHLC, and PHLC for univariate outliers. Are there any minor or extreme outliers? Discuss your answer in detail.
8. Use the variable PHLC as a criterion and check the data for multivariate outlier cases. Are there any multivariate outlier cases? Discuss your answer.
9. Examine the distributions of the variables PTSD, IHLC, CHLC, and PHLC. Are any of these distributions severely skewed? If yes, which distribution(s)? Discuss your answer in detail.
10. Conduct data transformation for each variable that is severely skewed. Does this transformation "fix" the problem? Discuss your answer in detail.

CHAPTER 3

Simple Linear Regression

LEARNING OBJECTIVES

1. Understand the purpose of simple linear regression
2. Understand the regression equation
3. Understand the definition and use of the confidence interval
4. Understand the assumptions underlying simple linear regression
5. Understand how to use SPSS to run the analysis
6. Understand how to interpret and present the results of the test

DATA SETS (APPENDIX)

Job Satisfaction
Mental Health

INTRODUCTION

Perhaps you already have learned to some extent about both the Pearson product-moment correlation coefficient and Spearman's *rho* coefficient tests. These tests are utilized to examine the linear relationship between two continuous variables measured at the same time (dependent and independent variables), that is, paired observations. Furthermore, the tests produce a correlation coefficient ranging between "−1" and "+1," which indicates the direction and the strength of the relationship between the two variables under study (e.g., the relationship between Years of Education and Income).

Yet, what if we want to know more about the relationship between these two variables? For example, can a financial advisor predict one's income given his or her level of education? Or can a university admissions officer predict students' grades in undergraduate school based on their high school GPA? Another question would be if a case manager can predict welfare recipients' level of depression given their physical health status. Or would it be possible for a psychologist to predict whether his or her customers become obese given their levels of self-esteem?

In these and similar cases, computing the Pearson correlation and/or Spearman *rho* is by itself a very important step in detecting whether the two variables share some variances, that is, coefficient of determination symbolized by r^2. These tests, however, do not allow us to make such a prediction. Therefore a more advanced statistical technique is needed to help us in our prediction. This technique is known as *simple linear regression.*

SIMPLE LINEAR REGRESSION

Purpose

Simple linear regression, simply known as *linear regression,* is an extension of the Pearson product-moment correlation coefficient; thus it is a bivariate statistical technique. It is utilized to further examine the relationship between two continuous variables, X and Y, where X is the independent variable and Y is the dependent variable. The independent variable (X) is also known as the *predictor, factor,* or *explanatory* variable, and the dependent variable (Y) is known as the *outcome* or *criterion* variable. In addition, linear regression analysis helps researchers to make a prediction about the outcomes based on the scores of the independent variables.

Linear regression, on the other hand, does not test for causality, that one variable is the cause of a second variable.[1] Neither does linear regression test whether the data from both variables form a linear correlation (relationship). The test assumes, however, that these variables have a significant linear relationship. This assumption must be examined prior to utilizing linear regression, usually using the Pearson correlation coefficient and the scatterplot. Otherwise, if no significant linear correlation exists between the two, it is unwise to use the linear regression to make a prediction, because the two variables have nothing in common.

Equation of Simple Linear Regression

Linear regression analysis uses the observed data for the independent variable (X) and the dependent variable (Y) to develop a linear equation that helps researchers in predicting an outcome $(\hat{Y})$ given existing data on both variables.

The linear equation, also known as the *regression equation,* is a straight line throughout the data that best fits these data. This fit line helps researchers to understand how a change in the X variable leads to a change in the Y variable. Mathematically, a linear equation is computed as follows:

---

[1]See Abu-Bader (2006), chapter 7.

Unstandardized Linear Equation

$$\hat{Y} = a + bX$$

Standardized Linear Equation

$$\hat{Y} = \beta Z_x$$

$\hat{Y}$ = Predicted score for the dependent variable; Y coordinate.

a = Intercept constant. It is a point where the fit line intercepts the Y axis. It is the value of Y when X equals zero. Its unstandardized coefficient (a) equals zero in standardized linear equation.

b = Slope of the regression line. It is the amount of change in the dependent variable (Y) for each one unit change in the independent variable (X). This is an unstandardized regression coefficient. Use "β" (*beta* = standardized regression coefficient) in standardized linear equation.

X = Score for the dependent variable; X coordinate.

Z_x = Z score for the X score.

Figure 3.1 illustrates a linear regression equation. Notice that each point (small circles) represents two measures, one for X (the independent variable) and another for Y (the dependent variable). The number of these points equals the number of participants in the study (sample size or N).

The coordinates (X_i, Y_i) for each point represent the scores of X and Y, respectively, for the ith person. The distance of Y_i from the fit line "ΔY_i" (read: Delta Y_i) represents how far the Y score of this person is from the fit line. The distance of X_i from the fit line (ΔX_i) represents how far the X score of this person is from the fit line.

Mathematically, the slope of a linear equation is computed by dividing the Y distance from the fit line by the X distance from the fit line for a particular person.

$$\text{Slope} = \frac{\Delta Y_i}{\Delta X_i}$$

Coefficients of Simple Linear Regression

Linear regression analysis computes a number of coefficients. Each coefficient provides valuable information about the relationship between the two variables. These coefficients include the following:

Correlation coefficient (R). R represents the correlation coefficient between the dependent variable (Y) and the independent variable (X). It is the same as r in Pearson's product-moment correlation.

Figure 3.1:   Scatterplot of Y on X

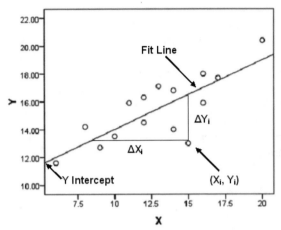

R square (R^2). R^2 represents the amount (%) of variance in the dependent variable explained by the independent variable. It is the same as the coefficient of determination (r^2) in Pearson's product-moment correlation. R square ranges between "0" and "1," with "0" indicating that the linear regression line does not fit the data at all and "1" indicating that the linear regression line fits the data perfectly. The complement of R^2 (that is, $1 - R^2$) is the amount of unexplained variance in the dependent variable, or errors.

Adjusted R square (Adjusted R^2).   Adjusted R^2 is a more conservative measure than the standard R^2. It is based on the number of factors entered in the regression analysis as opposed to the sample size. The greater the number of factors entered compared to the sample size, the smaller it becomes. When only one factor is entered (as in simple linear regression), it will be either equal or approximately equal to the standard R^2.

Regression constant (a).   It represents the intercept in the regression equation (a). It is the value of Y when the values of X equal zero.

Unstandardized regression coefficient (b).   It is the slope in the regression equation (b). In other words, it represents the proportion of change in the dependent variable (Y) for each one unit of change in the independent variable (X). The unstandardized regression coefficient is computed based on the actual raw scores of both variables in the regression analysis.

Standardized regression coefficient (beta, β).   Also known as *partial correlation coefficient,* it represents a linear correlation coefficient between the dependent and independent variables while controlling for the effect of other variables in the analysis. However, since there are only two variables in the simple linear regression analysis, one dependent and one independent, beta will be identical to the correlation coefficient (R).

Like the Pearson correlation coefficient, beta ranges from -1.00 (perfect negative correlation) to $+1.00$ (perfect positive correlation). A zero coefficient indicates no correlation between the criterion and the corresponding factor. The signs ($-/+$) indicate the direction of the relationship between the two variables.

The standardized regression coefficient (β) is more desirable than the unstandardized regression coefficient (b), because it is based on transforming the raw scores of variables under analysis to z scores. By transforming raw scores to z scores, the two variables will have the same units of measurement, making them more comparable.

Confidence Interval

As discussed earlier, linear regression analysis estimates (predicts) individual scores on the dependent variable based on knowing the scores of the independent variable. These scores are estimates driven from the data collected from a representative sample. The sample, however, is only an approximation of the population, and so are the predicted scores.

The only way that predicted scores could equal the true scores is if researchers studied every person (element) in the population, which is unlikely. On the other hand, it is possible to use the sample data and the level of significance (*alpha* = .05) to estimate a range of values that are more likely to contain the true predicted scores for the population. This range of scores is known as the *confidence interval* (CI).

Therefore, the confidence interval is a range of values (upper limit and lower limit) that researchers are confident contains the predicted scores for the outcome, dependent variable. How confident are they? It depends on the level of significance, alpha, which determines what researchers call levels of confidence.

The *level of confidence* is the degree of confidence researchers have that the confidence interval contains the true predicted scores. It is usually the complement of the level of significance (*alpha*). For example, if *alpha* is set at .05, then the level of confidence will be .95, or 95 percent. It is written as the *95th CI*.

Level of Confidence = 1 − *alpha*

Confidence statement is a statement of confidence in which researchers state their level of confidence in their data. It is usually written as follows: We are 95 percent confident that the interval [lower limit] to [upper limit] contains the true dependent variable predicted score for a particular individual or population. For example, we are 95 percent confident that the interval 45 to 55 contains the true predicted level of job satisfaction of John Doe.

Assumptions

As mentioned earlier, linear regression is an advanced technique of Pearson's correlation coefficient. In this sense, it requires the same set of assumptions. These assumptions include the following:

1. SAMPLE REPRESENTATION: The sample must be representative of the population from which it is drawn and to which generalization will be made.

2. LEVELS OF MEASUREMENT: The dependent and independent variables must be continuous data and measured at the interval level of measurement or higher.

3. NORMALITY: The shape of the distributions of both variables must approximate the shape of a normal curve (see chapter 2).

4. SAMPLE SIZE: The sample size should be large enough to conduct simple linear regression analysis. Although there is no clear-cut number of cases required to conduct the analysis, the *central limit theorem* has shown that variables are quite normally distributed based on sample sizes as low as 30 cases (see Landauer, 1997; Munro, 2005). Thus, as a general rule, a sample size of at least 30 subjects is needed for conducting this analysis.

Assumptions 1, 2, and 4 are methodological assumptions and therefore can be evaluated by referring to the research methodology. Assumption 3 can be evaluated by inspecting the histograms and the normal probability plots of both variables. If skewness exists in either or both variables, consider data transformation as outlined in chapter 2.

In addition to these four assumptions, the linear regression analysis requires the following assumptions:

5. LINEARITY: The relationship between the independent and dependent variables must be linear.

This assumption must be evaluated prior to utilizing a linear regression analysis. It can be tested by (a) examining the correlation coefficient between the two variables using Pearson's correlation coefficient and (b) constructing and inspecting a scatterplot displaying the relationship between the two variables.

With significant correlation and minor deviation from the fit line in the scatterplot, the problem is not severe. However, if deviation is throughout the plot, consider data transformation as discussed in chapter 2. On the other hand, if data transformation does not resolve the problem, linear regression analysis probably is not the right statistical method. Table 3.1 and figure 3.2 examine the assumption of linearity between the variables Job Satisfaction and Quality of Supervision (recall from chapter 2 that Supervision was transformed into the square root).

Table 3.1 shows a significant negative relationship between Job Satisfaction and Supervision. Lower scores in Supervision are associated with higher scores in

Table 3.1:   Pearson Correlation between Satisfaction and Supervision

		Satisfaction
SQRT_Super Pearson Correlation		−.356
	Sig. (1-tailed)	.000
	N	214

Job Satisfaction. Again, remember that Supervision was first reflected and then transformed. Therefore, lower scores mean greater quality of supervision. Thus the greater the quality of supervision is, the greater the levels of satisfaction among social workers.

Figure 3.2 also shows a negative relationship between the two variables. Notice that the fit line goes from the upper left corner to the lower right corner. In a positive relationship, the fit line goes from the lower left corner to the upper right corner. Notice also that most of the points are clustered around the fit line (with few deviations), indicating a linear relationship.

6.   HOMOSCEDASTICITY: Homoscedasticity is also known as the assumption of *homogeneity of variances* or *uniformity of variances*. It implies that for each value of the independent variable, the dependent variable should be normally distributed (equal variances). In other words, the variance around the regression line should be the same for all values of the independent variables.

Figure 3.2:   Scatterplot for Job Satisfaction by Supervision

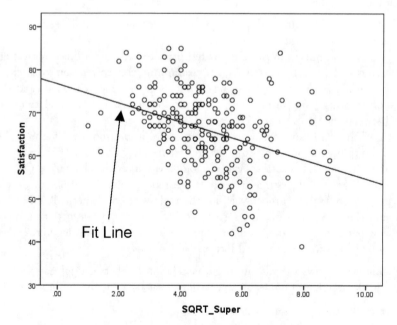

When the independent variable is a categorical (grouping) variable, homoscedasticity is simply tested using *Levene's test of equality* (or *homogeneity*) *of variances,* which is available in the independent *t*-test and analysis of variance tests.

In linear regression analysis, however, homoscedasticity can be evaluated by plotting the residuals (errors) against the predicted values. This plot is available in SPSS through the linear regression analysis (an illustration will be provided later in the chapter). A horizontal line parallel to the *X* axis indicates that the assumption of homoscedasticity is met. Departure from the line indicates heteroscedasticity. If heteroscedasticity happens, again consider data transformation.

Figure 3.3 displays a scatterplot of the standardized predicted scores by the standardized residual scores. If homoscedasticity exists, the scores should be distributed somewhat equally around the horizontal line. Figure 3.3 shows that the data are homoscedastic, however with minor deviation. Minor deviation from the line can be ignored; it will not impact the analysis.

7.   NORMALITY OF ERROR: Errors, also called residuals, are the differences between the predicted and observed scores. Linear regression analysis requires that the errors be normally distributed. If the analysis is perfect, the difference between the observed scores and predicted scores will be zero.

This assumption is easily detected by inspecting the histogram and normal probability plots for the residuals. These graphs are available in SPSS and most statistical software. If residuals are normally distributed, they should fall on the straight diagonal line of the normal probability plot.

Figure 3.3:   Scatterplot for Predicted and Residual Scores

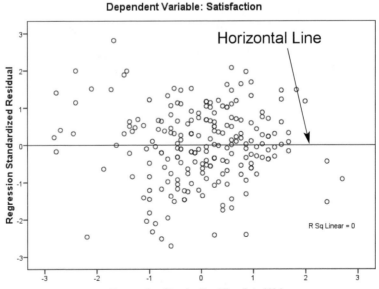

Dependent Variable: Satisfaction

Figures 3.4.A and 3.4.B display a histogram with a normal curve and a normal probability plot, respectively, for the standardized residuals.

Figure 3.4.A indicates that the shape of the distribution of the residuals (errors) approaches that of a normal curve. Also, this is consistent with figure 3.4.B, which shows a normal distribution. Notice that most of the residual points fall on the straight diagonal line.

Figure 3.4.A: Histogram of the Residuals—Dependent Variable Job Satisfaction

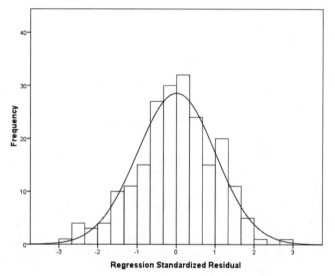

Figure 3.4.B: Normal Probability Plot of Standardized Residuals—
Dependent Variable Job Satisfaction

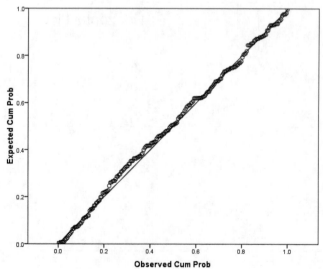

PRACTICAL EXAMPLE

To demonstrate the utilization of linear regression analysis using SPSS, we will analyze the relationship between physical health and emotional balance from the Mental Health SPSS data file. To do so, we will follow the steps in hypothesis testing.[2]

Hypothesis Testing

Step 1: State the Null and Alternative Hypotheses.

H_0: There is no significant relationship between emotional balance and physical health in the sample's population. That is:

$\beta = 0$

H_a: Physical health will be a significant predictor of emotional balance in the sample's population. That is:

$\beta \neq 0$

Step 2: Set the Criteria for Rejecting the Null Hypothesis.
We will set alpha at .05 ($\alpha = .05$). That is, reject H_0 only if $p \leq .05$.

Step 3: Choose the Appropriate Statistical Test.
As it appears in the research hypothesis, the purpose of this analysis is to examine whether knowing the scores in physical health predicts the scores in emotional balance. Thus a linear regression analysis seems most appropriate. However, before we perform this analysis, we must evaluate the test's assumptions.

1. SAMPLE REPRESENTATIVENESS: The data in this study were collected from a representative sample of 155 participants (see appendix).

2. LEVELS OF MEASUREMENT: Linear regression requires that both variables consist of continuous data and are measured at the interval level of measurement. In this study, both the independent variable (Physical Health) and the dependent variable (Emotional Balance) were measured using well-known scales, thus their total scores are measured at the interval level.

3. NORMALITY: The distributions of both independent and dependent variables must approach a normal curve. To examine the distributions, we will examine the skewness coefficients, histograms, and probability plots for both variables (see chapter 2 on how to use SPSS to generate these plots). Table 3.2 displays the descriptive statistics for both emotional balance and physical health.

---

[2]For further discussion of the steps in hypothesis testing, see Abu-Bader (2006).

Table 3.2:   Measures of Skewness and Kurtosis

	Emotional Balance	Physical Health
Valid	153	154
Missing	2	1
Skewness	−.196	−.259
Std. Error of Skewness	.196	.195
Kurtosis	.091	.134
Std. Error of Kurtosis	.390	.389

Applying the rules for skewness and kurtosis (see chapter 2), we find that neither distribution exceeds the ±1.96 cutoff normal value.

<table>
<tr><td colspan="2" align="center">General Rule</td></tr>
<tr><td colspan="2" align="center">Skewness: $-1.96 < \dfrac{S}{SES} < 1.96$</td></tr>
<tr><td colspan="2" align="center">Kurtosis: $-1.96 < \dfrac{K}{SEK} < 1.96$</td></tr>
<tr><td align="center">Emotional Balance</td><td align="center">Physical Health</td></tr>
<tr>
<td>✓ Skewness $= \dfrac{-.196}{.196} = -1$

✓ Kurtosis $= \dfrac{.091}{.390} = .23$</td>
<td>✓ Skewness $= \dfrac{-.259}{.195} = -1.63$

✓ Kurtosis $= \dfrac{.134}{.389} = .34$</td>
</tr>
</table>

Figures 3.5 and 3.6 display the histograms and the probability plots for both physical health and emotional balance. Eyeballing these plots, we find nor-

Figure 3.5:   Histogram and Normal Q-Q Plot for Physical Health

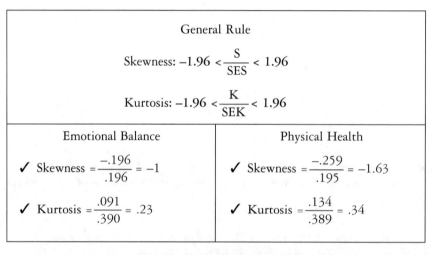

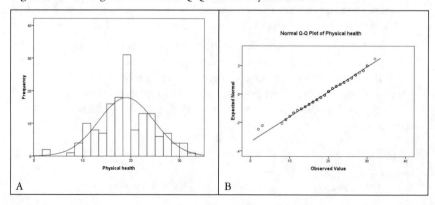

Figure 3.6:   Histogram and Normal Q-Q Plot for Emotional Balance

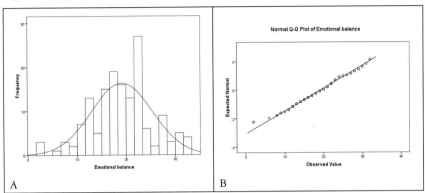

A   B

mal distributions, with minor deviations. Thus both measures of skewness and kurtosis and plots indicate that the shape of the distributions approaches the shape of a normal curve.

4. LINEARITY: This assumption implies that Emotional Balance (dependent variable) and Physical Health (independent variable) have a linear relationship.

    We will examine this assumption by utilizing the Pearson's correlation coefficient test and by creating a scatterplot for emotional balance on physical health. Pearson's correlation can be utilized in SPSS through the *Analyze, Correlate,* and *Bivariate* commands. A scatterplot can be generated in SPSS through the *Graphs, Legacy Dialogs,* and *Scatter/Dot* commands.[3] As a reminder, the following are the SPSS syntax for both Pearson's correlation and scatterplots.

SPSS Pearson's Correlation Syntax

CORRELATIONS
/VARIABLES=EB PH
/PRINT=TWOTAIL NOSIG
/MISSING=PAIRWISE.

SPSS Scatterplot Syntax

GRAPH
/SCATTERPLOT(BIVAR)=PH WITH EB
/MISSING=LISTWISE.

Table 3.3 displays the results of Pearson's correlation, and figure 3.7 displays a scatterplot for emotional balance and physical health. As it appears in

---

[3]For more on these commands, see Abu-Bader (2006).

Table 3.3:   Correlation between Emotional Balance and Physical Health

		Emotional Balance	Physical Health
Emotional Balance	Pearson Correlation	1.00	.536**
	Sig. (1-tailed)		.000
	N	153	153
Physical Health	Pearson Correlation	.536**	1.00
	Sig. (1-tailed)	.000	
	N	153	154

** $p < .01$

Figure 3.7:   Scatterplot for Emotional Balance and Physical Health

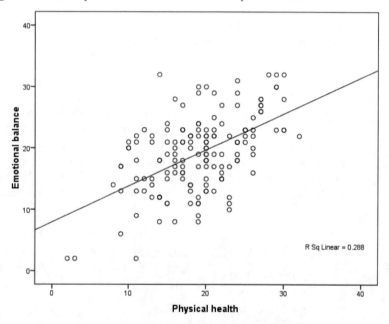

both table 3.3 and figure 3.7, physical health and emotional balance have a significant positive linear relationship ($r = .54, p < .001$).

5.   HOMOSCEDASTICITY: As discussed, this assumption implies that the dependent variable is normally distributed for each level of the independent variable.

To examine this assumption, we will plot the residuals against the predicted values. To request this plot in SPSS we will use the SPSS *Regression* commands:

a.   Open the Mental Health SPSS data file.

b.   Click on *Analyze, Regression,* and *Linear.*

Screen 3.1:   SPSS Linear Regression Dialog Box

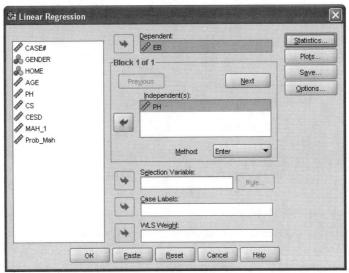

c.   Click on *EB* (Emotional Balance) in the variable list, and click on the top arrow to move *EB* into the *Dependent* box.

d.   Click on *PH* (Physical Health) in the variable list, and click on the second arrow to move *PH* into the *Independent(s)* box (see screen 3.1).

e.   Click on *Plots*. A "Linear Regression: Plots" screen will open (see screen 3.2).

f.   Click on the *ZPRED* (Standardized Predicted) in the left box and move it into the *X* box.

g.   Click on *ZRESID* (Standardized Residuals) in the left box and move it into the *Y* box.

Screen 3.2:   SPSS Linear Regression Plots Dialog Box

h.   Check both the *Histogram* and *Normal Probability Plot* boxes under "Standardized Residual Plots." This command will be used to evaluate the next assumption, normality of residuals.

i.   Click on *Continue* and *OK.*

You also can request these plots using the SPSS syntax:

SPSS Linear Regression Plots Syntax

```
REGRESSION
/DEPENDENT EB
/METHOD=ENTER PH
/SCATTERPLOT=(*ZRESID, *ZPRED)
/RESIDUALS HIST(ZRESID) NORM(ZRESID).
```

Once these commands are executed, SPSS produces a number of tables and graphs. Only one graph is discussed here. This graph is the scatterplot for predicted and residual scores. Others are discussed later in this chapter. Figure 3.8.A displays this graph. It is missing a fit line. To insert a fit line on the graph, follow these steps:

a.   Double-click anywhere on the graph.

b.   A new dialog box called "Chart Editor" will open.

c.   Click on *Elements* in the main menu, and click on *Fit Line at Total.* This command will insert a horizontal line on the graph.

d.   Click on *X* to close the "Chart Editor" dialog box and return to SPSS output.

Figure 3.8.B displays a scatterplot with a fit line for emotional balance and physical health. Inspecting this plot, we find that the points are almost equally

Figure 3.8:   Scatterplot for Predicted Scores and Residual Scores

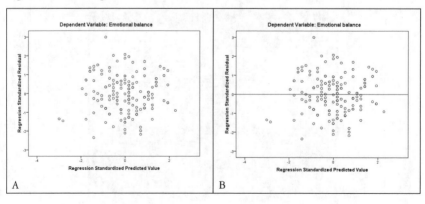

clustered around the line (half above and half below) with minor deviation. This finding indicates that emotional balance is equally distributed on each level of physical health.

Remember, if severe deviation exists, consider data transformation, as discussed in chapter 2.

6. NORMALITY OF ERROR: This assumption implies that the residuals are normally distributed. To examine this assumption, we will utilize SPSS to generate two graphs, a histogram and a normal probability plot.

To generate these graphs, follow the same steps discussed for homoscedasticity (particularly step h). These graphs are figures 3.9.A and 3.9.B. Figure 3.9.A shows that the residuals are normally distributed. Figure 3.9.B, the normal probability plot, shows that almost all residuals are clustered on a straight diagonal line, indicating a normal distribution. Again, if normality is violated, consider data transformation.

Evaluation of data reveals that none of the assumptions was violated, and therefore it is safe to conduct a linear regression analysis.

However, let's say, for instance, that one or more of the assumptions of normality, linearity, or homoscedasticity was severely violated. Transformation of one or both variables (as discussed for missing data and outlier cases in chapter 2) is likely to fix the problem. If not, try another type of transformation. If the problem(s) continue to exist, linear regression may not be the right technique.

How to Use SPSS to Run Linear Regression Analysis

Step 4: Run the Linear Regression Analysis.

Next we will utilize SPSS to run a linear regression analysis to predict emotional balance (EB) based on physical health (PH). To use SPSS to run linear regression analysis, follow these steps:

Figure 3.9: Histogram and Normal P-P Probability Plot for Residuals

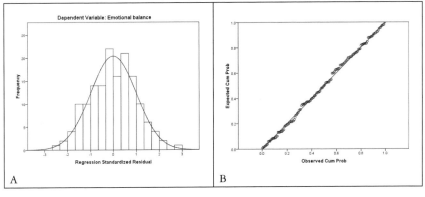

1.   Follow steps a through d for homoscedasticity (see screen 3.1).

2.   After moving *PH* into the *Independent(s)* box and *EB* into the *Dependent* box, click on *Statistics.* A new dialog box called "Linear Regression: Statistics" will open (see screen 3.3).

Screen 3.3:   SPSS Linear Regression Statistics Dialog Box

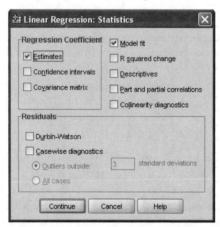

3.   Make sure that *Estimates* and *Model Fit* are checked (the SPSS defaults).

4.   Click on *Continue* to return to the main "Linear Regression" dialog box.

5.   Click on *Save.* A "Linear Regression: Save" dialog box will open (see screen 3.4).

6.   Check *Unstandardized* under "Predicted Values," and check *Individual* under "Prediction Intervals." The first computes each predicted score based on the independent variable, and the latter computes the 95th confidence interval for each individual's predicted score.

7.   You may also request other descriptive statistics, such as *Unstandardized* residuals. This is the same screen we used to compute the Mahalanobis distance to evaluate multivariate outliers (see chapter 2).

8.   Click on *Continue,* and click on *OK.*

You can request these analyses using the SPSS syntax commands:

Linear Regression SPSS Syntax

```
REGRESSION
/DEPENDENT EB
/METHOD=ENTER PH
/SCATTERPLOT=(*ZRESID, *ZPRED)
/SAVE PRED ICIN.
```

Screen 3.4:   SPSS Linear Regression Save Dialog Box

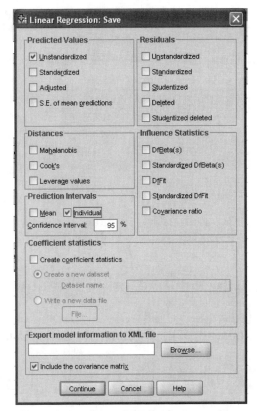

Reading SPSS Output

Execution of these commands produces five tables, all of which provide valuable information about the relationship between the independent and dependent variables and the type of analyses executed. In addition, three new variables will be added to the data file as a result of the execution of these commands. These variables are individuals' predicted scores (PRE_1), lower boundary for the 95th confidence interval (LICI_1), and the upper boundary for the 95th confidence interval (UICI_1) (see screen 3.5).

The tables include methods of variables entered in the analysis (table 3.4), overall model summary (table 3.5), analysis of variance (table 3.6), standardized and unstandardized coefficients (table 3.7), and residuals statistics (table 3.8). They are described in the following.

Table 3.4 describes the methods in which variables were entered in the analysis. This table, however, is important only if multiple regression analysis was conducted, where two or more independent variables are used to predict an

Screen 3.5:   SPSS Data File Showing New Predicted Scores

Table 3.4:   Methods of Entry

Variables Entered/Removed[b]

Model	Variables Entered	Variables Removed	Method
1	PH Physical Health[a]	.	Enter

[a]All requested variables entered.
[b]Dependent variable: EB Emotional Balance

outcome. These methods will be discussed along with multiple regression analysis in chapter 4.

Table 3.5, labeled "Model Summary," conveys the correlation coefficient (R), the coefficient of determination (R^2 and Adjusted R^2), and the standard error of estimate. It also lists the predictor variable and the dependent variable.

Table 3.5 shows that emotional balance and physical health have a correlation of .54 ($R = .536$).

Table 3.5:   Model Summary

Model Summary[b]

Model	R	R Square	Adjusted R Square	Std. Error of the Estimate
1	.536[a]	.288	.283	5.273

[a]Predictors: (constant), PH Physical Health
[b]Dependent variable: EB Emotional Balance

Squaring the correlation coefficient (R) produces the variance in the dependent variable (outcome) that is explained by the predictor (factor). In this case, physical health accounts for 28.8 percent of the variance in emotional balance (R^2 = .288).

Next table 3.5 displays the adjusted R^2. As discussed, when one factor is analyzed, the R^2 and the adjusted R^2 are approximately the same. In this case, the adjusted R^2 is .283 (compared to R^2 = .288).

Table 3.5 also displays the *standard error of the estimate* ($S_{Y.X}$). It represents the standard deviation of the observed values about the regression line; it measures the accuracy of predictions. In general, the larger the correlation between the dependent and independent variables, the smaller the standard error of estimate and the greater the accuracy of the prediction. It is used to compute the confidence interval.

Lastly, the table lists the predictor variable (Physical Health) and the dependent variable (Emotional Balance) in the bottom.

Table 3.6 conveys the results of ANOVA. This ANOVA table examines whether the overall regression model is significant at the preset alpha (see step 2). We are interested only in the last two columns, F and *Sig.* values. These columns show the F ratio (F is the test statistic) and the level of significance (*Sig.* is the p value).

In this case, F is 60.95 with a p value of .000 (or less than .001). As you may remember, a p value of .05 or less indicates a significant result. Therefore these results indicate that physical health is a significant predictor of emotional balance.

Table 3.6:   Analysis of Variance

ANOVA[b]

Model		Sum of Squares	df	Mean Square	F	Sig.
1	Regression	1694.790	1	1694.790	60.950	.000[a]
	Residual	4198.753	151	27.806		
	Total	5893.542	152			

[a]Predictors: (constant), PH Physical Health
[b]Dependent variable: EB Emotional Balance

Table 3.7:   Standardized and Unstandardized Coefficients

Coefficients[a]

Model		Unstandardized Coefficients		Standardized Coefficients		
		B	Std. Error	Beta	t	Sig.
1	(Constant)	7.950	1.497		5.312	.000
	PH Physical Health	.588	.075	.536	7.807	.000

[a]Dependent variable: EB Emotional Balance

Table 3.7 conveys the standardized and unstandardized linear equation coefficients and their levels of significance. For our discussion we are interested in the unstandardized B coefficients, Beta, and their corresponding t and $Sig.$ values.

The joint cell of the first row and first column (Constant and B) represents the unstandardized equation intercept (a = 7.95).

The joint cell of the second row and first column (PH Physical Health and B) represents the unstandardized equation slope (b = .588 or .59).

The joint cell of the first row and third column (Constant and Beta) represents the standardized equation intercept (a). Because this cell is empty, a = 0 (this is always the case in standardized regression equation).

The joint cell of the second row and third column (PH Physical Health and Beta) represents the standardized equation slope ($beta$, β = .536). $Beta$ is also called partial correlation coefficient, the correlation between the dependent and independent variables when controlling for all other factors in the analysis. However, since there are no other factors entered in the linear regression analysis, beta and the correlation coefficient are identical (β = .536, R = .536).

The joint cells of the second row and the fourth and fifth columns (PH, t, and $Sig.$) represent the results of the t-test examining whether the relationship between the dependent and independent variables (or $beta$) is significant. Here $Sig.$ is .000 (p < .001), which indicates that the two are significantly correlated.

The last table produced by the linear regression SPSS commands (table 3.8) describes the residuals range, their means, standard deviation, and total number. These statistics include the predicted values of the residuals, standardized values, standard errors of these residuals, and other information. These are only descriptive statistics and have no significance in our discussion.

Lastly, screen 3.5 displays the SPSS data file after linear regression analysis was executed. Recall that we requested predicted scores for each subject and their 95th confidence interval. These values are usually displayed at the end of the data file. Notice that each predicted score falls within their corresponding confidence intervals. This is always true; that is, the intervals will always contain the estimated value whether it is a correlation, a mean, or a predicted score.

Table 3.8:   Summary of Residuals Statistics

Residuals Statistics[a]

	Minimum	Maximum	Mean	Std. Deviation	N
Predicted Value	9.13	26.77	19.15	3.339	153
Std. Predicted Value	−3.002	2.281	.000	1.000	153
Standard Error of Predicted Value	.426	1.353	.578	.174	153
Adjusted Predicted Value	9.63	26.97	19.15	3.324	153
Residual	−12.419	15.817	.000	5.256	153
Std. Residual	−2.355	3.000	.000	.997	153
Stud. Residual	−2.379	3.017	.000	1.003	153
Deleted Residual	−12.669	16.005	.000	5.327	153
Stud. Deleted Residual	−2.417	3.102	.000	1.009	153
Mahal. Distance	.000	9.012	.993	1.385	153
Cook's Distance	.000	.071	.007	.011	153
Centered Leverage Value	.000	.059	.007	.009	153

[a]Dependent variable: EB Emotional Balance

Step 5: Write the Results.

Guidelines.   When writing the results of a linear regression analysis, first you need to show that you have examined the test assumptions, especially normality, linearity, and homoscedasticity. In addition, report whether a transformation was carried out and how it changed the variable(s).

Next report the correlation coefficient, the proportion of variance in the dependent variable explained by the independent variable, and the error variances. Finally, report the partial correlation, its level of significance, and the overall level of significance for the general model (equation).

Writing the Results

Evaluation of assumptions.   A linear regression analysis was conducted to estimate a linear equation that predicts levels of emotional balance among immigrant Muslims based on their physical health. Prior to conducting the analysis, several descriptive statistics and graphs were generated to examine the test assumptions.

A Pearson's correlation coefficient and a scatterplot show a significant linear relationship ($r = .54, p < .05$) between emotional balance and physical health. In addition, inspections of both the histogram and the normal probability plots of the residuals indicate that the errors were normally distributed. Moreover, inspection of the scatterplot of predicted scores and the residuals reveals that emotional balance scores were distributed equally on each level of physical health, thus satisfying the assumption of homoscedasticity.

Results of simple linear regression.   The results of the linear regression analysis revealed a significant correlation between emotional balance and physical health ($F = 60.95, p < .001$). With a beta of .54 ($t = 7.81, p < .001$), physical health accounted for about 29 percent of the variance in emotional balance, indicating a significant predictor of emotional balance. In other words, individuals with better physical health are more likely to be emotionally balanced.

Presentation of results in a summary table.   It is also helpful to present the results of a linear regression analysis in a summary table. In this table, report the correlation coefficient R and R square (from the model summary, table 3.5), the *beta,* the t value, the level of significance for the dependent variable (from the coefficients, table 3.7), the overall F ratio, and the level of significance (from the ANOVA, table 3.6). Table 3.9 illustrates a summary table.

Writing the regression equation.   After you conduct the analysis and compute all coefficients, you should be able to write the regression equation, which helps you to predict an individual's score on emotional balance knowing his or her score in physical health.

This equation is written simply by replacing both a and b in the linear equation discussed earlier with the actual values for a and b obtained by the analysis, as follows:

Unstandardized	$\hat{Y} = a + bX$	$\hat{Y} = 7.95 + .59\,X$
Standardized	$\hat{Y} = \beta X$	$\hat{Y} = .54\,X$

EXAMPLE: If Sam has a score of 16 on the physical health scale, what will be Sam's score on emotional balance (EB)?

ANSWER: Simply replace X with 16 in either equation. That is:

$$EB = 7.95 + .59\,X$$
$$Sam_{(EB)} = 7.95 + .59 * 16 = 17.39$$

Table 3.9:   Results of Linear Regression Analysis—Emotional Balance and Physical Health

Factor	R	R^{2*}	β	t	p	F	p
Physical Health	.54	.29	.54	7.81	.000	60.95	.000

*Adjusted R^2 = .28

SUMMARY

Linear regression analysis is an extension version of the Pearson's correlation coefficient. It allows researchers to predict a single outcome measured at the interval level of measurement based on knowledge of a single factor also measured at the interval level of measurement.

Chapter 3 is the first of three chapters dealing with predicting a single outcome based on single or multiple variables (factors). The chapter began by discussing the purpose of simple linear regression followed by a presentation of the regression equation, which follows the equation for a straight line.

Next the chapter presented various regression coefficients produced by the simple linear regression and their interpretation. These coefficients include the correlation coefficient (R), standard and adjusted R square, regression constant (line intercept), and regression coefficients (standardized and unstandardized). The chapter then discussed the confidence interval in simple linear regression.

Chapter 3 then listed the assumptions of linear regression analysis and discussed methods of evaluating these assumptions. They include sample selection, level of measurement of both dependent and predictor variables, normality of distributions, sample size, linearity of relationship, homoscedasticity, and normality of residuals.

Finally, the chapter presented a research example discussing the steps of utilizing simple linear regression. This example began with stating the hypotheses and progressed through selecting the appropriate test, evaluating its assumptions, writing the results, and writing the regression equation.

Chapter 4 will introduce an extension of the simple linear regression analysis, that is, the multiple regression analysis. It will follow the same outline as this chapter and will present a detailed example demonstrating the utilization of this important advanced technique.

PRACTICAL EXERCISES

A health care researcher was interested in predicting students' levels of depression (Depression) based on their self-perception (SelfPerception) of their body weight. To examine this prediction, the researcher collected data from 182 college students who completed the *Well-Being* survey (see appendix, Data File 6).

Access the Well-Being SPSS data file and use the variables SelfPerception and Depression to answer the following questions:

1. State the null and alternative hypotheses.

2. What statistical test will you utilize to examine the null hypothesis? Why? Discuss your answer in detail.

3. Write the SPSS syntax file for the test statistic.

4. Run the statistical test you selected in question 2.

5. What is your decision with regard to the null hypothesis? Discuss your answer in detail.

6. Present the results in a summary table and a scatterplot.

7. Write the regression equation.

8. If Mary scored 42 on the self-perception scale, what would Mary's score on depression be? What would the 95th confidence interval for Mary's predicted score be?

CHAPTER 4

Multiple Regression Analysis

LEARNING OBJECTIVES

1. Understand the purpose of multiple regression analysis

2. Understand the regression equation

3. Understand the coefficients of multiple regression

4. Understand the assumptions underlying multiple regression

5. Understand how to select the variables to be entered in multiple regression

6. Understand forward, stepwise, and backward regression methods

7. Understand how to use SPSS to compute the coefficients of multiple regression

8. Understand how to interpret and present the results of the test

DATA SET (APPENDIX)

Job Satisfaction

INTRODUCTION

The previous chapter discussed simple linear regression analysis. Recall that the purpose of simple linear regression is to estimate a regression model that predicts one outcome variable (dependent variable) based on one factor (independent variable).

Yet in real life, a single outcome can be a result of numerous factors. For example, a director of a graduate school admissions office would like to predict applicants' graduate GPA given their undergraduate GPA, GRE score (verbal and analytical), and letters of recommendation. The predicted GPA scores will help the director to admit only those applicants with, say, a GPA of 3.25 and above. A social work researcher wants to predict the levels of depression among welfare recipients based on their age, education, social support, and physical health. Welfare recipients with the highest predicted levels of depression will be recommended for immediate intervention. A social work administrator would like to predict the levels of turnover among his or her employees based on their gender, age, salary, physical environment, and workload. Social workers with the highest predicted levels of burnout will be referred for intervention.

Notice that in these three examples the main purpose is to predict a single outcome (graduate GPA, depression, and burnout, respectively) based on multiple factors (independent variables). An early prediction of the outcome helps social work professionals and others develop a treatment or intervention strategies.

In these and similar cases, however, a simple linear regression is not appropriate, because the relationship between multiple independent variables (2+) and one dependent variable is being examined. Instead, an advanced statistical technique is more suitable to examine such relationships. This technique is the *multiple linear regression analysis,* an extension of simple linear regression.

This chapter discusses the purpose of multiple regression analysis and the regression equation. Next it presents the coefficients produced by multiple regression analysis and discusses the assumptions underlying it and how to select the variables that should be entered in multiple regression. In addition, the chapter describes three regression methods of data entry: forward, stepwise, and backward. Finally, the chapter discusses how to use SPSS to compute the coefficients of multiple regression analysis and how to interpret, write, and present the results in a summary table.

MULTIPLE LINEAR REGRESSION ANALYSIS

Purpose

Multiple regression analysis is an advanced statistical technique. It is an extension of the simple linear regression analysis and the correlation coefficient. It was first used by Pearson in 1908. It is widely used in social sciences research and is perhaps the most used advanced statistical technique in social work research.

The purpose of multiple regression analysis is to examine the effect of multiple independent variables (two or more) on only one dependent variable. As with linear regression analysis, the dependent variable is known as a *criterion* and the independent variables are known as *factors* or *predictors.* The criterion is symbolized by the English capital letter Y, and each predictor is symbolized by the capital letter X with a subscript i that represents the number of each factor. For example, X_1 represents the first factor, X_2 represents the second factor, and X_i represents the ith factor.

In general, multiple regression analysis estimates a model of multiple factors that best predicts the criterion. Thus multiple regression analysis allows researchers to answer the following general research question:

What set of the following factors best predicts Y: X_1, X_2, X_3, . . . X_i?

Y = criterion

X_1 = 1st factor; X_2 = 2nd factor; X_3 = 3rd factor; X_i = i^{th} factor.

EXAMPLE: What set of the following factors best predicts *levels of depression* (criterion) among former welfare recipients: age, marital status, race, level of education, number of years on welfare, physical health, and social support (factors)?

By using multiple regression analysis, the researcher's aim is to predict levels of depression among welfare recipients based on their age, marital status, race, level of education, number of years on welfare, physical health, and social support. In other words, the researcher wants to know which set of these factors best predicts recipients' levels of depression. Knowing which factors predict depression can help practitioners and therapists to plan early intervention and prevention strategies for recipients who are likely to experience higher levels of depression.

Equation of Multiple Regression

As with simple linear regression analysis, the results of multiple regression analysis are expressed in a regression equation that represents a combination of the best factors predicting the criterion. This equation simply follows a straight line equation. It can be either unstandardized scores (raw scores) or standardized scores (z scores). They are expressed as follows:

Unstandardized Regression Equation

$$Y = a + b_1X_1 + b_2X_2 + b_3X_3 + \ldots + b_iX_i$$

Y = criterion (dependent variable)

a = Y intercept (the value of Y when all X's values are zero)

b = unstandardized regression coefficient

X = factors (independent variables)

Standardized Regression Equation

$$Z_Y = \beta_1Z_{X1} + \beta_2Z_{X2} + \beta_3Z_{X3} + \ldots + \beta_iZ_{Xi}$$

Z_Y = Z score for criterion (dependent variable)

β (*beta*) = standardized regression coefficient

Z_X = Z score for each factor (independent variable)

For example, levels of depression could be expressed as follows:

1. Unstandardized regression equation:

    Depression = a + (b_1 * Age) + (b_2 * Marital Status) + (b_3 * Race) + (b_4 * Education) + (b_5 * Years on Welfare) + (b_6 * Physical Health) + (b_7 * Social Support)

2. Standardized regression equation:

    $Z_{Depression}$ = (β_1 * Z_{Age}) + (β_2 * $Z_{Marital\ Status}$) + (β_3 * Z_{Race}) + (β_4 * $Z_{Education}$) + (β_5 * $Z_{Years\ on\ Welfare}$) + (β_6 * $Z_{Physical\ Health}$) + (β_7 * $Z_{Social\ Support}$)

The purpose of a multiple regression analysis is thus to find out what set of the seven factors best predicts depression and what their regression coefficients are.

Coefficients of Multiple Regression Analysis

Multiple regression analysis generates several coefficients; they are the same as in simple linear regression analysis. They are correlation coefficient (R), R square (R^2), adjusted R square (*adjusted R^2*), regression constant (a), unstandardized regression coefficient (B), and standardized regression coefficient (β).

Whereas there will be only one R, one R^2, one *adjusted R^2*, and one a, there will be one B and one β for each factor.

The interpretations of these coefficients are the same as in linear regression analysis except for the following:

Multiple correlation coefficient (R). R represents the correlation coefficient between the criterion (Y) and *all* factors entered in the regression equation (X's). It ranges between "0" (no linear relationship) and "1" (perfect linear relationship).

In order to find the size and the direction of the relationship between the criterion and each factor, simply look at the size and the sign (plus or minus) of the standardized regression coefficients (*beta*).

Multiple R square (R^2). R^2 is the proportion of the variance in the criterion that is explained by the multiple factors in the regression equation. The complement of R^2 (that is, $1 - R^2$) represents the proportion of the unexplained variance in the criterion.

Adjusted R square (adjusted R^2).   As discussed for simple linear regression, adjusted R^2 is based on the number of factors entered in the regression analysis as opposed to the sample size. The greater the number of factors entered compared to the sample size is, the smaller it becomes. Since in multiple regression analysis multiple factors are examined, adjusted R^2 is more appropriate than the standard R^2. Simply report both.

Regression constant (a).   This constant is the Y axis intercept, the value of Y when the values of all X's are zero.

Unstandardized regression coefficients (b).   These coefficients are the unstandardized regression coefficients between the criterion and each factor, the slope of the regression line.

Standardized regression coefficients (β).   These coefficients represent linear correlation coefficients between the criterion and each factor while controlling for the effects of all other factors in the analysis.

Unlike in simple linear regression analysis, multiple regression analysis also produces three more important values to changes in the regression equation due to adding more factors in the analysis. They are R *square change,* F *change,* and *significance of change.*

R square change.   This change represents the amount of variance in the criterion due to the addition of another factor. If only one factor is entered in the analysis, then R square change and R square values will be identical (0% change).

F change and significance of change.   They represent the F ratio (ANOVA) and whether the R square change is statistically significant.

Assumptions

Because multiple regression analysis is an extension of the simple linear regression analysis, it requires the same assumptions of the Pearson r. These assumptions include the following:

1. SAMPLE REPRESENTATIVENESS: The sample must represent the population from which it is selected and to which generalization will be made.

2. LEVEL OF MEASUREMENT: The criterion (dependent variable) must be continuous data and measured at the interval level of measurement or higher.

3. NORMAL DISTRIBUTION: (a) The shape of the distribution of the criterion must approximate the shape of a normal curve, and (b) the shape of the distribution of the residuals must approach the shape of a normal curve. This assumption can be evaluated by inspecting both the histogram and normal probability plots (see chapter 2).

4. LINEARITY: The relationship between the criterion and all factors is assumed to be a linear relationship.

Practically, it is almost impossible to confirm the assumption of linearity. However, as with simple linear regression, this assumption can be evaluated by (a) examining the correlation coefficient between the criterion and each factor using Pearson's correlation coefficient and (b) inspecting a scatterplot displaying the relationship between the criterion and each factor independently (see chapter 3).

5. HOMOSCEDASTICITY: For each value of the independent variables (factors), the dependent variable (criterion) should be normally distributed (have equal variance). Homoscedasticity can also be tested by inspecting the plot for the residuals against the predicted values (see chapter 3).

In addition to these assumptions, multiple regression analysis requires these three assumptions:

6. FACTORS (INDEPENDENT VARIABLES): Whereas the criterion must be measured at the interval level of measurement or higher, the factors can be measured at any level of measurement (nominal, ordinal, interval, or ratio). However, if a nominal variable (categorical) is used in multiple regression analysis, it *must* be recoded to *dummy* variables prior to entering it in the analysis.

A *dummy variable* is a dichotomous variable that is coded as "0" and "1." It is simply expressed in terms of "X" versus "Not X." For example, if gender is coded as "1" for males and "2" for females, then you may recode "2" into "0" (Not Males) and leave "1" as is. You may also recode "1" into "0" (Males) and "2" into "1" (Not Males) prior to entering gender in the regression analysis.

Furthermore, a nominal variable with three or more levels must be recoded into one or more dummy variables. For example, if Race is classified as 1 = Whites, 2 = African Americans, 3 = Asian Americans, and 4 = Hispanics, then you may create up to four dummy variables as follow: (1) 1 = Whites versus 0 = Not Whites; (2) 0 = African Americans versus 1 = Not African Americans; (3) 0 = Asians versus 1 = Not Asians; and (4) 0 = Hispanics versus 1 = Not Hispanics.

7. MULTICOLLINEARITY: Multicollinearity occurs when two independent variables (factors) are highly correlated. When this occurs, both variables measure essentially the same thing.

   a. DETECTING MULTICOLLINEARITY: To check the data for multicollinearity, you may use one of the following two options:

      i. Run and examine the Pearson correlation coefficient for each pair of independent variables (factors). A correlation coefficient that is greater than .80 ($r > .80$) indicates a multicollinearity problem.

      ii. Check the variance inflation factor (VIF) and tolerance. VIF is the reciprocal of tolerance, which is the proportion of variance in one factor that is unexplained by the other factors ($1 - R^2$). They can be computed along with the multiple regression coefficients in SPSS or any other statistical program. A VIF value that is greater than 10 usually indicates a multicollinearity problem. A tolerance value smaller than .10 also indicates a multicollinearity problem.

$$\text{Tolerance} = \frac{1}{VIF}$$

Multicollinearity exists *if* VIF > 10 or tolerance < .10.

---

   b. SOLVING THE PROBLEM: When two variables appear to be highly correlated, you may consider one of the following two methods:

      i. REMOVING ONE VARIABLE: If you believe that one of the two variables that are highly correlated doesn't appear to be necessary for the regression analysis, consider removing it from the regression analysis. For example, if Physical Health and Mental Health were to be used in predicting Life Satisfaction among elderly and both are highly correlated, you may consider removing the one that you believe is less important for Life Satisfaction and entering the second one in the regression analysis.

ii. CREATING COMPOSITE VARIABLES: If it is feasible, consider creating a new variable that combines the scores of both variables. In the above example, you may merge the scores of Physical Health and Mental Health to create a new variable (e.g., Health in General). However, if the two variables have different units of measures (e.g., 1 to 10 for Physical Health and 10 to 50 for Mental Health), you should transform their raw scores to standard scores (z scores) before creating the new variable.

8. SAMPLE SIZE: There is no clear agreement among researchers on the sample size required to utilize multiple regression analysis. Researchers have used anywhere between 10 and 50 cases per factor. Ideally, the larger the sample size is, the better the generalizability of the results to the population. Large samples are especially important if the data are not normally distributed. However, as a rule of thumb, a sample size of at least $50 + 8m$ (that is, $N \geq 50 + 8m$, where m = number of factors) is needed to utilize multiple regression analysis. For example, to examine the relationship between one criterion and six factors you need at least 98 subjects; that is, $N \geq 50 + (8 \times 6) \geq 50 + 48 \geq 98$.

Selecting Appropriate Factors for Regression

Because the purpose of multiple regression analysis is to produce the most significant set of factors that predicts a criterion, it is logical to assume that each factor to be entered in the regression analysis should have a significant bivariate relationship with the criterion. If the two do not have a significant relationship to begin with, it is unlikely that one will predict the other. In fact, this is the assumption of linearity.

Selecting only factors that are significantly correlated with the criterion could decrease the number of factors entered in the regression analysis and, in turn, decrease the required sample size. Thus, prior to entering factors in the regression analysis, researchers should examine the bivariate relationship between each factor and the criterion. In order to examine this relationship, first determine the appropriate bivariate statistical test (Pearson's correlation, t-test, ANOVA, etc.) to examine the relationship (see Abu-Bader, 2006) and then run the test. Factors that are significantly correlated with the criterion are then entered in the regression analysis whereas factors that are not significantly correlated with the criterion will not be entered in the analysis.

Methods of Data Entry in Multiple Regression Analysis

Whereas some researchers may decide to enter all factors in the regression analysis at once, others may decide to enter them based on specific criteria. There are a number of ways in which researchers choose to enter the factors in the regression analysis. The most common methods follow:

Forward method.   At the beginning, the bivariate correlation coefficient between each factor and the criterion is computed. Next the factor with the largest correlation coefficient is entered in the regression analysis. The next factor entered in the equation is the one that has the second largest correlation coefficient. In this method, once a factor is entered in the regression analysis, it remains in the equation. This procedure continues until no more factors contribute significantly to the variance in the criterion.

Backward method.   This method begins with entering all factors at once in the regression analysis. Then, multiple R square (R^2) and partial correlation coefficients (*betas*) are computed. In the next step, the factor that has the smallest partial correlation coefficient with the criterion is removed from the analysis. Then the factor that has the second smallest partial correlation coefficient is removed. This procedure stops when the variance in the criterion significantly drops.

Stepwise method.   This method is perhaps the most used method of regression analysis. It combines both the forward and backward methods, and thus it overcomes the problems that arise with each of these two methods. Like the forward method, in stepwise method, factors are entered based on the size of their partial correlation coefficients; the one with the largest correlation coefficient is entered first in the analysis. The factor with the second largest correlation coefficient is entered next. Unlike the forward method, after a new factor is entered in the analysis, the contribution of the factors that are already in the analysis is reassessed. Like the backward method, factors that no longer contribute significantly to the variance in the criterion are removed from the regression equation. The procedure stops when no more factors contribute significantly to the variance in the criterion. The stepwise method will be used in this chapter.

PRACTICAL EXAMPLE

We will use the Job Satisfaction SPSS data file (see appendix) to predict levels of job satisfaction among social workers based on a number of factors. In particular, we will examine the following research question: What set of the following factors best predicts levels of job satisfaction among professional social workers: gender, ethnicity, level of education, region of employment, working with colleagues, quality of supervision, promotion, and workload?

Hypothesis Testing

Step 1: State the Research Question.

Unlike in simple linear regression, in multiple regression analysis it is unnecessary to state a null and alternative hypothesis simply because researchers' aim is not to verify or falsify a research hypothesis but rather to develop a regression model that best predicts a criterion. Thus in multiple regression analysis simply state the research question under study. In this case, the research question is as follows: What set of the following factors best predicts levels of job satisfaction (Satisfaction) among professional social workers: gender (Gender), ethnicity (Ethnicity), level of education (Education_Rec), region of employment (Location), working with colleagues (Colleague), quality of supervision (SQRT_Super), promotion (Promotion), and workload (Workload)?

Step 2: Choose Alpha.

We will set alpha at .05 (α = .05). That is, results will be significant only if $p \leq .05$.

Step 3: Select the Appropriate Statistical Test.

Because the purpose here is to predict a single outcome based on a number of factors, we obviously will utilize multiple regression analysis. However, before starting this analysis we need to evaluate the data and examine whether they meet the assumptions for multiple regression analysis.

1. LEVEL OF MEASUREMENT: The dependent variable must be measured at the interval level or higher.

   In this research question, job satisfaction is the criterion and is measured at the interval level of measurement.

2. NORMALITY OF CRITERION: The shape of the distribution of the criterion must approach the shape of a normal curve.

   To evaluate this assumption, we should evaluate measures of skewness and kurtosis and inspect the histogram of job satisfaction. Table 4.1 displays measures of skewness and kurtosis, and figure 4.1 describes the distribution of job satisfaction.

   Figure 4.1.A shows that the shape of the distribution is not severely skewed.[1] It appears to approach the shape of a normal curve. Figure 4.1.B, the Q-Q plot, also shows that job satisfaction scores are clustered on a straight diagonal line with minor deviations.

   Dividing the skewness by its standard error reveals that it is slightly more than twice the standard error (outside the normal range of ±1.96). On the other

---

[1]If the distribution is severely skewed, consider transforming job satisfaction to the square root or using any other methods of transformation.

Figure 4.1:   Histogram and Normal Q-Q Plot for Job Satisfaction

A

B

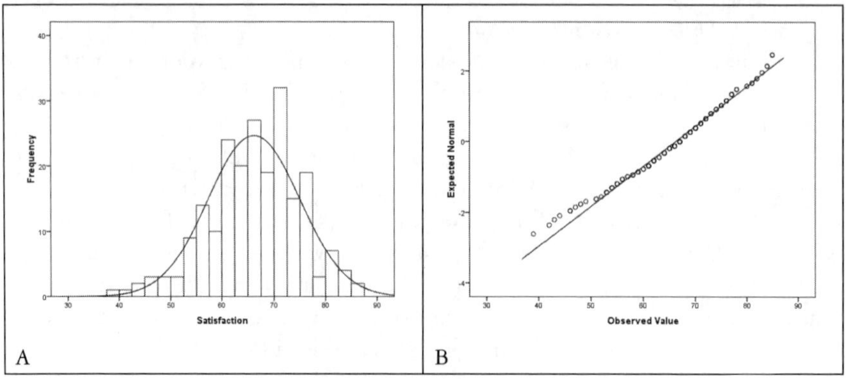

Table 4.1:   Measures of Skewness and Kurtosis for Job Satisfaction

Statistics		
Satisfaction		
N	Valid	218
	Missing	.00
	Skewness	−.392
	Std. Error of Skewness	.165
	Kurtosis	.148
	Std. Error of Kurtosis	.328

hand, kurtosis is smaller than twice its standard error (within the ±1.96 normal range). Also, when eyeballing the histogram of job satisfaction, you find that it appears to approach the shape of a normal curve. Thus this histogram is normally distributed.

3.   LINEARITY: The relationship between the criterion and the factors is assumed to be a linear relationship.

As said earlier, this assumption is evaluated by looking at the scatterplot for each factor with the criterion. Here we should consider only factors with continuous data. In this case, there are four continuous factors: working with colleagues, quality of supervision,[2] promotion, and workload. Thus we will use SPSS to create four scatterplots (see chapter 3). Figure 4.2 presents a scatterplot for job satisfaction and working with colleagues (A), square root quality of supervision (B), promotion (C), and workload (D).

---

[2]Recall from chapter 2 that quality of supervision was reflected and transformed into the square root (SQRT_Supervision).

Figure 4.2:   Scatterplots for Colleagues, Supervision, Promotion, and Workload with
Job Satisfaction

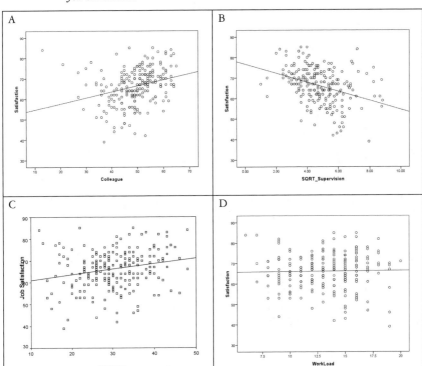

When eyeballing these scatterplots, you find a linear relationship (a straight line with the points clustered around it) between job satisfaction and each factor with minor deviation (few points appear to be far from the line).

4. NORMALITY OF RESIDUALS: The shape of the distribution of the residuals must approach the shape of a normal curve.

As mentioned earlier, this assumption can be evaluated by inspecting the histogram of the residuals and the normal plot.

We will use the SPSS *Analyze, Regression,* and *Linear* subcommands to request this plot (see chapter 3). In this case, Job Satisfaction will be entered in the *Dependent Variable* box, and all factors will be entered in the *Independent(s)* box. Figure 4.3 displays a histogram (A) and a normal probability plot (B). Inspection of these two plots indicates that the residuals are normally distributed. Notice that the shape in figure 4.3.A follows the shape of a normal curve and that the points in figure 4.3.B fall on a straight diagonal line.

Figure 4.3:   Histogram and Probability Plot for the Residuals

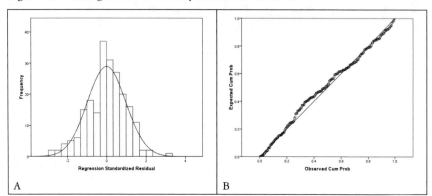

5. HOMOSCEDASTICITY: The variance around the regression line should be the same for all values of the independent variables.

   This assumption can be evaluated by looking at the scatterplot of the residuals against the predicted values. Figure 4.4 displays a scatterplot for the residuals with the predicted scores (this plot is produced along with the histogram and normal plot of the residuals; see chapter 3).

   In figure 4.4, the points appear to distribute equally along the horizontal line for each level of the multiple factors (X axis), thus indicating that the data are homoscedastic.

Figure 4.4:   Scatterplot for the Residuals and Predicted Scores

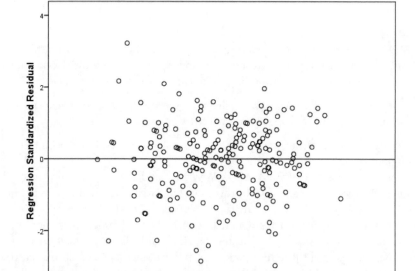

6.   MULTICOLLINEARITY: The relationship between all pairs of the independent variables must not exceed .80.

To examine the assumption of multicollinearity, we will run Pearson correlation coefficients (see Abu-Bader, 2006, chap. 7) between all factors (*do not include the dependent variable*). Table 4.2 displays the Pearson correlation coefficients between all factors.

Table 4.2 shows that the correlation coefficients between the independent variables range between −.006 (Gender and Location) and −.487 (Working with Colleagues and Supervision). No correlation coefficient exceeds .80, thus indicating that no multicollinearity exists among the factors.

Also, we can evaluate the assumption of multicollinearity by inspecting the VIF and tolerance values produced by the regression analysis (see "How to Use SPSS to Compute Multiple Regression Coefficients"). Table 4.3 displays these values. It shows the VIF and tolerance values for each factor with all other factors.

Table 4.2:   Pearson Correlation Coefficients

		Gender	Ethnicity	Location	Education	Colleague	Supervision	Promotion	WorkLoad
Gender	Pearson	1.000							
	Sig. (1-tailed)								
Ethnicity	Pearson	-.475	1.000						
	Sig. (1-tailed)	.000							
Location	Pearson	-.006	-.388	1.000					
	Sig. (1-tailed)	.467	.000						
Education	Pearson	-.053	-.053	.033	1.000				
	Sig. (1-tailed)	.216	.218	.314					
Colleague	Pearson	.133	-.232	.082	-.092	1.000			
	Sig. (1-tailed)	.025	.000	.116	.089				
Supervision	Pearson	-.024	.174	-.077	.118	-.487	1.000		
	Sig. (1-tailed)	.365	.005	.133	.042	.000			
Promotion	Pearson	-.146	-.042	.215	-.122	.449	-.321	1.000	
	Sig. (1-tailed)	.015	.271	.001	.036	.000	.000		
WorkLoad	Pearson	.174	-.123	.043	.041	-.045	.051	-.060	1.000
	Sig. (1-tailed)	.005	.035	.263	.274	.254	.228	.191	

Table 4.3:   VIF and Tolerance Values for Each Factor

	Collinearity Statistics	
	Tolerance	VIF
(Constant)		
Gender	.685	1.461
Ethnicity	.587	1.704
Education_Rec	.961	1.040
Location	.768	1.302
Colleague	.623	1.605
SQRT_Supervision	.734	1.362
Promotion	.706	1.417
WorkLoad	.958	1.044

Table 4.3 shows that none of the VIF exceeds the cutoff value of 10. Also, none of the tolerance values is smaller than .10. Thus no multicollinearity problem exists.

7.   DUMMY VARIABLES: Factors to be entered in the regression analysis can be measured at any level of measurement (nominal, ordinal, interval, or ratio). However, if nominal variables (categorical) are used in multiple regression analysis, they *must* be recoded to *dummy* variables before they are entered in the analysis.

The factors (independent variables) in this research question are Gender, Ethnicity, Level of Education, Region of Employment, Working with Colleagues, Quality of Supervision, Promotion, and Workload. The variables Working with Colleagues, Quality of Supervision, Promotion, and Workload are continuous variables. They are measured at the interval level of measurement.

On the other hand, Gender, Ethnicity, Level of Education, and Region of Employment are categorical variables. Thus they must be coded as "0" and "1." Looking at the SPSS data file, Gender, Ethnicity, and Level of Education are coded as "0" and "1." Region of employment (Location), however, is coded as "1 = North," "2 = Center," and "3 = South." In this case, it must be recoded to three dummy variables as follow: North (1 = North and 0 = Others); Center (1 = Center and 0 = Others); and South (1 = South and 0 = Others).

SPSS Syntax for Recoding Location to Three New Variables

RECODE LOCATION (SYSMIS=SYSMIS) (1=1) (2=0) (3=0) INTO NORTH.
RECODE LOCATION (SYSMIS=SYSMIS) (1=0) (2=1) (3=0) INTO CENTER.
RECODE LOCATION (SYSMIS=SYSMIS) (1=0) (2=0) (3=1) INTO SOUTH.

---

8.   SAMPLE SIZE: There are eight factors in this research question (Gender, Ethnicity, Region, Education, Supervision, Colleagues, Promotion, and Workload). Applying the sample size formula, we need a sample size of 114 cases or more $(50 + 8m = 50 + (8 \times 8) = 114)$ to utilize multiple regression analysis. In this case, 218 social workers completed and returned the Job Satisfaction survey, which exceeds the minimum required sample size.

Step 4: Select Factors That Will Be Entered in the Analysis.

The next step after evaluating the assumptions is to select what factors should be entered in the regression analysis. This is especially important because (1) if the variable shows no bivariate relationship with the criterion, it will likely not contribute to the variance in the criterion, and (2) the less the number of factors entered in the analysis is, the smaller the sample size required for the regression analysis.

In our example there are eight factors of which four are categorical variables and four are continuous variables. Of the four categorical variables, three are dichotomous (Gender, Ethnicity, and Education) and one has three groups (Region of Employment).

Recall that the criterion (Job Satisfaction) is measured at the interval level of measurement and is normally distributed. Thus we will run three independent t-tests to test the relationship between Job Satisfaction and Gender, Ethnicity, and Education (see chapter 1). We will also run a one-way ANOVA to test the relationship between Region and Job Satisfaction. The results of the three independent t-tests and ANOVA are presented in tables 4.4.A through 4.7.B.

Table 4.4.B shows no significant difference (*Sig.* = .276) between male and female social workers with regard to their levels of job satisfaction. Both males and females have similar mean scores in job satisfaction, 64.69 and 66.45, respectively (table 4.4.A). This variable, thus, will *not* be included in the regression analysis.

Table 4.5.B shows a significant difference (*Sig.* = .000) between Arab and Jewish social workers with regard to their levels of job satisfaction. Table 4.5.A shows that Jewish social workers have higher levels of job satisfaction (mean = 67.69) than Arab social workers (mean = 63.03). This variable, thus, *will* be included in the regression analysis.

Table 4.4.A: Descriptive Statistics for Job Satisfaction by Gender

Group Statistics					
	Gender	N	Mean	Std. Deviation	Std. Error Mean
Satisfaction	0 MALE	36	64.69	8.783	1.464
	1 FEMALE	182	66.45	8.829	.654

Table 4.4.B: Independent t-Test for Job Satisfaction by Gender

Independent Samples Test		Levene's Test for Equality of Variances		t-test for Equality of Means						
									95% Confidence Interval of the Difference	
		F	Sig.	t	df	Sig. (2-tailed)	Mean Difference	Std. Error Difference	Lower	Upper
Satisfaction	Equal variances assumed	.036	.849	-1.091	216	.276	-1.756	1.609	-4.928	1.415
	Equal variances not assumed			-1.095	50.005	.279	-1.756	1.603	-4.977	1.464

Table 4.5.A: Descriptive Statistics for Job Satisfaction by Ethnicity

Group Statistics					
	Ethnicity	N	Mean	Std. Deviation	Std. Error Mean
Satisfaction	0 JEWS	145	67.69	8.156	.677
	1 ARABS	72	63.03	9.391	1.107

Table 4.5.B: Independent *t*-Test for Job Satisfaction by Ethnicity

Independent Samples Test

| | | Levene's Test for Equality of Variances | | t-test for Equality of Means | | | | | | |
| | | | | | | | | | 95% Confidence Interval of the Difference | |
		F	Sig.	t	df	Sig. (2-tailed)	Mean Difference	Std. Error Difference	Lower	Upper
Satisfaction	Equal variances assumed	2.292	.132	3.767	215	.000	4.662	1.238	2.223	7.101
	Equal variances not assumed			3.593	125.464	.000	4.662	1.298	2.094	7.230

Table 4.6.B shows a significant difference (*Sig.* = .088/2 = .044, which is smaller than .05)[3] between undergraduate and graduate social workers with regard to their levels of job satisfaction. Table 4.6.A shows that graduate social workers have higher levels of job satisfaction (mean = 68.58) than undergraduate social workers (mean = 65.73). This variable *will* also be included in the regression analysis.

Table 4.7.A shows a significant overall difference (*Sig.* = .000) between the three regions of employment (North, Center, and South) with regard to levels of

Table 4.6.A: Descriptive Statistics for Job Satisfaction by Education

Group Statistics

	Education	N	Mean	Std. Deviation	Std. Error Mean
Satisfaction	0 Undergraduate	185	65.73	8.798	.647
	1 Graduate	33	68.58	8.718	1.518

Table 4.6.B: Independent *t*-Test for Job Satisfaction by Education

Independent Samples Test

| | | Levene's Test for Equality of Variances | | t-test for Equality of Means | | | | | | |
| | | | | | | | | | 95% Confidence Interval of the Difference | |
		F	Sig.	t	df	Sig. (2-tailed)	Mean Difference	Std. Error Difference	Lower	Upper
Satisfaction	Equal variances assumed	.198	.657	-1.714	216	.088	-2.846	1.660	-6.118	.426
	Equal variances not assumed			-1.725	44.428	.091	-2.846	1.650	-6.170	.478

Table 4.7.A: One-Way ANOVA for Job Satisfaction by Region

ANOVA

Satisfaction

	Sum of Squares	df	Mean Square	F	Sig.
Between Groups	1294.728	2	647.364	8.885	.000
Within Groups	15591.843	214	72.859		
Total	16886.571	216			

---

[3]Remember, you need to divide the *p* value by 2 if you have a one-tailed hypothesis. In this case, we would hypothesize that graduate social workers will have higher job satisfaction than undergraduate social workers.

Table 4.7.B: Post Hoc Bonferroni for Job Satisfaction by Region

Satisfaction
Bonferroni

(I) Location Region	(J) Location Region	Mean Difference (I-J)	Std. Error	Sig.	95% Confidence Interval	
					Lower Bound	Upper Bound
1 NORTH	2 CENTER	-1.993	1.611	.652	-5.88	1.89
	3 SOUTH	-5.750*	1.450	.000	-9.25	-2.25
2 CENTER	1 NORTH	1.993	1.611	.652	-1.89	5.88
	3 SOUTH	-3.757*	1.377	.021	-7.08	-.44
3 SOUTH	1 NORTH	5.750*	1.450	.000	2.25	9.25
	2 CENTER	3.757*	1.377	.021	.44	7.08

*. The mean difference is significant at the 0.05 level.

job satisfaction. The *post hoc* Bonferroni test (table 4.7.B) shows that there is no significant difference between the North and Center regions (*Sig.* = .652). On the other hand, there is a significant difference between North and South (*Sig.* = .000). The second row shows a significant difference between the Center and South regions (*Sig.* = .021). These findings suggest that social workers in the South are significantly different than social workers from the other two regions.

Recall that a categorical variable with three or more levels must be recoded to one or more dummy variables prior to entering it in the regression analysis. In this case, because the one-way ANOVA and the post hoc test show that South is significantly different than the other two regions, we will create a new dummy variable that has South as one group (coded as "1") and All Others as the second group (coded as "0"). Recall that we already created three new dummy variables. However, we will enter only South in the regression analysis.

Next we will select the continuous factors that will be entered in the analysis. To select these factors, we will simply run a Pearson correlation between Job Satisfaction (criterion) and each factor (Supervision, Colleagues, Promotion, and Workload). Table 4.8 presents the Pearson correlation coefficients generated by SPSS.

Table 4.8 shows that Job Satisfaction has a significant correlation with Working with Colleagues ($r = .283, p < .05$), Promotion ($r = .213, p < .05$), and

Table 4.8:   Correlation between Job Satisfaction and the Factors

		Satisfaction	Colleague	Promotion	WorkLoad	SQRT_Super
Satisfaction	Pearson Correlation	1.000				
	Sig. (1-tailed)					
Colleague	Pearson Correlation	.283**	1.000			
	Sig. (1-tailed)	.000				
Promotion	Pearson Correlation	.213**	.449**	1.000		
	Sig. (1-tailed)	.001	.000			
WorkLoad	Pearson Correlation	.016	-.045	-.060	1.000	
	Sig. (1-tailed)	.407	.254	.191		
SQRT_Super	Pearson Correlation	-.356**	-.487**	-.321**	.051	1.000
	Sig. (1-tailed)	.000	.000	.000	.228	

**. Correlation is significant at the 0.01 level (1-tailed).

Quality of Supervision[4] ($r = -.356$, $p < .05$). On the other hand, no significant correlation is found between Job Satisfaction and Workload ($r = .016$, $p > .05$). Thus Workload will *not* be entered in the regression analysis.

To conclude, the variables Ethnicity, Education, South, Colleagues, Supervision, and Promotion have significant bivariate relationships with Job Satisfaction. Thus they will be entered in the regression analysis. The variables Gender and Workload have no significant relationships with Job Satisfaction. Therefore they will be excluded from the analysis.

How to Use SPSS to Compute Multiple Regression Coefficients

Step 5: Run Multiple Regression Analysis.

The multiple regression procedures in SPSS enable us to select and compute many statistics and coefficients and create various plots in which each can provide valuable information. For our purpose here, we will request only the statistics and coefficients that we have discussed.

In our research question, the dependent variable is Job Satisfaction (Satisfaction), and the independent variables are Ethnicity (Ethnicity), Education (Education_Rec), Region (South), Supervision (SQRT_Super), Colleagues (Colleague), and Promotion (Promotion).

To run the multiple regression analysis in SPSS, follow these steps:

1. Open the Job Satisfaction SPSS data file.
2. Click on *Analyze* in the SPSS main toolbar.
3. Scroll down to and click on *Regression* and then *Linear.*
4. A dialog box called "Linear Regression" will open (see screen 4.1).
5. Scroll down in the variables list, click on *Satisfaction,* and click on the upper arrow button to move it into the *Dependent* box.
6. Scroll down in the variables list, click on *Ethnicity,* and click on the arrow button corresponding with *Independent(s)* to move it into the *Independent(s)* box. Repeat this step to move South, Education_Rec, SQRT_Super, Colleague, and Promotion into the *Independent(s)* box.
7. Click on the *Method* drop-down arrow to select the method of data entry in the regression (forward, stepwise, backward, etc.). Select *Stepwise* (you may choose any other method).
8. Click on *Statistics* in the upper right corner of the "Linear Regression" dialog box. A new dialog box called "Linear Regression: Statistics" will open (see screen 4.2).
9. Make sure that the *Estimates* box (SPSS default) under "Regression Coefficient" is checked. If not, check it. This command computes the standardized (β) and unstandardized (b) regression coefficients, their levels of significance (t and p values), and the regression constant (a).

---

[4]Remember, Quality of Supervision was first reflected and then transformed into the square root.

Screen 4.1: SPSS Linear Regression Dialog Box

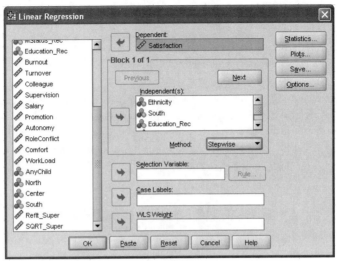

Screen 4.2: SPSS Linear Regression Statistics Dialog Box

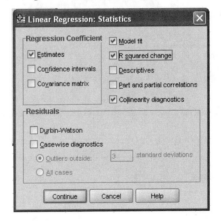

10. Also make sure that the *Model Fit* box is checked (SPSS default). This command computes the multiple correlation coefficient (R), R square, and adjusted R square. It also computes ANOVA table and the level of significance for the overall model.

11. Check the *R Squared Change* box. This command computes the change in the proportion of the variance in the criterion due to the addition of a new factor and whether the change is significant.

12. Check the *Collinearity Diagnostics* box. This command computes the tolerance and the variance inflation factor (VIF). You need these values to evaluate the assumption of multicollinearity (see the discussion of assumptions under "Step 3: Select the Appropriate Statistical Test").

13. Click on *Continue* to return to the "Linear Regression" dialog box.

14. Click on *Plots*. A new dialog box called "Linear Regression: Plots" will open (see screen 4.3).

15. Under "Standardized Residual Plots," check the *Histogram* and *Normal Probability Plot* boxes. You need these plots to check the assumption of normality of residuals.

16. Click on *ZRESID* and click on the top arrow to move it into the *Y* box. Also click on *ZPRED* and the second arrow to move it into the *X* box. This command will create a scatterplot for the predicted and the residuals. You need this plot to evaluate the assumption of homoscedasticity.

17. Click on *Continue* and then *OK*.

Screen 4.3:   SPSS Linear Regression Plots Dialog Box

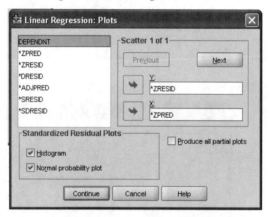

You can also request these outputs using the SPSS syntax commands:

SPSS Syntax for Stepwise Multiple Regression Analysis

REGRESSION
/MISSING LISTWISE
/STATISTICS COEFF OUTS R ANOVA COLLIN TOL CHANGE
/CRITERIA=PIN(.05) POUT(.10)
/NOORIGIN
/DEPENDENT Satisfaction
/METHOD=STEPWISE Ethnicity Education_Rec South Colleague
SQRT_Super Promotion
/SCATTERPLOT=(*ZRESID, *ZPRED)
/RESIDUALS HIST(ZRESID) NORM(ZRESID).

To select a different regression method, change *STEPWISE* (seventh line) to *BACKWARD* or *FORWARD*.

Reading the Output

The following output presents the results of multiple regression procedures. These results include four tables (4.9–4.12) and two graphs (figures 4.3 and 4.4). Other tables that were produced by SPSS were omitted because they are not necessary for our purpose at this level.

Table 4.9 displays the number, the order, and the regression method in which factors are entered in and removed from the regression equation. It has four columns:

1. The Model column shows the number of steps the regression method utilized to produce the best regression model predicting the dependent variable (criterion). Table 4.9 shows (first column, Model) that the regression method utilized three steps to produce a final regression model, equation.

2. The second column (Variables Entered) in table 4.9 shows the order in which the factors were entered in the regression equation. As discussed earlier, in the stepwise method the variable that has the largest correlation coefficient with the dependent variable will be entered first followed by the second, the third, and so on. The process stops when no more independent variables contribute significantly to the variance in the criterion.

   Table 4.9 (second column, Variables Entered) shows that in all only three factors were entered: Quality of Supervision (SQRT_Super) was entered first, then Region (South), and last Level of Education (Education_Rec).

   Notice that no other factor was entered after Education because Ethnicity, Promotion, and Colleague (recall that six variables were entered in the analysis) did not contribute significantly to the variance in Job Satisfaction.

   This column thus displays the number and order of the factors that best predict job satisfaction. In this example, three factors are shown: Supervision, Region, and Education.

3. The third column (Variables Removed) summarizes the variables that no longer contribute significantly to the variance in job satisfaction after a new variable is entered in the regression equation. In this example the list is empty because all variables entered in the regression equation remain significant after each entry (e.g., Supervision remained significant after South was entered; Supervision and South remained significant after Education was entered).

Table 4.9:   Results of Multiple Regression Analysis—Methods of Variable Entry

Variables Entered/Removed[a]

Model	Variables Entered	Variables Removed	Method
1	SQRT_Super	.	Stepwise (Criteria: Probability-of-F-to-enter <= .050, Probability-of-F-to-remove >= .100).
2	South	.	Stepwise (Criteria: Probability-of-F-to-enter <= .050, Probability-of-F-to-remove >= .100).
3	Education_Rec	.	Stepwise (Criteria: Probability-of-F-to-enter <= .050, Probability-of-F-to-remove >= .100).

a. Dependent Variable: Satisfaction

4. The fourth column (Method) describes the regression method in which variables are entered in the regression equation (stepwise, forward, backward, etc.). In this case, variables were entered based on the stepwise method. The column also shows that variables are entered only if their correlation with the criterion is significant at alpha of .05 or less.

Table 4.10 has ten columns of which *six* are appropriate for our discussion at this level:

1. The Model (first) column conveys the number and order of the best factors entered in the regression equation, predicting the criterion.

2. The R (second) column conveys the correlation coefficient between the criterion and the factor(s) at each step.

3. The R Square (third) column conveys the proportion of the variance in the criterion that is accounted for by all factors entered in the equation at each step.

4. The Adjusted R Square (fourth) column conveys the adjusted proportion of the variance in the criterion due to sample size and number of factors.

5. The R Square Change (sixth) column conveys the change in the proportion of the variance in the criterion as a result of entering a new factor. When only one factor is entered, R square and R square change are identical.

6. The Sig. F Change (tenth) column conveys the level of significance for the R square change. A *Sig.* value of .05 or less indicates a significant change in the R square.

Table 4.10 shows that there were three steps in which factors were entered in the regression equation:

1. MODEL 1: Quality of Supervision (SQRT_Super) was entered at the first step. The first row and second column (R = .355) show that the correlation between supervision and job satisfaction is .355. The R Square column shows that supervision contributes 12.6 percent to the variance in job satisfaction (first row, third column, R^2 = .126). The fourth column shows that

Table 4.10:   Results of Multiple Regression Analysis—Model Summary

Model Summary[d]

Model	R	R Square	Adjusted R Square	Std. Error of the Estimate	R Square Change	F Change	df1	df2	Sig. F Change
1	.355[a]	.126	.122	8.244	.126	30.498	1	211	.000
2	.423[b]	.179	.171	8.011	.053	13.492	1	210	.000
3	.454[c]	.206	.195	7.896	.027	7.148	1	209	.008

a. Predictors: (Constant), SQRT_Super

b. Predictors: (Constant), SQRT_Super, South

c. Predictors: (Constant), SQRT_Super, South, Education_Rec

d. Dependent Variable: Satisfaction

the adjusted R square is 12.2 percent (first row, fourth column, adjusted R^2 = .122). The sixth column (R Square Change) shows that supervision added 12.6 percent to the variance in job satisfaction. Since this is the first step in the analysis, the R^2 and R^2 change are the same (only one variable is in the regression equation, Supervision). The tenth column shows that this proportion (R^2 change) is significant at alpha of .05 (first row, tenth column, Sig. F Change = .000).

2. MODEL 2: Region of Employment (South) was entered at the second step. Table 4.10 shows that the multiple correlation between all variables in the equation at Model 2 (step 2) and job satisfaction is .423 (second row, second column, R = .423). These factors are Supervision (entered at step 1) and Region of Employment (entered at step 2). The two variables together accounted for 17.9 percent of the variance in job satisfaction (second row, third column, R square = .179). The adjusted R square is still similar to the standard R square (second row, fourth column, Adjusted R square = .171). The second variable (Region of Employment) added 5.3 percent to the variance in job satisfaction (second row, sixth column, R square change = .053).[5] This R square change is still significant at alpha of .05 (second row, tenth column, Sig. F change = .000).

3. MODEL 3: Finally, Level of Education (Education_Rec) was entered at the third step. Table 4.10 shows that the multiple correlation between all factors in the equation and job satisfaction is .454 (third row, second column, R = .454). These variables are Supervision (entered at step 1), Region of Employment (entered at step 2), and Level of Education (entered at step 3). The three variables accounted for 20.6 percent of the variance in job satisfaction (third row, third column, R square = .206). This R square is still similar to the adjusted R square (third row, fourth column, Adjusted R square = .195). The third variable (Level of Education) added 2.7 percent to the variance in job satisfaction (third row, sixth column, R square change = .027). This R square change is still significant at alpha of .05 (third row, tenth column, Sig. F change = .008).

The model summary table is followed by footnotes. The first three footnotes list the variables in each step (a = SQRT_Super, b = SQRT_Super, South, etc.). The last footnote shows the dependent variable (Satisfaction).

To sum up, this table shows that quality of supervision is the best predictor of job satisfaction, followed by region of employment and level of education.

Table 4.11 displays the results of the one-way ANOVA. Multiple regression analysis uses one-way ANOVA to examine the overall level of significance for each regression model. There will be one ANOVA test for each model.

---

[5]You can also compute the variance that each variable contributes simply by subtracting the R square at the previous step from the R square at the current step.

Table 4.11:   Results of Multiple Regression Analysis—ANOVA

ANOVA[d]

Model		Sum of Squares	df	Mean Square	F	Sig.
1	Regression	2072.925	1	2072.925	30.498	.000[a]
	Residual	14341.554	211	67.969		
	Total	16414.479	212			
2	Regression	2938.719	2	1469.360	22.898	.000[b]
	Residual	13475.760	210	64.170		
	Total	16414.479	212			
3	Regression	3384.337	3	1128.112	18.095	.000[c]
	Residual	13030.142	209	62.345		
	Total	16414.479	212			

a. Predictors: (Constant), SQRT_Super
b. Predictors: (Constant), SQRT_Super, South
c. Predictors: (Constant), SQRT_Super, South, Education_Rec
d. Dependent Variable: Satisfaction

Table 4.11 lists the order of the models in the first column (Model) and then provides the sum of squares (second column), degrees of freedom (third column), mean square (fourth column), ANOVA F ratio (fifth column), and overall level of significance (sixth column). Here we are interested in only the last two columns.

1. MODEL 1: The first row shows the results of ANOVA for the first model (Supervision). With only one factor in (Supervision), the model is a significant predictor of job satisfaction (first row, last two columns, $F = 30.498$, $Sig. = .000$).

2. MODEL 2: The second row shows the results of ANOVA for the second model (Supervision and Region). With these two factors in, the model is also a significant predictor of job satisfaction (second row, last two columns, $F = 22.898$, $Sig. = .000$).

3. MODEL 3: The third row shows the results of ANOVA for the third model (Supervision, Region, and Education). With these three factors in, the model is still a significant predictor of Job Satisfaction (third row, last two columns, $F = 18.095$, $Sig. = .000$).[6]

To sum up, the results of ANOVA show that the three-factor model significantly predicts job satisfaction ($F = 18.10, p < .001$).

Table 4.12 displays the unstandardized and standardized regression coefficients, their levels of significance, and the collinearity statistics. It has eight columns:

1. The first column (Model) conveys the number and order of the models and lists the variables that entered into the regression equation at each step (model). This column is consistent with the previous two tables.

---

[6]Notice that the more variables entered into the analysis, the smaller the F value.

Table 4.12:   Results of Multiple Regression Analysis—Coefficients

Coefficients[a]

Model		Unstandardized Coefficients		Standardized Coefficients	t	Sig.	Collinearity Statistics	
		B	Std. Error	Beta			Tolerance	VIF
1	(Constant)	76.686	2.001		38.321	.000		
	SQRT_Super	-2.197	.398	-.355	-5.522	.000	1.000	1.000
2	(Constant)	74.243	2.055		36.126	.000		
	SQRT_Super	-2.092	.388	-.338	-5.398	.000	.995	1.005
	South	4.047	1.102	.230	3.673	.000	.995	1.005
3	(Constant)	74.167	2.026		36.610	.000		
	SQRT_Super	-2.211	.385	-.358	-5.748	.000	.981	1.019
	South	4.124	1.086	.235	3.796	.000	.994	1.006
	Education_Rec	4.078	1.525	.166	2.673	.008	.985	1.015

a. Dependent Variable: Satisfaction

2. The second and third columns (*B* and Std. Error, respectively) convey the unstandardized regression coefficients (*b*'s) and their standard errors for each factor entered in the analysis. The table also reports the constant (*a*) for each model: first line in each row (Constant) and first column (*B*).

3. The fourth column (*Beta*) conveys the standardized regression coefficients (β). This column reports the size and direction of the partial correlation between each factor and the criterion (in this case, Job Satisfaction).

4. The fifth and sixth columns (*t* and *Sig.*, respectively) convey the *t* value and the level of significance (*p*) for each regression coefficient. This statistic examines whether the partial correlation between the criterion and the corresponding factor is significant.

5. The seventh and eighth columns (Tolerance and VIF, respectively) convey the collinearity measures. These measures evaluate the assumption of multicollinearity. They were presented and discussed earlier in table 4.3.

These coefficients and statistics are reported for each factor entered in the regression equation and reassessed once a new variable is entered. We will need only the last row, which displays the coefficients for all factors that best contribute to the variance in the criterion (Job Satisfaction), that is, model 3.

1. The first line in model 3 (Constant) conveys the regression constant (the *a* value in the unstandardized regression equation). The second column shows that the constant for this model is 74.167 (first line in third row, second column, *B* = 74.167) with a standard error of 2.026 (first line in third row, third column, Std. error = 2.026).

Table 4.12 does not report the standardized coefficient for the constant (first line in third row, fourth column, *Beta* =), because, as you may recall from the formula of the regression equation, the constant (*a*) for a standardized regression equation is zero.

2. The second line in model 3 reports the coefficients and statistics for the strongest factor in the equation, Supervision. The unstandardized regression coefficient for Supervision is −2.211 with a standard error of .385 (that is, $b_{\text{SUPERVISION}} = -2.211$).

    Table 4.12 shows that the partial correlation (*Beta*) between supervision and job satisfaction is −.358 (that is, $\beta_{\text{SUPERVISION}} = -.358$). *Beta* indicates a negative partial correlation between supervision and job satisfaction; the better the supervision is, the higher the levels of job satisfaction.[7] This correlation is significant (second line in model 3, fifth and sixth columns; $t = -5.748$, *Sig.* = .000).

3. The third line in model 3 reports the coefficients and statistics for the second strongest factor in the equation, Region of Employment (South). The unstandardized regression coefficient is 4.124 with a standard error of 1.086 (that is, $b_{\text{SOUTH}} = 4.124$).

    The partial correlation (*Beta*) between region of employment and job satisfaction is .235 ($\beta_{\text{SOUTH}} = .235$), which indicates that social workers from the South (coded as "1") tend to be more satisfied than social workers from other regions (coded as "0"). This correlation is significant (third line in model 3, fifth and sixth columns: $t = 3.796$, *Sig.* = .000).

4. Finally, the fourth line in model 3 reports the coefficients and statistics for the third and last strongest factor in the equation, Level of Education. The unstandardized regression coefficient is 4.078 with a standard error of 1.525 (that is, $b_{\text{EDUCATION}} = 4.078$).

    The partial correlation (*Beta*) between level of education and job satisfaction is .166 ($\beta_{\text{EDUCATION}} = .166$), which indicates that graduate social workers (coded as "1") tend to be more satisfied than undergraduate social workers (coded as "0"). This correlation is significant (fourth line in model 3, fifth and sixth columns: $t = 2.673$, *Sig.* = .008).

Next, SPSS commands produce a table labeled "Excluded Variables" and three graphs. The table displays the factors that are excluded from the analysis at each step (Model). It is not of importance. The first two graphs are a histogram and a normal probability plot for the residuals, which are used to evaluate the assumption of normality of residuals. The third graph is a scatterplot for the residuals with the predicted scores, which is used to evaluate the assumption of homoscedasticity. These graphs were discussed under evaluation of assumptions (see figures 4.3 and 4.4).

Step 6: Write the Results.

As with linear regression analysis, prior to reporting the results, show that you have examined the assumptions of multiple regression, especially normality,

---

[7]Remember, Supervision was first reflected and then transformed into the square root. Thus low scores indicate better supervision.

linearity, homoscedasticity, and multicollinearity. In addition, report whether a transformation was carried out and how it changed the variable(s).

Next you should report the number of factors that best predicts the criterion, their order from the most significant to the least significant, the proportion of the variance each contributes to the criterion, their partial correlation coefficients, and the level of significance. In our example, the results can be summarized as follows.

Writing the Results

Evaluation of assumptions.   A stepwise multiple regression analysis was conducted to estimate a regression model that best predicts levels of job satisfaction among social workers based on six factors: ethnicity, education, location, working with colleagues, quality of supervision, and opportunities for promotion.

Prior to conduction of the analysis, several descriptive statistics and graphs were generated to examine the test assumptions, including normality of distributions, linear relationship between job satisfaction and factors, normality of residuals, homoscedasticity, and multicollinearity.

Measures of skewness and kurtosis, histograms, and Q-Q plots show that the shapes of the distributions of job satisfaction, working with colleagues, and promotions approach that of a normal curve. On the other hand, supervision was significantly skewed to the left. Therefore a square root transformation was conducted on supervision after it was reflected due to the negative skewness. Evaluation of the newly transformed supervision indicates it was close to a normal curve.

Pearson's correlation coefficients and scatterplots show a linear relationship between job satisfaction and all factors. In addition, inspections of both the histogram and the normal probability plots of the residuals indicate that the errors were normally distributed. Moreover, inspection of the scatterplot of predicted scores against the residuals confirms that the assumption of homoscedasticity was met. Finally, evaluation of the correlation matrix and both VIF and tolerance values show no multicollinearity exists among the six factors.

Results of multiple regression analysis.   The results of the stepwise multiple regression analysis revealed that three of the six factors emerged as significant predictors of job satisfaction ($F = 18.10, p < .001$). With a beta of $-.36$ ($p < .001$), quality of supervision emerged as the strongest predictor of job satisfaction, accounting for 12.6 percent of the variance in job satisfaction. The second strongest factor was region of employment ($\beta = .24, p < .001$), accounting for an additional 5.3 percent of the variance in job satisfaction. The third strongest factor was level of education ($\beta = .17, p < .001$). Education, however, accounted for only 2.7 percent of the variance in job satisfaction.

These results indicate that higher job satisfaction is a function of better quality of supervision, employment in the southern region, and higher levels of education. Overall, the model explains almost 21 percent of the variance in job satisfaction ($R = .45$). On the other hand, about 79 percent of the variance in job satisfaction is still unaccounted for in this model.

Presentation of results in a summary table. When presenting the results of multiple regression analysis in a summary table, report the multiple correlation coefficient and R square for each factor (from the model summary table); the partial correlation coefficient, the t value, and the level of significance for each factor (from the coefficients table); and the overall F ratio and level of significance for each model (from the ANOVA table). The table should be part of the results section. Factors should be presented based on their partial correlation, from the largest to the smallest beta. For example, table 4.13 presents the results of the multiple regression analysis for job satisfaction.

In table 4.13, the first two columns (R and R^2) are from the model summary table (table 4.10), the next three columns (β, t, and p) are from the coefficients table (table 4.12), and the last two columns (F and p) are from the ANOVA table (table 4.11).

Writing the regression equation. Once a regression model has been estimated and all coefficients have been computed, you should be able to write the regression equation. This equation helps you to compute the level of job satisfaction for an individual social worker. Recall that job satisfaction was found to be a function of quality of supervision, region of employment, and level of education. The regression equation for job satisfaction is thus as follows:

REGRESSION EQUATION:
$Y = a + b_1X_1 + b_2X_2 + b_3X_3 + \ldots + b_iX_i$
Job Satisfaction = 74.17 + (-2.21 × Square Root of Supervision)
$+ (4.12 \times \text{South}) + (4.08 \times \text{Education})$

EXAMPLE:
If John (a social worker) is employed in the southern region (a score of 1), has a BSW (a score of 0), and has a score of 60 on the supervision scale, then what will be John's level of job satisfaction?

Table 4.13:   Results of Multiple Regression Analysis—Predictors of Job Satisfaction

Factor	R	R^{2a}	β	t	p	F	p
Supervision[b]	.36	.13	$-.36$	-5.75	<.001	30.50	<.001
Region—South	.42	.18	.24	3.80	<.001	22.90	<.001
Education	.45	.21	.17	2.67	<.010	18.10	<.001

Note: all coefficients are rounded to the nearest two decimals.
[a]*Adjusted R^2* = .20
[b]Square root of Supervision

ANSWER:

First we have to reflect and compute the square root for supervision using the same methods we used in reflecting and transforming the scores of supervision (see chapter 2). (Remember, always use in the equation the same type of scores used in the regression analysis.)

REFLECT:
John's Score = 80 − 60 = 20

SQUARE ROOT:
John's Score = $\sqrt{20}$ = 4.47
Job Satisfaction = 74.17 + (−2.21 × 4.47) + (4.12 × 1) + (4.08 × 0) = 68.41

SUMMARY

Multiple regression analysis is perhaps the most used advanced statistical technique in social sciences research. It allows researchers and practitioners to predict a specific outcome (criterion) based on several observed factors (independent variables). For example, by predicting which clients are more likely to be drug addicts, to be clinically depressed, or to experience anxiety, clinicians and practitioners can plan in advance intervention techniques that will result in reducing or preventing the occurrence of such problems.

This chapter began with an introduction and a discussion of the purpose of multiple regression analysis and the regression equation. Two equations were introduced, the unstandardized and the standardized regression equations. The unstandardized regression equation is based on the actual raw scores, whereas the standardized regression equation is based on the transformation of the scores of all factors to standard scores (z scores).

The chapter then introduced and discussed major coefficients that are produced by the regression analysis. These coefficients include the unstandardized regression coefficient (b), standardized regression coefficient ($beta$), multiple correlation coefficient (R), multiple R square (R^2), adjusted R square, and regression constant (a).

The chapter also presented and discussed the assumptions underlying multiple regression analysis. These assumptions include the level of measurement of the dependent variable, normality of the distributions of the criterion and the residuals, linearity of the relationship between the criterion and the factors, multicollinearity, homoscedasticity, and the assumption for the sample size. The chapter also discussed various methods for evaluating each assumption.

Because multiple regression analysis predicts one criterion based on multiple factors, the chapter discussed how to select for inclusion in the regression analysis only the factors that are more likely to contribute to the variance in the criterion. This section was followed by a discussion of the different regression methods, which include forward, stepwise, and backward. Finally, the chapter presented a practical example based on actual research data to illustrate the use of multiple regression analysis in social sciences research. This chapter then discussed how to use SPSS to analyze the data and how to interpret the output and write and present the results of multiple regression analysis.

Chapter 5 will introduce an equivalent technique to multiple regression analysis used to predict a single outcome based on multiple factors, yet this outcome consists of two possible outcomes, either yes or no. This technique is the logistic regression analysis. Chapter 5 will follow outlines similar to those presented in chapter 4 to illustrate the purpose of logistic regression; its equation, coefficients, and assumptions; and the utilization of SPSS to conduct the analysis.

PRACTICAL EXERCISES

A mental health researcher was interested in predicting levels of depression (CESD) among older immigrants based on their gender (Gender), age (Age), owning a home (Home), emotional balance (EB), physical health (PH), and cognitive status (CS). For this purpose, the researcher collected data from a sample of 155 immigrants ages fifty and older who completed the *Mental Health* survey (see appendix, Data File 4).

Access the Mental Health data file; use the variables CESD, Gender, Home, EB, PH, and CS; and answer the following questions:

1. Write a research question predicting levels of depression among older immigrants based on the above factors.
2. What statistical test(s) will you utilize to examine the research question? Why? Discuss your answer in detail.
3. Write the SPSS syntax file for the test statistic.
4. Run the test statistic you selected in question 2.
5. What is your decision? Discuss your answer in detail.
6. Present the results in a summary table.
7. Write the regression equation.
8. What would be Maria's level of depression if she is seventy-two years old, has no home, and scored 32 on the emotional balance, 30 on the physical health, and 27 on the cognitive status scales?
9. What would be Edward's level of depression if he is eighty years old, owns his home, and scored 28 on the emotional balance, 16 on the physical health, and 18 on the cognitive status scales?

CHAPTER 5

Logistic Regression Analysis

LEARNING OBJECTIVES

1. Understand the purpose of the logistic regression analysis

2. Understand the logistic regression equation

3. Understand the tests and coefficients of the logistic regression

4. Understand the assumptions underlying the logistic regression

5. Understand how to select the appropriate factors for the logistic regression

6. Understand the methods of factor entry in the logistic regression

7. Understand how to use SPSS to compute the logistic regression

8. Understand how to interpret and present the results of the test

DATA SET (APPENDIX)

Well-Being

INTRODUCTION

In chapters 3 and 4, you were introduced to the simple linear regression and the multiple linear regression statistical techniques. Both techniques are utilized to predict a single outcome knowing the scores of one factor (simple linear regression analysis) or of multiple factors (multiple regression analysis). In both cases, however, the outcome (dependent variable) must consist of continuous data.

Sometimes, however, not all outcomes are classified as continuous data. Consider these scenarios:

A therapist is interested in predicting whether his or her client will be clinically depressed (versus not depressed) based on the client's gender, age, socioeconomic status, level of education, physical health, family support, and self-esteem.

A physician is interested in whether or not an individual will develop a certain disease given his or her age, weight, number of cigarettes smoked, number of alcoholic drinks consumed, and cholesterol level.

A real estate agent is interested in the likelihood that an individual will buy a house next year given his or her income, marital status, number of dependents, interest rate, and property taxes.

A Ph.D. admissions office is interested in predicting whether a first-year doctoral student will pass the qualifying exam given his or her gender, GPA, GRE scores, number of hours spent in the library, and student income.

These examples, and many others, are somewhat similar to those discussed in the previous chapter. Their aim is to predict a single outcome (criterion) based on one or more factors (independent variables). So why can we not simply utilize multiple regression analysis to predict these outcomes?

The answer is simple. Looking at these cases, we can see that, unlike in chapter 4, the outcome variables (criteria) consist of two possible outcomes: depressed versus not depressed, development of disease versus no development of disease, buy a house versus not buy a house, and pass versus not pass the qualifying exam. In other words, these criteria consist of dichotomous data: dummy variables. Therefore these criteria violate the assumption of continuous data, they cannot approach the normal distribution, and their errors cannot be normal.

Recall that multiple regression analysis requires that the outcome variables be measured at the interval level of measurement and that both raw scores and errors be normally distributed. Thus multiple regression analysis cannot be utilized to predict these categorical outcomes. The question is then, what statistical technique would be most suitable to address these and similar cases?

This chapter will introduce a new form of regression analysis that is most appropriate to analyze such cases. This technique is the logistic regression analysis. The chapter will present the purpose of this technique and its assumptions. A detailed practical example will follow to illustrate how to utilize SPSS to run the analysis, read the output, and write the results.

LOGISTIC REGRESSION ANALYSIS

Purpose

Logistic regression analysis, also known as *binary logistic regression,* is an extension of multiple regression analysis. It is utilized to predict a single outcome (dependent variable or criterion) based on multiple factors (independent variables or predictors).

Unlike multiple regression analysis, the criterion in logistic regression must be a categorical (discrete) variable with only two groups, that is, a dichotomous variable coded as "0" and "1." Thus logistic regression analysis is utilized to predict an individual's membership in one of the two groups of the dependent variable based on a number of factors.

In other words, logistic regression analysis is used primarily to examine the probability of an event to occur or not, the probability that an individual will fall into one of the two groups. For example, what is the *probability* that an individual will pass (coded as "1") the GRE test given a number of factors? Or, what is the *probability* that an individual will develop a certain disease (coded as "1") given a number of factors?

Logistic regression thus *always* examines the probability of the occurrence of the outcome (event) that is coded as "1." Therefore the probability of no event coded as "0" (e.g., *fail* or *no disease*) is the complement of 1 or 100 percent.

$$P(\text{no event}) = 1 - P(\text{event})$$
$$P = \text{probability}$$

Probability ranges between 0 and 1 (0% to 100%), with 0 (0%) indicating that it is unlikely that the outcome will occur and 1 (100%) indicating that it is certain that the outcome will occur. *Remember,* the predicted outcome in multiple regression can take any value ($-\infty$ to $+\infty$).

Equation of Logistic Regression

As you learned in the previous two chapters, one of the purposes of regression analyses is to develop a regression equation that best fits the data. This is also the purpose of logistic regression analysis.

As discussed in chapter 4, the multiple regression equation is useful to predict an individual score based on a number of factors. The predicted score can take any value, and the predicted variable is composed of continuous data. In a logistic regression analysis, however, the equation is used to predict the *odds ratio* that an event will occur.

Logistic Regression Equation

$$ln(Odds) = a + b_1X_1 + b_2X_2 + \ldots + b_iX_i$$

ln(Odds) = odds ratio of event to occur
a = Y intercept
b = regression coefficient
X = factors

The odds ratio is used to compare the probability of an event to occur (e.g., buy a house) and the probability of no event to occur (e.g., not buy a house).

Mathematically, it is expressed as follows:

Odds Formula

$$Odds = \frac{P(event)}{1 - P(event)}$$

Mathematically, the *ln(Odds)* is the natural logarithm of the odds ratio, and the quantity of *ln(Odds)* is called the *Logist.*

An odds ratio of 1 indicates that the probability that an event will occur is the same as the probability that no event will occur. In other words, both groups ("0" and "1") have equal probability to occur, that is, a 50/50 chance.

An odds ratio that is *greater* than 1 indicates that the probability that an event (e.g., pass GRE) will occur is *greater* than the probability that no event (e.g., fail GRE) will occur. On the other hand, an odds ratio that is *smaller* than 1 indicates the probability that an event will occur is smaller than the probability that no event will occur.

The probability that an event will occur can be computed using the following mathematical formula:

Probability of Event

$$P(event) = \frac{1}{1 + e^{-(a + b_1X_1 + b_2X_2 + \ldots + b_iX_i)}}$$

e = constant = 2.718

Research Questions of Logistic Regression

As discussed, logistic regression analysis is utilized to predict the probability an event will occur given certain factors. In other words, although logistic regression still tests research hypotheses, it is more likely to address research questions than to test hypotheses.

The following are examples of research questions:

1. What is the *probability* that a client will be clinically depressed (versus not depressed) knowing his or her gender, age, socioeconomic status, level of education, physical health, family support, and self-esteem?

2. What is the *likelihood* an individual will be considered obese (versus not obese) given his or her age, race, amount of weekly exercise, number of cigarettes smoked, number of alcoholic drinks consumed, and level of cholesterol?

3. What is the *likelihood* an individual will buy a house in the next six months knowing his or her income, marital status, number of dependents, interest rate, and property taxes?

4. What set of the following factors *correctly predicts* whether a first-year doctoral student will pass a qualifying exam given his or her gender, GPA, GRE scores, number of hours spent in the library, and income?

Statistical Tests in Logistic Regression

Logistic regression analysis uses several statistics to evaluate the accuracy of the regression model and to estimate the probability of occurrence of a specific event. These statistics include the omnibus tests of model coefficients, likelihood-ratio test ($-2LL$), Cox and Snell R square, Nagelkerke R square, Hosmer and Lemeshow test, and Wald test.

Omnibus tests of model coefficient.   This is a test of the overall regression model. It uses the chi-square test to examine the level of significance for each model produced by the logistic regression. It is the same as the ANOVA test in multiple regression analysis.

Likelihood-ratio test.   This test is a statistical technique that examines the goodness-of-fit between the observed and predicted models. In other words, it examines how well the data fit the population. Mathematically, the natural logarithm of the likelihood-ratio is computed due to the fact that the likelihood-ratio is smaller than 1. The natural logarithm is then multiplied by "-2." This term is known as "$-2LL$." The smaller the "$-2LL$" is, the better the model fits the population (predicts the outcome).

Cox and Snell R square and Nagelkerke R square.   Similar to the R square in multiple regression analysis, they estimate the proportion of variance in the outcome variable that is accounted for by the factors entered in the logistic regression analysis. Cox and Snell R square usually serves as the lower limit of proportion, and Nagelkerke R square serves as the upper limit of the variance. The two measures are also known as *Pseudo R^2*.

Hosmer and Lemeshow test.   This test is the chi-square goodness-of-fit test. It examines the overall goodness-of-fit of the predicted model. It divides subjects into ten cells based on their predicted probability and then computes the chi-square given both observed and predicted probabilities for both levels of outcomes ("0" and "1"). In other words, the Hosmer and Lemeshow test forms a 2x10 contingency table and tests the hypothesis that no significant difference exists between the observed model and the expected model. A nonsignificant chi-square value is thus desired ($p > .05$).

Wald test.   This test is analogous to the t-test in multiple regression analysis. It examines the level of significance for each regression coefficient (b) in the regression model. Unlike the t-test, it is calculated using standard z scores and the chi-square distribution.

Assumptions

Due to the nature of the outcome variable as a dichotomous variable, many of the assumptions required for multiple regression analysis and simple linear regression are *not* required for logistic regression. Those assumptions not required follow:

1. LINEARITY: The relationship between the dependent variable (outcome) and the independent variables (factors) does not need to be linear.

2. NORMAL DISTRIBUTION: The distribution of the dependent variable does not need to be normal.

3. HOMOSCEDASTICITY: The variances of the dependent variable for each level of the independent variables do not need to be equal or homoscedastic.

4. NORMALITY OF RESIDUALS: The distribution of the residuals does not need to follow the normal curve.

Yet, as with any statistical technique, logistic regression still requires some assumptions to be satisfied, mainly related to sample selection, sample size, and multicollinearity among the independent variables. These assumptions are as follows:

1. SAMPLE REPRESENTATIVENESS: The sample must be representative of the population to which generalization will be made.

This assumption is a methodological one and should be addressed accordingly. Violation of this assumption could affect the generalizability of the results.

2. LEVELS OF MEASUREMENT: Whereas the dependent variable must be dichotomous and coded as "0" and "1," the independent variables can be any level of measurement. However, as in multiple regression analysis, if categorical factors are to be used, they need to be recoded into dummy variables.

This assumption is also a methodological one and should be addressed accordingly. Sometimes researchers must recode nominal variables into dummy variables if they decide to enter them in the analysis. This recoding can be done through the SPSS *Transform* and *Recode into Different Variables* commands (see chapter 4).

3. MULTICOLLINEARITY: The correlation between the factors should not be greater than .80.

Multicollinearity can be evaluated by inspecting the correlation matrix and the VIF and tolerance values using a multiple regression analysis (see chapter 4). If the problem exists, try to solve it using one of the methods discussed in chapter 4.

4. SAMPLE SIZE: The Hosmer and Lemeshow goodness-of-fit measure assumes that no more than 20 percent of all cells should have expected frequencies of less than five cases. This is a chi-square goodness-of-fit test assumption

(see Abu-Bader, 2006, chap. 11). Also, no cell should have an expected value of less than 1.

Recall that Hosmer and Lemeshow divides the data into a 2x10 table, that is, twenty cells in total. In other words, a maximum of four cells can have expected values less than 5 (but not less than 1).

This assumption can be evaluated by inspecting the *contingency table for Hosmer and Lemeshow test* (a *2x10 table*) produced along with the logistic regression outputs (see "Practical Example," p. 134).

Selecting Appropriate Factors for Logistic Regression

As with multiple regression analysis, it is essential to select only factors that are most likely to increase the probability that an event will occur. That is, factors that do not have significant association with the criterion are less likely to correctly predict the criterion (outcome).

Therefore, prior to entering factors in the logistic regression analysis, researchers should examine whether a significant difference exists between the two outcome groups with regard to each factor.

Since the outcome variable in logistic regression consists of two groups (0 and 1), use the independent *t*-test (or its alternative Mann-Whitney *U*) to examine the difference between these two groups with regard to continuous factors. You can use the chi-square test of significance to examine the relationship between the outcome variable and categorical factors (see chapter 1).

Factors that show significant correlation with the criterion will be included in the logistic regression analysis whereas factors that are not significantly correlated with the criterion will be excluded from the analysis.

Methods of Data Entry in Logistic Regression Analysis

As in multiple regression analysis, researchers conducting logistic regression need to decide how factors should be entered in the analysis. The decision of what method to use is solely a researcher's preference based on his or her own judgment. SPSS provides seven methods of data entry:

Enter. All factors in the analysis are entered at once regardless of their importance in predicting the outcome variable. They all are treated equally.

Forward-conditional. This is a stepwise method. Factors are entered in the analysis based on their likelihood-ratio values using conditional parameter estimates.

Forward-LR. This is perhaps the most used method of data entry. It is parallel to the stepwise method in multiple regression analysis. In this case, factors are entered in the analysis based not on their likelihood-ratio values but on the maximum partial likelihood-ratio estimates. The factor with the highest likelihood-ratio values is entered first, followed by the second highest likelihood-ratio, and so on. SPSS stops adding factors when no additional contribution to the variance in the outcome is founded.

Forward-Wald.   This is another form of a stepwise method. However, factors are entered in the analysis based on the Wald test value.

Backward-conditional.   As in multiple regression analysis, all factors are entered at once. Once they are in the analysis, factors with the smallest likelihood-ratio value will be removed one at a time using conditional parameter estimates.

Backward-LR.   In this method, all factors are entered at once. Next, factors with the smallest likelihood-ratio value will be removed one at a time using the maximum partial likelihood estimates.

Backward-Wald.   As in the backward-LR, all factors will be entered at once. However, factors with the least significant Wald value will be removed one at a time.

PRACTICAL EXAMPLE

To demonstrate the utilization of logistic regression and how to use SPSS to compute the statistics, we will use the Well-Being SPSS data file (see appendix) to predict the probability of a student becoming overweight given certain conditions. In particular, we will examine the following research question: What is the *probability* that a university student is considered overweight (Overweight) knowing his or her gender (Gender), age (Age), race (Race), physical health (Physical-Health), life satisfaction (LifeSatisfaction), and self-perception (SelfPerception)?

In this research question, there is one outcome variable, Overweight (0 = no, 1 = yes), and six factors: Gender (0 = male, 1 = female), Age (actual age), Race (1 = African American, 2 = White, 3 = others), Physical Health (scale), Life Satisfaction (scale), and Self-Perception (scale).

Hypothesis Testing

Step 1: State the Research Question.
As discussed earlier, the purpose here is to predict the probability that a student will be considered overweight knowing a number of factors. Thus null and alternative hypotheses are unnecessary. We should only state the research question as follows:

What is the *probability* that a university student is classified as overweight knowing his or her gender, age, race, physical health, life satisfaction, and self-perception?
OR

What set of the following factors *correctly predicts* whether a university student is classified as overweight: gender, age, race, physical health, life satisfaction, and self-perception?

Step 2: Choose the Level of Significance.

We will set alpha at .05 (α = .05). That is, results will be significant only if $p \le .05$.

Step 3: Select the Appropriate Statistical Test.

Because our purpose here is to predict a dichotomous outcome (overweight vs. not overweight) based on various factors, it is obvious that we will utilize logistic regression analysis. However, before we run the test, we should address its assumptions.

As discussed earlier, logistic regression analysis does not require most of the assumptions required in multiple regression analysis. However, basic assumptions related to sample selection, sample size, and multicollinearity still need to be evaluated.

1. SAMPLE REPRESENTATIVENESS: The sample must be representative of the population.

    In the Well-Being study, data were collected from a sample of 182 students randomly selected from two university campuses. As a result, the sample is representative of the population.

2. LEVEL OF MEASUREMENT: The dependent variable must be dichotomous and coded as "0" and "1." The independent variables can be continuous variables and/or dummy variables.

    There are six factors in the research question. Four consist of continuous data (Age, Physical Health, Life Satisfaction, and Self-Perception), and two are categorical variables. Gender is a dichotomous variable coded as "0" and "1," and Race consists of three groups. Race therefore needs to be recoded into a dummy variable (1 = African American and 0 = others).

3. MULTICOLLINEARITY: The correlation between the six factors should not be greater than .80.

    To evaluate this assumption, we will simply run the VIF and tolerance values using multiple regression SPSS commands (see chapter 4). Here we will enter any continuous variable that is not part of our factors in the *Dependent* variable box and the six factors in the *Independent(s)* variable box.

    Table 5.1 displays the collinearity statistics produced by SPSS multiple regression commands. Notice that we used Depression as our dependent variable. The dependent variable will not affect the collinearity measures, because these measures examine the relationship among the factors.

    Notice that all tolerance values are greater than .10 and all VIF values are smaller than 10. Thus multicollinearity is not a problem.

Table 5.1: VIF and Tolerance Values

		Collinearity Statistics	
Model		Tolerance	VIF
1	(Constant)		
	Gender	.983	1.018
	Race	.953	1.049
	Age	.986	1.014
	Physical Health	.836	1.196
	Life Satisfaction	.915	1.093
	Self-perception	.787	1.270

4. SAMPLE SIZE: None of the cells should have an expected value less than 1. Also, no more than 20 percent of all cells should have expected frequencies of less than five cases.

We will evaluate this assumption by inspecting the contingency table for the Hosmer and Lemeshow test (a 2x10 table), produced along with the logistic regression.

Table 5.2 displays the contingency table for the Hosmer and Lemeshow test (this table is part of the logistic regression output discussed under "How to Compute Logistic Regression Tests in SPSS").

Table 5.2 is a 2x10 table (two overweight groups and ten rows). Each group has two values, observed and expected.[1] For our purpose of evaluating the assumption of sample size, (a) none of the expected values should be less than 1 and (b) no more than 20 percent of these cells (20% x 20 cells = 4) should have expected values less than 5.

As it appears in table 5.2, the smallest expected value is 2.425. Also, there are four cells with expected values less than 5. Therefore, the data satisfy the two conditions.

Step 4: Select Factors That Will Be Included in the Analysis.

After we examine the test assumptions, we need to decide what factors are more likely to correctly predict students' weight. To do this, we will use the independent t-test to compare those who are overweight with those who are not overweight with regard to their age, life satisfaction, physical health, and self-perception. Table 5.3 displays the results of the independent t-test.

Table 5.3 shows a significant difference between overweight and not over-weight students with regard to age ($t = -2.249$, $p = .026$), physical health ($t =$

---

[1] See Abu-Bader (2006), chapter 11 for more on the chi-square test.

Remember: Independent *t*-Test SPSS Syntax

T-TEST GROUPS=Overweight(0 1)
/MISSING=ANALYSIS
/VARIABLES=Age PhysicalHealth LifeSatisfaction SelfPerception
/CRITERIA=CI(.9500).

Table 5.2: Contingency Table for Hosmer and Lemeshow Test

		Overweight = 0 No		Overweight = 1 Yes		Total
		Observed	Expected	Observed	Expected	
Step 4	1	14	15.575	4	2.425	18
	2	14	13.563	4	4.437	18
	3	13	12.206	5	5.794	18
	4	15	11.839	4	7.161	19
	5	9	10.052	9	7.948	18
	6	8	9.345	11	9.655	19
	7	8	7.374	10	10.626	18
	8	6	5.934	12	12.066	18
	9	4	4.569	14	13.431	18
	10	2	2.543	16	15.457	18

Table 5.3: Results of the Independent *t*-Test

Independent Samples Test

		Levene's Test for Equality of Variances		t-test for Equality of Means							
										95% Confidence Interval of the Difference	
		F	Sig.	t	df	Sig. (2-tailed)	Mean Difference	Std. Error Difference	Lower	Upper
Age	Equal variances assumed	5.268	.023	-2.249	180	.026	-2.145	.954	-4.027	-.263
	Equal variances not assumed			-2.238	168.461	.027	-2.145	.958	-4.037	-.253
Physical Health	Equal variances assumed	.294	.588	3.084	180	.002	.395	.128	.142	.648
	Equal variances not assumed			3.078	177.190	.002	.395	.128	.142	.648
Life Satisfaction	Equal variances assumed	.166	.684	.230	180	.818	.182	.792	-1.381	1.746
	Equal variances not assumed			.230	178.217	.819	.182	.793	-1.383	1.748
Self Perception	Equal variances assumed	.178	.674	2.518	180	.013	2.799	1.111	.606	4.992
	Equal variances not assumed			2.521	180.000	.013	2.799	1.110	.608	4.990

3.084, $p = .002$), and self-perception ($t = 2.518$, $p = .013$). On the other hand, no significant difference exists between the two groups with regard to life satisfaction ($t = .230$, $p = .818$). Thus the first three factors will be entered in the analysis and the last will be excluded.

Next we will examine the association between the overweight groups and their gender and race. For this examination, we will conduct a chi-square test (both variables are categorical variables).

Table 5.4 displays the results of the chi-square test between overweight and gender, and table 5.5 displays the results between overweight and race.

Table 5.4 shows a significant association between overweight and gender (chi-square = 12.62, p = .000), and table 5.5 shows a significant association between overweight and race (chi-square = 8.75, p = .003). Thus these two factors, Gender and Race, will be included in the analysis.

Remember: Chi-Square SPSS Syntax

CROSSTABS
/TABLES=Gender Race BY Overweight
/FORMAT=AVALUE TABLES
/STATISTICS=CHISQ
/CELLS=COUNT
/COUNT ROUND CELL.

Table 5.4:   Results of the Chi-Square—Gender by Overweight

Chi-Square Tests

	Value	df	Asymp. Sig. (2-sided)	Exact Sig. (2-sided)	Exact Sig. (1-sided)
Pearson Chi-Square	12.623[a]	1	**.000**		
Continuity Correction[b]	11.581	1	.001		
Likelihood Ratio	12.772	1	.000		
Fisher's Exact Test				.001	.000
Linear-by-Linear Association	12.554	1	.000		
N of Valid Cases	182				

a. 0 cells (.0%) have expected count less than 5. The minimum expected count is 38.14.

b. Computed only for a 2x2 table

Table 5.5:   Results of the Chi-Square—Race by Overweight

Chi-Square Tests

	Value	df	Asymp. Sig. (2-sided)	Exact Sig. (2-sided)	Exact Sig. (1-sided)
Pearson Chi-Square	8.747[a]	1	**.003**		
Continuity Correction[b]	7.891	1	.005		
Likelihood Ratio	8.817	1	.003		
Fisher's Exact Test				.005	.002
Linear-by-Linear Association	8.699	1	.003		
N of Valid Cases	182				

a. 0 cells (.0%) have expected count less than 5. The minimum expected count is 43.03.

b. Computed only for a 2x2 table

How to Compute Logistic Regression Tests in SPSS

Step 5: Run Logistic Regression Analysis.

Now that we have examined the test assumptions and have decided on the factors that are more likely to predict students' overweight group, we will utilize SPSS to run the analysis.

Recall that our dependent variable is Overweight and our factors are Gender, Race, Age, Physical Health, and Self-Perception. Notice that we will exclude Life Satisfaction from the regression analysis.

To use SPSS to compute logistic regression tests, follow these steps:

1. Open the Well-Being SPSS data file.

2. Click on *Analyze* in the SPSS main toolbar.

3. Click on *Regression,* and click on *Binary Logistic* (see screen 5.1).

4. A "Logistic Regression" dialog box will open (see screen 5.2).

5. Click on *Overweight* in the variable list, and click on the upper arrow to move it into the *Dependent* box.

Screen 5.1:   SPSS Logistic Regression Main Menu

Screen 5.2:   SPSS Logistic Regression Dialog Box

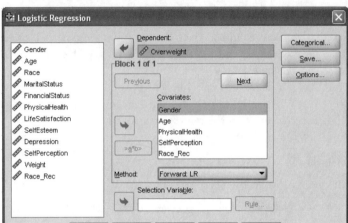

6.   Click on *Gender,* and click on the middle arrow to move it into the *Covari-ates* box. Repeat this step to move *Age, Race_Rec, PhysicalHealth,* and *Self-Perception* into the *Covariates* box.

7.   If you are interested in analyzing the demographic variables (Gender, Race, and Age) as one set and the other two as a second set, then move *Gender, Age,* and *Race* into the *Covariates* box. Then click on *Next* under "Block 1 of 1" and move *PhysicalHealth* and *SelfPerception* into the *Covariates* box. You can have as many blocks as you need. Here we will enter all factors in only one block.

8.   Click on the *Method* drop-down arrow and click on *Forward: LR* to request the method of factor entry in the analysis. This method is the same as step-wise in multiple regression analysis.

9.   Click on *Categorical* on the upper right side of the dialog box. A new dia-log box labeled "Logistic Regression: Define Categorical Variables" will open (see screen 5.3).

10.   Click on *Gender* in the *Covariates* box, and click on the arrow to move it into the *Categorical Covariates* box. Repeat this process to move *Race_Rec* into the *Categorical Covariates* box. You should move all categorical vari-ables into the *Categorical Covariates* box. This function will evaluate the codes of groups in each categorical factor.

11.   Click on *Continue* to return to the "Logistic Regression" dialog box.

12.   Click on *Save* on the upper right side. A "Logistic Regression: Save" dia-log box will open (see screen 5.4).

Screen 5.3: SPSS Logistic Regression Define Categorical Variables Dialog Box

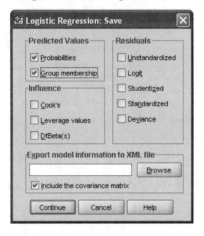

Screen 5.4: SPSS Logistic Regression Save Dialog Box

13.   Check the *Probabilities* and *Group Membership* boxes under "Predicted Values." This command will create two new variables, PRE_1 (predicted probability for an event to occur) and PGR_1 (predicted group membership).

14.   Click on *Continue* to return to the "Logistic Regression" dialog box.

15.   Click on *Options* in the upper right side to open the "Logistic Regression: Options" dialog box (see screen 5.5).

16.   Check the *Hosmer-Lemeshow Goodness-of-Fit* box under "Statistics and Plots."

17.   Click on *Continue,* and click on *OK.*

Screen 5.5:   SPSS Logistic Regression Options Dialog Box

You can also use the SPSS syntax commands to request these statistics:

SPSS Logistic Regression Syntax Commands

LOGISTIC REGRESSION VARIABLES Overweight
/METHOD=FSTEP(LR) Gender Age Race PhysicalHealth SelfPerception
/CONTRAST (Gender)=Indicator
/CONTRAST (Race_Rec)=Indicator
/SAVE=PRED PGROUP
/PRINT=GOODFIT
/CRITERIA=PIN(0.05) POUT(0.10) ITERATE(20) CUT(0.5).

Reading Logistic Regression SPSS Output

Both the SPSS logistic regression main menu and the syntax commands produce a number of tables, each of which examines different aspects of the relationship between the criterion and the factors. Mainly these outputs are divided in three parts: (1) descriptive statistics, (2) block 0: beginning block, and (3) block 1: method = forward stepwise (likelihood ratio).

The first part (tables 5.6–5.8) describes the number of cases in the analysis, the criterion and its coding, and factors that are classified as categorical data.

The second part (block 0: beginning block) examines a hypothetical model, also known as a constant model. In this case, no factor yet has been entered in the analysis. This block is not of interest, and thus it will not be discussed.

The third part (block 1: method) examines the regression coefficients and statistics of all factors (tables 5.9–5.14).

If factors were entered into two sets in the analysis (e.g., set 1 = Gender, Age, and Race; set 2 = Physical Health and Self-Perception), then set 1 would be labeled as block 1 and set 2 would be labeled as block 2.

Table 5.6 ("Case Processing Summary") displays the number of cases included in the analysis, missing cases, total cases, unselected cases, and overall total. Usually report the number of cases included in the analysis. In this case, $N = 182$.

Table 5.7 describes the coding of the dependent variable, original coding, and SPSS internal coding. In this case, Overweight was coded as "0" (no) and "1" (yes). The internal coding is not changed.

Table 5.8 lists all categorical factors, their frequencies, and their coding. In our case, there are two categorical factors, Race and Gender.

Table 5.8 shows that Gender consists of two groups. Originally they were coded as "0" (male) and "1" (female). Notice, however, under Parameter Coding (1) that the SPSS program reversed the coding for gender to be "1" for male and "0" for female. Race coding was also reversed. The new coding shows African American as "0" and others as "1." This new coding is important to remember because the remaining analysis is based on it.

Table 5.6:   Case Processing Summary

Case Processing Summary

Unweighted Cases[a]		N	Percent
Selected Cases	Included in Analysis	182	100.0
	Missing Cases	0	.0
	Total	182	100.0
Unselected Cases		0	.0
Total		182	100.0

a. If weight is in effect, see classification table for the total number of cases.

Table 5.7:   Dependent Variable Coding

Dependent Variable Encoding

Original Value	Internal Value
0 No	0
1 Yes	1

Table 5.8:   Categorical Factors Coding

Categorical Variables Codings

		Frequency	Parameter coding (1)
Race_Rec	0 Others	94	**1.000**
	1 African American	88	.000
Gender	0 MALE	78	**1.000**
	1 FEMALE	104	.000

Table 5.9 conveys the results of the stepwise logistic regression. It is similar to the ANOVA table in multiple regression analysis. It describes the level of significance for each factor entered in the analysis. In all, table 5.9 shows that four factors were entered in the analysis. Recall that in stepwise (or forward: LR) method, the factor with the highest likelihood-ratio values is entered first, followed by the second highest likelihood-ratio, until no further variance is added to the dependent variable.

In this case, there are four rows corresponding with four significant factors. Each row has four columns. The columns display the step in which each factor was entered (first column), its chi-square value (second column), number of degrees of freedom (*df*) (third column), and the level of significance of the chi-square (*Sig.*) (fourth column).

Each row has three lines, *step, block,* and *model:*

1. *Step* describes the statistics for the particular factor entered in the corresponding step and whether it is significant in predicting the probability of an event to occur (versus no event).

2. *Block* describes the statistics and level of significance of the factor(s) entered in the analysis within the particular block. *Remember,* if you divide factors into two (or more) sets, demographic factors and other factors, then you should have two (or more) blocks. In our case, all factors were entered in one block.

3. *Model* displays the statistics and level of significance for all factors in the model in the corresponding step. When factors are entered in one block, the results of the block and model are identical.

Note: when only one factor is entered in the analysis, the results of step, block, and model are identical.

STEP 1: Table 5.9 shows the results of the step, block, and model in step 1 are the same. The table indicates that the first factor entered in the analysis is a

Table 5.9:   Omnibus Tests of Regression Model Coefficients

Omnibus Tests of Model Coefficients

		Chi-square	df	Sig.
Step 1	Step	12.772	1	.000
	Block	12.772	1	.000
	Model	12.772	1	.000
Step 2	Step	10.967	1	.001
	Block	23.739	2	.000
	Model	23.739	2	.000
Step 3	Step	8.685	1	.003
	Block	32.424	3	.000
	Model	32.424	3	.000
Step 4	Step	5.056	1	.025
	Block	37.480	4	.000
	Model	**37.480**	**4.000**	**.000**

significant predictor of the probability of being overweight (chi-square = 12.772, *Sig.* = .000).

STEP 2: When a second factor was entered in the analysis, the results show that the second factor is also significant (step 2, first line: chi-square = 10.967, *Sig.* = .001). The results of the model (step 2, third line) indicate that with two factors in the analysis, the overall model is significant (chi-square = 23.739, *Sig.* = .000).

STEP 3: When a third factor was entered, the results show that this factor is also significant (step 3, first line: chi-square = 8.685, *Sig.* = .003). The results of the model (step 3, third line) indicate that with three factors in the analysis, the overall model is significant (chi-square = 32.424, *Sig.* = .000).

STEP 4: When a fourth factor was entered, the results show that this factor is also significant (step 4, first line: chi-square = 5.056, *Sig.* = .025). The results of the model (step 4, third line) indicate that with four factors in the analysis, the overall model is significant (chi-square = 37.480, *Sig.* = .000).

Overall, the results show that a four-factor model is a significant predictor of the probability of students becoming overweight.

To summarize, as with multiple regression analysis, we are interested in only the last row. This row includes the results for the final model, in this case, step 4.

Table 5.10 conveys the results of the likelihood-ratio (−2 log likelihood) (second column), Cox and Snell *R* square (third column), and the Nagelkerke *R* square (fourth column). The order and number of steps (models) are consistent with those in table 5.9. As it appears in table 5.10, the more factors entered in the analysis, the smaller the likelihood-ratio and the larger the *R* square values.

STEP 1 (FIRST LINE): With only one factor in the analysis, the likelihood-ratio is 239.446 and the proportion of variance in the criterion due to this factor ranges between 6.8 and 9 percent (Cox and Snell *R* square = .068, Nagelkerke *R* square = .090).

STEP 2 (SECOND LINE): With two factors in the analysis, the likelihood-ratio is 228.479 and the proportion of variance in the criterion due to these two factors ranges between 12.2 and 16.3 percent (Cox and Snell *R* square = .122, Nagelkerke *R* square = .163). In other words, the second factor added between 5.4 and 7.3 percent to the variance in the dependent variable (.122 − .068 = .054 and .163 − .090 = .073, respectively).

Table 5.10: Regression Model Summary

Model Summary

Step	-2 Log likelihood	Cox & Snell R Square	Nagelkerke R Square
1	239.446[a]	.068	.090
2	228.479[b]	.122	.163
3	219.794[b]	.163	.218
4	**214.738[b]**	**.186**	**.248**

a. Estimation terminated at iteration number 3 because parameter estimates changed by less than .001.

b. Estimation terminated at iteration number 4 because parameter estimates changed by less than .001.

Table 5.11:   Hosmer and Lemeshow Test of Goodness-of-Fit

Hosmer and Lemeshow Test

Step	Chi-square	df	Sig.
1	.000	0	.
2	4.431	6	.619
3	9.996	7	.189
4	**4.592**	**8**	**.800**

STEP 3 (THIRD LINE): With three factors in the analysis, the likelihood-ratio is 219.794 and the proportion of variance in the criterion due to these three factors ranges between 16.3 and 21.8 percent (Cox and Snell R square = .163, Nagelkerke R square = .218). In other words, the third factor added between 4.1 and 5.5 percent to the variance in the dependent variable (.163 − .122 = .041 and .218 − .163 = .055, respectively).

STEP 4 (FOURTH LINE): Finally, with four factors in the analysis, the likelihood-ratio is 214.738 and the proportion of the variance in the criterion due to these three factors ranges between 18.6 and 24.8 percent (Cox and Snell R square = .186, Nagelkerke R square = .248). In other words, the fourth factor only added between 2.3 and 3.0 percent to the variance in the dependent variable (.186 − .163 = .023 and .248 − .218 = .030, respectively).

Table 5.11 conveys the results of the Hosmer and Lemeshow chi-square test of goodness-of-fit. It compares the observed model with the predicted (expected) model. In other words, it examines how well the four-factor model identified in table 5.10 fits the population from which the data were collected. A nonsignificant p value ($p > .05$) thus indicates that the two models are not significantly different; they are equal.

STEP 4: Table 5.11 also has four lines corresponding with the four steps in the previous two tables. Each line examines how well the factor(s) in the corresponding step fit(s) the population. Here we are interested in the overall model, that is, step 4.

The results show that the four-factor model is not significantly different than the expected population's model (fourth line, chi-square = 4.592, *Sig.* = .800 which is greater than .05). In other words, this model has a very good fit of the population.

Table 5.12 displays the Hosmer and Lemeshow observed and expected probability values for each overweight group ("0" and "1") for each step. We are interested in the observed and expected values only for the last model (step 4). We will use this information to evaluate the assumption of number of cases per cell that was discussed earlier during evaluation of assumptions (see table 5.2).

Table 5.13 displays the results of the level of accuracy of the model in classifying individuals in one of the two weight groups (overweight versus not overweight) per step. In other words, it examines how correct the model is in predicting students' weight group. Thus it has four rows associated with the four steps identified in the previous tables. Again we are interested only in the final model (step 4), the four-factor model.

Table 5.12:   Hosmer and Lemeshow Contingency Table

Contingency Table for Hosmer and Lemeshow Test

		Overweight = 0 No		Overweight = 1 Yes		
		Observed	Expected	Observed	Expected	Total
Step 4	1	14	15.575	4	**2.425**	18
	2	14	13.563	4	**4.437**	18
	3	13	12.206	5	5.794	18
	4	15	11.839	4	7.161	19
	5	9	10.052	9	7.948	18
	6	8	9.345	11	9.655	19
	7	8	7.374	10	10.626	18
	8	6	5.934	12	12.066	18
	9	4	**4.569**	14	13.431	18
	10	2	**2.543**	16	15.457	18

STEP 4: This row has three lines and three columns. It displays the observed and predicted frequency in each weight group. Table 5.13 also displays the *success rate* of correctly predicting individuals in the corresponding weight group (Percentage Correct).

1. Table 5.13 shows that of the 93 (that is, 70 + 23) observed "no overweight" students, the model correctly predicted 70; that is a *success rate* of 75 percent; 70/93 = .75. On the other hand, the model missed 25 percent of the cases (23 cases predicted as "overweight" when in fact they should be "no overweight"; 23/93 = .25).

2. Table 5.13 also shows that of the 89 (that is, 28 + 61) observed "overweight" students, the model correctly predicted 61; that is a *success rate* of 69 percent; 61/89 = .69. On the other hand, the model missed 31 percent of the cases (28 cases predicted as "no overweight" when in fact they should be "overweight"; 28/89 = .31).

Table 5.13:   Logistic Regression Accuracy of Prediction

Classification Table[a]

			Predicted		
			Overweight		
	Observed		0 No	1 Yes	Percentage Correct
Step 1	Overweight	0 No	65	28	69.9
		1 Yes	39	50	56.2
		Overall Percentage			63.2
Step 2	Overweight	0 No	70	23	75.3
		1 Yes	37	52	58.4
		Overall Percentage			67.0
Step 3	Overweight	0 No	66	27	71.0
		1 Yes	28	61	68.5
		Overall Percentage			69.8
Step 4	Overweight	0 No	**70**	23	**75**
		1 Yes	28	**61**	**69**
		Overall Percentage			**72.0**

a. The cut value is .500

3.   The table shows that the four-factor model has an overall accuracy rate (success rate) of 72 percent (see table 5.13, step 4, third line [Overall Percentage], and last column [Percentage Correct]).

Table 5.14 conveys the logistic regression coefficients (B), standard error (SE), results of Wald test (*Wald, df, Sig.*), and odds ratio values [*Exp(B)*] for each factor in each step. It is equivalent to the coefficient table in multiple regression analysis. It has four rows, corresponding with the four steps, and seven columns. Again, we are interested only in the results of step 4, the full model. We need steps 1, 2, and 3 only to find out the order in which factors were entered in the analysis. You also can get this information by looking at the footnotes immediately under the table (a. Variable(s) entered on step . . ., etc.). You need these factors to create a regression summary table (discussed later).

STEP 4:

1.   Gender (first line) was entered in the *first* step (based on its likelihood ratio). The regression coefficient (B) indicates a positive relationship between gender and weight (step 4, first line and second column joint cell: $B = 1.3$). In other words, males are more likely to be overweight than females ("1" in Gender, male, is associated with "1," yes, in Overweight).

The results of the Wald test show that gender is a significant predictor of the probability of a student being overweight (see step 4, first line and fourth, fifth, and sixth joint cells: $Wald = 14.38, df = 1, Sig. = .000$).

Table 5.14 shows that gender correctly predicts the probability of classifying a student in the "overweight" group about four times *more* often than predicting the probability of classifying a student as "no overweight"; this

Table 5.14:   Logistic Regression Coefficient

Variables in the Equation

		B	S.E.	Wald	df	Sig.	Exp(B)
Step 1[a]	Gender(1)	1.091	.311	12.296	1	.000	2.976
	Constant	-.511	.203	6.360	1	.012	.600
Step 2[b]	Gender(1)	1.204	.326	13.618	1	.000	3.332
	PhysicalHealth	-.604	.190	10.114	1	.001	.547
	Constant	1.562	.674	5.371	1	.020	4.768
Step 3[c]	Gender(1)	1.250	.335	13.928	1	.000	3.492
	PhysicalHealth	-.598	.194	9.521	1	.002	.550
	Race_Rec(1)	-.949	.327	8.410	1	.004	.387
	Constant	2.005	.712	7.928	1	.005	7.430
Step 4[d]	Gender(1)	**1.3**	.343	14.380	1	.000	3.678
	PhysicalHealth	**-0.43**	.208	4.199	1	.040	.653
	SelfPerception	**-0.06**	.026	4.658	1	.031	.946
	Race_Rec(1)	**-1.11**	.343	10.569	1	.001	.328
	Constant	4.08	1.221	11.137	1	.001	58.932

a. Variable(s) entered on step 1: Gender.
b. Variable(s) entered on step 2: PhysicalHealth.
c. Variable(s) entered on step 3: Race_Rec.
d. Variable(s) entered on step 4: SelfPerception.

is the odds ratio value (step 4, first line and seventh column joint cell; $Exp(B)$ = 3.678).

2. The Physical Health variable (second line) was entered in the second step. The regression coefficient (B) shows a negative relationship between physical health and weight (see step 4, second line and second column joint cell: B = −.43). In other words, students with poorer physical health are more likely to be classified as overweight than healthier students (lower scores in Physical Health are associated with "1," yes, in Overweight).

    The results of the Wald test show that physical health is a significant predictor of the probability of a student being overweight (see step 4, second line and fourth, fifth, and sixth joint cells: $Wald$ = 4.199, df = 1, $Sig.$ = .040).

    Table 5.14 also shows that physical health correctly predicts the probability of classifying a student as "overweight." This probability is smaller than the probability of predicting a student as "no overweight"; this is the odds ratio value (see step 4, second line and seventh column joint cell: $Exp(B)$ = .653).

3. Race (fourth line) was entered in the third step. The regression coefficient (B) shows a negative relationship between race and overweight (step 4, fourth line and second column joint cell: B = −1.11). In other words, African American students are more likely to be classified as overweight than non–African Americans (a score of "0" in Race, African American, is associated with a score of "1," yes, in Overweight).

    The results of the Wald test show that race is a significant predictor of the probability of a student being overweight (see step 4, fourth line and fourth, fifth, and sixth joint cells: $Wald$ = 10.569, df = 1, $Sig.$ = .001).

    The table shows that race is less likely to correctly classify a student as "overweight" than "no overweight"; this is the odds ratio value (step 4, fourth line and seventh column joint cell: $Exp(B)$ = .328).

4. Self-Perception (third line) was entered in the fourth step. The regression coefficient (B) also shows a negative relationship between self-perception and weight (see step 4, third line and second column joint cell: B = −.06). In other words, students with lower self-perception are more likely to be classified as overweight than students with higher self-perception (lower scores in Self-Perception are associated with a score of "1," yes, in Overweight).

    The results of the Wald test show that self-perception is a significant predictor of the probability of a student being overweight (see step 4, third line and fourth, fifth, and sixth joint cells: $Wald$ = 4.658, df = 1, $Sig.$ = .031).

    The table shows that self-perception is almost equally likely to correctly predict the probability of a student as "overweight" or as "no overweight"; that is the odds ratio value (step 4, third line and seventh column joint cell: $Exp(B)$ = .946).

5. In the fifth line (Constant) table 5.14 provides the regression equation's intercept value (*a*). In this case, *a* = 4.08 (see step 4, fifth line and second column).

Finally, the SPSS commands, as said earlier, compute the probability scores and group membership for each case based on the regression model. These values will be added to the data file in the last two columns (see screen 5.6). They are PRE_1 (predicted probability) and PGR_1 (predicted group membership).

Note the three cases emphasized with boxes on screen 5.6. These cases were observed as overweight (see under Overweight). However, the model predicted them as "not overweight" (see under PGR_1). Their probability of being overweight ranges only between .11 and .13 (see under PRE_1). Recall that the model misclassified twenty-eight out of the observed eighty-nine overweight cases.

Step 6: Write the Results.

As we have done when writing the results of each test, remember to discuss that you have examined the basic assumptions of the logistic regression concerning the sample size and multicollinearity.

Screen 5.6:   SPSS Data View

Also, as with multiple regression analysis, report the number of factors that best predict the probability of occurrence of the particular outcome group (i.e., overweight). Also state variable order based on stepwise data entry, the proportion of the variance each contributes to the criterion, and their odds ratio values. Results from the practical example are found in the following section.

Writing the Results

Evaluation of assumptions.   A stepwise likelihood ratio (forward LR) logistic regression analysis was conducted to estimate a regression model that correctly predicts the probability of university students' weight groups (overweight versus not overweight). In all, six factors were entered in the analysis: Gender, Race, Age, Physical Health, Life Satisfaction, and Self-Perception.

Prior to conducting the analysis, chi-square and independent t-tests were utilized to examine the bivariate relationship between weight and each factor. The results of the chi-square and the independent t-test show significant relationships between weight and gender, race, age, physical health, and self-perception. On the other hand, no significant relationship was detected between weight and life satisfaction, and thus life satisfaction was excluded from the analysis.

Furthermore, tolerance and VIF values were computed for all factors to examine the assumption of multicollinearity. Both tolerance and VIF values show no multicollinearity problem exists among the factors.

Finally, the Hosmer and Lemeshow test contingency table shows that only four cells (20%) had expected values greater than 5. No cell, however, had an expected value smaller than 1.

Results of logistic regression.   The results of the stepwise likelihood ratio logistic regression reveal that four factors emerged as significant predictors of students' weight group. These factors are Gender ($Wald_{(df = 1)} = 14.38, p < .001$), Physical Health ($Wald_{(df = 1)} = 4.20, p < .05$), Race ($Wald_{(df = 1)} = 10.57, p < .01$), and Self-Perception ($Wald_{(df = 1)} = 4.66, p < .05$). In other words, African American male students with poorer physical health and lower self-perception are more likely to be correctly classified as overweight than non–African American female students with greater physical health and higher self-perception.

The results show that the overall model significantly improves the prediction of the occurrence of excess weight among university students ($\chi^2_{(df = 4)} = 37.48, p < .001$). This model has a very good fit (-2 log likelihood = 214.74, Hosmer and Lemeshow, $\chi^2_{(df = 8)} = 4.59, p = .800$).

The results of the Cox and Snell and the Nagelkerke R^2 indicate that gender accounted for 6.8 to 9.0 percent of the variance in weight. Physical health accounted for another 5.4 to 7.3 percent of the variance. Race and self-perception added 4.1 to 5.5 percent and 2.3 to 3.0 percent, respectively, to the variance in weight. Overall, the model accounted for 18.6 to 24.8 percent of the variance in weight.

Finally, the model correctly classified 75 percent of the "no overweight" cases and 69 percent of the "overweight" cases. Overall, this model has a success rate of .72.

Presentation of results in a summary table.   When presenting the results of the logistic regression analysis in a summary table, report the correlation coefficient (B), Wald value, *df,* level of significance, and odds ratio for each factor from the variables in the equation table (see table 5.14). Also, report both the likelihood ratio (–2LL) and the R square values from the model summary table (see table 5.10). Factors should be listed based on their entry in the stepwise analysis, from the largest –2LL to the smallest –2LL. For example, table 5.15 presents the results of the logistic regression analysis.

Writing the regression equation.   As with multiple regression analysis, after a logistic regression model has been identified, you should be able to write the odds ratio regression equation. This equation helps you to compute the probability that an individual will fall in one outcome group knowing certain information about this individual. In this example, the equation will help us to compute the probability of a student being classified as overweight given his or her gender, race, physical health, and self-perception.

Remember: Probability of Event

$$P(event) = \frac{1}{1 + e^{-(a + b_1X_1 + b_2X_2 + \ldots + b_iX_i)}}$$

e = constant = 2.718

Table 5.15:   Results of Logistic Regression[a, b]

Factor	B	Wald	df	p	–2LL	R^2	Odds-Ratio
Gender	1.30	14.38	1	.000	239.45	.068–.090	3.68
Physical Health	–.43	4.20	1	.040	228.48	.122–.163	.65
Race	–1.11	10.57	1	.001	219.79	.163–.218	.33
Self-perception	–.06	4.66	1	.031	214.74	.186–.248	.95
Constant	3.10	6.03	1	.014			58.93

[a]Overall model: $\chi^2_{(df = 4)} = 37.48, p < .001$.
[b]Goodness-of-fit: $-2LL = 214.74; \chi^2_{(df = 8)} = 4.59, p = .800$.

Given the information presented in table 5.15, we can rewrite the equation as follows:

$$P(event) = \frac{1}{1 + 2.718^{- (4.08 + 1.30 * G + -.43 * PH + -1.11 * R - .06 * SP)}}$$

G = gender; PH = physical health; R = race; SP = self-perception

EXAMPLE:

Lisa is an African American student in a northeastern university (Race = 0; Gender = 0) (see table 5.8 for categorical variables coding). Lisa scored 2 on a 5-point physical health scale and 20 on a self-perception scale ranging from 12 to 60. What is the probability that Lisa is considered overweight? Not overweight?

ANSWER:

Probability of Event

$$P(Overweight) = \frac{1}{1 + 2.718^{-(4.08 + 1.30 * 0 - .43 * 2 - 1.11 * 0 - .06 * 40)}}$$

$$P(Overweight) = \frac{1}{1 + 2.718^{-(4.08 + 0 - .86 - 0 - 2.4)}}$$

$$P(Overweight) = \frac{1}{1 + 2.718^{-(.82)}} = \frac{1}{1 + .44} = .69$$

That is, the probability that Lisa is classified as overweight is .69, or 69 percent.

Probability of No Event

$$P(Not\ Overweight) = 1 - P(Overweight) = 1 - .69 = .31$$

That is, the probability that Lisa is not overweight is .31, or 31 percent.

SUMMARY

Logistic regression analysis is parallel to multiple regression analysis. It allows social science researchers to predict the probability of the occurrence of a specific outcome based on multiple factors. For example, it helps clinicians, practitioners, and other professionals in predicting the likelihood that a client will develop certain mental health diseases, become obese, or consider committing suicide. By predicting the likelihood of the occurrence of these events, human services and health providers can take the appropriate measures to intervene in the lives of their clients and treat them accordingly.

This chapter introduced the logistic regression analysis and discussed its use. The chapter then discussed the logistic regression equation and how it is used in predicting a specific outcome. Next, the chapter presented the logistic regression coefficient and tests. Unlike in multiple regression analysis, logistic regression analysis examines how well the data fit the population and how well the factors predict the outcome variable. The first is examined by the Hosmer and Lemeshow test and uses the chi-square goodness-of-fit test to compare the observed model to the predicted model. The second is examined using omnibus tests and the $-2LL$ to examine the overall significance of the regression model. In addition, the individual factors are examined by the Wald test, which is analogous to the t-test in multiple regression analysis. Logistic regression analysis also provides the proportion of variance in the outcome variable accounted for by each factor. The proportion of variance is found by performing the Cox and Snell and the Nagelkerke R square tests.

The chapter also presented the assumptions underlying logistic regression analysis. Logistic regression technique makes fewer assumptions than multiple regression analysis. These assumptions relate to the level of measurement of the dependent variable, sample selection, number of cases per cell, and the correlation between the factors (multicollinearity). The chapter discussed how to evaluate each assumption.

Next, the chapter discussed how to select only the factors that are more likely to increase the probability of an event to occur, or the success rate. This section was followed by a discussion of the different regression methods. These methods include enter, forward (stepwise), and backward. Finally, the chapter presented a practical example based on an actual research data set to illustrate in detail the use of logistic regression analysis in social sciences research. This example illustrated how to use SPSS to analyze the data, interpret the output, write and present the results in a summary table, and compute the probability of an event to occur.

Chapters 6, 7, 8, and 9 will introduce new advanced techniques of data analysis. They are based on the analysis of variance (ANOVA). Chapter 1 reviewed the one-way ANOVA, pointing out that it examines the mean differences of three or more groups.

Chapter 6 will discuss an advanced method of the one-way ANOVA, the two-way ANOVA. The chapter will present the test's purpose, advantages, sources of variation, research questions, hypotheses, assumptions, and post hoc techniques. The chapter then will present a detailed example from real data explaining the utilization of the two-way ANOVA. This example will begin with writing the hypotheses. It will also address utilization of SPSS to generate the output, and it will cover writing the results and presenting them in a summary table.

PRACTICAL EXERCISES

Use the information from the practical exercises in chapter 4. Recode levels of depression (CESD) into a new variable called Depression, and code all scores between 0 and 15 as "0" (Not Depressed) and all scores 16 and above as "1" (Depressed). Now answer the following questions:

1. Write a research question predicting the probability that an older immigrant is more likely to be depressed based on gender, age, owning a home, emotional balance, physical health, and cognitive status.

2. What statistical test(s) will you utilize to examine this research question? Why? Discuss your answer in detail.

3. Write the SPSS syntax file for the test statistic.

4. Run the test statistic you selected in question 2.

5. What is your decision? Discuss your answer in detail.

6. Present the results in a summary table.

7. Write the regression equation.

8. What is the probability that Maria is considered depressed if she is seventy-two years old, has no home, and scored 32 on the emotional balance, 30 on the physical health, and 27 on the cognitive status scales?

9. What is the probability that Edward is not depressed if he is eighty years old, owns his home, and scored 28 on the emotional balance, 16 on the physical health, and 18 on the cognitive status scales?

10. Compare your results for this research question with the results you obtained in the practical exercises for chapter 4.

CHAPTER 6

Two-Way Analysis of Variance

LEARNING OBJECTIVES

1. Understand the purpose of the two-way ANOVA
2. Understand the assumptions underlying the two-way ANOVA
3. Understand the post hoc tests
4. Understand how to use SPSS to compute the statistics
5. Understand how to interpret, write, and present the results of the test

DATA SET (APPENDIX)

Job Satisfaction

INTRODUCTION

Chapter 1 reviewed some useful bivariate statistical tests utilized to examine the differences between the means of two groups (independent t-test) and the differences between the means of three or more groups (one-way ANOVA).

For example, in chapter 1 we examined the mean differences in life satisfaction based on college students' marital status. In this case we utilized the one-way ANOVA and found significant differences between students who are single, married, and others with regard to their life satisfaction. A question that may arise is whether these differences are due to the influence of another variable, for example, the students' race (whites, African Americans, and others).

To answer this question, we would need to conduct another one-way ANOVA to examine the mean differences in life satisfaction based on students' race. However, although these analyses will examine the differences in life satisfaction based on each variable independently, they will fail to show any differences in levels of life satisfaction due to the interaction between the two variables, Marital Status and Race (e.g., single white, married white, single African American, married African American, etc.).

There are two ways to capture the differences due to this interaction. First, we can use race and marital status to create a new variable to produce all possible groups (single white, married white, other white, single African American, married African American, and other African American) and conduct a one-way ANOVA (or Kruskal-Wallis H test, based on the assumptions) to examine the mean differences between the groups. However, this method is limited in that it does not show the effect of each independent variable (Race and Marital Status).

The second method is to utilize a more advanced statistical technique that will capture the effect of each variable independently as well as the joint effect of both variables. This technique is known as the *two-way analysis of variance.*

TWO-WAY ANALYSIS OF VARIANCE

Purpose

The purpose of two-way ANOVA, also known as *between-subjects design, two-factor ANOVA, fixed-effects model,* and *two-way classification,* is to examine the differences between the mean scores of one continuous variable based on two categorical variables and whether these differences are statistically significant. Each categorical variable must have two or more groups.

The two-way ANOVA can also be expressed as *j * k ANOVA,* where *j* is the number of groups (or levels) in the first independent variable (Factor J) and *k* is the number of groups (or levels) in the second dependent variable (Factor K). A 3x4 ANOVA, for example, means that the first independent variable has three groups and the second independent variable has four groups.

EXAMPLE: A two-way ANOVA can be used to examine whether there are statistically significant differences in the levels of job satisfaction among social services workers based on their marital status and location of employment. Table 6.1 illustrates this example.

TOTAL ROW: mean scores of job satisfaction for each marital status (main effect 1).

EXAMPLE: μ_S = mean score of job satisfaction for single workers.

TOTAL COLUMN: mean scores of job satisfaction for each location (main effect 2).

EXAMPLE: μ_N = mean score of job satisfaction for workers living in the North.

Table 6.1:   Job Satisfaction Based on Marital Status and Location of Employment

	Marital Status			
Location	Single	Married	Divorced	Total
North	μ_{SN}	μ_{MN}	μ_{DN}	μ_N
Center	μ_{SC}	μ_{MC}	μ_{DC}	μ_C
South	μ_{SSO}	μ_{MSO}	μ_{DS}	μ_{SO}
Total	μ_S	μ_M	μ_D	μ_T

JOINT CELLS: mean scores of job satisfaction for each marital status by location (interaction effect).

EXAMPLE: μ_{SN} = mean score of job satisfaction for single workers living in the North.

Sources of Variation

The variance (SS) in a two-way ANOVA, as in a one-way ANOVA, is partitioned into two sources of variability: *within-subjects* variability (SS_W) and *between-subjects* variability (SS_B). The within-subjects variability is the same as in a one-way ANOVA. It refers to variations in the scores of subjects within each group in each independent variable. It is also known as errors or residuals.

Unlike in a one-way ANOVA, the between-subjects variability is the sum of variability in three sources: the variability in the first independent variable (Factor J, or SS_J), the variability in the second independent variable (Factor K, or SS_K), and the variability due to the interaction between these two variables (SS_{JK}).

The sum of *within-subjects variance* and *between-subjects variance* is the *total variance* (SS_T).

Formula

$$SS_B = SS_J + SS_K + SS_{JK}$$
$$SS_T = SS_W + SS_B$$

SS_B = between-subjects variance
SS_J = variance in first independent variable
SS_K = variance in second independent variable
SS_{JK} = variance in J by K interaction
SS_T = total variance
SS_W = within-subjects variance

Advantages

There are three main advantages to using the two-way ANOVA:

1. Unlike the one-way ANOVA, the two-way ANOVA allows researchers to examine the effects of two categorical variables on one dependent variable simultaneously; thus it is more efficient. For example, to examine if there are statistically significant differences in the levels of job satisfaction among workers based on their marital status and based on their location of employment, a researcher would need to conduct two separate one-way ANOVA analyses, one for marital status and job satisfaction and a second analysis for location and job satisfaction. On the other hand, with a two-way ANOVA,

researchers need to conduct only one analysis to capture the effects of both marital status and location on job satisfaction.

2. By examining both categorical variables simultaneously, researchers control for the effect of one independent variable (e.g., Location) over the second independent variable (e.g., Marital Status). Otherwise, if one-way ANOVA is used and a significant result is revealed between the dependent variable and the independent variable under analysis, this significant result could be attributed to the second variable. A two-way ANOVA eliminates this confusion.

3. By utilizing a two-way ANOVA, not only are researchers able to examine the effect of each independent variable on the dependent variable (*main effect 1* and *main effect 2*), but they also are able to examine whether there are significant differences on the mean scores of the dependent variable between the groups of one independent variable across the groups of the second independent variable. These differences are referred to as *interaction effect*. (Hinkle, Wiersma, & Jurs, 2003)

Research Questions and Hypotheses

The purpose of a two-way ANOVA is to examine the effects of two independent variables on one dependent variable. These effects include two main effects and one interaction effect:

Main effect 1 is the effect of the first independent variable on the dependent variable (e.g., Marital Status on Job Satisfaction).

Main effect 2 is the effect of the second independent variable on the dependent variable (e.g., Location of Employment on Job Satisfaction).

Interaction effect is the effect of the joint cells (first independent variable by second independent variable) on the dependent variable (e.g., Marital Status by Location on Job Satisfaction).

Therefore, a two-way ANOVA is utilized to address three research questions/hypotheses. They are as follows:

RESEARCH QUESTION 1: Are there significant differences between the levels of the first independent variable on the dependent variable?

EXAMPLE: Are there significant differences between single, married, and divorced social services workers with regard to their levels of job satisfaction?

RESEARCH QUESTION 2: Are there significant differences between the levels of the second independent variable on the dependent variable?

EXAMPLE: Are there significant differences between workers who live in the north, center, and south with regard to their levels of job satisfaction?

RESEARCH QUESTION 3: Are there significant differences between the levels of the first independent variable on the dependent variable across the levels of the second independent variable?

EXAMPLE: Are there significant differences between workers who are single living in the north, single living in the center, single living in the south, married living in the north, married living in the center, married living in the south, divorced living in the north, divorced living in the center, and divorced living in the south with regard to their job satisfaction?

The simplest way to write this question is as follows: Are there significant marital status by location interaction effects (or differences) with regard to job satisfaction?

The research hypotheses for the two-way ANOVA follow:

RESEARCH HYPOTHESIS 1: There are significant differences in the levels of the first independent variable on the dependent variable.

EXAMPLE: There are statistically significant differences between single, married, and divorced workers with regard to their levels of job satisfaction.

RESEARCH HYPOTHESIS 2: There are significant differences in the levels of the second independent variable on the dependent variable.

EXAMPLE: There are statistically significant differences between workers who live in the north, center, and south with regard to their levels of job satisfaction.

RESEARCH HYPOTHESIS 3: There are significant differences in the levels of the first independent variable on the dependent variable across the levels of the second independent variable.

EXAMPLE: There is a statistically significant marital status by location interaction effect on workers' job satisfaction.

Assumptions

As discussed, the two-way ANOVA is an extension of the one-way ANOVA in that it examines the effect of two categorical variables on one dependent variable at the same time. Therefore, it requires the same assumptions as the one-way ANOVA. These assumptions include the following:

1. SAMPLE REPRESENTATIVENESS: The sample must be representative of the population to which generalization will be made.

2. LEVEL OF MEASUREMENT: The dependent variable must be continuous and measured at the interval level or higher. The two independent variables must be nominal with two or more groups for each (e.g., Marital Status = single, married, and divorced; Location = north, center, and south). Sometimes, however, researchers may recode continuous data into categorical data to compare groups on the dependent variable. If recoded, make sure that groups are mutually exclusive and exhaustive.

These two assumptions are methodological ones and can be inspected through the research design of the study.

3.   NORMALITY OF DISTRIBUTION: The shape of the distribution of the dependent variable must approximate the shape of a normal curve.

To evaluate this assumption, inspect measures of skewness and kurtosis, histograms, and normal probability plots for the dependent variable (see chapter 2).

4.   SAMPLE SIZE: The sample size must be adequate. Although there is no agreement among statisticians on the minimum sample size required for ANOVA, a minimum of 30 cases should be sufficient to utilize ANOVA. It is also recommended that each cell have 5 cases or more.

For example, in a 3x3 ANOVA (Marital Status and Location; each has three levels), a sample of 45 (or more) should be adequate (that is, 3 x 3 x 5 = 45). In general, the larger the sample size is, the greater the power of the test.

Although it is preferred to have groups (cells) with equal frequencies, it is not a requirement, because, mathematically, different types of ANOVA can be used to adjust for unequal sample sizes. These methods are available in the SPSS General Linear Model (GLM), such as *Type III Source of Variance,* which is the default in SPSS GLM. We will return to SPSS options in the practical example.

5.   PAIRED OBSERVATION: Data for all groups must be collected at the same time (e.g., data on levels of job satisfaction were collected simultaneously from married, single, and divorced workers from the three locations).

This assumption is also a methodological one and can be evaluated accordingly.

6.   HOMOSCEDASTICITY: The variances of all groups on the dependent variable should be equal, which is also called the assumption of *homogeneity of variances* and *equality of variances.*

This assumption can be evaluated by examining the results of Levene's test of equality of variances, which can be requested along with the results of ANOVA. As a general rule and because Levene's test of equality of error variances is a very conservative test, the level of significance (*Sig.*) should be greater than .001 for this assumption to be satisfied.

Post Hoc Tests

Like the one-way ANOVA, the two-way ANOVA examines whether there are overall significant differences between the groups of each independent variable on the dependent variable. Yet when the number of groups in one or both independent variables exceeds two, a post hoc test must be utilized to pinpoint what groups are significantly different.

SPSS is equipped with eighteen post hoc tests, fourteen of which are appropriate when data meet the assumption of homogeneity of variances. Four tests are appropriate when the assumption is not met, that is, when the variances are not equal.

The four most frequently reported post hoc tests when *equality of variances is assumed* include the LSD (least significant difference), Bonferroni (also known as Bonferroni correction), Scheffe, and Tukey. The Tamhane's T2 is another post hoc test that is based on the independent *t*-test. However, it is most appropriate when *equality of variances is not assumed.*

PRACTICAL EXAMPLE

To demonstrate the utilization of the two-way ANOVA, we will examine the effects of marital status and location of employment on job satisfaction. We will follow the steps of hypothesis testing (data file: Job Satisfaction).

Hypothesis Testing

Step 1: State the Null and Alternative Hypotheses.

MAIN EFFECT 1:

H_{o1}: There are no statistically significant differences between single, married, and divorced workers with regard to their levels of job satisfaction.

$\mu_S = \mu_M = \mu_D$

H_{a1}: There are statistically significant differences between single, married, and divorced workers with regard to their levels of job satisfaction.

$\mu_S \neq \mu_M \neq \mu_D$; for at least two groups

MAIN EFFECT 2:

H_{o2}: There are no statistically significant differences between social services workers living in the north, center, and south with regard to their levels of job satisfaction.

$\mu_N = \mu_C = \mu_{SO}$

H_{a2}: There are statistically significant differences between workers living in the north, center, and south with regard to their levels of job satisfaction.

$\mu_N \neq \mu_C \neq \mu_{SO}$; for at least two groups

INTERACTION EFFECT:

H_{o3}: There is no statistically significant marital status by location interaction effect among workers with regard to their levels of job satisfaction.

$\mu_{SN} = \mu_{MN} = \mu_{DN} = \mu_{SC} = \mu_{MC} = \mu_{DC} = \mu_{SSO} = \mu_{MSO} = \mu_{DSO}$

H_{a3}: There is a statistically significant marital status by location interaction effect among workers with regard to their levels of job satisfaction.

$\mu_{SN} \neq \mu_{MN} \neq \mu_{DN} \neq \mu_{SC} \neq \mu_{MC} \neq \mu_{DC} \neq \mu_{SSO} \neq \mu_{MSO} \neq \mu_{DSO}$; for at least two groups

Step 2: Set the Criteria for Rejecting the Null Hypotheses.
We will set alpha at .05 ($\alpha = .05$). That is, reject H_o only if $p \leq .05$.

Step 3: Select the Appropriate Statistical Test.

In this study, there are two categorical independent variables (Marital Status and Location of Employment) and one continuous dependent variable (Job Satisfaction). Therefore, we will consider a two-way ANOVA to examine the main and interaction effects. However, first we must examine the test assumptions to ensure its appropriateness to examine these effects.

1. LEVEL OF MEASUREMENT: The independent variables, Marital Status and Location of Employment, are nominal variables. Each variable has three groups (Marital Status: single, married, and divorced; Location: north, center, and south). The dependent variable, Job Satisfaction, is continuous and measured at the interval level.

2. NORMALITY OF DISTRIBUTION: To evaluate the assumption of normality, use SPSS to compute measures of skewness and kurtosis and to create a histogram and a normal probability plot for job satisfaction (see chapter 2). Table 6.2 presents measures of skewness and kurtosis, and figure 6.1 displays both a histogram (A) and a normal probability plot (B) for job satisfaction.

Evaluation of the measure of skewness (skewness/standard error of skewness = −2.375) shows that it falls outside the normal range (±1.96) and thus indicates severe skewness. Kurtosis, on the other hand, shows that the distribution falls within the normal range (kurtosis/standard error of kurtosis = .451). Furthermore, both the histogram and the normal probability plot (see figure 6.1) show

Table 6.2:   Measures of Skewness and Kurtosis for Job Satisfaction

Statistics

Satisfaction

N	Valid	218.000
	Missing	.000
	Skewness	-.392
	Std. Error of Skewness	.165
	Kurtosis	.148
	Std. Error of Kurtosis	.328

Figure 6.1:   Histogram and Normal Probability Plot for Job Satisfaction

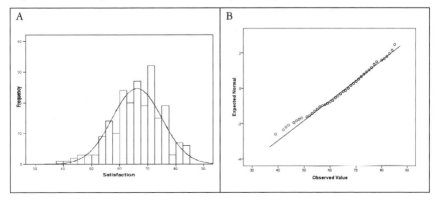

Table 6.3:   Levene's Test of Equality of Error Variances

Levene's Test of Equality of Error Variances[a]

Dependent Variable:Satisfaction

F	df1	df2	Sig.
1.341	8	208	.225

Tests the null hypothesis that the error variance of the dependent variable is equal across groups.

a. Design: Intercept + MStatus + Location + MStatus * Location

that the shape of the distribution of job satisfaction appears to approach the shape of a normal curve, with few minor deviations from the horizontal line. Thus we can conclude that the distribution of job satisfaction approaches the shape of a normal curve.

3.   HOMOGENEITY OF VARIANCES: To evaluate this assumption, we will inspect the results of Levene's test of equality of variances. Table 6.3 presents these results.

Table 6.3 shows that the level of significance for Levene's test (*Sig.*) is .225, which is greater than .001. Thus the assumption of homogeneity of variances is met.

4.   SAMPLE SIZE: Two hundred and eighteen social services workers participated in the Job Satisfaction study.

To conclude, we will utilize the two-way ANOVA (3x3 ANOVA) to examine the three hypotheses.

How to Use SPSS to Run Two-Way ANOVA

Step 4: Compute the Two-Way ANOVA Test Statistic.
To run the two-way ANOVA in SPSS, follow these steps:

1.   Open the Job Satisfaction SPSS data file.

2.   Click on *Analyze* in the SPSS main toolbar.

3.   Scroll down to and click on *General Linear Model* and then *Univariate.*

4.   A dialog box called "Univariate" will open (see screen 6.1).

5.   Scroll down in the variables list, click on *Satisfaction* (dependent variable), and click on the upper arrow button to move *Satisfaction* into the *Dependent Variable* box.

6.   Scroll down in the variables list, click on *MStatus* (first independent variable), and click on the second arrow button to move it into the *Fixed Factor(s)* box.

7.   Scroll down in the variables list, click on *Location* (second independent variable), and click on the second arrow button to move it into the *Fixed Factor(s)* box.

Screen 6.1:   SPSS Two-Way ANOVA Univariate Dialog Box

8. Click on *Post Hoc* at the right of the "Univariate" dialog box to request one or more post hoc tests. A new dialog box called "Univariate: Post Hoc Multiple Comparisons for Observed Means" will open (see screen 6.2). These tests are organized into two groups: "Equal Variances Assumed" and "Equal Variances not Assumed."

9. Click on *MStatus,* and click on the middle arrow button to move it into the *Post Hoc Tests For* box.

Screen 6.2:   SPSS Univariate Post Hoc Tests Dialog Box

10.   Click on *Location*, and click on the middle arrow button to move it into the *Post Hoc Tests For* box. Remember, you need post hoc only for independent variables with three or more groups.

11.   Check the *Bonferroni* box (you may also select *LSD, Scheffe,* etc.).

12.   Click on *Continue* to go back to the "Univariate" dialog box (see screen 6.1).

13.   Click on *Options* in the "Univariate" dialog box. A new dialog box called "Univariate: Options" will open (see screen 6.3).

14.   Click on *Overall*, and click on the middle arrow button to move it into the *Display Means For* box.

15.   Repeat this step to move all variables into the *Display Means For* box.

16.   Under "Display," check the boxes for *Descriptive Statistics* (generates descriptive statistics for each group), *Estimates of Effect Size* (computes the variances in the dependent variable accounted by each independent variable and by their interaction), *Observed Power* (produces the power for each analysis; power is the probability of rejecting the null hypothesis when in fact it is false), and *Homogeneity Tests* (Levene's test of equality of variances).

17.   Click on *Continue* to go back to the "Univariate" dialog box.

18.   Click on *Plots*. A new dialog box called "Univariate: Profile Plots" will open (see screen 6.4).

Screen 6.3:   SPSS Univariate Options Dialog Box

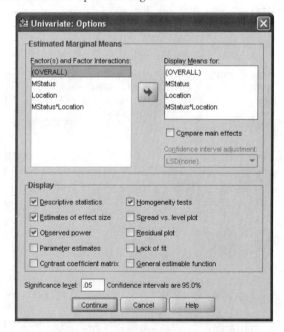

Screen 6.4: SPSS Univariate Plots Dialog Box

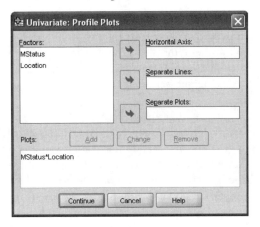

19. Click on *MStatus*, and click on the upper arrow to move it into the *Horizontal Axis* box.

20. Click on *Location*, and click on the middle arrow to move it into the *Separate Lines* box.

21. Click on *Add* to move both variables into the *Plots* box. This command will generate a plot for both variables and their interaction.

22. Click on *Continue* to return to the "Univariate" dialog box.

23. Click on *OK* in the "Univariate" dialog box.

SPSS Syntax for Two-Way ANOVA

UNIANOVA
Satisfaction BY MStatus Location
/METHOD = SSTYPE(3)
/INTERCEPT = INCLUDE
/POSTHOC = MStatus Location (BONFERRONI)
/PLOT = PROFILE (MStatus*Location)
/EMMEANS = TABLES(OVERALL)
/EMMEANS = TABLES(MStatus)
/EMMEANS = TABLES(Location)
/EMMEANS = TABLES(MStatus*Location)
/PRINT = DESCRIPTIVE ETASQ OPOWER HOMOGENEITY
/CRITERIA = ALPHA(.05)
/DESIGN = MStatus Location MStatus*Location .

Reading the SPSS Output of the Two-Way ANOVA

Tables 6.4 through 6.9 and figure 6.2 display the results of the two-way ANOVA generated by SPSS. The results follow.

Table 6.4 displays the number of subjects in each group within each independent variable. In this study, 140 subjects were married, 47 were single, and 30 were divorced. Also, 52 subjects were located in the north, 61 in the center, and 104 in the south.

Table 6.5 displays the descriptive statistics (means, standard deviations, and number of subjects) for each group of the first independent variable (Marital Status), for each group of the second independent variable (Location), and for their interaction (Marital Status by Location).

Table 6.5 has four rows. The number of rows equals the number of groups in the first independent variable (Marital Status = 3 groups) plus one row displaying the means for all groups in the second independent variable (Location). The means for the groups in the first independent variable are presented in the last line of each row, Total.

Table 6.4:   Between-Subjects Factors

Between-Subjects Factors

		Value Label	N
MStatus	1	MARRIED	140
	2	SINGLE	47
	3	DIVORCED	30
Location	1	NORTH	52
	2	CENTER	61
	3	SOUTH	104

Table 6.5:   Descriptive Statistics

Descriptive Statistics

Dependent Variable:Satisfaction

MStatus	Location	Mean	Std. Deviation	N
1 MARRIED	1 NORTH	62.66	8.303	32
	2 CENTER	62.18	7.875	45
	3 SOUTH	67.73	8.272	63
	Total	64.79	8.527	140
2 SINGLE	1 NORTH	62.83	7.846	18
	2 CENTER	73.57	7.934	7
	3 SOUTH	67.68	10.803	22
	Total	66.70	9.886	47
3 DIVORCED	1 NORTH	65.50	.707	2
	2 CENTER	71.22	6.119	9
	3 SOUTH	72.42	6.371	19
	Total	71.60	6.212	30
Total	1 NORTH	62.83	7.920	52
	2 CENTER	64.82	8.780	61
	3 SOUTH	68.58	8.684	104
	Total	66.14	8.842	217

In this study, as an example, 32 subjects were married and lived in the north (first row, first line, Married–North). Their mean score on job satisfaction was 62.66 with a standard deviation of 8.303. In all, 140 subjects were married (first row, fourth line, Married–Total). Their mean score on job satisfaction was 64.79 (SD = 8.527).

Also, of the 30 divorced subjects (third row, fourth line, Divorced–Total), 19 subjects were located in the south (third row, third line, Divorced–South). Their mean score on job satisfaction was 72.42 (SD = 6.371).

The fourth row, Total, presents the descriptive statistics for each group in the second variable. For example, the mean score on job satisfaction among subjects who lived in the center (second line) was 64.82 with a standard deviation of 8.78 ($N = 61$).

Table 6.6 displays the results of the overall two-way ANOVA test. As with one-way ANOVA, the two-way ANOVA table shows the sum of square deviations (SS), the degrees of freedom (df), and the mean square deviations. The table also shows the F ratio and the level of significance (*Sig.*, or p value). In addition, table 6.6 shows the partial eta squared and the observed power.

Explanation of Terms

The *Type III Sum of Squares* column displays the total variances due to each one of the analyses. Notice that this is *Type III* (SPSS default). This type is appropriate when cells have unequal frequencies, like in our case where we do not have equal cells (see table 6.4). You can use different types by clicking on *Model* in the SPSS "Univariate" dialog box (see screen 6.1); then click on the *Sum of Squares* drop-down arrow and choose your desired type (see screen 6.5) and click on *Continue* to return to the main dialog box.

There are four sources of variations of interest: MStatus (first independent variable or main effect 1; SS_J), Location (second independent variable or main effect 2; SS_K), MStatus * Location (interaction effect; SS_{JK}), and Error (within-

Table 6.6:   Results of the Two-Way Analysis of Variance

Tests of Between-Subjects Effects

Dependent Variable:Satisfaction

Source	Type III Sum of Squares	df	Mean Square	F	Sig.	Partial Eta Squared	Noncent. Parameter	Observed Power[b]
Corrected Model	2872.688[a]	8	359.086	5.330	.000	.170	42.638	.999
Intercept	375643.050	1	375643.050	5575.453	.000	.964	5575.453	1.000
MStatus	698.059	2	349.030	5.180	.006	.047	10.361	0.82
Location	414.331	2	207.166	3.075	.048	.029	6.150	0.59
MStatus * Location	685.885	4	171.471	2.545	.041	.047	10.180	0.71
Error	14013.883	208	67.374					
Total	966235.000	217						
Corrected Total	16886.571	216						

a. R Squared = .170 (Adjusted R Squared = .138)

b. Computed using alpha = .05

Screen 6.5:   SPSS Univariate Model Dialog Box

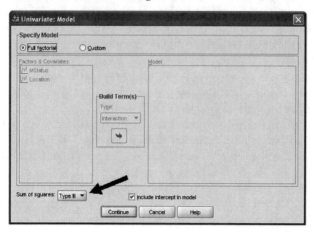

variances; SS_W). The sum of these variances is the total corrected variance, or, in SPSS, the *corrected total* (total variances; SS_T).

The *df* column displays the number of degrees of freedom associated with each analysis (first independent variable, second independent variable, interaction, error, and total).

Formula for Degrees of Freedom

df (variable J) = df_J = j − 1
df (variable K) = df_K = k − 1
df (interaction) = df_{JK} = (j − 1) * (k − 1)
df (error) = df_W = N − (j * k)
df (total) = df_T = N − 1

j = number of groups of first independent variable
k = number of groups in the second independent variable
N = number of subjects in the study

The *mean square* of variances is the sum of squared variances due to a particular analysis divided by the degrees of freedom of the particular analysis. For example, the mean square of variances due to marital status is equal to the sum of square of variances due to marital status divided by the number of degrees of freedom associated with marital status.

The **F** value column displays the *F* statistic for each analysis. It is the ratio of the mean square of variances due to a particular analysis divided by the within-subjects (error) variances. For example, the *F* statistic for location is equal

Formulas

$$MS_J = SS_J/df_J$$
$$MS_K = SS_K/df_K$$
$$MS_{JK} = SS_{JK}/df_{JK}$$
$$MS_W = SS_{JK}/df_W$$

MS_J = mean square of variances due to variable J
SS_J = sum of square of variances due to variable J
MS_K = mean square of variance due to variable K
SS_K = sum of square of variance due to variable K
MS_{JK} = mean square of variance due to interaction of J by K
SS_{JK} = sum of square of variance due to interaction of J by K
MS_W = mean square of variance due to error
SS_W = sum of square of variance due to error

to the mean square of variances due to location divided by the mean square of variances due to error.

Formulas

$$F_J = MS_J/MS_W$$
$$F_K = MS_K/MS_W$$
$$F_{JK} = MS_{JK}/MS_W$$

The *Sig.* column displays the p value, the probability of rejecting the null hypothesis when, in fact, it is true. Usually, unless a different alpha is specified, a p value of .05 or less is considered significant, thus supporting the rejection of the null hypothesis.

The *partial eta squared,* symbolized by the Greek letter η^2 (read: eta square), represents the total variance in the dependent variable that is accounted for by the particular analysis (each independent variable and the interaction).

The *observed power,* last column, displays the power for each analysis. Whereas type I error (*alpha*) is the probability of rejecting the null hypothesis when, in fact, it is true, power is the probability of rejecting the null hypothesis when, in fact, it is false. Thus power is a function of type I error. Mathematically, usually a desired power is equal to $(1 - 4 * alpha)$. For example, if alpha is set at .05, the desired power is $(1 - 4 * .05 = .80)$.

Reading the Table

Main effect 1—MStatus (line 3).   Table 6.6 shows a significant difference between at least two marital status groups with regard to their levels of job satisfaction (third line, MStatus, $F = 5.180$, $df = 2$, $Sig.$ = .006). In this example, 4.7 percent (third line, partial eta squared value = .047) of the variance in job satisfaction is accounted for by (or is due to) marital status. This analysis has a power of .82, which exceeds the cutoff of .80 (observed power = .82).

Main effect 2—Location (line 4).   Table 6.6 also shows a significant difference between at least two locations with regard to their levels of job satisfaction (fourth line, Location, $F = 3.075$, $df = 2$, $Sig.$ = .048). In this example, 2.9 percent (fourth line, partial eta squared value = .029) of the variance in job satisfaction is accounted for by (or is due to) location of employment. This analysis has a power of .59 (observed power = .59).

Interaction effect—MStatus * Location (line 5).   Table 6.6 shows a significant marital status by location interaction effect on levels of job satisfaction (fifth line, MStatus * Location, df, F, and $Sig.$ values: $F = 2.545$, $df = 4$, $Sig.$ = .041). In this study, 4.7 percent (fifth line, partial eta squared value = .047) of the variance in job satisfaction is accounted for by (or is due to) the interaction of marital status and location of employment. This analysis, however, has a power of .71 (observed power = .71).

Overall variance.   Finally, table 6.6 shows that 17 percent ($\bar{R}$ squared = .170) of the variance in job satisfaction is accounted for by (or is due to) marital status, location of employment, and their interaction.

Estimated Marginal Means

Next, SPSS calculates the estimated marginal means. They include the overall mean of the dependent variable, Job Satisfaction, known as the grand mean (see table 6.7.A); the mean for each group in the first independent variable, Marital Status (see table 6.7.B); the mean for each group in the second independent variable, Location (see table 6.7.C); and the mean for each group in the first independent variable, Marital Status, by each group in the second independent variable, Location (see table 6.7.D). These means represent the interaction means.

Table 6.7.A: Estimated Job Satisfaction Grand Mean

1. Grand Mean

Dependent Variable: Satisfaction

		95% Confidence Interval	
Mean	Std. Error	Lower Bound	Upper Bound
67.310	.901	65.533	69.088

Table 6.7.B: Estimated Job Satisfaction by Marital Status Means

2. MStatus

Dependent Variable: Satisfaction

MStatus	Mean	Std. Error	95% Confidence Interval	
			Lower Bound	Upper Bound
1 MARRIED	64.188	.721	62.768	65.608
2 SINGLE	68.029	1.351	65.365	70.693
3 DIVORCED	69.714	2.229	65.320	74.109

Table 6.7.C: Estimated Job Satisfaction by Location Means

3. Region

Dependent Variable: Satisfaction

Region	Mean	Std. Error	95% Confidence Interval	
			Lower Bound	Upper Bound
1 NORTH	63.663	2.096	59.531	67.795
2 CENTER	68.990	1.438	66.156	71.825
3 SOUTH	69.278	.924	67.457	71.099

Table 6.7.D: Estimated Job Satisfaction by Marital Status by Location Means

4. MStatus * Region

Dependent Variable: Satisfaction

MStatus	Region	Mean	Std. Error	95% Confidence Interval	
				Lower Bound	Upper Bound
1 MARRIED	1 NORTH	62.656	1.451	59.796	65.517
	2 CENTER	62.178	1.224	59.766	64.590
	3 SOUTH	67.730	1.034	65.691	69.769
2 SINGLE	1 NORTH	62.833	1.935	59.019	66.647
	2 CENTER	73.571	3.102	67.455	79.688
	3 SOUTH	67.682	1.750	64.232	71.132
3 DIVORCED	1 NORTH	65.500	5.804	54.058	76.942
	2 CENTER	71.222	2.736	65.828	76.616
	3 SOUTH	72.421	1.883	68.709	76.133

In general, these estimated marginal means, also known as *unweighted means* or *adjusted means,* are computed to adjust the actual means due to unequal sample sizes. When all cells have equal sample sizes, both actual means and estimated marginal means will be identical. Thus when cells are unequal, it is recommended to report the adjusted means and their standard errors.

Multiple Comparisons Analysis

Recall that each independent variable, Marital Status and Location of Employment, has more than two groups (each has three groups). Thus when significant results are detected, a post hoc analysis is needed to pinpoint what groups are significantly different.

In our example, both marital status and location of employment were found to be significant. Therefore, two post hoc analyses were conducted, one for each variable. Tables 6.8 and 6.9 display the results of the Bonferroni post hoc test for marital status and location, respectively.

Table 6.8 displays the results of multiple comparisons for all of marital status's pairs. These pairs are shown in the first column. The table displays the mean difference for each pair (second column), standard error (third column), the *Sig.,* or *p* value, (fourth column), and the 95% confidence interval (last two columns).

The first row of table 6.8 compares married and single (first line) and married and divorced (second line) with regard to their levels of job satisfaction. The table shows that the mean difference between married and single is −1.92 with a standard error of 1.384. This difference is not significant at the .05 level (*Sig.* = .503).

The first row also shows that the mean difference between married and divorced is −6.81 with a standard error of 1.651. This mean difference is, however, significant at the .05 level[1] (*Sig.* = .000). Recall from the descriptive table (table 6.5) that the mean score for married is 64.79 and the mean score for divorced is 71.60 (mean difference = 64.79 − 71.60 = −6.81). This statistic indicates that divorced workers were significantly more satisfied with their work than married workers.

Table 6.8:   Results of the Bonferroni Post Hoc for Marital Status

Multiple Comparisons

Satisfaction
Bonferroni

(I) MStatus	(J) MStatus	Mean Difference (I-J)	Std. Error	**Sig.**	95% Confidence Interval Lower Bound	Upper Bound
1 MARRIED	2 SINGLE	-1.92	1.384	.503	-5.26	1.42
	3 DIVORCED	-6.81*	1.651	.000	-10.80	-2.83
2 SINGLE	1 MARRIED	1.92	1.384	.503	-1.42	5.26
	3 DIVORCED	-4.90*	1.918	.034	-9.53	-.27
3 DIVORCED	1 MARRIED	6.81*	1.651	.000	2.83	10.80
	2 SINGLE	4.90*	1.918	.034	.27	9.53

Based on observed means.
The error term is Mean Square(Error) = 67.374.

*. The mean difference is significant at the .05 level.

[1] By default, results that are significant at the .05 level or less will be marked by a single asterisk.

The second row of table 6.8 compares single and married (first line). This line of the second row is redundant of the first line in the first row. The second row also compares single and divorced (second line). The table shows that the mean difference between the two groups is –4.90 with a standard error of 1.918 and a *p* value (*Sig.*) of .034. Again, this *p* value indicates a significant difference between the two groups, with divorced workers being significantly more satisfied with their work than single workers.

The third row of table 6.8 compares divorced with married and divorced with single. These comparisons are redundant of the comparisons already presented in the first two rows.

Table 6.9 displays the results of multiple comparisons for all location pairs. The first row compares north and center (first line) and north and south (second line) with regard to their levels of job satisfaction. The table shows that the mean difference between northern workers and central workers is –1.99 with a standard error of 1.549. This difference is not significant at the .05 level (*Sig.* = .599).

The first row also shows that the mean difference between northern workers and southern workers is –5.75 with a standard error of 1.394. This mean difference is significant at the .05 level (*Sig.* = .000). This statistic indicates that southern workers were significantly more satisfied with their work than northern workers.

The second row of table 6.9 compares center and north (first line). This line and row is redundant of the first line in the first row. The row also compares center and south (second line). The table shows that the mean difference between the two groups is –3.76 with a standard error of 1.324 and a *p* value (*Sig.*) of .015. Again, this *p* value indicates a significant difference between the two groups, with southern workers being significantly more satisfied with their work than central workers.

The third row of table 6.9 compares south with north and south with center. These comparisons are redundant of the previous two rows.

Table 6.9:   Results of the Bonferroni Post Hoc for Location

Multiple Comparisons

Satisfaction
Bonferroni

(I) Region	(J) Region	Mean Difference (I-J)	Std. Error	Sig.	95% Confidence Interval Lower Bound	Upper Bound
1 NORTH	2 CENTER	-1.99	1.549	.599	-5.73	1.75
	3 SOUTH	-5.75*	1.394	.000	-9.11	-2.39
2 CENTER	1 NORTH	1.99	1.549	.599	-1.75	5.73
	3 SOUTH	-3.76*	1.324	.015	-6.95	-.56
3 SOUTH	1 NORTH	5.75*	1.394	.000	2.39	9.11
	2 CENTER	3.76*	1.324	.015	.56	6.95

Based on observed means.
The error term is Mean Square(Error) = 67.374.

*. The mean difference is significant at the .05 level.

Interaction Means Plot

SPSS also produces a graph displaying the mean scores for each group in the independent variables and whether these means interact together. This graph is referred to as an interaction means plot. If significant interaction effect is detected, the lines connecting the group means of the first independent variable on the second independent variable will intersect. If no significant interaction is found, the lines will not intersect. They will be somewhat parallel to each other, depending on the sampling distribution.

Figure 6.2 displays three lines. Each line presents the mean scores of the three marital status groups (married, single, and divorced) on one location. Line A displays the means of married, single, and divorced workers who live in the center. Line B displays the means of married, single, and divorced workers who live in the south. Line C displays the means of married, single, and divorced workers who live in the north.

Notice that the segments of lines B and C are parallel. When this pattern occurs, it indicates no significant interaction between the two variables. However, in this example, location has three groups, and thus three lines. Line A (center), on the other hand, intersects with both lines B and C. This pattern means there is a significant interaction between the two variables. In other words, the significant interaction between marital status and location is due to the center group.

Step 5: Write the Results.

When writing the results of a two-way ANOVA, you must first discuss the assumptions of the test statistic and whether these assumptions are fulfilled. Then you need to present the *F* ratio, degrees of freedom (*df*), and *p* value for each effect (main effect 1, main effect 2, and interaction effect). Moreover, you need to report the percentage of variance in the dependent variable that is accounted for by each effect (eta squared). In addition, when either or both variable(s) have

Figure 6.2:   Interaction Means Plot for Marital Status by Location

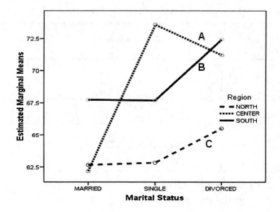

more than two groups and significant results are found, you need to report the results of the post hoc tests. In addition, you must report the means and standard deviations of all groups and their interactions. Further, you should present the results of the ANOVA (also called summary ANOVA). Finally, you may display the interaction mean scores in an interaction means plot. This plot is especially important for readers who prefer visualizing the results.

Writing the Results

The following section presents the written results of the two-way ANOVA for Job Satisfaction based on marital status and location of employment.

Evaluation of assumptions.   Prior to the two-way ANOVA analysis, data were screened to ensure that the two-way ANOVA assumptions were met. Descriptive statistics, histograms, and normal probability plots show that the dependent variable was normally distributed. In addition, the results of Levene's test of equality of variances show that the variances of all groups on the dependent variable were equal, thus satisfying the assumption of homogeneity of variance.

Results of the two-way ANOVA.   A two-way ANOVA (or a 3x3 ANOVA) was utilized to examine the effects of marital status, location, and marital status by location on levels of job satisfaction among a sample of 218 social workers.

MAIN EFFECT 1 (MARITAL STATUS):
The results of the two-way ANOVA show an overall significant difference in social workers' levels of job satisfaction based on their marital status ($F_{(2, 216)}$ = 5.18, $p < .010$, $\eta^2 = .047$).

The results of the post hoc Bonferroni test show a significant difference between married and divorced workers ($p < .001$), with divorced workers reporting significantly higher levels of job satisfaction (mean = 71.60) than married workers (mean = 64.79). Divorced workers also reported significantly greater levels of satisfaction ($p < .05$) than single workers (mean = 66.70). No significant difference, on the other hand, was found between married and single workers ($p > .05$).

Overall, marital status accounted for only 4.7 percent of the variance in job satisfaction, indicating weak relationships between the two variables.

MAIN EFFECT 2 (LOCATION):
The results of the two-way ANOVA also show an overall significant difference in the levels of job satisfaction among social workers based on their employment location ($F_{(2, 216)}$ = 3.08, $p < .05$, $\eta^2 = .029$).

The results of the post hoc Bonferroni test show a significant difference between northern workers and southern workers ($p < .001$), with southern workers being significantly more satisfied with their jobs (mean = 68.58) than northern workers (mean = 62.83). Southern workers also reported significantly greater levels of satisfaction ($p < .05$) than workers located in the center (mean = 64.82). No significant difference, on the other hand, was found between northern and central workers ($p > .05$).

Overall, location of employment accounted for only 2.9 percent of the variance in job satisfaction, indicating weak relationships between the two variables.

INTERACTION EFFECT (MARITAL STATUS BY LOCATION):

The results of the two-way ANOVA also show a significant marital status by location interaction effect on job satisfaction ($F_{(4, 216)} = 2.55$, $p < .05$, $\eta^2 = .047$). However, this interaction effect accounted for only 4.7 percent of the variance in job satisfaction.

Finally, overall, the three effects accounted for a total of 17 percent of the variance in job satisfaction.

Presentation of results in summary tables.   The results of the two-way ANOVA should be presented in two summary tables. The first table should present the mean scores for each level of each independent variable, their interactions, and the total means. The second table should convey the sum of squares and mean squares of all sources of variation and their degrees of freedom. Finally, the table should convey the F ratio and level of significance for each main effect.

For this example, tables 6.10.A and 6.10.B and figure 6.2 display the results of the two-way ANOVA.

Table 6.10.A: Descriptive Statistics of Job Satisfaction by Region and Marital Status

Marital Status	Region	N	Mean	SD
Married	North	32	62.66	8.30
	Center	45	62.18	7.88
	South	63	67.73	8.27
	Total	140	64.79	8.53
Single	North	18	62.83	7.85
	Center	7	73.57	7.93
	South	22	67.68	10.80
	Total	47	66.70	9.89
Divorced	North	2	65.50	.71
	Center	9	71.22	6.12
	South	19	72.42	6.37
	Total	30	71.60	6.21
Total	North	52	62.83	7.92
	Center	61	64.82	8.78
	South	104	68.58	8.68
	Total	217	66.14	8.84

Table 6.10.B: Two-Way ANOVA Summary Table

Source of Variance	SS	df	MS	F^a	p
Marital Status	698.06	2	349.03	5.18	.006
Region	414.33	2	207.17	3.08	.048
Interaction	685.89	4	171.47	2.55	.041
Error	14013.88	208	67.37		
Total	16886.57	216			

$^aR^2 = .17$

SUMMARY

Chapter 6 discussed the purpose and advantages of the two-way ANOVA, a more advanced statistical technique than the one-way ANOVA. As an advantage over the one-way ANOVA, the two-way ANOVA examines the mean differences based on *two* categorical variables simultaneously. In addition, it examines the mean differences between the groups of the first independent variable across the groups of the second independent variable.

The chapter then discussed the sources of variation in two-way ANOVA. These sources include the within-subjects variability and between-subjects variability. The first is due to the groups within each factor, and the latter includes variability due to the first factor, variability due to the second factor, and variability due of the factors' interaction.

The chapter next presented the research questions and hypotheses addressed by the two-way ANOVA. They examine the mean differences based on the first independent variable (main effect 1), the second independent variable (main effect 2), and their interaction (interaction effect).

Chapter 6 then presented and discussed the test assumptions. These assumptions are similar to those of the one-way ANOVA. They include sample representativeness, levels of measurement of the variables, normality of distribution of the dependent variable, equality of variances (also known as homoscedasticity), and sample size.

Finally, the chapter covered post hoc tests, which allow researchers to pinpoint what groups or joint cells are significantly different, if any. These tests are known as multiple comparison tests. A detailed example was discussed to demonstrate how to utilize the test, examine the assumptions, use the SPSS, write the results, and construct summary tables.

Chapter 7 will introduce a new data analysis technique that combines two-way ANOVA (chapter 6) and multiple regression analysis (chapter 4). This technique is the two-way analysis of covariance (ANCOVA). The chapter will follow the outlines used in this chapter to illustrate the purpose, advantages, research questions, and hypotheses. It will then present a detailed example illustrating the use of the two-way ANCOVA.

PRACTICAL EXERCISES

A health care researcher was interested in the impact of race (Race) and body weight (Overweight) on the levels of self-esteem (SelfEsteem) among college students. For this purpose, the researcher collected data from 182 college students who completed the *Well-Being* survey (see appendix, Data File 6).

Access the Well-Being data file; use the variables Race, Overweight, and SelfEsteem; and answer the following questions:

1. What is the research question being examined?

2. State the null and alternative hypotheses.

3. What statistical test(s) will you utilize to examine the null hypotheses? Why? Discuss your answer in detail.

4. Write the SPSS syntax file for the test statistic.

5. Run the statistical test you chose in question 3.

6. What is your decision with regard to the null hypotheses? Discuss your answer in detail.

7. Present the results in summary table(s) and graph(s).

CHAPTER 7

Two-Way Analysis of Covariance

LEARNING OBJECTIVES

1. Understand the purpose of two-way ANCOVA

2. Understand the assumptions underlying ANCOVA

3. Understand the post hoc tests

4. Understand how to use SPSS to compute the statistics

5. Understand how to interpret, write, and present the results of the tests

DATA SET (APPENDIX)

Job Satisfaction

INTRODUCTION

Chapters 1 and 6 reviewed and discussed the one-way and the two-way ANOVA, respectively. The one-way ANOVA is utilized to examine the mean differences on one categorical variable. The two-way ANOVA is utilized to examine the mean differences on two categorical variables and their interaction effect on the dependent variable.

Now imagine that you, as a clinical therapist, were asked to conduct group therapy to reduce the levels of anxiety among new refugees of political torture. For this purpose you selected 45 men and 45 women who arrived in the country within the past six months to escape political torture in their countries. You divided them equally into three groups based on their country of origin: Africans, Asians, and Hispanics. In preparation for the therapy, you pretested participants' levels of anxiety using a standardized measure. Also, you asked participants to report the number of years of education they completed prior to arriving in the country.

After collecting and entering the data in statistical software and evaluating the data, you conducted a two-way ANOVA and found significant mean differences in levels of anxiety based on the participants' country of origin as well as their gender.

As an experienced therapist/researcher you began to question these results, especially since all participants in the study were political refugees who went through similar unfortunate experiences. On the other hand, you noticed based on your data that refugees who have higher levels of education have significantly lower levels of anxiety than those with lower levels of education. Given this fact, you began to question your findings with regard to anxiety and began to speculate that levels of education may be responsible for the anxiety differences in both gender and country of origin. The question is then, is it possible to rule out this option, that is, to examine the mean differences in anxiety based on gender and country of origin while keeping levels of education constant?

The answer to this question is yes. One option is to select participants who meet certain criteria. In this case, the therapist/researcher could select refugees who have, for example, elementary education. However, by doing so, the therapist/researcher will exclude other refugees because they have more education, and thus he or she will exclude them from receiving therapy.

To prevent this ethical dilemma and provide therapy to participants regardless of their education, the therapist could rule out the effect of education on anxiety without selecting only individuals with similar education by using an advanced statistical procedure. This procedure is the *analysis of covariance* (ANCOVA).

ANALYSIS OF COVARIANCE

Purpose

Analysis of covariance, also known as *univariate general linear model* (GLM), is an advanced statistical technique of the analysis of variance (ANOVA). As with one-way and two-way ANOVA, ANCOVA allows researchers to examine the differences in a *single* dependent variable based on *one* or *more* categorical variables. Unlike ANOVA, ANCOVA allows researchers to *control for* the effect of *one* or *more* extraneous variables on the dependent variable. In other words, ANCOVA is utilized to examine the mean differences in the dependent variable based on one or more independent variables after removing the impact of one or more variables on the dependent variable. These variables are known as *control* variables or *covariates*.

Analysis of covariance thus examines the differences between groups on the dependent variable after *adjusting* the imbalance between the groups on the dependent variable due to the impact of a third (or fourth) variable.

In the previous example, Gender and Country of Origin are the independent variables, level of Anxiety is the dependent variable, and Education is the control variable, or covariance. By conducting ANCOVA in this case, the therapist/researcher will be able to examine the anxiety differences due to country of origin and gender after *controlling* or *adjusting* for the effect of education on anxiety. Table 7.1 summarizes these comparisons. Notice that table 7.1 is similar to table 6.1; however, unlike table 6.1, which compares the actual means, table 7.1 uses the adjusted means due to the addition of a third variable (Education).

Table 7.1:   Anxiety Based on Gender and Country of Origin

Country	Males	Females	Total
Africans	μ'_{AFM}	μ'_{AFF}	μ'_{AF}
Asians	μ'_{ASM}	μ'_{ASF}	μ'_{AS}
Hispanics	μ'_{HM}	μ'_{HF}	μ'_{H}
Total	μ'_{M}	μ'_{F}	μ'_{T}

1. μ' = adjusted means

2.   TOTAL COLUMN: mean scores of anxiety for each country (main effect 1); EXAMPLE: μ'_{AF} = adjusted mean score of anxiety for African refugees

3.   TOTAL ROW: mean scores of anxiety for each gender (main effect 2); EXAMPLE: μ'_{M} = adjusted mean score of anxiety for male refugees

4.   JOINT CELLS: adjusted mean scores of anxiety for each country of origin by gender (interaction effect); EXAMPLE: μ'_{ASM} = adjusted mean score of anxiety for Asian male refugees

Analysis of covariance, thus, examines the relationship between three types of variables simultaneously. They are dependent, independent, and control variables. In a sense, any ANOVA test can become an ANCOVA test simply by adding a control variable.

One-way ANCOVA is parallel to the one-way ANOVA. It requires *one* dependent variable, *one* independent variable, and *one or more* control variables.

Two-way ANCOVA is parallel to the two-way ANOVA. It requires *one* dependent variable, *two* independent variables, and *one or more* control variables.

Factorial ANCOVA is parallel to the factorial ANOVA. It requires *one* dependent variable, *three or more* independent variables, and *one or more* control variables.

Multivariate ANCOVA (MANCOVA) is parallel to the multivariate ANOVA (MANOVA, see chapter 9). It requires *two or more* dependent variables, *one or more* independent variables, and *one or more* control variables.

This chapter focuses on the two-way ANCOVA. The assumptions, analysis, and interpretations of both one-way and factorial ANCOVA are the same as the two-way ANCOVA, so by understanding the two-way ANCOVA, you will be able to conduct and interpret both the one-way and factorial ANCOVA. MANCOVA will be discussed in chapter 9.

Sources of Variation

Unlike with two-way ANOVA, the variance in a two-way ANCOVA is partitioned into three sources of variability: *within-groups, between-groups,* and *covariate.*

The within-groups variability is the variation in the scores of subjects within each group in each independent variable. The between-groups variability is the sum of variability in three sources: variability in the first independent variable, variability in the second independent variable, and variability due to the

Figure 7.1:   ANCOVA Sources of Variation

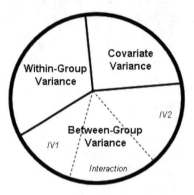

Note: the proportion of area representing each source of variance does not necessarily reflect the actual proportion each source contributes to the variation in the dependent variable; it is only for visualization purposes.

interaction between these two variables. The covariate variability is the variation due to the covariance.

The sum of within-groups variance, between-groups variance, and covariate variance is the total variance. Figure 7.1 illustrates these sources of variation.

Advantages

The utilization of analysis of covariance has several advantages over the analysis of variance. One of the most important advantages of ANCOVA is that it allows researchers to control for a third variable believed to affect the relationship between the independent and dependent variables. This ability is especially important in experimental designs when it is impossible to control for an extraneous variable in the design itself, which could affect the internal validity of the experiment (treatment).

A second advantage of ANCOVA over ANOVA is that it examines the variations in the dependent variable due not only to the independent variable but also to the control variable.

A third advantage is that by adjusting the mean differences due to the addition of a covariate (control variable), ANCOVA reduces the sampling errors and, in turn, increases the statistical power, that is, the likelihood to reject the null hypothesis when in fact it is false (make the correct decision) (see Hinkle, Wiersma, & Jurs, 2003). In other words, ANCOVA has greater power than ANOVA.

Finally, ANCOVA combines both ANOVA and multiple regression (MR) analysis. Recall that MR analysis examines the relationship between the dependent (criterion) and independent (factor) variables while controlling for other factors (the beta coefficient). ANCOVA also examines the relationship between the independent and dependent variables while controlling for other factors.

Research Questions and Hypotheses

As said, the purpose of a two-way ANCOVA is to examine the effects of two independent variables on one dependent variable while controlling for the effect of a third variable. Thus, unlike two-way ANOVA, ANCOVA examines three effects. They include one covariate's effect, two independent variables' effects, and one interaction's effect. They are as follows:

Covariate effect is the effect of the covariate on the dependent variable (e.g., Education on Anxiety).

Main effect 1 is the effect of the first independent variable on the dependent variable controlling for a third variable (e.g., Country of Origin and Anxiety controlling for Education).

Main effect 2 is the effect of the second independent variable on the dependent variable controlling for a third variable (e.g., Gender and Anxiety controlling for Education).

Interaction effect is the effect of the joint cells (first independent variable by second independent variable) on the dependent variable controlling for a third variable (e.g., Gender by Country of Origin controlling for Education).

In other words, the purpose of a two-way ANCOVA is to test four research questions/hypotheses. Consider the following examples:

RESEARCH QUESTION 1: Is there a significant correlation between the covariate and the dependent variable? (*Remember*, this is one of the assumptions of ANCOVA.)

EXAMPLE: Is there a significant correlation between refugees' number of years of education and their levels of anxiety?

RESEARCH QUESTION 2: Controlling for the covariate, are there significant differences between the levels of the first independent variable on the dependent variable?

EXAMPLE: Controlling for levels of education, are there significant differences between African, Asian, and Hispanic political refugees with regard to their levels of anxiety?

RESEARCH QUESTION 3: Controlling for the covariate, are there significant differences between the levels of the second independent variable on the dependent variable?

EXAMPLE: Controlling for levels of education, are there significant differences between male and female political refugees with regard to their levels of anxiety?

RESEARCH QUESTION 4: Controlling for the covariate, are there significant differences between the levels of the first independent variable on the dependent variable across the levels of the second independent variable?

EXAMPLE: Controlling for levels of education, are there significant differences between African male, African female, Asian male, Asian female, Hispanic male, and Hispanic female political refugees with regard to their levels of anxiety? Or, controlling for levels of education, are there significant gender by country of origin interaction effects (or differences) with regard to levels of anxiety?

The research hypotheses are as follows:

RESEARCH HYPOTHESIS 1: There is a significant correlation between the covariate and the dependent variable.

EXAMPLE: There is a significant correlation between refugees' number of years of education and their levels of anxiety.

RESEARCH HYPOTHESIS 2: Controlling for the covariate, there are significant differences between the levels of the first independent variable on the dependent variable.

EXAMPLE: Controlling for levels of education, there are significant differences between African, Asian, and Hispanic political refugees with regard to their levels of anxiety.

RESEARCH HYPOTHESIS 3: Controlling for the covariate, there are significant differences between the levels of the second independent variable on the dependent variable.

EXAMPLE: Controlling for levels of education, there are significant differences between male and female political refugees with regard to their levels of anxiety.

RESEARCH HYPOTHESIS 4: Controlling for the covariate, there are significant differences between the levels of the first independent variable on the dependent variable across the levels of the second independent variable.

EXAMPLE: Controlling for levels of education, there are significant differences between African male, African female, Asian male, Asian female, Hispanic male, and Hispanic female political refugees with regard to their levels of anxiety. Or, controlling for levels of education, there are significant gender by country of origin interaction effects (or differences) with regard to levels of anxiety.

Assumptions

Recall that the two-way ANCOVA is an advanced technique that combines the two-way ANOVA and multiple regression analysis. Thus it requires certain assumptions of these two tests. These assumptions include the following:

1. SAMPLE REPRESENTATIVENESS: The sample must represent the population to which results will be generalized.

2. PAIRED OBSERVATION: Data for all groups must be collected at the same time (e.g., data on gender, country of origin, levels of anxiety, and education should be collected simultaneously).

3. LEVEL OF MEASUREMENT:

    a. The dependent variable and covariate must be continuous data and measured at the interval level of measurement or higher.

b.   The two independent variables must be nominal with two or more groups for each (e.g., Country of Origin = African, Asian, and Hispanic; Gender = male and female).

4.   SAMPLE SIZE: As with two-way ANOVA, the sample size must be adequate. In general, a sample size of 30 cases or more is sufficient to utilize ANCOVA. Furthermore, it is also recommended that each cell have five cases or more. For example, for a 3x4 ANCOVA (that is, three levels in the first independent variable and four levels in the second independent variable), a sample size of 60 would be sufficient (3 x 4 x 5 = 60).

In addition, all cells should have an equal number of cases. On the other hand, if cells have unequal numbers of cases, consider using type III sum of square (see chapter 6) to adjust for inequality among cells.

The above four assumptions are methodological issues and can be evaluated in the research methodology and design and by inspecting the number of valid cases in the specific data file.

5.   NORMALITY OF DISTRIBUTION: The distributions of the dependent variable and the covariate must approximate a normal curve.

Normality can be evaluated by inspecting measures of skewness and kurtosis, histograms, and normal probability plots for both the dependent variable and the covariate (see chapter 2).

6.   LINEARITY: The relationship between the covariate and the dependent variable should be linear.

Linearity can be examined by inspecting the Pearson's correlation coefficient and the scatterplot of the covariate and dependent variable.

7.   HOMOGENEITY OF VARIANCES: The variances of all groups on the dependent variable should be equal. This is also known as the assumption of homoscedasticity.

This assumption can be evaluated using Levene's test of equality of variances (see chapter 6). It can be requested along with the results of ANCOVA (discussed later). As said in chapter 6, a p value greater than .001 indicates that the assumption is satisfied.

In addition, ANCOVA requires the following:

8.   RELIABILITY OF COVARIATE: The covariate should have no measurement errors. In reality, it is almost impossible to have measurement without errors.

Statistically, it is hard to examine this assumption. However, as a general rule, this assumption can be ignored when the covariate has a reliability coefficient of .80 or above.

9.   MULTICOLLINEARITY: If more than one covariate is used, the relationship between these covariates should not exceed .80; that is the assumption of multicollinearity.

Multicollinearity can be evaluated simply by inspecting the Pearson's correlation coefficients between the covariates or by inspecting both tolerance and VIF, as discussed for multiple regression analysis.

10.   HOMOGENEITY OF REGRESSION: The relationship between the dependent variable and covariate should be the same for each group of the independent variables. In other words, there should be no relationship between the independent variable and covariate (or no interaction between the independent variable and covariate).

Homogeneity of regression is evaluated by inspecting the interaction effect between the independent variable and the covariate on the dependent variable. A nonsignificant p value is needed for the assumption to be met. It also can be examined by plotting the dependent variable on the covariate for each group in the independent variable.

In this case, parallel lines indicate no interaction between the two variables (figure 7.2.A). Intersecting lines, on the other hand, indicate a violation of the assumption (figure 7.2.B). If this assumption is violated, ANCOVA is not the appropriate technique. In this case, consider recoding the covariate into groups, add it as another independent variable, and conduct a factorial ANOVA. Another option is to conduct a hierarchical multiple regression analysis with the two independent variables entered in the first step and the covariate in the second step. We will return to this assumption when we discuss the ANCOVA SPSS commands and outputs.

Post Hoc Tests

As discussed, two-way ANCOVA is an advanced version of the two-way ANOVA. It examines whether there are overall significant differences between the groups in each independent variable on the dependent variable while adjust-

Figure 7.2:   Homogeneity and Heterogeneity of Regression

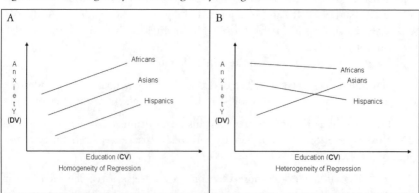

ing for the variation due to a third variable. Yet when the number of groups in one or both independent variables exceeds two, pairwise comparisons must be utilized to detect the groups that are significantly different. Unlike ANOVA, these post hoc comparisons use the adjusted group means to compute the t values and levels of significance.

Unlike in ANOVA, where SPSS provides eighteen post hoc tests, only three post hoc tests are available in SPSS when a covariate is used. They are the LSD (least significant difference), Bonferroni (also known as Bonferroni correction), and Sidak. The three tests are preferred because they adjust the p value when conducting multiple comparisons.

PRACTICAL EXAMPLE

We will use the SPSS Job Satisfaction data file to demonstrate the use of the two-way ANCOVA. For this purpose, we will examine the differences in levels of burnout among professional social services workers based on ethnicity and marital status while ruling out the effect of promotions on their satisfaction.

Thus our research question is as follows: Controlling for opportunities for promotions, are their significant differences in the levels of burnout among professional social services workers due to their ethnicity and marital status?

Hypothesis Testing

Step 1: State the Null and Alternative Hypotheses.

H_{o1}: Controlling for the effect of promotions, there are no statistically significant differences between Arab and Jewish social services workers with regard to their levels of burnout.

   $\mu'_A = \mu'_J$; adjusted burnout mean scores are equal.

H_{a1}: Controlling for the effect of promotions, there are statistically significant differences between Arab and Jewish social services workers with regard to their levels of burnout.

   $\mu'_A \neq \mu'_J$; adjusted burnout mean scores are not equal.

H_{o2}: Controlling for the effect of promotions, there are no statistically significant differences between single, married, and divorced social services workers with regard to their levels of burnout.

   $\mu'_S = \mu'_M = \mu'_D$; adjusted burnout mean scores are equal.

H_{a2}: Controlling for the effect of promotions, there are statistically significant differences between single, married, and divorced social services workers with regard to their levels of burnout.

   $\mu'_S \neq \mu'_M \neq \mu'_D$; adjusted burnout mean scores are not equal for at least two marital statuses.

H_{o3}: Controlling for the effect of promotions, there are no statistically significant ethnicity by marital status interaction effects among social services workers with regard to their levels of burnout.

$\mu'_{AM} = \mu'_{AS} = \mu'_{AD} = \mu'_{JM} = \mu'_{JS} = \mu'_{JD}$; adjusted burnout mean scores are equal for each ethnicity on each marital status.

H_{a3}: Controlling for the effect of promotions, there are statistically significant ethnicity by marital status interaction effects among social services workers with regard to their levels of burnout.

$\mu'_{AM} \neq \mu'_{AS} \neq \mu'_{AD} \neq \mu'_{JM} \neq \mu'_{JS} \neq \mu'_{JD}$; adjusted burnout mean scores are not equal for at least two joint cells.

Step 2: Set the Criteria for Rejecting the Null Hypotheses.
We will set alpha at .05 ($\alpha = .05$). That is, reject H_o only if $p \leq .05$.

Step 3: Select the Appropriate Statistical Test.
Our interest here is in comparing levels of burnout among social services workers based on their ethnicity and marital status while ruling out the effect of a third variable, Promotion, on levels of burnout. Thus we have four variables under analysis in which one is the dependent variable, two are independent variables (Ethnicity and Marital Status), and one is a control variable or covariate (Promotion). Therefore, we should utilize the two-way analysis of covariance. However, before doing so, we need to examine its assumptions and whether they are fulfilled. These assumptions include the following:

1.   SAMPLE REPRESENTATIVENESS: Data for the Job Satisfaction file were collected from a random sample of 218 professional social workers (see appendix).

2.   PAIRED OBSERVATION: Data on workers' gender, ethnicity, levels of burnout, promotion, and others were collected at the same time.

3.   LEVEL OF MEASUREMENT: The dependent variable, Level of Burnout, and the covariate, Promotion, were collected using standardized scales. Thus their total scores are continuous data and measured at the interval level of measurement.

The two independent variables, Ethnicity and Marital Status, are categorical variables. Ethnicity consists of two groups (0 = Jews and 1 = Arabs). Marital status consists of three levels (1 = married, 2 = single, and 3 = divorced).

4.   SAMPLE SIZE: The sample size must be large enough to conduct ANCOVA. Also, all cells should have an equal number of cases.

In this example, there are 217 participants who completed measures on both burnout and promotion. Table 7.7 (discussed later) shows unequal frequencies among cells; the smallest has six cases (divorced Arabs), and the largest has ninety-five cases (married Jews). Thus, although the sample size is large enough and all cells have at least six cases, they are unequal. Therefore, type III sum of squares will be used to adjust for these unequal cells. (This method is the default in SPSS.)

5.   NORMALITY OF DISTRIBUTION: The distributions of both dependent control
     variables must approximate a normal curve.

To examine this assumption, we will inspect measures of skewness and kurtosis, histograms, and normal probability plots for both variables (see chapters 2 and 6 on how to request and evaluate this assumption).

Table 7.2 conveys measures of skewness and kurtosis for both the covariate and dependent variable. Figure 7.3 displays a histogram and normal probability plot for the covariate, and figure 7.4 displays a histogram and normal probability plot for the dependent variable Burnout.

Evaluation of measures of skewness and kurtosis for promotion indicates that both coefficients are within the normal range (smaller than twice their standard error, respectively). Thus, based on these coefficients, the distribution of promotion is not severely skewed.

The histogram and the Q-Q plot for promotion also confirm that the shape of the distribution of promotion appears to approach the shape of a normal curve.

On the other hand, measures of both skewness and kurtosis (see table 7.2), indicate that the distribution of burnout is severely skewed (both skewness and kurtosis are greater than twice their standard errors, respectively). On the other hand, eyeballing the histogram of burnout (figure 7.4.A) shows a positive, yet not severe, skewness. The normal Q-Q plot (figure 7.4.B) also shows that most of the data points are clustered on a straight line, with few points departing from

Table 7.2:   Measures of Skewness and Kurtosis for Burnout and Promotion

Statistics

		Promotion	Burnout
N	Valid	218	218
	Missing	0	0
	Skewness	-.049	1.000
	Std. Error of Skewness	.165	.165
	Kurtosis	-.361	2.084
	Std. Error of Kurtosis	.328	.328

Figure 7.3:   Histogram and Q-Q Plot for Promotion (Covariate)

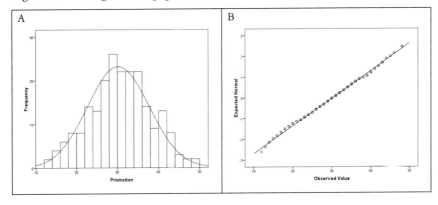

Figure 7.4:   Histogram and Q-Q Plot for Burnout

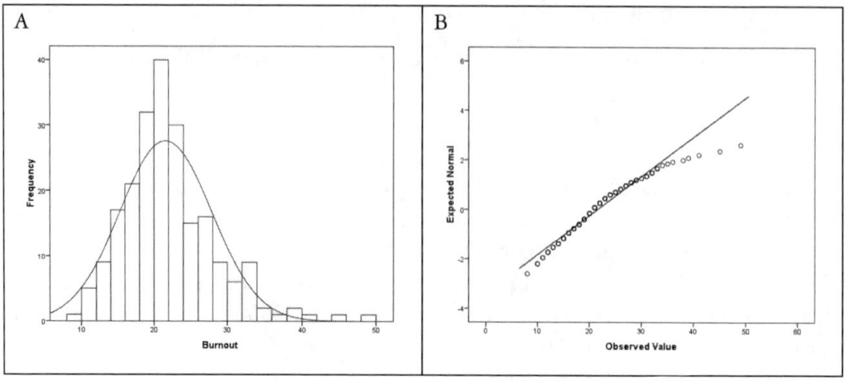

the line. Recall that skewness and kurtosis coefficients are very sensitive for minor outlier cases. Thus they need to be interpreted with caution.

6.   LINEARITY: The relationship between Promotion (covariate) and Burnout (dependent variable) should be linear.

To examine this assumption we will examine the Pearson's correlation coefficient and the scatterplot for burnout on promotion (see chapter 6).

Table 7.3 displays the correlation between burnout and promotion. As it appears, both have a significant relationship ($r = -.311, p < .01$).

Figure 7.5 displays a scatterplot for burnout on promotion. The figure shows a negative linear relationship between burnout and promotion.

7.   HOMOGENEITY OF VARIANCES: The variances of ethnicity by marital status on burnout should be equal.

To evaluate this assumption, we will inspect the results of Levene's test of equality of variances. Levene's test can be requested along with the results of ANCOVA.

Table 7.4 presents the results of Levene's test of equality of variances. (We will return to this assumption under "How to Use SPSS to Examine the Test Assumptions and Run the Analysis.")

Table 7.3:   Correlation between Burnout and Promotion

Correlations

		Burnout	Promotion
Burnout	Pearson Correlation	1.000	-.311**
	Sig. (2-tailed)		.000
	N	218.000	218
Promotion	Pearson Correlation	-.311**	1.000
	Sig. (2-tailed)	.000	
	N	218	218.000

**. Correlation is significant at the 0.01 level (2-tailed).

Figure 7.5:   Scatterplot for Burnout and Promotion

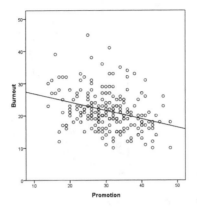

Table 7.4:   Levene's Test of Equality of Variances

Levene's Test of Equality of Error Variances[a]

Dependent Variable:Burnout

F	df1	df2	Sig.
.498	5	211	.777

Tests the null hypothesis that the error variance of the dependent variable is equal across groups.

a. Design: Intercept + MStatus + Ethnicity + Promotion + MStatus * Ethnicity * Promotion

The results of Levene's test of equality of error variances show no significant differences in group variances on the burnout scores ($F = .498$, *Sig.* = .777, $p >$ .001). Thus the assumption of homogeneity of variances (homoscedasticity) in this case is fulfilled.

8.   RELIABILITY OF COVARIATE: Burnout should have no measurement errors. As said earlier, this assumption is unrealistic. However, a covariate should have reliability of .80 or above to satisfy this assumption. In this case, promotion has a reliability coefficient of .86 (see Abu-Bader, 2006).

9.   MULTICOLLINEARITY: This assumption applies only if there are two or more covariates. In this case, there is only one covariate (Promotion), and therefore, multicollinearity is not an issue.

10.   HOMOGENEITY OF REGRESSION: The relationship between burnout and promotion should be the same for each ethnicity on each level of marital status. In other words, there should be an ethnicity by marital status by promotion interaction.

To examine this assumption, we will inspect the ANCOVA custom table for interaction between ethnicity, marital status, and promotion. This table can be requested through the SPSS *GLM Univariate* commands (discussed under "How to Use SPSS to Examine the Test Assumptions and Run the Analysis").

Table 7.5:   ANCOVA Custom Table—Homogeneity of Regression

Tests of Between-Subjects Effects

Dependent Variable:Burnout

Source	Type III Sum of Squares	df	Mean Square	F	Sig.
Corrected Model	2072.492[a]	9	230.277	7.277	.000
Intercept	6069.582	1	6069.582	191.803	.000
MStatus	353.313	2	176.656	5.582	.004
Ethnicity	43.084	1	43.084	1.361	.245
Promotion	375.800	1	375.800	11.876	.001
MStatus * Ethnicity * Promotion	328.877	5	65.775	**2.079**	**.069**
Error	6550.503	207	31.645		
Total	109642.000	217			
Corrected Total	8622.995	216			

a. R Squared = .240 (Adjusted R Squared = .207)

Table 7.5 presents the results of the ANCOVA custom table. In this table we are interested in only the sixth line under Source: MStatus * Ethnicity * Promotion. This line represents the interaction between the independent variables and the covariate(s). A nonsignificant p value (*Sig.* > .05) is needed to satisfy the assumption of homogeneity of regression.

Table 7.5 shows no significant marital status by ethnicity by promotion interaction on the dependent variable, Burnout ($F_{(df = 5, 207)} = 2.079, p > .05$), indicating that the assumption is met. Note that if there is interaction between the independent variables and the covariate (i.e., $p < .05$), you should *stop*! ANCOVA is not the right test. Consider conducting multiple regression analysis by treating the covariate as an independent variable. Another alternative is to recode the covariate into a categorical variable and then conduct factorial ANOVA.

To conclude, our data and variables appear to satisfy all the assumptions of two-way ANCOVA. Next we will carry out the analysis.

How to Use SPSS to Examine the Test Assumptions and Run the Analysis

Step 4: Compute the Two-Way ANCOVA Test Statistic.
First, we will utilize SPSS to examine the assumptions of homogeneity of regression and homogeneity of variances. To do so, follow these SPSS steps:

1.   Open the Job Satisfaction SPSS data file.

2.   Click on *Analyze* in the SPSS main toolbar.

3.   Scroll down to and click on *General Linear Model,* and click on *Univariate.*

4.   A dialog box called "Univariate" will open (see screen 7.1, which is the same as screen 6.1).

5.   Scroll down in the variables list, click on *Burnout* (dependent variable), and click on the upper arrow button to move *Burnout* into the *Dependent Variable* box.

Screen 7.1:   SPSS Two-Way ANOVA Univariate Dialog Box

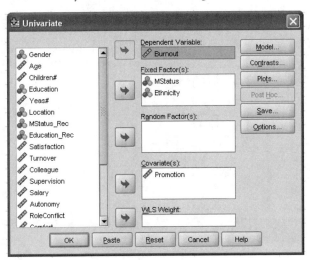

6. Scroll down in the variables list, click on *MStatus* (first independent variable), and click on the second arrow button to move it into the *Fixed Factor(s)* box.

7. Scroll down in the variables list, click on *Ethnicity* (second independent variable), and click on the second arrow button to move it into the *Fixed Factor(s)* box.

8. Scroll down in the variables list, click on *Promotion* (control variable), and click on the fourth arrow button to move it into the *Covariate(s)* box.

9. Click on *Model* at the upper right corner. A new dialog box called "Univariate: Model" will open.

10. Check *Custom* under "Specify Model."

11. Click on *Ethnicity* in the *Factors and Covariates* box, and click on the arrow under "Build Term(s)" to move *Ethnicity* into the *Model* box. Repeat this process for *MStatus* and *Promotion*.

12. Continue to hold down the *Ctrl* button on the keyboard while clicking on *Ethnicity, MStatus,* and *Promotion*. Click on the arrow to move them into the *Model* box (see screen 7.2). This command tests the assumption of homogeneity of regression.

13. Make sure that *Type III* (SPSS default) appears next to *Sum of Squares*. If not, click on the drop-down arrow of *Sum of Squares* and click on *Type III*. This type adjusts for unequal cell frequencies.

14. Click on *Continue,* and click on *Options*. A new dialog box called "Univariate: Options" will open.

Screen 7.2:   SPSS Univariate Custom Model Dialog Box

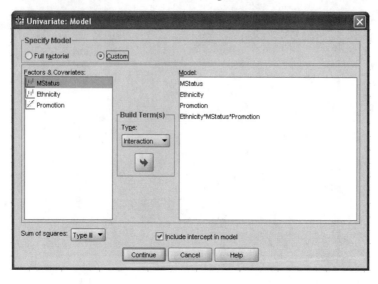

15.   Check the *Homogeneity Tests* box (see screen 7.3). This command will run Levene's test of equality of variances to test the assumption of homogeneity of variances (homoscedasticity).

16.   Click on *Continue,* and click *OK.*

Screen 7.3:   SPSS Univariate Options Dialog Box

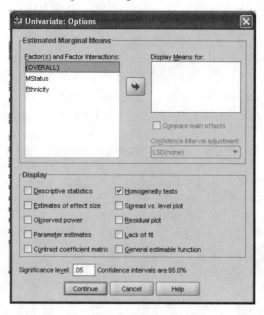

Homogeneity of Regression and Variances SPSS Syntax Commands

UNIANOVA Burnout BY MStatus Ethnicity WITH Promotion
/METHOD=SSTYPE(3)
/INTERCEPT=INCLUDE
/PRINT=HOMOGENEITY
/CRITERIA=ALPHA(.05)
/DESIGN=MStatus Ethnicity Promotion
Ethnicity*MStatus*Promotion.

The execution of these commands will produce three tables. They are between-subjects factors, Levene's test of equality of error variances, and tests of between-subjects effects. The first simply displays the levels of each independent group and the number of cases within the particular level. The second table tests the assumption of homogeneity of variances (see table 7.4). The third table tests the assumption of homogeneity of regression (see table 7.5).

Now that we have examined the test's assumptions, we will run the two-way ANCOVA to examine our research hypotheses. To utilize SPSS to conduct the analysis, follow these steps:

1. Click on *Analyze* in the SPSS main toolbar.

2. Scroll down to and click on *General Linear Model,* and click on *Univariate.*

3. The "Univariate" dialog box will open (see screen 7.1).

4. Click on *Model* to open the "Univariate: Model" dialog box (see screen 7.4).

Screen 7.4:   SPSS Univariate Full Factorial Model Dialog Box

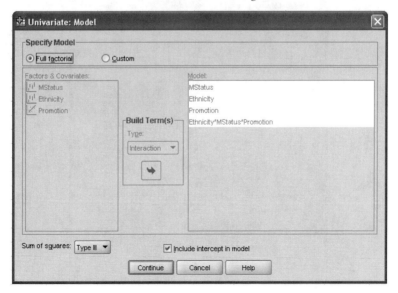

5.   Click on *Full Factorial* under "Specify Model." This command will dim all variables in both boxes.

6.   Click on *Continue* to return to the main "Univariate" dialog box.

7.   Click on *Options.* A new dialog box called "Univariate: Options" will open.

8.   Uncheck the *Homogeneity Tests* box (we checked this box when we examined the assumptions of homogeneity of regression and homogeneity of variances).

9.   Check the *Descriptive Statistics* and *Estimates of Effect Size* boxes under "Display." The first generates statistics for all groups on the dependent variable. The second computes the proportion of variance in the dependent variable accounted for by each factor and covariate in the analysis.

10. Click on each factor and their interactions in the *Factor(s) and Factor Interactions* box, and click on the arrow to move them into the *Display Means For* box.

11. Check the *Compare Main Effects* box (this is the post hoc test in ANCOVA).

12. Click on the drop-down arrow under *Confidence Interval Adjustment,* and click on *Bonferroni* (see screen 7.5).

13. Click on *Continue* and then *Plots.* This command opens a "Univariate: Profile Plots" dialog box (see screen 7.6).

14. Click on *Ethnicity,* and click on the top arrow to move it into the *Horizontal Axis* box.

Screen 7.5:   SPSS Univariate Options Dialog Box

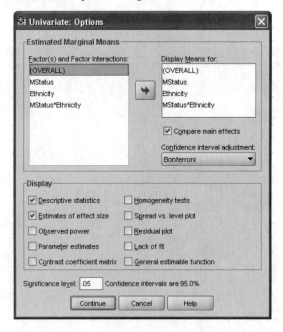

Screen 7.6:   SPSS Univariate Profile Plots Dialog Box

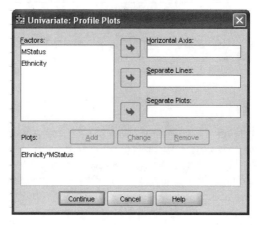

15. Click on *MStatus*, and click on the middle arrow to move it into the *Separate Lines* box.

16. Click on *Add* next to *Plots*. This command will generate a mean plot for each ethnicity by each marital status on the dependent variable.

17. Click on *Continue*, and click *OK*.

Analysis of Covariance SPSS Syntax Commands

UNIANOVA Burnout BY MStatus Ethnicity WITH Promotion
/METHOD=SSTYPE(3)
/INTERCEPT=INCLUDE
/PLOT=PROFILE(Ethnicity*MStatus)
/EMMEANS=TABLES(OVERALL) WITH(Promotion=MEAN)
/EMMEANS=TABLES(MStatus) WITH(Promotion=MEAN) COMPARE
    ADJ(BONFERRONI)
/EMMEANS=TABLES(Ethnicity) WITH(Promotion=MEAN) COMPARE
    ADJ(BONFERRONI)
/EMMEANS=TABLES(MStatus*Ethnicity) WITH(Promotion=MEAN)
/PRINT=ETASQ DESCRIPTIVE
/CRITERIA=ALPHA(.05)
/DESIGN=Promotion MStatus Ethnicity MStatus*Ethnicity.

Reading the SPSS Output of the Two-Way ANCOVA

The execution of the above SPSS commands or syntax will produce eleven tables and one figure; each displays different information concerning the relationship between the independent, dependent, and control variables. These tables and the figure are similar to those produced by a two-way ANOVA, however adjusting for the addition of a third variable, in this case Promotion.

Table 7.6: Frequencies of Between-Subjects Factors

Between-Subjects Factors

		Value Label	N
MStatus	1	MARRIED	140
	2	SINGLE	47
	3	DIVORCED	30
Ethnicity	0	JEWS	145
	1	ARABS	72

Table 7.6 displays the number of cases in each group within each independent variable. In this study, 140 subjects were married, 47 were single, and 30 were divorced. Of the total, 145 were Jewish workers and 72 were Arab workers.

Table 7.7 displays the actual (unadjusted) means, standard deviations, and number of subjects for each level of marital status on each ethnicity. It also displays the overall mean, standard deviation, and number of subjects in each level of each independent variable.

In this study, for example, 140 participants were married (first row, Married; third line, Total; last column, N). Of them, 95 were Jewish workers and 45 were Arab workers. Their burnout means and standard deviations are 20.78 (SD = 5.98) and 25.09 (SD = 5.58), respectively. Overall, the mean of burnout among married workers was 22.16 (SD = 6.177) (first row, Married; third line, Total; Mean and Std. Deviation columns).

The fourth row displays the descriptive statistics for each level of the second independent variable, Ethnicity. In this case, the overall burnout mean among the 145 Jewish workers was 20.27 with a standard deviation of 6.0 (fourth row, Total; first line, Jews). In comparison, the mean score among Arabs (N = 72) was 24.21 (SD = 6.14).

The last line (Total) of the fourth row (Total) displays the grand mean of burnout, overall standard deviation, and total sample size. They are 21.58,

Table 7.7: Descriptive Statistics for Burnout on Ethnicity and Marital Status

Descriptive Statistics

Dependent Variable:Burnout

MStatus	Ethnicity	Mean	Std. Deviation	N
1 MARRIED	0 JEWS	20.78	5.983	95
	1 ARABS	25.09	5.583	45
	Total	22.16	6.177	**140**
2 SINGLE	0 JEWS	19.73	5.731	26
	1 ARABS	24.10	7.134	21
	Total	21.68	6.692	**47**
3 DIVORCED	0 JEWS	18.83	6.363	24
	1 ARABS	18.00	2.098	6
	Total	18.67	5.744	**30**
Total	0 JEWS	20.27	6.008	145
	1 ARABS	24.21	6.141	72
	Total	21.58	6.318	**217**

Table 7.8:   Results of Two-Way ANCOVA

Tests of Between-Subjects Effects

Dependent Variable:Burnout

Source	Type III Sum of Squares	df	Mean Square	F	Sig.	Partial Eta Squared
Corrected Model	1843.232[a]	6	307.205	9.516	.000	.214
Intercept	9560.994	1	9560.994	296.147	.000	.585
Promotion	748.497	1	748.497	23.184	.000	.099
MStatus	310.263	2	155.131	4.805	.009	.044
Ethnicity	193.855	1	193.855	6.005	.015	.028
MStatus * Ethnicity	99.616	2	49.808	1.543	.216	.014
Error	6779.763	210	32.285			
Total	109642.000	217				
Corrected Total	8622.995	216				

a. R Squared = .214 (Adjusted R Squared = .191)

6.318, and 217, respectively. Remember, these are unadjusted means and standard deviations.

Table 7.8 displays the results of the two-way ANCOVA test. As with two-way ANOVA, the two-way ANCOVA table shows source of variations, sum of square deviations (SS) due to a particular source, degrees of freedom (*df*), mean square deviations, *F* ratio, level of significance (*Sig.*), and partial eta squared.

Although the two-way ANCOVA table has the same sources of variation as a two-way ANOVA, the ANCOVA table reports an additional source of variation. This source is the variation in the dependent variable due to the addition of a control variable, in this case Promotion.

Explanation of Terms

These terms are interpreted in the same way as they are for the two-way ANOVA (see chapter 6), except the extra source of variance due to the inclusion of the covariate. The terms are briefly reviewed:

The *Type III Sum of Squares* column displays the variances in the dependent variable due to each source of variation. The table lists five sources of variation:

1. Variation due to the first independent variable (MStatus)

2. Variation due to the second independent variable (Ethnicity)

3. Variation due to the interaction between the two independent variables (MStatus * Ethnicity)

4. Variation due to the control variable (Promotion)

5. Variation due to within-subjects variations (Error)

As shown in figure 7.1, we divided these sources into three main sources of variations: between-group variance (MStatus + Ethnicity + MStatus * Ethnicity), within-subjects variance (error), and covariate variance (Promotion).

The *df* column displays the number of degrees of freedom associated with each source of variance.

The *mean square* refers to the mean of the sum of square deviations (that is, sum of squares for each source divided by its degrees of freedom).

The *F* value column displays the *F* statistic for each source of variance (mean squares for each source divided by the error).

The *Sig.* column displays the level of significance for each source of variance.

Partial eta squared (η^2) represents the proportion of variance in the dependent variable accounted for by each source of variance.

Reading the Table

Covariate—Promotion (line 3).   Table 7.8 shows a significant relationship between promotion and the levels of burnout (third line, Promotion: F = 23.18, *Sig.* = .000). Recall that one of the assumptions of ANCOVA is that the covariate and dependent variable have a linear relationship. In this case, promotion accounted for 9.9 percent of the variance in burnout (third line, Partial Eta Squared = .099). This measure is similar to the coefficient of determination of Pearson's correlation (table 7.3, r = −.311; r^2 = .097).

Main effect 1—Marital Status (line 4).   Table 7.8 shows a significant difference between at least two levels of marital status with regard to burnout (fourth line, MStatus: F = 4.805, *df* = 2, *Sig.* = .009). Marital status accounted for 4.4 percent of the variance in burnout (fourth line, Partial Eta Squared = .044).

Main effect 2—Ethnicity (line 5).   Table 7.8 also shows a significant burnout based on workers' ethnicity (fifth line, Ethnicity: F = 6.005, *df* = 1, *Sig.* = .015). In this case, however, ethnicity accounted for only 2.8 percent of the variance in burnout (fifth line, Partial Eta Squared = .028).

Interaction effect—MStatus * Ethnicity (line 6).   Table 7.8, on the other hand, shows no significant marital status by ethnicity interaction effect on burnout (sixth line, MStatus * Ethnicity: F = 1.543, *df* = 2, *Sig.* = .216). In this study, marital status by ethnicity accounted for only 1.4 percent of the variance in burnout (sixth line, Partial Eta Squared = .014).

Overall variance.   Finally, table 7.8 shows that 21.4 percent of the variance in burnout (R squared = .214) is accounted for by marital status, ethnicity, their interaction, and promotion.

Estimated Marginal Means

Unlike two-way ANOVA, two-way ANCOVA relies on the adjusted mean scores of the dependent variable in computing test statistics and the level of significance. Means are adjusted to account for errors due to (1) the effect of the covariate and (2) unequal sample sizes in cells. Still, if sample sizes in all cells are equal, means will be adjusted in ANCOVA to account for errors due to the covariate.

Table 7.9 shows that the adjusted grand mean for burnout is 21.135, slightly below the actual grand mean reported in table 7.7.

Table 7.10 reports the adjusted burnout mean scores for each level of marital status. In addition, the table reports the standard error and the 95th confidence interval for burnout for each level of marital status. Notice that these means (married = 22.769, single = 22.194, divorced = 18.443) are somewhat different than the actual means reported in table 7.7 (married = 22.16, single = 21.68, divorced = 18.67).

Table 7.11 conveys the results of the Bonferroni post hoc test. It compares each level of marital status with all other levels. These comparisons are as follows:

Table 7.9: Estimated Marginal Means—Grand Mean

1. Grand Mean

Dependent Variable:Burnout

		95% Confidence Interval	
Mean	Std. Error	Lower Bound	Upper Bound
21.135[a]	.542	20.067	22.203

a. Covariates appearing in the model are evaluated at the following values: Promotion = 30.21.

Table 7.10: Estimated Marginal Means—Marital Status

Estimates

Dependent Variable:Burnout

			95% Confidence Interval	
MStatus	Mean	Std. Error	Lower Bound	Upper Bound
1 MARRIED	22.769[a]	.515	21.753	23.785
2 SINGLE	22.194[a]	.836	20.546	23.841
3 DIVORCED	18.443[a]	1.297	15.887	20.999

a. Covariates appearing in the model are evaluated at the following values: Promotion = 30.21.

Table 7.11: Results of Bonferroni Post Hoc Test for Marital Status

Pairwise Comparisons

Dependent Variable:Burnout

(I) MStatus	(J) MStatus	Mean Difference (I-J)	Std. Error	Sig.[a]	95% Confidence Interval for Difference[a]	
					Lower Bound	Upper Bound
1 MARRIED	2 SINGLE	.575	.984	1.000	-1.799	2.949
	3 DIVORCED	4.326[*]	1.395	0.01	.958	7.694
2 SINGLE	1 MARRIED	-.575	.984	1.000	-2.949	1.799
	3 DIVORCED	3.751[*]	1.542	0.04	.028	7.473
3 DIVORCED	1 MARRIED	-4.326[*]	1.395	0.01	-7.694	-.958
	2 SINGLE	-3.751[*]	1.542	0.04	-7.473	-.028

Based on estimated marginal means

a. Adjustment for multiple comparisons: Bonferroni.

*. The mean difference is significant at the .05 level.

1. The table shows no significant difference between married and single work-ers with regard to their burnout (first row, Married; first line, Single: *Sig.* = 1.000). Married workers scored only about a half point more than single workers (first row, Married; first line, Single: mean difference = .575).

2. The table shows a significant difference between married and divorced workers with regard to their levels of burnout (first row, Married; second line, Divorced: *Sig.* = .01). Married scored 4.326 points higher than divorced in the burnout scale (first row, Married; second line, Divorced: mean difference = 4.326).

3. Finally, the table also shows a significant difference between single and divorced workers with regard to their burnout, with single reporting greater burnout than divorced workers (second row, Single; second line, Divorced: mean difference = 3.751, *Sig.* = .04).

The two-way ANCOVA also uses a one-way ANOVA to conduct univari-ate groups comparison. It uses the one-way ANOVA to examine the differences in the *adjusted* mean scores of the dependent variable based on each inde-pendent variable, independently. Because there are two independent variables, two one-way ANOVA tests will be used, one for Marital Status and another for Ethnicity.

Table 7.12 shows an overall significant difference in the adjusted means of burnout between at least two levels of marital status ($F = 4.805$, *Sig.* = .009). Of course, these findings are consistent with the results of the two-way ANCOVA for marital status (main effect 1).

Table 7.13 reports the adjusted mean scores for the second independent variable, Ethnicity. As it appears in the table, the mean for Jews is 19.808 and for Arabs is 22.462. In comparison, the actual mean for Jews is 20.27 and for

Table 7.12:   Univariate Tests—Burnout on Marital Status

Univariate Tests

Dependent Variable:Burnout

	Sum of Squares	df	Mean Square	F	Sig.	Partial Eta Squared
Contrast	310.263	2	155.131	4.805	**.009**	.044
Error	6779.763	210	32.285			

The F tests the effect of MStatus. This test is based on the linearly independent pairwise comparisons among the estimated marginal means.

Table 7.13:   Estimated Marginal Means—Ethnicity

Estimates

Dependent Variable:Burnout

Ethnicity	Mean	Std. Error	95% Confidence Interval	
			Lower Bound	Upper Bound
0 JEWS	19.808[a]	.570	18.684	20.932
1 ARABS	22.462[a]	.921	20.647	24.278

a. Covariates appearing in the model are evaluated at the following values: Promotion = 30.21.

Table 7.14:   Results of Bonferroni Post Hoc Test for Ethnicity

Pairwise Comparisons

Dependent Variable:Burnout

(I) Ethnicity	(J) Ethnicity	Mean Difference (I-J)	Std. Error	Sig.[a]	95% Confidence Interval for Difference[a]	
					Lower Bound	Upper Bound
0 JEWS	1 ARABS	-2.655*	1.083	**0.02**	-4.790	-.519
1 ARABS	0 JEWS	2.655*	1.083	**0.02**	.519	4.790

Based on estimated marginal means

*. The mean difference is significant at the .05 level.

a. Adjustment for multiple comparisons: Bonferroni.

Table 7.15:   Univariate Tests—Burnout on Ethnicity

Univariate Tests

Dependent Variable:Burnout

	Sum of Squares	df	Mean Square	F	Sig.	Partial Eta Squared
Contrast	193.855	1	193.855	6.005	.015	**.028**
Error	6779.763	210	32.285			

The F tests the effect of Ethnicity. This test is based on the linearly independent pairwise comparisons among the estimated marginal means.

Arabs is 24.21 (see table 7.7). Notice that the mean score for Arabs dropped about 1.75 points after adjustments were made for unequal sample size and the addition of the covariate (Promotion).

Table 7.14 reports the results of the Bonferroni post hoc test for the second independent variable, Ethnicity. However, because Ethnicity has only two groups, the results of this post hoc test are redundant of the results of the two-way ANCOVA (main effect 2). Still, for clarification, the table shows a significant difference between Jewish and Arab workers with regard to burnout (*Sig.* = .02), with Jews reporting 2.65 points on average below Arabs (mean difference = −2.655).

Table 7.15 is the second one-way ANOVA test that examines the differences between Arab and Jewish workers with regard to their adjusted means of burnout. The table shows a significant difference between the two groups with regard to burnout (*F* = 6.005, *Sig.* = .015). These results are consistent with the results of the two-way ANCOVA (main effect 2).

Table 7.16 reports the adjusted means, standard error, and 95th confidence interval for burnout for each level of marital status by each level of ethnicity. It is also called interaction means. Comparing these means with the means reported in table 7.7 shows slight differences, with four means slightly increasing (married Jews, single Jews, single Arabs, and divorced Arabs) and two decreasing (married Arabs and divorced Jews).

Table 7.16:   Estimated Marginal Means—Marital Status by Ethnicity Interaction Means

4. MStatus * Ethnicity

Dependent Variable:Burnout

MStatus	Ethnicity	Mean	Std. Error	95% Confidence Interval	
				Lower Bound	Upper Bound
1 MARRIED	0 JEWS	20.861[a]	.583	19.711	22.011
	1 ARABS	24.677[a]	.851	22.998	26.355
2 SINGLE	0 JEWS	19.833[a]	1.115	17.636	22.030
	1 ARABS	24.555[a]	1.244	22.103	27.006
3 DIVORCED	0 JEWS	18.730[a]	1.160	16.443	21.016
	1 ARABS	18.156[a]	2.320	13.583	22.729

a. Covariates appearing in the model are evaluated at the following values: Promotion = 30.21.

Interaction Means Plot

As with two-way ANOVA, the results of a two-way ANCOVA can be plotted in a graph that is known as an interaction means plot. This plot displays the adjusted mean scores of the dependent variable for each level of the first independent variable on each level of the second independent variable.

Figure 7.6 displays three lines. Each line presents the adjusted mean scores of burnout for marital status groups (married, single, and divorced) for both Arabs and Jews. As it appears in the graph, married workers (Arabs and Jews) have higher burnout than divorced workers (Arabs and Jews, respectively). Married and single Arabs also appear to have greater burnout than married and single Jews, respectively.

Figure 7.6:   Means Plot for Ethnicity by Marital Status on Burnout

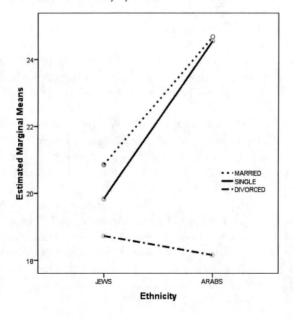

The graph, on the other hand, shows that the lines do not intersect, thus indicating that no marital status and ethnicity interaction effect on burnout exists. This graph confirms the results of the two-way ANCOVA, interaction effect.

Step 5: Write the Results.

Writing the results of the two-way ANCOVA is the same as for the two-way ANOVA. You should begin this section by reporting your methods for evaluation of the test assumptions, including normality, linearity, homoscedasticity, multicollinearity, and homogeneity of regression, and whether you conducted any data transformation.

Then you need to present the F ratio, degrees of freedom (df), and p value for each source of variation (covariate, main effect 1, main effect 2, and interaction effect). Moreover, you also need to report the percentage of variance in the dependent variable that is accounted for by each effect (eta squared). Furthermore, you need to report the results of the post hoc tests, if any. In addition, you need to report the adjusted means and standard errors for all groups and their interaction. Finally, you may display the interaction mean scores in an interaction means plot.

Writing the Results

The following presents the results of the two-way ANCOVA for burnout based on marital status and ethnicity while controlling for promotion.

Evaluation of assumptions.   Prior to the two-way ANCOVA analysis, data were screened to ensure that the two-way ANCOVA assumptions were met. Descriptive statistics including skewness and kurtosis, histograms, and normal Q-Q plots were examined to ensure that the assumption of normality of both the covariate and the dependent variable was fulfilled. Inspection of a scatterplot of Burnout (dependent variable) on Promotion (covariate) also shows a linear relationship between the covariate and the dependent variable.

Furthermore, the assumption of homoscedasticity was evaluated by Levene's test of equality of variances, which shows equal variances among all groups ($F = .498, p = .777$). Finally, the assumption of homogeneity of regression was evaluated by the two-way ANCOVA custom model. The results show no significant interaction between the covariate and the independent variable ($F = 2.079$, $p > .05$).

Results of two-way ANCOVA.   A two-way ANCOVA (or a 2x3 ANCOVA) was utilized to examine the effects of marital status, ethnicity, and marital status by ethnicity on burnout among a sample of 218 social services workers while holding their opportunities for promotion constant.

COVARIATE:

The results of the two-way analysis of covariance show a significant relationship between Promotion (covariate) and Burnout ($F_{(1, 216)}$ = 23.18, p < .001). In this study, the covariate accounted for about 10 percent of the variance in burnout (η^2 = .099).

MAIN EFFECT 1 (MARITAL STATUS):

The results of the two-way ANCOVA show overall significant burnout differences based on marital status among social services workers ($F_{(2, 216)}$ = 4.81, p < .010).

The results of the Bonferroni pairwise comparisons show a significant difference between married and divorced social workers (p < .010), with married workers reporting significantly higher levels of burnout (mean = 22.77, SE = .52) than divorced workers (mean = 18.44, SE = 1.30). Single workers also reported significantly higher burnout (mean = 22.19, SE = .84) than divorced social workers (p < .05). No significant burnout difference, on the other hand, was found between married and single workers (p > .05).

Overall, marital status accounted for less than 5 percent of the variance in burnout (η^2 = .044), indicating a weak relationship between the two variables while controlling for promotion.

MAIN EFFECT 2 (ETHNICITY):

The results of the two-way ANCOVA also show a significant burnout difference between Arab and Jewish workers ($F_{(1, 216)}$ = 6.01, p < .05).

In this study, Arab social services workers reported significantly higher levels of burnout (mean = 22.46, SE = .92) than Jewish workers (mean = 19.81, SE = .57). On the other hand, ethnicity accounted for less than 3 percent of the variance in burnout (η^2 = .028), indicating a weak relationship between ethnicity and burnout while controlling for promotion.

INTERACTION EFFECT (MARITAL STATUS BY ETHNICITY):

The results of the two-way ANCOVA show no significant marital status by ethnicity interaction effect on burnout ($F_{(2, 216)}$ = 1.54, p > .05). In this case, marital status by ethnicity interaction accounted for only 1.4 percent of the variance in burnout.

Finally, the two-way ANCOVA full factorial model accounted for a total of 21 percent of the variance in burnout.

Presentation of results in summary tables.   The summary tables of the two-way ANCOVA are similar to those of the two-way ANOVA. In ANCOVA, unlike in ANOVA, the first table should present the adjusted means. The second table should also report the sum of squares and mean squares of variation due to the covariate and its F ratio and level of significance.

In this example, tables 7.17.A and 7.17.B and figure 7.6 display the results of the two-way ANCOVA.

Table 7.17.A: Adjusted Means of Burnout by Ethnicity and Marital Status

Marital Status	Ethnicity	N	Mean	SE
Married	Jewish	95	20.86	.58
	Arab	45	24.68	.85
	Total	140	22.77	.52
Single	Jewish	25	19.83	1.12
	Arab	21	24.56	1.24
	Total	47	22.19	.84
Divorced	Jewish	24	18.73	1.16
	Arab	6	18.16	2.32
	Total	30	18.44	1.30
Total	Jewish	145	19.81	.57
	Arab	72	22.46	.92
	Total	217	21.14	.54

Table 7.17.B: Two-Way ANCOVA Summary Table

Source of Variance	SS	df	MS	F^a	p
Promotion (covariate)	748.50	1	748.50	23.18	.000
Marital Status	310.26	2	155.13	4.81	.009
Ethnicity	193.86	1	193.86	6.01	.015
Interaction	99.62	2	49.81	1.54	.216
Error	6779.76	210	32.29		
Total	8622.10	216			

$^aR^2 = .21$

SUMMARY

A two-way analysis of covariance (ANCOVA) is an advanced statistical technique that combines two-way analysis of variance and multiple regression analysis. First, it allows researchers to examine the differences among groups with regard to one dependent variable (like a two-way ANOVA) while holding constant the effect of a third variable on the dependent variable, known as the covariate (like the regression coefficient in multiple regression analysis).

Chapter 7 discussed the purpose and advantages of the two-way ANCOVA, followed by a discussion of the sources of variation in the two-way ANCOVA (within-groups variability, between-groups variability, and covariate variability).

The chapter then discussed the research questions and hypotheses examined by the two-way ANCOVA. In addition to the questions examined in the two-way ANOVA (main effect 1, main effect 2, and interaction effect), two-way ANCOVA examines the effects of a third variable (or more) on the dependent variable.

Chapter 7 then discussed the assumptions of the two-way ANCOVA. They are the same assumptions as in two-way ANOVA; however, ANCOVA requires three additional assumptions. They are the assumptions of linearity, homogeneity of regression, and multicollinearity. The first refers to the relationship between the covariate and dependent variable; they need to have a linear relationship. The second implies no interaction between the covariate and the independent variable on the dependent variable. The third refers to the relationship between covariates and is required only if there is more than one covariate.

Next, chapter 7 presented the post hoc tests that allow researchers to pinpoint what groups or joint cells are significantly different when overall significant results are obtained. These tests are known as multiple comparisons. Finally, a detailed example was given to demonstrate how to utilize the two-way ANCOVA, examine the assumptions, use the SPSS main menu and syntax commands, and write and present the results in summary tables.

Chapter 8 will introduce another type of analysis of variance known as repeated measures analysis of variance (RANOVA). The chapter will follow the outline of this chapter to discuss the purpose of RANOVA and its advantages, research questions, and hypotheses and will then present a detailed example illustrating the use of the test in social sciences research.

PRACTICAL EXERCISES

The researcher in the practical exercises in chapter 6 was also interested in examining whether students' life satisfaction (LifeSatisfaction) contributes to the differences in students' levels of self-esteem. Answer the following questions:

1. Rewrite the research question being examined.
2. Restate the null and alternative hypotheses.
3. What statistical test(s) will you utilize to examine the null hypotheses? Why? Discuss your answer in detail.
4. Write the SPSS syntax file for the test statistic.
5. Run the statistical test you selected in question 3.
6. What is your decision with regard to the null hypotheses? Discuss your answer in detail.
7. Present the results in summary table(s) and graph(s).
8. Compare the results for this research question with those obtained in the practical exercises for chapter 6. Are there any differences? If yes, discuss them.

CHAPTER 8

Repeated Measures Analysis of Variance

LEARNING OBJECTIVES

1. Understand the purpose of repeated measures ANOVA

2. Understand the differences between within-subjects ANOVA and mixed between-within-subjects ANOVA

3. Understand the sources of variations in repeated measures ANOVA

4. Understand the advantages of repeated measures ANOVA

5. Understand the assumptions underlying repeated measures ANOVA

6. Understand the post hoc tests

7. Understand how to use SPSS to compute the test statistics

8. Understand how to interpret, write, and present the results of the tests

DATA SET (APPENDIX)

Health Control

INTRODUCTION

In its review of bivariate statistical methods, chapter 1 discussed the dependent *t*-test. The purpose of the dependent *t*-test is to compare the difference between the mean scores of two repeated measures of the same sample or to compare the mean scores of two related variables or conditions. The question is then, what statistical test(s) could be used if there are more than two repeated measures?

For example, a therapist claimed that he or she developed a new anxiety reduction technique that could significantly reduce levels of anxiety for victims of torture. To prove his or her claim, the therapist utilized a pretest-posttest pre-experiment design with a six-month follow-up. For this purpose, he or she recruited 40 victims (20 males and 20 females) of torture from the local Center for Victims of Torture and asked them to complete a standardized ten-item anxiety scale (pretest). All subjects then participated in an eight-week therapy for

Table 8.1:   Pre-experiment Pretest-Posttest Design with Follow-up

Group	Pretest	Posttest	Follow-up
Males	μ_{M1}	μ_{M2}	μ_{M3}
Females	μ_{F1}	μ_{F2}	μ_{F3}

μ (Miu) = mean score for anxiety

anxiety. All participants then completed the ten-item scale at the conclusion of the therapy (posttest) and six months later (follow-up). Table 8.1 summarizes this group design.

In this design, the therapist wants to examine (1) whether posttest and follow-up scores of anxiety are significantly lower than pretest scores and (2) whether males and females are significantly different with regard to levels of anxiety over time.

1. $\mu_{M1} = \mu_{F1}$; the means of the two groups are equal at the pretest (baseline).

2. $\mu_{M1} > \mu_{M2} \geq \mu_{M3}$; posttest and follow-up scores of males are lower than their pretest scores.

3. $\mu_{F1} > \mu_{F2} \geq \mu_{F3}$; posttest and follow-up scores of females are lower than their pretest scores.

4. $\mu_{M2} \neq \mu_{F2}$; the mean scores of males and females are different at posttest.

5. $\mu_{M3} \neq \mu_{F3}$; the mean scores of males and females are different at follow-up.

Consider another example in which a gerontology researcher was interested in exploring how older people perceive the causes of the changes in their health: internal causes, external causes (powerful others), or causes due to chance. For this purpose, the researcher administered the Multidimensional Health Locus of Control Scale (Wallston, Wallston, & DeVellis, 1978) to a random sample of 60 participants ages sixty and above. The scale has eighteen items measuring three sources of health locus of control: internal, external (powerful others), and chance. In this case, the researcher was interested to find out which locus of control older people believed caused the changes in their health. In other words, is there a significant difference between internal, external, and chance health locus of control among the older population? The researcher hypothesized the following:

$\mu_I \neq \mu_E \neq \mu_C$; the mean scores of internal (μ_I), external (μ_E), and chance (μ_C) health locus of control are different.

In the first example, there are two groups in which each is measured at three different times. Thus there are two main comparisons: (1) within-subjects differences between pretest, posttest, and follow-up and (2) between-subjects differences (males vs. females) with regard to these three times. For the first case, inexperienced researchers may utilize a number of dependent *t*-tests to compare pretest scores with posttest scores, posttest scores with follow-up scores, and pretest scores with follow-up scores. Also, they may utilize three independent *t*-tests to compare the two genders with regard to pretest scores, posttest scores, and follow-up scores.

In the second example, there is only one group that is measured at one time, however on three *related* variables. Here, researchers may utilize three dependent *t*-tests to compare the mean scores of the three health variables.

However, conducting multiple dependent *t*-tests and/or independent *t*-tests on the same data is not only *time consuming,* especially with too many repeated measures or groups, but also statistically *inflates* the probability of making *type I error (alpha)* (see Abu-Bader, 2006). In other words, the more tests that are utilized to examine the data, the greater the likelihood of making type I error. Furthermore, neither the dependent *t*-test nor the independent *t*-test will examine the *interaction effect* of group (males and females) by time (pretest, posttest, and follow-up) on the dependent variable (Anxiety).

To avoid these problems, researchers may utilize a more advanced technique that will (1) prevent the inflation of alpha, (2) examine group by time interaction effect on the dependent variable, (3) enhance the statistical power of the results, and (4) take less time to complete. This technique is the *repeated measures analysis of variance.*

This chapter will present two types of repeated measures analysis of variance (RANOVA), discuss the purpose of RANOVA, examine the assumptions underlying RANOVA, and present two examples to illustrate how to utilize SPSS to run the analysis, read the output, and write the results.

REPEATED MEASURES ANALYSIS OF VARIANCE

Purpose

Repeated measures analysis of variance (RANOVA) is an advanced statistical technique that builds upon the dependent *t*-test and analysis of variance. It is used to examine the (1) changes in a dependent variable measured repeatedly three or more times (*occasions*) among the same subjects (also known as longitudinal research), (2) changes in a dependent variable measured under three or more conditions among the same subjects (*different conditions*), and (3) performance, views, or attitudes of the same subjects on three or more related topics (*related variables*). Each subject is exposed to all measures of the dependent variable. The following paragraphs discuss these types in greater detail.

Repeated measures (occasions).   Repeated measures ANOVA can be used to examine changes in levels of anxiety among subjects before, during, and after they receive treatment. Here, each subject is measured on three occasions: before, during, and after. This case is also an example of a longitudinal research in which each subject is measured on the same variable over time.

Different conditions.   Repeated measures ANOVA is also appropriate to examine changes in the magnitude of migraine headaches among subjects after taking Imitrex, Tylenol, and Advil (headache medications) at different times. Here the magnitude of migraine headaches is measured under three different conditions.

Related topics.   In addition, repeated measures ANOVA can be used to examine differences between subjects' English proficiency based on their performance on reading, writing, and speaking English. In this example, each subject is measured on three related topics (variables): reading, writing, and speaking.

As you may have already noticed, the primary purpose of these examples is to examine whether significant differences exist between the subject's own scores (his or her anxiety scores before, during, or after treatment; his or her magnitude of headache after taking Imitrex, Tylenol, or Advil; and his or her English performance in reading, writing, or speaking).

Therefore, unlike analysis of variances (one-way, two-way, and factorial ANOVA), which are used to examine *between-subjects* (*groups*) differences (e.g., Caucasians, African Americans, and others) on the dependent variable, repeated measures ANOVA is used to examine *within-subjects* differences due to one of the above-mentioned three conditions. In other words, in repeated measures ANOVA, each subject serves as his or her own *control* group.

Types of Analysis of Variance

Chapters 1 and 6 presented the one-way ANOVA and two-way ANOVA. As you may recall, these ANOVA tests are also called between-subjects designs. In the current chapter, the discussion extends to two additional types of ANOVA, *within-subjects* ANOVA and *mixed between-within-subjects* ANOVA. Both are types of repeated measures ANOVA.

Within-subjects design, as already said, is used to examine changes or differences in the dependent variable measured over time, under different conditions, or on related variables on the same sample.

Mixed between-within-subjects design combines between-subjects and within-subjects designs. It is used to examine changes in a dependent variable measured over time, under different conditions, or on related variables for the same sample. At the same time, it examines whether these changes are significantly different based on a categorical independent variable (e.g., whether changes in levels of anxiety scores over time differ between males and females).

Sources of Variation

Recall that there are two sources of variation in ANOVA (see chapter 6). These sources are within-subjects variability and between-subjects variability. The primary interest in ANOVA, as you may remember, is the *between-subjects* variation. The *within-subjects* variability is then labeled as errors for that test.

In RANOVA, however, we are interested in three sources of variability. Unlike ANOVA, the primary interest in RANOVA is on scores of the same subject over time (Time 1, Time 2, etc.), under different conditions (Condition 1, Condition 2, etc.), or on related topics (Topic 1, Topic 2, etc.). These scores are dependent on each other (e.g., scores of Time 2 depend on scores of Time 1, etc.). Thus the *main source* of variability is taking the test more than one time, hereafter referred to as *occasions* (SS_O).

In addition, there are individual differences among subjects with regard to the dependent variable (Subject 1, Subject 2, Subject 3, etc.). These scores are independent of each other. Thus the second source of variation is due to differences among subjects, hereafter referred to as *subjects* (SS_I).

The third source of variability is variations due to errors or residuals, hereafter referred to as *errors* (SS_E). The *sum* of these three variations is the total variance (SS_T). Figure 8.1 describes these sources of variation.

Figure 8.1:   Sources of Variability in Repeated Measures ANOVA

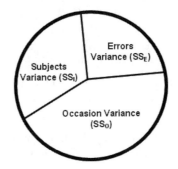

Accordingly, the degrees of freedom for RANOVA are:

1. For $SS_O = K - 1$; K = number of occasions (measures)

2. For $SS_I = n - 1$; n = number of subjects in each occasion (measure)

3. For $SS_E = (n - 1) * (K - 1)$

4. For $SS_T = N - 1$; N = total sample size (remember, each individual has repeated measures; thus, $N = n * K$)

If 10 subjects completed the pretest, posttest, and follow-up; then $n = 10$, $K = 3$, and $N = 10 * 3 = 30$.

Advantages

RANOVA has several advantages over ANOVA. Unlike analysis of variance, repeated measures ANOVA examines changes in each single subject's scores over time, under different conditions, or on related variables. Thus as a first advantage over ANOVA, repeated measures ANOVA *controls* for errors due to differences between subjects.

A second advantage is that by controlling for errors due to between-subjects differences, repeated measures ANOVA is able to extract one more source of variation than ANOVA, that is, within-subjects variation.

On the other hand, by explaining more sources of variation, repeated measures ANOVA, as a third advantage, reduces the error variance. This reduction in the error variance, in turn, creates a fourth advantage by increasing the power of RANOVA in testing the null hypothesis, in other words, rejecting the null hypothesis when in fact it is false.

Research Questions and Hypotheses

The main interest of both within-subjects ANOVA and mixed between-within-subjects ANOVA is to examine the differences in the mean scores of the dependent variable between all occasions, conditions, or related topics. These differences are also known as *occasion effect.*

Occasion effect (within-subjects effect).   It is the effect of time/conditions/topics on the dependent variable, that is, the change in the dependent variable due to occasion (e.g., levels of anxiety at pretest, posttest, and follow-up; or English proficiency in reading, writing, and speaking).

RESEARCH QUESTION: Are there significant differences in the dependent variable between all occasions among participants in the study?
EXAMPLES:

1. Is there a significant decrease in the levels of anxiety between pretest, posttest, and follow-up among participants in the therapy?

2. Are there significant differences in immigrants' English performance in reading, writing, and speaking?

RESEARCH HYPOTHESIS: There are significant differences in the dependent variable between all occasions among participants in the study.
EXAMPLES:

1. There are significant decreases (or changes) in the levels of anxiety between pretest, posttest, and follow-up among participants in the therapy.

$$H_a: \ \mu_{Pr} \neq \mu_{Po} \neq \mu_{Fo}; \text{ for some } i, \ k$$

2. There are significant differences in immigrants' English performance in reading, writing, and speaking.

$$H_a: \mu_R \neq \mu_W \neq \mu_S; \text{ for some } i, k$$

R = reading, W = writing, S = speaking

Group effect (between-within-subjects effect). Mixed between-within-subjects ANOVA examines two additional effects, group effect and interaction effect. It is the effect of the grouping variable on the dependent variable (e.g., differences in levels of anxiety between males and females at pretest, posttest, and follow-up; or the difference in English proficiency between males and females).

RESEARCH QUESTION: Are there significant differences between the levels of the grouping variable with regard to the dependent variable on each occasion, condition, or topic?

EXAMPLES:

1. Are there significant differences between males and females with regard to their levels of anxiety at the pretest, posttest, and follow-up?

2. Are there significant differences between male and female immigrants with regard to their English performance in reading, writing, and speaking?

RESEARCH HYPOTHESIS: There are significant differences between the levels of the grouping variable with regard to the dependent variable on each occasion, condition, or topic.

EXAMPLES:

1. There are significant differences between males and females with regard to their levels of anxiety at the pretest, posttest, and follow-up.

$$H_{a1}: \mu_{M1} \neq \mu_{F1}$$
$$H_{a2}: \mu_{M2} \neq \mu_{F2}$$
$$H_{a3}: \mu_{M3} \neq \mu_{F3}$$

M = male, F = female
1 = pretest, 2 = posttest, 3 = follow-up

---

2. There are significant differences between male and female immigrants with regard to their English performance in reading, writing, and speaking.

$$H_{a1}: \mu_{MR} \neq \mu_{FR}$$
$$H_{a2}: \mu_{MW} \neq \mu_{FW}$$
$$H_{a3}: \mu_{MS} \neq \mu_{FS}$$

M = male, F = female
R = reading, W = writing, S = speaking

Interaction effect (occasion by group effect).   This effect is also known as *within-subjects by between-subjects interaction effect.* It is the effect of occasion by group interaction (joint cells) on the dependent variable (e.g., the differences in the levels of anxiety between the males at pretest, females at pretest, males at posttest, females at posttest, males at follow-up, and females at follow-up; or the differences between males and females on each level of English proficiency in reading, writing, and speaking: males reading, females reading, males writing, females writing, males speaking, and females speaking).

RESEARCH QUESTION: Are there significant differences between each level of the grouping variable on the dependent variable across each occasion, condition, and topic?

EXAMPLES:

1.   Are there significant differences in the levels of anxiety between males at pretest, females at pretest, males at posttest, females at posttest, males at follow-up, and females at follow-up?

2.   Are there significant English performance differences between males' reading, females' reading, males' writing, females' writing, males' speaking, and females' speaking scores?

The simplest way to write these questions is as follows:

1.   Are there significant occasion (pretest, posttest, and follow-up) by gender (male and female) interaction effects on levels of anxiety?

2.   Are there significant performance (reading, writing, and speaking) by gender (male and female) interaction effects on their English proficiency?

RESEARCH HYPOTHESIS: There are significant differences between each level of the grouping variable on the dependent variable across each occasion, condition, or topic.

EXAMPLES:

1.   There are significant differences in the levels of anxiety between males at pretest, females at pretest, males at posttest, females at posttest, males at follow-up, and females at follow-up.

2.   There are significant English performance differences between males' reading, females' reading, males' writing, females' writing, males' speaking, and females' speaking scores.

The simplest way to write these hypotheses is as follows:

1. There are significant occasion (pretest, posttest, and follow-up) by gender (male and female) interaction effects on levels of anxiety.

$$H_a: \mu_{M1} \neq \mu_{M2} \neq \mu_{M3} \neq \mu_{F1} \neq \mu_{F2} \neq \mu_{F3}; \text{ for some } i, k$$

2. There are significant performance (reading, writing, and speaking) by gender (male and female) interaction effects on English proficiency.

$$H_a: \mu_{MR} \neq \mu_{FR} \neq \mu_{MW} \neq \mu_{FW} \neq \mu_{MS} \neq \mu_{FS}; \text{ for some } i, k$$

Assumptions

Recall that repeated measures ANOVA is an advanced technique of the dependent t-test and analysis of variance. Thus it requires the same set of assumptions as both the dependent t-test and the analysis of variance. These assumptions are as follows:

1. SAMPLE REPRESENTATIVENESS: The sample must be representative of the population to which generalization of results will be made. Also, if experiment designs are used, subjects should be randomly assigned to each group.

2. LEVEL OF MEASUREMENT: The dependent variable for all occasions, conditions, and related variables must be continuous data and measured at the interval level of measurement or higher.

3. SAMPLE SIZE: The sample should be large enough to utilize the repeated measures ANOVA. As with ANOVA, a sample size of 30 subjects or more is considered generally acceptable for RANOVA. RANOVA examines within-subjects scores. Therefore, each subject must have valid scores on all occasions, conditions, or related variables.

These three assumptions are methodological issues and can be evaluated by referring to the research methodology and design and by inspecting the number of valid cases in the specific data file.

4. NORMAL DISTRIBUTION: The distributions of the dependent variable over time or under different conditions must approach the shape of a normal distribution.

Normality of the distribution of the dependent variable can be evaluated by inspecting measures of skewness and kurtosis, histograms, and normal probability plots for the dependent variable for all occasions, conditions, and related topics (see chapter 2).

5.   ASSUMPTION OF SPHERICITY: This assumption is similar to the assumption of homogeneity of variance in ANOVA; however, it implies that the variances of the *difference scores* of all pairs of occasions, conditions, or related topics should be equal. For example, if there are three levels of the dependent variable, say, pretest, posttest, and follow-up, then there should be three pairs of differences ($D1$ = pretest–posttest; $D2$ = pretest–follow-up; and $D3$ = posttest–follow-up). Then the assumption implies that the variances of $D1$, $D2$, and $D3$ should be equal.

The assumption of sphericity can be evaluated by inspecting the results of the *Mauchly's* W *test of sphericity* computed along with the results of RANOVA in SPSS. The assumption is met if $p > .05$. If there are only two repeated measures of the dependent variable (e.g., pretest and posttest), two conditions, or two related topics, then the Mauchly's W will be "1" and the p value will be "." because there is only one difference score (e.g., D = posttest–pretest). In other words, sphericity is not an issue when there are only two measures of the dependent variable.

When, however, there are *more* than two measures of the dependent variable, violation of the assumption of sphericity is severe. It inflates type I error, which leads to inaccurate conclusions. On the other hand, as with the independent *t*-test in which alternative tests are used to adjust for unequal variances, repeated measures ANOVA also provides alternative tests to correct for violation of sphericity, namely, *Greenhouse-Geisser, Huynh-Feldt,* and *lower-bound* (discussed under "Correction for Sphericity").

In addition to these assumptions, RANOVA requires two additional assumptions:

6.   COMPOUND SYMMETRY: Because data in repeated measures are from the same subjects, not only the variances of all pairs of difference scores need to be equal (assumption of sphericity) but also the covariances of all pairs of difference scores should be similar (e.g., the covariance between $D1$ and $D2$, $D1$ and $D3$, and $D2$ and $D3$ should be similar).

As with the assumption of sphericity, when there are only two measures of the dependent variable, compound symmetry is not an issue. On the other hand, when there are *more* than two measures of the dependent variable, violation of the assumption is critical. Unfortunately, SPSS does not yet provide a statistical test to evaluate the assumption. However, although it is time consuming and tedious, the assumption can be evaluated by creating new variables for all possible difference scores and computing and inspecting the covariances of all pairs of the new variables.

Researchers, however, have focused greatly on the assumption of sphericity and less on the assumption of compound symmetry. When data violate this assumption, researchers have reported the results of the alternative tests which overcome the violations of both assumptions.

7. RANGE OF SCORES: Measures for all repeated measures, conditions, and related variables should have equal possible ranges (minimum and maximum scores) and the same interpretations. If a high score means greater value in one measure, it should be the same in all others. If not, they should be transformed into standard scores so they have similar scales.

This assumption can be evaluated by referring to the research methodology and instruments used to find out if the same instrument is used to measure the dependent variable on all occasions, conditions, or related topics. If not, transform the scores of all occasions, conditions, or related topics into standard scores (see chapter 2 for data transformation).

In addition to these assumptions, when *mixed between-within-subjects ANOVA* is utilized, the following three assumptions must be fulfilled:

8. NORMALITY OF DISTRIBUTION: The distribution of all measures of the dependent variables should be normal for each level of the independent variable.

Normality can be evaluated, as said, by computing measures of skewness and kurtosis and inspecting both histograms and normal probability plots for each group on each measure (see the second practical example in this chapter).

9. HOMOGENEITY OF VARIANCE: The variances on all measures of the dependent variable (all occasions, conditions, or related topics) should be equal across all groups.

Homogeneity of variance can be evaluated simply by inspecting the results of Levene's test of equality of variances, computed along with the results of RANOVA. Remember, a $p > .001$ indicates that the variances are equal.

10. HOMOGENEITY OF VARIANCE-COVARIANCE MATRICES: This assumption implies that the covariance matrices on all measures of the dependent variable should be equal across all levels of the independent variable. This assumption is needed only if groups have unequal sample sizes.

The assumption can be evaluated by inspecting the results of *Box's M test of equality of covariance matrices,* computed along with the results of RANOVA. As a general rule, a $p > .001$ indicates that the assumption is fulfilled.

Correction for Sphericity

As said previously, repeated measures ANOVA requires that all pairs of the difference scores of all measures of the dependent variable have equal variances, that is, the assumption of sphericity.

SPSS provides three alternative methods that are more powerful when the assumption of sphericity is violated. These tests correct for unequal variances by reducing the degrees of freedom, which, in turn, increase the critical value for the

F ratio and lower type I error. These tests include Greenhouse-Geisser (G-G), Huynh-Feldt (H-F), and lower-bound (L-B).

Although the discussion of the theory behind each test is beyond the scope of this book, you do need to know which one is to be used when the assumption of sphericity is violated. As you will see in the discussion of SPSS, all three tests compute correction factors ranging between 0 and 1. The closer the correction's value to 1, the closer the data fulfill the assumption of sphericity.

Recommendations: When the assumption of sphericity is violated, report the correction test with the largest value. If all correction tests are equal, report the results of the Huynh-Feldt (H-F) because it is less conservative than both Greenhouse-Geisser (G-G) and lower-bound (L-B). On the other hand, if all correction tests are the same as the results of the *sphericity assumed* test, report the results of the latter.

In addition to these correction tests, within-subjects ANOVA also uses multivariate tests to examine the hypothesis. These tests include Pillai's trace, Wilks' lambda, Hotelling's trace, and Roy's largest root (see chapter 9). Multivariate tests, on the other hand, do not require the fulfillment of either sphericity or compound symmetry and therefore can be reported when the assumptions are violated.

Recommendation: when the assumption(s) are violated, report the results of one correction test (as discussed in this section) and the results of Wilks' lambda.

Post Hoc Tests

Post hoc tests in RANOVA, such as LSD, Bonferroni, Tukey, and Scheffe, serve two purposes. First, post hoc tests identify what levels of the dependent variable are significantly different when significant results occur between all measures of the dependent variable (e.g., pretest, posttest, and follow-up). Second, when mixed between-within-subjects ANOVA is utilized where the independent variable has more than two groups, post hoc tests pinpoint what groups, if any, are significantly different.

As with ANOVA, there are eighteen post hoc tests available in SPSS, four of which are appropriate when the assumption of homogeneity of variances is not met. In RANOVA, however, these tests are available to compare all levels of the independent variable. In contrast with the analysis of covariance (see chapter 7), only three post hoc tests available in SPSS compare levels of the dependent variable. They are LSD, Bonferroni, and Sidak.

FIRST PRACTICAL EXAMPLE: WITHIN-SUBJECTS ANALYSIS OF VARIANCE

This example will illustrate the utilization of within-subjects ANOVA. Using the Health Control SPSS data file, we will examine the differences among older Muslim American immigrants' health locus of control. In this data file, there are three health locus of control variables: internal (IHLC), external or powerful others (PHLC), and chance (CHLC). The research question is as follows: Are there significant differences between internal, external (powerful others), and chance health locus of control scores among older Muslim American immigrants?

Hypothesis Testing

Step 1: State the Null and Alternative Hypotheses.

H_o: There are no significant differences between internal (I), powerful others (P), and chance (C) health locus of control scores among older Muslim American immigrants.

$$\mu_I = \mu_P = \mu_C$$

H_a: There are significant differences between internal, powerful others, and chance health locus of control scores among older Muslim American immigrants.

$$\mu_I \neq \mu_P \neq \mu_C; \text{ for at least two means}$$

Step 2: Set the Criteria for Rejecting the Null Hypothesis.
We will set alpha at .05 ($\alpha = .05$). That is, reject H_o only if $p \leq .05$.

Step 3: Select the Appropriate Statistical Test.
In this example, we are examining whether older Muslim American immigrants have different perceptions of what causes the changes in their current health: are they due to internal causes, powerful others, or chance? In other words, we are interested in the differences among three related topics, health locus of control, measured on the same subjects.

Therefore, we will consider utilizing a one-way repeated measure ANOVA to analyze these differences (one-way RANOVA because there is technically only one independent variable, which is Occasions). Since there are no group comparisons, we will use the within-subjects ANOVA to examine the aforementioned research question. Before we conduct the test, we must evaluate the test's assumptions and determine whether they are fulfilled. The evaluation follows.

1. SAMPLE REPRESENTATIVENESS: The sample in this study was randomly selected from various Islamic community centers and mosques in three northeastern states.

2. LEVEL OF MEASUREMENT: The three measures of health locus of control (internal, external, and chance) are continuous data and measured at the interval level of measurement.

3. SAMPLE SIZE: In this study, 60 participants completed all three measures of health locus of control. This number is greater than 30, and the assumption is met.

Table 8.2:   Measures of Skewness and Kurtosis

Statistics

		IHLC	PHLC	CHLC
N	Valid	60	60	60
	Missing	0	0	0
	Skewness	-.168	-.347	.192
	Std. Error of Skewness	.309	.309	.309
	Kurtosis	.825	.810	.751
	Std. Error of Kurtosis	.608	.608	.608

4.   NORMAL DISTRIBUTION: The distributions of the three measures of the health locus of control should approach the shape of a normal distribution.

To examine this assumption, we will compute measures of skewness and kurtosis of the three variables. We will also inspect their histograms and normal probability plots.

Table 8.2 displays measures of skewness and kurtosis for each measure of health locus of control.

The table shows that both skewness and kurtosis coefficients for each measure are smaller than twice their standard error. In other words, these coefficients show that the three health locus of control measures fall within the normal range (e.g., skewness/standard error of skewness is not greater than ±1.96). This indicates that the distributions of internal, external, and chance health locus of control approach the normal curve. Next, we will eyeball both histograms and normal probability plots of these measures (see figures 8.2, 8.3, and 8.4).

Both the histograms and the normal probability plots of the three measures also show that the distributions appear to approach the shape of a normal curve. The distribution of powerful others (figure 8.3) has minor deviations, however.

5.   SPHERICITY: The variances of the three measures of health locus of control should be equal.

Figure 8.2:   Histogram and Q-Q Plot for Internal Health Locus of Control

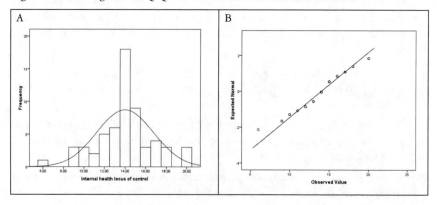

Figure 8.3: Histogram and Q-Q Plot for Powerful Others Health Locus of Control

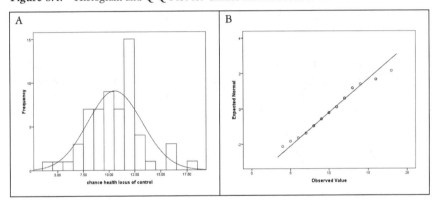

Figure 8.4: Histogram and Q-Q Plot for Chance Health Locus of Control

We will evaluate this assumption by inspecting the results of Mauchly's W test of sphericity, which is produced along with the results of RANOVA (see "How to Use SPSS to Run Within-Subjects ANOVA"). Table 8.3 presents the results of Mauchly's W test. As indicated in the discussion of assumptions, a p value greater than .05 indicates that the assumption is fulfilled. In our case, $Sig.$ = .063. This value indicates that the variances of the three health locus of

Table 8.3: Results of the Mauchly's W Test of Sphericity

Mauchly's Test of Sphericity[b]

Measure MEASURE_1

Within Subjects Effect	Mauchly's W	Approx. Chi-Square	df	Sig.	Epsilon[a]		
					Greenhouse-Geisser	Huynh-Feldt	Lower-bound
Health	.909	5.518	2	.063	0.92	0.94	.500

Tests the null hypothesis that the error covariance matrix of the orthonormalized transformed dependent variables is proportional to an identity matrix.

a. May be used to adjust the degrees of freedom for the averaged tests of significance. Corrected tests are displayed in the Tests of Within-Subjects Effects table.

b. Design: Intercept
Within Subjects Design: Health

control scores are equal, and therefore, the assumption of sphericity is met. Notice that both epsilon Greenhouse-Geisser and Huynh-Feldt correction values are very close to 1 (.92 and .94, respectively). If, on the other hand, the assumption was violated, we would report the results of Huynh-Feldt (see step 4).

6. COMPOUND SYMMETRY: The correlation between all pairs of the three measures of health locus of control (internal and external, internal and chance, and external and chance) should be equal.

As said earlier, we will relate this assumption to the assumption of sphericity. In other words, since the assumption of sphericity is fulfilled, we will report the results accordingly.

7. RANGE OF SCORES: Internal, external, and chance health locus of control scores should have equal range and the same interpretations.

In this study, the Multidimensional Health Locus of Control Scale was used to measure participants' health locus of control. This is an eighteen-item instrument with three subscales, internal, external, and chance health locus of control. Total scores for each measure range between 8 and 32, with higher scores indicating more external beliefs in locus of control (see appendix for more detail).

To conclude, it appears that the data satisfy all assumptions for the within-subjects ANOVA test. Next we will use SPSS to execute the repeated measures within-subjects ANOVA.

How to Use SPSS to Run Within-Subjects ANOVA

Step 4: Compute the Within-Subjects ANOVA Test Statistic.
We will utilize SPSS to run within-subjects ANOVA. To conduct the analysis in SPSS, follow these steps:

1. Open the Health Control SPSS data file.

2. Click on *Analyze* in the SPSS main toolbar.

3. Scroll down to and click on *General Linear Model,* and click on *Repeated Measures* (see screen 8.1).

4. A dialog box called "Repeated Measures Define Factor(s)" will open.

5. You can either keep "factor(1)" or type any name you wish. Highlight and change "factor(1)," which is SPSS default, to "Health" in the *Within-Subject Factor Name* box.

6. Type "3" in the *Number of Levels* box (this is the number of measures in the dependent variable), and click on *Add* (see screen 8.2).

7. Click on *Define.* A new dialog box labeled "Repeated Measures" will open.

8. Click on *IHLC,* and click on the third arrow from the bottom to move *IHLC* into the *Within-Subjects Variables (Health)* box. *IHLC* will replace "_?_(1)."

Screen 8.1: SPSS Repeated Measures ANOVA Main Menu

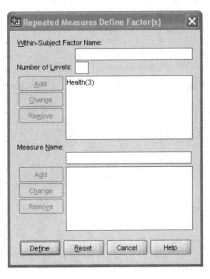

Screen 8.2: SPSS Repeated Measures Define Factor(s) Dialog Box

9. Repeat step 8 to move *PHLC* and *CHLC* into the *Within-Subjects Variables (Health)* box (see screen 8.3).

10. Click on *Options* on the right side menu, which will open the "Repeated Measures: Options" dialog box.

Screen 8.3:   SPSS Repeated Measures Dialog Box

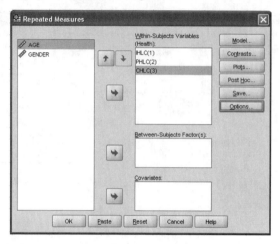

11.   Click on *Overall* in the *Factor(s) and Factor Interactions* box, and click on the middle arrow to move *Overall* into the *Display Means For* box.

12.   Repeat step 11 to move *Health* into the *Display Means For* box.

13.   Check the *Compare Main Effects* box. Click on the drop-down arrow for *Confidence Interval Adjustment,* and click on *Bonferroni.* This is the post hoc test to compare the means of all possible pairs of the three measures.

14.   Check both the *Descriptive Statistics* and the *Estimates of Effect Size* boxes (see screen 8.4).

Screen 8.4:   SPSS Repeated Measures Options Dialog Box

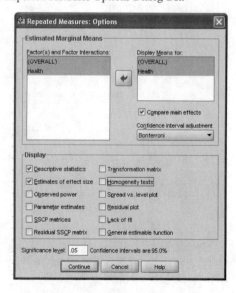

Screen 8.5: SPSS Repeated Measures Profile Plots Dialog Box

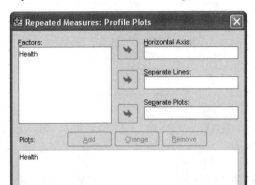

15. Click on *Continue* to return to the "Repeated Measures" main menu.

16. Click on *Plots* on the right side menu. A "Repeated Measures: Profile Plots" dialog box will open.

17. Click on *Health* in the *Factors* box and move it into the *Horizontal Axis* box, and click on *Add* to move *Health* into the *Plots* box (see screen 8.5).

18. Click on *Continue,* and click on *OK* in the "Repeated Measures" main dialog box.

Within-Subjects ANOVA SPSS Syntax Commands

GLM IHLC PHLC CHLC
/WSFACTOR=Health 3 Polynomial
/METHOD=SSTYPE(3)
/PLOT=PROFILE(Health)
/EMMEANS=TABLES(OVERALL)
/EMMEANS=TABLES(Health) COMPARE ADJ(BONFERRONI)
/PRINT=DESCRIPTIVE ETASQ
/CRITERIA=ALPHA(.05)
/WSDESIGN=Health.

Reading the Output of Within-Subjects ANOVA

The execution of these SPSS commands will produce eleven tables and one graph. Of them, three will not be discussed because they are unnecessary. A fourth table, Mauchly's M test, was discussed earlier (see table 8.3). The remaining tables (8.4–8.10) and the graph (figure 8.5) follow.

Table 8.4 displays the number of factors (measures) of the dependent variable. As you may recall, we called the dependent variable Health. It has three

Table 8.4: Measures of Health Locus of Control

Within-Subjects Factors

Measure:MEASURE_1

Health	Dependent Variable
1	IHLC
2	PHLC
3	CHLC

factors. They are (1) IHLC, (2) PHLC, and (3) CHLC. It is important to remember this order, because some tables use this order (1, 2, and 3) to refer to the factors.

Table 8.5 displays the number of cases, mean, and standard deviation for each factor (measure) of the dependent variable. Remember, the number of cases should be equal for all factors because each subject was measured on all measures. The table shows that powerful others locus of control has the highest mean (mean = 16.18, SD = 4.01), followed by internal health locus of control (mean = 14.0, SD = 2.74) and chance health locus of control (mean = 10.57, SD = 2.64).

Table 8.6 presents the results of the multivariate tests. These results are appropriate if the data violate either the assumption of sphericity or the assumption of compound symmetry. The data do not violate these assumptions, so these results will not be used. Just for clarification, all of the multivariate tests (Pillai's trace, Wilks' lambda, Hotelling's trace, and Roy's largest root) show significant differences between at least two measures of health locus of control (*Sig.* = .000).

Table 8.7 conveys the results of the within-subjects ANOVA. The table has seven columns and two rows.

Table 8.5: Descriptive Statistics for Health Locus of Control

Descriptive Statistics

	Mean	Std. Deviation	N
IHLC	14.0000	2.74325	60
PHLC	16.1833	4.01477	60
CHLC	10.5667	2.63848	60

Table 8.6: Results of Repeated Measures Multivariate Tests

Multivariate Tests[b]

Effect		Value	F	Hypothesis df	Error df	Sig.	Partial Eta Squared
Health	Pillai's Trace	.788	107.552[a]	2.000	58.000	.000	.788
	Wilks' Lambda	.212	107.552[a]	2.000	58.000	.000	.788
	Hotelling's Trace	3.709	107.552[a]	2.000	58.000	.000	.788
	Roy's Largest Root	3.709	107.552[a]	2.000	58.000	.000	.788

a. Exact statistic

b. Design: Intercept
Within Subjects Design: Health

Table 8.7:   Results of Within-Subjects Analysis of Variance

Tests of Within-Subjects Effects

Measure:MEASURE_1

Source		Type III Sum of Squares	df	Mean Square	F	Sig.	Partial Eta Squared
Health	Sphericity Assumed	962.033	2.000	481.017	88.141	.000	.599
	Greenhouse-Geisser	962.033	1.834	524.671	88.141	.000	.599
	Huynh-Feldt	962.033	1.889	509.149	88.141	.000	.599
	Lower-bound	962.033	1.000	962.033	88.141	.000	.599
Error (Health)	Sphericity Assumed	643.967	118.000	5.457			
	Greenhouse-Geisser	643.967	108.182	5.953			
	Huynh-Feldt	643.967	111.480	5.777			
	Lower-bound	643.967	59.000	10.915			

These columns are the same as in analysis of variance and covariance (see chapters 6 and 7). They include *Source* of variability; *Sum of Squares* of variance; number of degrees of freedom, *df; Mean Square* of variances; *F* ratio; level of significance, *Sig.;* and proportion of variance in the dependent variable due to each particular source of variability, *Partial Eta Squared.*

The two rows display the results for two of the three sources of variability: *within-subjects* variance (occasion variance) and *errors* variance, respectively (see figure 8.1).

Each row reports the results of four different tests examining the mean differences of all factors of the dependent variable, in this case, Health Locus of Control.

The first line, Sphericity Assumed, reports the results of repeated measures ANOVA without correction for violation of the assumption of sphericity. Thus report this line and the first line in the second row (Error) when the assumption is met, that is, when Mauchly's *W* test is *not significant (Sig. > .05)*.

Table 8.7 shows that there are significant differences between at least two measures of health locus of control (*F* = 88.14, *Sig.* = .000). The table also shows that almost 60 percent of the variance in Health Locus of Control (dependent variable) is due to occasions, or variance due to within-subject differences between the three measures (partial eta squared = .599).

The next three lines report the results of the correction tests, Greenhouse-Geisser, Huynh-Feldt, and lower-bound, respectively. Notice here that each correction test slightly reduces the actual degrees of freedom (*df* = 2). Because our data met the assumption of sphericity, we should report the results of the first lines (Sphericity Assumed). Note that all tests report similar results (*F* = 88.14, *Sig.* = .000).

For clarity, if sphericity was not met, we would still report the results of Sphericity Assumed because they are consistent with the results of the correction tests, especially Huynh-Feldt.

Table 8.8 reports the results of the third source of variability, subjects' variance (see figure 8.1). This variance is due to differences between subjects (e.g.,

Table 8.8:   Tests of Between-Subjects Effects-Subjects Variation

Tests of Between-Subjects Effects

Measure:MEASURE_1
Transformed Variable:Average

Source	Type III Sum of Squares	df	Mean Square	F	Sig.	Partial Eta Squared
Intercept	33211.250	1	33211.250	1686.648	.000	.966
Error	**1161.750**	**59**	**19.691**			

subject 1 and subject 2, subject 1 and subject 3, etc.). We are interested in only the *Sum of Squares, df,* and *Mean Square* of variances of Error (second line).

Table 8.9 displays the mean, standard error, and 95th confidence interval (lower and upper limits) for each measure of health locus of control. Remember, 1 is internal, 2 is powerful others, and 3 is chance health locus of control (see table 8.4).

Table 8.10 conveys the results of the Bonferroni post hoc test. As in ANOVA, Bonferroni compares each level of the dependent variable with each other level.

FIRST ROW AND FIRST LINE: The table shows a significant difference (*Sig.* = .000) between internal health locus of control (health = 1) and powerful others

Table 8.9:   Estimates of Descriptive Statistics of Measures of Health Locus of Control

Estimates

Measure:MEASURE_1

Health	Mean	Std. Error	95% Confidence Interval	
			Lower Bound	Upper Bound
1	14.000	.354	13.291	14.709
2	16.183	.518	15.146	17.220
3	10.567	.341	9.885	11.248

Table 8.10:   Results of Bonferroni Post Hoc Test

Pairwise Comparisons

Measure:MEASURE_1

(I) Health	(J) Health	Mean Difference (I-J)	Std. Error	Sig.[a]	95% Confidence Interval for Difference[a]	
					Lower Bound	Upper Bound
1	2	-2.183*	.483	.000	-3.374	-.992
	3	3.433*	.375	.000	2.510	4.356
2	1	2.183*	.483	.000	.992	3.374
	3	5.617*	.414	.000	4.595	6.638
3	1	-3.433*	.375	.000	-4.356	-2.510
	2	-5.617*	.414	.000	-6.638	-4.595

Based on estimated marginal means

*. The mean difference is significant at the .05 level.

a. Adjustment for multiple comparisons: Bonferroni.

health locus of control (health = 2). Participants reported 2.18 points (mean difference = −2.183) more, on average, on the powerful others health locus of control scale (mean = 16.183, see table 8.9) than on the internal health locus of control scale (mean = 14.00, see table 8.9).

FIRST ROW AND SECOND LINE: The table also shows a significant difference (*Sig.* = .000) between internal health locus of control (health = 1) and chance health locus of control (health = 3). On average, participants reported 3.43 points more (mean difference = 3.433) on the internal health locus of control scale (mean = 14.00, see table 8.9) than on the chance health locus of control scale (mean = 10.57, see table 8.9).

SECOND ROW AND SECOND LINE: The table shows a significant difference (*Sig.* = .000) between powerful others health locus of control (health = 2) and chance health locus of control (health = 3). On average, participants reported 5.62 points (mean difference = 5.617) more on the powerful others health locus of control scale (mean = 16.183, see table 8.9) than on the chance health locus of control scale (mean = 10.57, see table 8.9).

Note that the first line in the second row is redundant of the first line in the first row. Also note that the third row (both lines) is redundant of the second line in both the first and second rows.

Figure 8.5 displays a line graph comparing the means of the three measures of the health locus of control. As it appears in figure 8.5, powerful other health locus of control (2) has the highest mean score, followed by internal health locus of control and chance health locus of control.

Figure 8.5:   Means Plot for Measures of Health Locus of Control

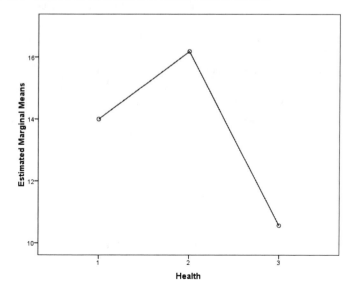

Step 5: Write the Results.

As you have done so far in the previous chapters, you begin this step by reporting evaluations of the assumptions of within-subjects ANOVA. Specifically, you evaluate the assumptions of normality, sphericity, and compound symmetry. You also state whether you conducted any data transformation.

Then, you should report the F ratio, degrees of freedom (df), and p value for within-subject variation of the uncorrected test (Sphericity Assumed), the corrected test (e.g., Huynh-Feldt), if any, or the multivariate test. Also, report the percentage of variance in the dependent variable that is accounted for by occasions. Moreover, report the results of the post hoc tests, if any, and the means and standard errors for all levels of the dependent variable. Finally, you may present the results in a graph that could help some readers to visualize the mean differences among all measures of occasions.

Writing the Results

The following presents the results of the within-subjects analysis of variance for measures of health locus of control among older Muslim American immigrants.

Evaluation of assumptions.   Prior to the repeated measures analysis, data were screened to ensure that the test's assumptions were met. Descriptive statistics, measures of skewness and kurtosis, histograms, and normal Q-Q plots were examined and showed that the assumption of normality was fulfilled among the three measures of health locus of control: internal, external, and chance. In addition, the results of Mauchly's W test show no significant differences between the variance of the three measures of health locus of control, thus satisfying the assumption of sphericity (Mauchly's $W = .91$, chi-square$_{(df = 2)} = 5.52, p > .05$).

Results of within-subjects ANOVA.   A one-way within-subjects ANOVA was used to examine the differences in health locus of control among a sample of 60 older Muslim American immigrants.

The results of repeated measures ANOVA show an overall significant difference between internal, powerful others, and chance health locus of control ($F_{(df = 2, 118)} = 88.14, p < .001, \eta^2 = .60$). The results of the multivariate Wilks' lambda test also show an overall significant difference between the three mean scores (Wilks' lambda $= .212$, $F_{(df = 2, 58)} = 107.55, p < .001, \eta^2 = .79$).

Note: If the assumption of sphericity was violated, we would report the results of one of the correction tests, as discussed earlier. For example, we may say, "The Huynh-Feldt test was utilized to adjust for the violation of the assumption of sphericity. The corrected results of the Huynh-Feldt test show an overall significant difference between . . . The results of the multivariate Wilks' lambda . . ."

In this study, the results of the Bonferroni pairwise comparisons show that all three measures of health locus of control were significantly different from each other. These results show that powerful others was significantly greater than both internal health locus of control ($p < .001$) and chance health locus of control ($p < .001$). In addition, internal health locus of control was significantly greater than chance health locus of control ($p < .001$). In other words, participants in this study significantly perceived that external causes (mean = 16.18, SE = .52) impact their current health, followed by internal causes (mean = 14.00, SE = .35) and then chance causes (mean = 10.57, SE = .34).

Finally, the results of the one-way repeated measures ANOVA show that almost 60 percent of the variance in health locus of control is accounted for by occasions, that is, within-subjects differences in the three measures.

Presentation of results in summary tables.   The summary tables for within-subjects ANOVA are similar to those of two-way ANOVA. The first table should convey the number of cases, mean, and standard error for each occasion. The second table should display the sum of squares, degrees of freedom, and mean squares for each source of variation and the overall F ratio and level of significance for occasions. Finally, it is recommended to report the overall results of the Wilks' lambda and the proportion of variance in the dependent variable accounted for by the occasions (η^2).

In this example, tables 8.11.A and 8.11.B and figure 8.5 display the results of within-subjects ANOVA.

Table 8.11.A: Results of One-Way Repeated Measures ANOVA—Descriptive Statistics

Locus of Control	n	M	SE
Internal Health	60	14.00	.35
External Health	60	16.18	.52
Chance Health	60	10.57	.34

Table 8.11.B: Results of One-Way Repeated Measures ANOVA—Summary Table

Source	SS	df	MS	F	p
Occasions[a]	962.03	2	481.02	88.14	.000
Subjects	1161.75	59	19.69		
Residuals	643.97	118	5.46		
Total	2767.75	179			

[a]Wilks' lambda = .212; $F_{(2, 58)} = 107.55$, $p < .001$; $\eta^2 = .60$

SECOND PRACTICAL EXAMPLE: MIXED BETWEEN-WITHIN-SUBJECTS ANALYSIS OF VARIANCE

This example will illustrate the utilization of mixed between-within-subjects ANOVA. We will use the same SPSS data file (Health Control) to examine the main effect discussed in the first example. Here, however, we will add a new independent variable (Gender) to the analysis. In other words, we will also examine if there are significant differences among males and females with regard to the three measures of health locus of control.

Therefore, we will utilize the mixed between-within-subjects ANOVA (two-way RANOVA; two independent variables: Occasions, or Times, and Gender). As said earlier, mixed between-within-subjects designs examine three research questions (effects). Therefore, in this example we will examine the following three research questions:

1. Are there significant differences between internal, external, and chance health locus of control among older Muslim American immigrants?

2. Are there significant differences between male and female older Muslim American immigrants with regard to their internal, external, and chance health locus of control?

3. Is there a significant interaction effect between gender and occasion on health locus of control levels among older Muslim American immigrants?

Hypothesis Testing

Step 1: State the Null and Alternative Hypotheses.

OCCASIONS (WITHIN-SUBJECTS) EFFECT (SAME AS IN FIRST EXAMPLE):

H_{o1}: There are no significant differences between internal (I), powerful others (P), and chance (C) health locus of control scores among older Muslim American immigrants.

$$\mu_I = \mu_P = \mu_C$$

H_{a1}: There are significant differences between internal, powerful others, and chance health locus of control scores among older Muslim American immigrants.

$$\mu_I \neq \mu_P \neq \mu_C; \text{ for at least two means}$$

GROUP (BETWEEN-GROUPS) EFFECT:

H_{o2}: There are no significant differences between male (M) and female (F) older Muslim American immigrants with regard to their internal (I), powerful others (P), and chance (C) health locus of control scores.

$$\mu_{MI} = \mu_{FI}; \mu_{MP} = \mu_{FP}; \mu_{MC} = \mu_{FC}$$

H_{a2}: There are significant differences between male (M) and female (F) older Muslim American immigrants with regard to their internal (I), powerful others (P), and chance (C) health locus of control scores.

$$\mu_{MI} \neq \mu_{FI}; \ \mu_{MP} \neq \mu_{FP}; \ \mu_{MC} \neq \mu_{FC}$$

INTERACTION (OCCASIONS BY GROUPS) EFFECT:

H_{o3}: There is not a significant interaction effect between gender and occasion on health locus of control scores among older Muslim American immigrants.

$$\mu_{MI} = \mu_{FI} = \mu_{MP} = \mu_{FP} = \mu_{MC} = \mu_{FC}$$

H_{a3}: There is a significant interaction effect between gender and occasion on health locus of control scores among older Muslim American immigrants.

$$\mu_{MI} \neq \mu_{FI} \neq \mu_{MP} \neq \mu_{FP} \neq \mu_{MC} \neq \mu_{FC}; \text{ for at least two means}$$

Step 2: Set the Criteria for Rejecting the Null Hypotheses.
We will set alpha at .05 ($\alpha = .05$). That is, reject H_o only if $p \leq .05$.

Step 3: Select the Appropriate Statistical Test.
The purpose of this mixed method is threefold: to examine (1) whether there are significant differences in health locus of control among older Muslim American immigrants, (2) whether there are significant differences between males and females on the three measures of health locus of control, and (3) whether there are significant interactions between occasions and gender on health locus of control.

In other words, we are interested in (1) within-subjects differences between internal, external, and chance health locus of control and (2) between-groups (subjects) differences on the three measures of health locus of control.

Therefore, we will consider mixed between-within-subjects analysis of variance to address the research hypotheses. However, to utilize this mixed design, we must examine the test's assumptions and whether they have been met. These assumptions include those assumptions evaluated in the first example and three more assumptions related to the addition of the between-subjects analysis. Thus we will evaluate these three assumptions. In addition, we will re-evaluate the assumption of sphericity because it may change due to the addition of the independent variable.

1. NORMAL DISTRIBUTION: In mixed between-within-subjects ANOVA, all measures of the dependent variable (internal, external, and chance health locus of control) for each level of the independent variable (male and female) should be normally distributed. In this example, we need to compute measures of skewness and kurtosis and inspect the histograms and

normal probability plots for internal, external (powerful others), and chance health locus of control for males as well as for females.

Measures of skewness and kurtosis, histograms, and normal probability plots can be generated in SPSS through the *Analyze, Descriptive Statistics,* and *Explore* commands, where you move all levels of the dependent variable (IHLC, PHLC, and CHLC) into the *Dependent List* box and the independent variable (Gender) into the *Factor List* box (see chapter 2 for SPSS "Explore" dialog box and commands).

SPSS Explore Syntax Commands

EXAMINE VARIABLES=IHLC PHLC CHLC BY GENDER
/PLOT HISTOGRAM NPPLOT
/STATISTICS DESCRIPTIVES
/CINTERVAL 95
/MISSING LISTWISE
/NOTOTAL.

Table 8.12 displays measures of skewness and kurtosis. Figures 8.6 through 8.11 display the histograms and normal probability plots for internal, powerful others, and chance health locus of control for male and female participants.

Dividing each skewness and kurtosis coefficient by its corresponding standard error shows that none of these coefficients is greater than twice its standard error. In other words, all calculations are within ±1.96, thus indicating that all histograms of the dependent variable for both genders approach the shape of a normal curve. Eyeballing the histograms and the normal probability plots also shows similar conclusions with minor deviation from normality in some cases, but not severe (e.g., see figure 8.8.B). Remember, when violation of normality occurs, consider data transformation as discussed in chapter 2.

Table 8.12:   Measures of Skewness and Kurtosis for Health by Gender

Statistics

GENDER		IHLC	PHLC	CHLC
Male	Valid	36	36	36
	Skewness	-.372	-.653	.145
	Std. Error of Skewness	.393	.393	.393
	Kurtosis	1.074	1.282	.609
	Std. Error of Kurtosis	.768	.768	.768
Female	Valid	24	24	24
	Skewness	.202	.089	.173
	Std. Error of Skewness	.472	.472	.472
	Kurtosis	.857	.643	1.127
	Std. Error of Kurtosis	.918	.918	.918

Figure 8.6:   Histogram and Q-Q Plot for Male—IHLC

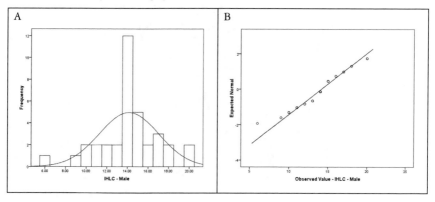

Figure 8.7:   Histogram and Q-Q Plot for Female—IHLC

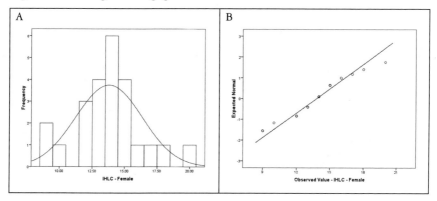

Figure 8.8:   Histogram and Q-Q Plot for Male—PHLC

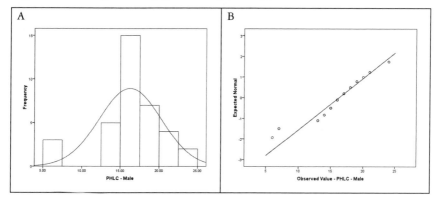

Figure 8.9:   Histogram and Q-Q Plot for Female—PHLC

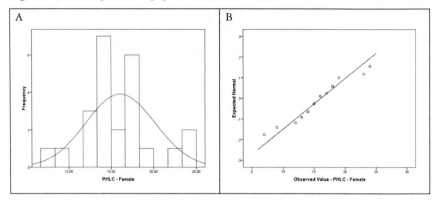

Figure 8.10:   Histogram and Q-Q Plot for Male—CHLC

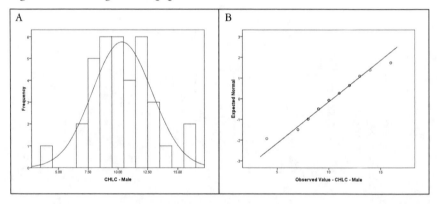

Figure 8.11:   Histogram and Q-Q Plot for Female—CHLC

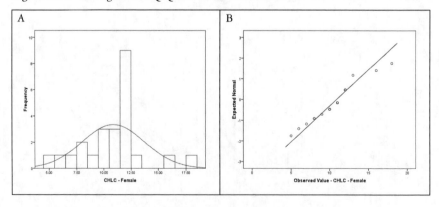

2. SPHERICITY: As in the previous example, we will inspect the results of Mauchly's W test. Table 8.13 displays these results.

Table 8.13 shows no significant differences between the variances of the three measures of health for both genders (Mauchly's W = .902, chi-square$_{(df = 2)}$ = 5.89, p > .05). Thus the assumption of sphericity is still met. *Remember, if,* on the other hand, it was violated, we would report the results of epsilon Huynh-Feldt; it has the highest correction factor (.95).

3. HOMOGENEITY OF VARIANCE: The variances of the dependent variable should be the same across all groups (male and female).

As with ANOVA and ANCOVA, we will evaluate this assumption by examining the results of Levene's test of equality of variances (produced along with the results of the mixed between-within-subjects ANOVA). Table 8.14 presents these results.

Table 8.14 shows that the variances of both males and females are the same on all three measures of health (p > .001). Thus the assumption of homogeneity of variances is met.

4. HOMOGENEITY OF VARIANCE-COVARIANCE MATRICES: As said, this assumption implies that covariance matrices of all measures of the dependent variables are the same across all groups. We will evaluate this assumption by inspecting the results of Box's M test (produced along with the results of the mixed design). Table 8.15 displays the results of Box's M test.

Table 8.13: Results of Mauchly's W Test of Sphericity

Mauchly's Test of Sphericity[b]

Measure:MEASURE_1

Within Subjects	Mauchly's W	Approx. Chi-Square	df	Sig.	Epsilon[a]		
					Greenhouse-Geisser	Huynh-Feldt	Lower-bound
Health	.902	5.891	2	.053	.911	0.95	.500

Tests the null hypothesis that the error covariance matrix of the orthonormalized transformed dependent variables is proportional to an identity matrix.

a. May be used to adjust the degrees of freedom for the averaged tests of significance. Corrected tests are displayed in the Tests of Within-Subjects Effects table.

b. Design: Intercept + GENDER
Within Subjects Design: Health

Table 8.14: Results of Levene's Test of Equality of Variances

Levene's Test of Equality of Error Variances[a]

	F	df1	df2	Sig.
IHLC	.120	1	58	.731
PHLC	.037	1	58	.848
CHLC	.068	1	58	.795

Tests the null hypothesis that the error variance of the dependent variable is equal across groups.

a. Design: Intercept + GENDER
Within Subjects Design: Health

Table 8.15:   Results of Box's M Test of Equality of Covariance Matrices

Box's Test of Equality of Covariance Matrices[a]

Box's M	6.049
F	.948
df1	6.000
df2	16318.844
Sig.	**.459**

Tests the null hypothesis that the observed covariance matrices of the dependent variables are equal across groups.

a. Design: Intercept + GENDER
Within Subjects Design: Health

The results of Box's M test show that the covariance matrices of all measures of health are equal across both genders ($p > .001$).

General Guideline

If you decide to report the results of the multivariate tests instead of the results of the repeated measures, follow this guideline:

Report the results of the multivariate Wilks' lambda test *if* Box's M test is *not significant* ($p > .001$).

Report the results of another multivariate test (e.g., Pillai's trace or Hotelling's trace) *if* Box's M test is *significant* ($p < .001$).

To conclude, data appear to meet all assumptions for mixed between-within-subjects ANOVA. If, on the other hand, some assumptions were violated, then the appropriate measures and/or alternative tests would be used as discussed earlier.

How to Use SPSS to Run Mixed Between-Within-Subjects ANOVA

Step 4: Compute the Mixed Between-Within-Subjects ANOVA.

Again, we will use SPSS to run the analysis. To conduct this mixed design analysis in SPSS, follow these steps:

1. Repeat steps 1 through 7 from the first example.

2. Click on *Gender,* and move it into the *Between-Subjects Factor(s)* box (see screen 8.6).

3. Click on *Options* to open the "Repeated Measures: Options" dialog box.

4. Highlight *Overall, Gender, Health,* and *Gender * Health* in the *Factor(s) and Factor Interactions* box, and click on the middle arrow to move them into the *Display Means For* box.

5. Check the *Compare Main Effects* box.

6. Click on the drop-down arrow for *Confidence Interval Adjustment,* and click on *Bonferroni.*

Screen 8.6:   SPSS Between-Within-Subjects Repeated Measures Dialog Box

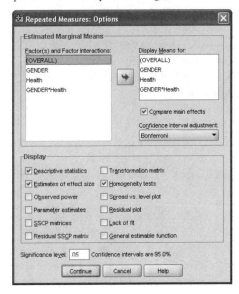

7.   Check the *Descriptive Statistics, Estimates of Effect Size,* and *Homogeneity Tests* boxes (see screen 8.7).

8.   Click on *Continue* to return to the "Repeated Measures" main menu.

9.   Click on *Plots* to go to the "Repeated Measures: Profile Plots" dialog box.

10. Click on *Gender* in the *Factors* box and move it into the *Separate Lines* box.

11. Click on *Health* in the *Factors* box and move it into the *Horizontal Axis* box.

12. Click on *Add* to move *Health * Gender* into the *Plots* box (see screen 8.8).

Screen 8.7:   SPSS Repeated Measures Options Dialog Box

Screen 8.8:   SPSS Repeated Measures Profile Plots Dialog Box

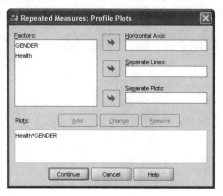

13.   Click on *Continue* to return to the "Repeated Measures" main menu.

14.   You can click on *Post Hoc* to request post hoc tests (this step is the same as in ANOVA). In this case, however, we do not need post hoc because the independent variable, Gender, has only two groups. As you may recall, post hoc tests are required only when there are more than two groups.

15.   Click on *OK*.

Mixed Between-Within-Subjects ANOVA SPSS Syntax Commands

GLM IHLC PHLC CHLC BY GENDER
/WSFACTOR=Health 3 Polynomial
/METHOD=SSTYPE(3)
/PLOT=PROFILE(GENDER*Health)
/EMMEANS=TABLES(OVERALL)
/EMMEANS=TABLES(GENDER) COMPARE ADJ(BONFERRONI)
/EMMEANS=TABLES(Health) COMPARE ADJ(BONFERRONI)
/EMMEANS=TABLES(GENDER*Health)
/PRINT=DESCRIPTIVE ETASQ HOMOGENEITY
/CRITERIA=ALPHA(.05)
/WSDESIGN=Health
/DESIGN=GENDER.

Reading the Output of Mixed Between-Within-Subjects ANOVA

These SPSS commands produce eighteen tables and one graph. Of them, three tables were already discussed: Box's M test (table 8.15), Mauchly's W test (table 8.13), and Levene's test of equality of variances (table 8.14). Of the remaining fifteen tables, six are unnecessary and thus will not be discussed. The other nine tables and the graph are discussed in the following.

Table 8.16 reports the levels of the independent variable, their SPSS value labels, and the number of participants in each group. Notice that the groups have unequal sample sizes (male = 36, female = 24). As said earlier, when groups have an unequal number of cases, the assumption of homogeneity of covariance matrices must be fulfilled. We examined this assumption in step 3 (Box's M test).

Table 8.17 displays the observed means, standard deviations, and number of cases for each measure of the dependent variable by each level of the independent variable (male and female) and for the total sample.

Notice that the mean scores and standard deviations for both males and females are similar on all levels of occasion: internal, powerful others, and chance health locus of control (e.g., first row, IHLC: Male: M = 14.14, SD = 2.89, n = 36; Female: M = 13.79, SD = 2.55, n = 24; Overall: M = 14.00, SD = 2.74, N = 60; etc.).

Table 8.18 displays the results of the multivariate tests. As said earlier, if we were to use this table as an alternative to the repeated measures ANOVA, we

Table 8.16:   Between-Subjects Factors

Between-Subjects Factors

		Value Label	N
GENDER	0	Male	36
	1	Female	24

Table 8.17:   Descriptive Statistics for Health by Gender

Descriptive Statistics

	GENDER	**Mean**	Std. Deviation	N
IHLC	**Male**	14.1389	2.88991	36
	Female	13.7917	2.55341	24
	Total	14.0000	2.74325	60
PHLC	**Male**	16.2500	4.02403	36
	Female	16.0833	4.08514	24
	Total	16.1833	4.01477	60
CHLC	**Male**	10.3611	2.49746	36
	Female	10.8750	2.86375	24
	Total	10.5667	2.63848	60

Table 8.18:   Results of the Multivariate Tests

Multivariate Tests[b]

Effect		Value	F	Hypothesis df	Error df	Sig.	Partial Eta Squared
Health	Pillai's Trace	.779	100.495[a]	2.000	57.000	.000	.779
	Wilks' Lambda	**.221**	**100.495[a]**	**2.000**	**57.000**	**.000**	.779
	Hotelling's Trace	3.526	100.495[a]	2.000	57.000	.000	.779
	Roy's Largest Root	3.526	100.495[a]	2.000	57.000	.000	.779
Health * GENDER	Pillai's Trace	.026	.772[a]	2.000	57.000	.467	.026
	Wilks' Lambda	**.974**	**.772[a]**	**2.000**	**57.000**	**.467**	**.026**
	Hotelling's Trace	.027	.772[a]	2.000	57.000	.467	.026
	Roy's Largest Root	.027	.772[a]	2.000	57.000	.467	.026

a. Exact statistic

b. Design: Intercept + GENDER
Within Subjects Design: Health

would report the results of Wilks' lambda because Box's M test was not signifi-cant. In general, the results of Wilks' lambda show an overall significant differ-ence between the three measures of health (first row, Health, and second line: Wilks' lambda = .22, $F_{(2, 57)}$ = 100.50, p < .001). The results of Wilks' lambda, on the other hand, show *no* significant health by gender interaction (second row, Health * Gender, and second line: Wilks' lambda = .97, $F_{(2, 57)}$ = .77, p = .467).

Table 8.19 displays the results of the within-subjects ANOVA tests. They include the uncorrected results (*sphericity* is *met*) and the corrected results (*spheric-ity* is *violated*). This table is similar to table 8.7 in the first example. However, in this example, it has three rows instead of two.

The first row (Health) is the same as in table 8.7, although the numbers are slightly different. It presents the results for the main effect of within-subjects variance. Because the assumption of sphericity was met, we will read the first line, Sphericity Assumed. These results show overall significant differences between measures of health locus of control ($F_{(df = 2, 116)}$ = 81.75, p = .000). The table also shows that 58.5 percent (partial eta squared = .585) of the within-subjects dif-ferences is accounted for by occasion.

The second row (Health * Gender) appears only with mixed design. It pre-sents the results for the interaction effect between occasions and gender. In other words, it examines the third research question/hypothesis. Again, because we reported the results of Sphericity Assumed in the first row, we must do the same here. The first line in the second row shows *no* significant occasion by gen-der interaction effect on health locus of control among participants in the study ($F_{(df = 2, 116)}$ = .54, p = .584). Table 8.19 shows that less than 1 percent (partial eta squared = .009) of the variance in health locus of control is due to the inter-action between occasion and gender.

The third row (Errors) is the same as the second row in table 8.7. It displays the amount of variance (sum of squares), degrees of freedom (*df*), and mean square of variances associated with the residuals (errors), the third source of variability.

Table 8.19:   Results of the Within-Subjects ANOVA

Tests of Within-Subjects Effects

Measure:MEASURE_1

Source		Type III Sum of Squares	df	Mean Square	F	Sig.	Partial Eta Squared
Health	Sphericity Assumed	899.272	2	449.636	81.748	.000	.585
	Greenhouse-Geisser	899.272	1.821	493.785	81.748	.000	.585
	Huynh-Feldt	899.272	1.909	470.958	81.748	.000	.585
	Lower-bound	899.272	1.000	899.272	81.748	.000	.585
Health * GENDER	Sphericity Assumed	5.939	2	2.969	.540	.584	.009
	Greenhouse-Geisser	5.939	1.821	3.261	.540	.568	.009
	Huynh-Feldt	5.939	1.909	3.110	.540	.576	.009
	Lower-bound	5.939	1.000	5.939	.540	.465	.009
Error(Health)	Sphericity Assumed	638.028	116	5.500			
	Greenhouse-Geisser	638.028	105.628	6.040			
	Huynh-Feldt	638.028	110.748	5.761			
	Lower-bound	638.028	58.000	11.000			

Table 8.20:   Results of the Between-Subjects ANOVA

Tests of Between-Subjects Effects

Measure:MEASURE_1
Transformed Variable:Average

Source	Type III Sum of Squares	df	Mean Square	F	Sig.	Partial Eta Squared
Intercept	31882.800	1	31882.800	1591.739	.000	.965
GENDER	.000	1	.000	.000	1.000	.000
Error	1161.750	58	20.030			

Table 8.20 conveys the results of the between-subjects (or group) effects. It is similar to one-way ANOVA. It examines whether there is an overall significant difference between the levels of the independent variable on the dependent variable (that is, the second research question/hypothesis). We are interested only in the second line, Gender.

The table shows *no* significant difference between male and female participants with regard to health locus of control (second line, Gender: $F_{(df = 1, 58)}$ = .000, p = 1.00). Table 8.20 shows that gender accounted for no variance in health locus of control (partial eta squared = .000).

Table 8.21 presents the estimated means, standard errors, and 95th confidence interval of overall health locus of control for males and females. This table usually follows the tests of between-subjects effect (table 8.20). The table shows that both genders do indeed have equal scores on health locus of control (which is why gender was not significant in table 8.20).

Note: When there are more than two groups in the independent variable, you should read the Bonferroni pairwise comparison table. It was omitted here because Gender has only two groups.

Table 8.22 presents the means, standard errors, and 95th confidence interval for all measures of health locus of control. It is the same as table 8.9 in the

Table 8.21:   Descriptive Statistics for Health by Gender

Estimates

Measure:MEASURE_1

GENDER	Mean	Std. Error	95% Confidence Interval	
			Lower Bound	Upper Bound
Male	13.583	.431	12.721	14.445
Female	13.583	.527	12.528	14.639

Table 8.22:   Descriptive Statistics for Health by Occasion

Estimates

Measure:MEASURE_1

Health	Mean	Std. Error	95% Confidence Interval	
			Lower Bound	Upper Bound
1	13.965	.364	13.237	14.694
2	16.167	.533	15.099	17.234
3	10.618	.349	9.919	11.317

first example, with slightly different values due to the adjustment for the independent variable. As in the first example, table 8.22 shows that powerful others has the highest mean (mean = 16.17, SE = .53), followed by internal health locus of control (mean = 13.97, SE = .36) and then chance health locus of control (mean = 10.62, SE = .35).

Table 8.23 displays the results of the Bonferroni pairwise comparisons. This table is the same as table 8.10 in the first example, with slightly different values. Table 8.23 shows, as in the first example, significant differences between all measures of health locus of control (*Sig.* = .000), with powerful others indicated as the most highly perceived locus of control, followed by internal locus of control and then chance locus of control.

Table 8.24 is the last in the SPSS mixed between-within-subjects ANOVA output. It is the same as table 8.17; however, this table displays the estimated means of measures of health locus of control across the two genders (interaction means).

Table 8.24 shows that males and females reported different mean scores on measures of health locus of control within each group (estimated means of IHLC, PHLC, and CHLC among males are different: 14.14, 16.25, and 10.36, respectively). On the other hand, males and females reported similar mean scores on

Table 8.23: Results of Bonferroni Pairwise Comparisons

Pairwise Comparisons

Measure:MEASURE_1

(I) Health	(J) Health	Mean Difference (I-J)	Std. Error	Sig.[a]	95% Confidence Interval for Difference[a] Lower Bound	Upper Bound
1	2	-2.201[*]	.497	.000	-3.428	-.975
	3	3.347[*]	.381	.000	2.407	4.288
2	1	2.201[*]	.497	.000	.975	3.428
	3	5.549[*]	.424	.000	4.502	6.595
3	1	-3.347[*]	.381	.000	-4.288	-2.407
	2	-5.549[*]	.424	.000	-6.595	-4.502

Based on estimated marginal means

*. The mean difference is significant at the .05 level.

a. Adjustment for multiple comparisons: Bonferroni.

Table 8.24: Descriptive Statistics for Gender by Occasions

GENDER * Health

Measure:MEASURE_1

GENDER	Health	Mean	Std. Error	95% Confidence Interval Lower Bound	Upper Bound
Male	1	14.139	.460	13.218	15.060
	2	16.250	.675	14.899	17.601
	3	10.361	.441	9.477	11.245
Female	1	13.792	.564	12.663	14.920
	2	16.083	.826	14.429	17.737
	3	10.875	.541	9.793	11.957

Figure 8.12:   Means Plot

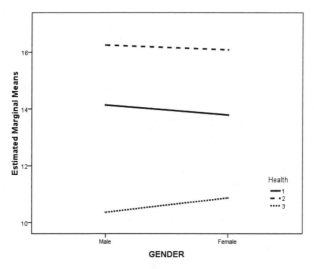

each measure of health locus of control (males and females have similar IHLC: 14.14 and 13.79, respectively). Recall that both Wilks' lambda and sphericity assumed tests show significant within-group differences but no significant gender by occasion interaction.

Finally, figure 8.12 displays three line graphs comparing males and females on the three means of measures of health locus of control. Figure 8.12 shows significant differences among the three measures overall. On the other hand, the figure shows no differences between the two genders on each measure.

Step 5: Write the Results of Mixed Designs.

The principles of writing the results of the mixed between-within-subjects ANOVA are the same as within-subjects ANOVA. Here, however, you should also address the evaluation of the assumptions of homogeneity of variances and homogeneity of covariance matrices. In addition, you should address all effects examined by the mixed between-within-subjects ANOVA: occasions, groups, and interaction effects.

Writing the Results of Mixed Between-Within-Subjects ANOVA

The following presents the results of the mixed between-within-subjects analysis of variance for measures of health locus of control among older Muslim American immigrants based on their gender.

Evaluation of assumptions.   Prior to conducting the analysis, data were screened to ensure that the assumptions of this mixed design were fulfilled.

Descriptive statistics, including skewness and kurtosis coefficients, histograms, and normal Q-Q plots, were examined for internal, powerful others, and chance health locus of control for both males and females. These measures and plots showed that the assumption of normality was fulfilled on the three measures of health locus of control across gender. In addition, the results of Mauchly's W test show that the assumption of sphericity is met (Mauchly's W = .0902, chi-square$_{(df = 2)}$ = 5.89, p > .05). Furthermore, the results of Levene's test of equality of variances (p > .05) and Box's M test (F = .95, p > .05) show that the assumptions of both homogeneity of variances and homogeneity of covariance matrices, respectively, were fulfilled.

Results of mixed between-within-subjects ANOVA.

A two-way repeated measures ANOVA (two-way RANOVA) was utilized to examine the differences between internal, powerful others, and chance health locus of control among older Muslim American immigrants and whether these measures are different based on gender.

WITHIN-SUBJECTS EFFECT: The results of the two-way RANOVA tests of within-subjects effects show an overall significant difference between internal, powerful others, and chance health locus of control ($F_{(df = 2, 116)}$ = 81.75, p < .001, η^2 = .59). The results of the multivariate Wilks' lambda test also show an overall significant difference between the three mean scores (Wilks' lambda = .22, $F_{(2, 57)}$ = 100.50, p < .001, η^2 = .78).

The results of the Bonferroni pairwise comparisons show that all three measures of health locus of control were significantly different from each other. These results show that scores for powerful others were significantly greater than both internal health locus of control (p < .001) and chance health locus of control (p < .001) scores. In addition, internal health locus of control scores were significantly greater than chance health locus of control scores (p < .001). In other words, participants in this study significantly perceived that external causes (mean = 16.17, SE = .53) impact their current health, followed by internal causes (mean = 13.97, SE = .36), followed by chance causes (mean = 10.62, SE = .35).

Overall, about 59 percent of the variance in health locus of control is accounted for by occasions.

GROUP (BETWEEN-SUBJECTS) EFFECT: The results of the two-way RANOVA tests of between-subjects effects show no significant differences between males and females on their overall health locus of control ($F_{(df = 1, 58)}$ = .00, p > .05, η^2 = .00). Both male and female participants reported similar mean scores on overall health locus of control (male: M = 13.58, SE = .43; female: M = 13.58, SE = .53). Overall, the results show that gender did not contribute any percentage to the variance in health locus of control.

INTERACTION (OCCASION BY GENDER) EFFECT: The results of the two-way RANOVA tests of within-subjects effects show no significant interaction between occasion and gender on health locus of control ($F_{(df = 2, 116)}$ = .54, p > .05,

$\eta^2 = .01$). The results of the multivariate Wilks' lambda test also show no significant occasion by gender interaction on health locus of control (Wilks' lambda $= .97$, $F_{(2, 57)} = .77$, $p > .05$, $\eta^2 = .03$).

Presentation of the results in summary tables.   Presentation of the results of the mixed between-within-subjects ANOVA in summary tables is the same as in two-way ANOVA. The first table should display the number of cases, mean score, and standard error for each level of the independent variable on each occasion. The table should also display the overall number of cases, mean, and standard error for each level of the independent variable and each occasion. The second table should present the sum of squares, degrees of freedom, and mean square for each source of variation. The table should also report the overall F ratio and level of significance for occasion, independent variable, and their interaction. Finally, the overall results of Wilks' lambda should also be reported.

In this example, tables 8.25.A and 8.25.B and figure 8.12 display the results of within-subjects ANOVA.

Description of tables.   The following describes in more detail the information presented in both table 8.25.A and 8.25.B:

1.   Table 8.25.A reports the number of cases, estimated mean, and standard error for each level of the dependent variable (Health) by each level of the independent variable (Gender).

Table 8.25.A: Results of Two-Way Repeated Measures ANOVA—Descriptive Statistics

Health	Male			Female			Total		
	n	Mean	SE	n	Mean	SE	N	Mean	SE
Internal	36	14.14	.46	24	13.79	.56	60	13.97	.36
External	36	16.25	.68	24	16.08	.83	60	16.17	.53
Chance	36	10.36	.44	24	10.88	.54	60	10.62	.35
Total	108	13.58	.43	72	13.58	.53	180	13.58	.34

Table 8.25.B: Results of Two-Way Repeated Measures ANOVA—Summary Table

Source	SS	df	MS	F	p
Occasions[a]	899.27	2	449.64	81.75	.000
Gender	.000	1	.000	.00	1.000
Interaction[b]	5.94	2	2.97	.54	.584
Subjects	1161.75	58	20.03		
Residuals	638.02	116	5.50		
Total	2704.99	179			

[a]Wilks' lambda $= .22$; $F_{(2, 57)} = 100.50$, $p < .001$; $\eta^2 = .59$
[b]Wilks' lambda $= .97$; $F_{(2, 57)} = .77$, $p > .05$; $\eta^2 = .03$

2.   The Total column in table 8.25.A reports the number of cases, estimated mean, and standard error for each level of the dependent variable (Health) regardless of the levels of the independent variable (Gender). Notice that the number of cases is the sum of the number of cases for all levels of the independent variable (e.g., total cases for internal = 36 + 24 = 60).

3.   The Total row in table 8.25.A reports the number of cases, estimated mean, and standard error for each level of the independent variable (Gender) regardless of the levels of the dependent variable (Health). Again, the total number of cases is the sum of the number of cases for all levels of the dependent variable (e.g., total cases for male = 36 + 36 + 36 = 108).

4.   The Total–Total joint cells in Table 8.25.A report the total number of cases (N), grand mean for all the measures of the dependent variable, and standard error for all the measures for all cases.

5.   In table 8.25.B, the variance for the total (SS–Total) is simply the sum of all sum of squares. Also, the number of degrees of freedom for the Total is the sum of all degrees of freedom, or simply, $N - 1$.

SUMMARY

Chapter 8 presented and discussed repeated measures analysis of variance (RANOVA), an advanced technique of the dependent t-test and analysis of variance. It is used for longitudinal research to examine the differences in the mean scores of three or more repeated measures of the same subjects. In addition, RANOVA can be used to examine the difference in three or more related measures of the same subject or the differences in subjects measured under three or more conditions.

The chapter discussed two types of RANOVA: within-subjects ANOVA and mixed between-within-subjects ANOVA. The first examines variations in the dependent variable due to within-subjects difference because of the repeated measures, related topics, and different conditions (occasions). The second type, mixed between-within-subjects ANOVA, as its name implies, combines both between-subjects ANOVA and within-subjects ANOVA. It examines not only within-subjects variations due to the repeated measures but also variations due to differences between groups. In addition, this mixed design allows researchers to examine variations in the dependent variable due to the interaction between groups and repeated measures (occasions).

Chapter 8 then discussed the advantages of RANOVA. As an advantage over ANOVA, RANOVA examines not only between-subjects variability but also within-subjects variability. This examination, in turn, reduces the likelihood of making type I error and increases the statistical power of the test.

Next, chapter 8 discussed research questions and hypotheses examined by each type of RANOVA. As said, within-subjects ANOVA examines one research question/hypothesis. On the other hand, the number of research questions and hypotheses examined by mixed design depends on the number of independent variables examined. For example, with only one independent variable, there are three hypotheses examining the within-subjects variability, one the between-subjects variability, and one the interaction variability (see the second practical example).

The chapter then discussed the assumptions of the RANOVA. They are the same assumptions as the dependent t-test and ANOVA. These assumptions include representative sample, continuous data, normal distributions, and sample size. In addition, RANOVA requires two major assumptions: sphericity and compound symmetry. The first is equivalent to homogeneity of variances in ANOVA, yet it compares the variances of the difference scores. The second refers to the equality of the covariances of all pairs of difference scores. Finally, mixed designs require that the covariance-variance matrices are equal.

Next, the chapter presented the post hoc tests, which allow researchers to compare not only group differences like in ANOVA (Whites with African Americans, Whites with Asians, etc.) but also all possible pairs of the dependent variable (pretest with posttest, pretest with follow-up, etc.). As in ANCOVA, these tests are known as multiple comparisons tests.

Finally, chapter 8 presented two examples illustrating the use of both types of ANOVA, within-subjects RANOVA and mixed between-within-subjects ANOVA. In each example, we examined the test assumptions, discussed how to use the SPSS main menu and syntax commands, illustrated how to write the results of RANOVA, and presented the results in summary tables.

Chapter 9 will introduce a new way of analyzing multiple variables in a single analysis. This technique is the multivariate analysis of variances (MANOVA). The chapter will discuss the purpose of MANOVA, its advantages, assumptions, research questions, and hypotheses. It will also present a detailed example from real data illustrating the utilization of MANOVA in social sciences research.

PRACTICAL EXERCISES

As part of its requirements for admission of international students to its undergraduate programs, a community college admissions office administered the English as a Second Language (ESL) proficiency test to 60 international applicants (30 males and 30 females). The test measures applicants' ability to speak, read, and write in English. The test is used to determine the level of English proficiency for applicants in order to place them in the appropriate English course.

Total scores in each area range between 5 and 40, with higher scores indicating greater proficiency in the particular area. The following are the raw scores of male and female applicants on the three areas of English proficiency.

Gender	Speaking	Writing	Reading	Gender	Speaking	Writing	Reading
Male	10	17	10	Female	11	10	16
Male	12	10	10	Female	12	16	10
Male	12	10	28	Female	15	15	14
Male	15	11	11	Female	16	14	15
Male	17	17	14	Female	17	10	13
Male	17	14	12	Female	18	13	10
Male	18	15	13	Female	18	11	11
Male	19	20	16	Female	21	14	19
Male	21	14	16	Female	22	20	13
Male	22	15	10	Female	22	12	30
Male	22	19	19	Female	23	18	21
Male	23	24	14	Female	23	18	15
Male	24	10	20	Female	24	10	14
Male	25	12	13	Female	26	14	23
Male	26	18	18	Female	26	16	20
Male	26	16	14	Female	26	11	21
Male	26	13	18	Female	27	19	20
Male	27	10	14	Female	27	11	10
Male	28	17	17	Female	28	15	17
Male	28	18	21	Female	28	14	19
Male	28	14	18	Female	29	11	25
Male	29	15	18	Female	29	17	19
Male	29	15	18	Female	30	13	18
Male	30	13	23	Female	30	14	16
Male	30	14	19	Female	30	22	17
Male	25	12	13	Female	26	14	23
Male	26	18	18	Female	26	16	20
Male	26	16	14	Female	26	11	21
Male	26	13	18	Female	27	19	20
Male	27	10	14	Female	27	11	10

Part 1

RESEARCH QUESTION: Are there significant differences between speaking, writing, and reading English among international students?

1. Enter the raw data into an SPSS program.

2. State the null and alternative hypotheses.

3. What statistical test(s) will you utilize to examine the null hypothesis(es)? Why? Discuss your answer in detail.

4. Write the SPSS syntax file for the test statistic.

5. Run the statistical test you chose in question 3.

6. What is your decision with regard to the null hypothesis(es)? Discuss your answer in detail.

7. Present the results in summary table(s) and graph(s).

Part 2

RESEARCH QUESTION: Are there significant differences in the levels of English proficiency between international male and female students?

1. State the null and alternative hypotheses.

2. What statistical test(s) will you utilize to examine the null hypotheses? Why? Discuss your answer in detail.

3. Write the SPSS syntax file for the test statistic.

4. Run the statistical test you chose in question 2.

5. What is your decision with regard to the null hypotheses? Discuss your answer in detail.

6. Present the results in summary table(s) and graph(s).

Multivariate Analysis of Variance and Covariance

LEARNING OBJECTIVES

1. Understand the purpose of multivariate analysis of variance (MANOVA) and covariance (MANCOVA)
2. Understand the advantages of MANOVA and MANCOVA
3. Understand the sources of variation in MANOVA and MANCOVA
4. Understand the multivariate tests of MANOVA and MANCOVA
5. Understand the post hoc tests of MANOVA and MANCOVA
6. Understand the research questions and hypotheses examined by MANOVA and MANCOVA
7. Understand the assumptions underlying MANOVA and MANCOVA
8. Understand how to use SPSS to compute the coefficients of MANOVA and MANCOVA
9. Understand how to interpret and present the results of MANOVA and MANCOVA

DATA SET (APPENDIX)

Mental Health

INTRODUCTION

Up to this point, this book has reviewed and discussed a number of bivariate statistical techniques (Pearson's r correlation, Student's t-tests, ANOVA, chi-square test of association, and simple linear regression). The purpose of these statistical tests is to examine the relationship between one independent variable and one dependent variable. Next, the book discussed five advanced statistical techniques (multiple regression analysis, logistic regression analysis, two-way

ANOVA, two-way ANCOVA, and repeated measures ANOVA). As said, the purpose of these tests is to examine the relationship between multiple independent variables and *one* dependent variable. In other words, all tests discussed so far focus on the relationship between one or more independent variables and only *one* dependent variable and, in one case, one or more covariances (two-way ANCOVA).

Social sciences researchers sometimes, however, examine several outcome (dependent) variables simultaneously and whether they are affected by one or more independent variable(s). For example, a clinical researcher was interested in the differences in overall well-being among immigrants based on their gender and level of education, just to name two factors. The researcher was also interested in *ruling out* any differences on immigrants' well-being due to their age and socioeconomic status.

For this purpose, the researcher conceptualized well-being as immigrants' life satisfaction, self-esteem, and levels of depression. The researcher then decided to select a random sample of 100 immigrants from four local community centers and asked them to complete three standardized measures on life satisfaction, self-esteem, and depression. Participants also reported their gender, age, level of education, and socioeconomic status. After data collection was completed, entered in a statistical program, and checked for missing values and outliers (see chapter 2), the researcher began to consider what statistical test(s) to use.

Based on what this book has discussed so far, the researcher could consider conducting three tests of two-way ANOVA, one for gender and education on life satisfaction, another for gender and education on self-esteem, and a third for gender and education on depression. Moreover, to *rule out* the effect of age and socioeconomic status on well-being, the researcher could use three tests of a two-way ANCOVA instead of ANOVA.

However, as you may already know, conducting multiple tests on the same data is more likely to inflate type I error (rejecting the null hypothesis when in fact it is true) and thus leads to incorrect decisions. Furthermore, three two-way ANOVA or ANCOVA tests may examine the differences in each variable separately based on participants' gender and education, but they will not address the main purpose of the study, differences in the overall well-being, which is a *composite* of the three variables. Thus the researcher needs a more advanced and comprehensive technique that not only overcomes these problems but also has a greater statistical power than the ordinary ANOVA or ANCOVA tests.

This chapter will introduce and discuss two new statistical techniques that allow researchers to examine group differences on a composite variable of two or more dependent variables and, at the same time, control for the effect of one or more extraneous factors. These techniques are the *multivariate analysis of variance* and the *multivariate analysis of covariance*.

MULTIVARIATE ANALYSIS OF VARIANCE AND COVARIANCE

Purpose

Multivariate analysis of variance (MANOVA) and covariance (MANCOVA) are probably the most used multivariate techniques in social sciences research. They are extensions of ordinary ANOVA and ANCOVA, respectively. The word *multivariate* implies the simultaneous analysis of several dependent variables.

Thus the purpose of MANOVA is to examine the mean differences between levels of *one or more* independent variables on *two or more* dependent variables (several dependent variables).

As in MANOVA, the purpose of MANCOVA is to examine mean differences between levels of *one or more* independent variables on *two or more* dependent variables while controlling (holding constant) for one or more extraneous variables.

In other words, the purpose of MANOVA and MANCOVA is the same as ANOVA and ANCOVA, respectively. However, MANOVA and MANCOVA consider *multiple* dependent variables, outcome measures.

The following are examples of MANOVA:

1. Are there significant differences between Caucasian, African American, and Hispanic students with regard to their overall GRE scores (quantitative, analytical, and verbal tests)?
2. Are there significant differences in the overall levels of well-being (life satisfaction, self-esteem, and depression) based on immigrants' gender and levels of education?

The following are examples of MANCOVA:

1. Controlling for the effect of financial status and parents' education, are there significant differences between Caucasian, African American, and Hispanic students with regard to their overall GRE scores (quantitative, analytical, and verbal tests)?
2. Controlling for age and socioeconomic status, are there significant differences in the overall levels of well-being (life satisfaction, self-esteem, and depression) based on immigrants' gender and levels of education?

As with ANOVA and ANCOVA, MANOVA and MANCOVA can be utilized to examine differences on several dependent variables on one independent variable, two independent variables, or several independent variables. Table 9.1 compares multivariate analysis of variance and covariance with bivariate analysis of variance and covariance.

Advantages

Multivariate analysis of variance and covariance have several advantages over the ordinary analysis of variance and covariance. These advantages include the following:

Table 9.1:   Comparisons of ANOVA and MANOVA

Test	# of IVs	# of DVs	# of COVs
One-Way ANOVA	1 categorical	1 continuous	0
One-Way ANCOVA	1 categorical	1 continuous	1+ continuous
Two-Way ANOVA	2 categorical	1 continuous	0
Two-Way ANCOVA	2 categorical	1 continuous	1+ continuous
Factorial ANOVA	3+ categorical	1 continuous	0
Factorial ANCOVA	3+ categorical	1 continuous	1+ continuous
One-Way MANOVA	1 categorical	2+ continuous	0
One-Way MANCOVA	1 categorical	2+ continuous	1+ continuous
Two-Way MANOVA	2 categorical	2+ continuous	0
Two-Way MANCOVA	2 categorical	2+ continuous	1+ continuous
Factorial MANOVA	3+ categorical	2+ continuous	0
Factorial MANCOVA	3+ categorical	2+ continuous	1+ continuous

1. As the name implies, MANOVA and MANCOVA allow researchers to examine multiple dependent variables in one shot without the need to conduct multiple ordinary ANOVA or ANCOVA tests.

2. Both MANOVA and MANCOVA protect for the inflation of type I error. When several dependent variables are considered for analysis, multivariate analysis mathematically creates one composite variable of a linear combination (centroids) of all dependent variables. It then compares all levels of the independent variable(s) on this composite variable (MANOVA), while adjusting for the effect of the control variables (MANCOVA). This method eliminates the need to conduct multiple ordinary ANOVA or ANCOVA tests and thus protects against the inflation of type I error.

    For example, with three dependent variables and one categorical variable, three one-way ANOVA/ANCOVA tests would be needed. However, with three one-way ANOVA/ANCOVA tests and alpha is .05, the probability of making type I error (*alpha*) would increase to $[1 - (1 - .05)^3 = .14]$ .14, instead of .05 (Abu-Bader, 2006). However, with one composite variable, only one test (MANOVA/MANCOVA) that will examine the differences among all levels of the independent variable is needed.

3. Both MANOVA and MANCOVA allow researchers to examine not only group differences on each dependent variable but also group differences on the combined construct: centroids of all dependent variables (e.g., overall well-being, overall GRE).

4. Creating a composite variable of the centroids of all dependent variables maximizes the differences between levels of the independent variable(s) on the dependent variables. In such cases, MANOVA and MANCOVA are more likely to capture group differences that otherwise would not be captured by ordinary ANOVA/ANCOVA tests.

    In addition to these advantages over ordinary ANOVA/ANCOVA, MANCOVA has two extra advantages over MANOVA:

1. MANCOVA allows researchers to control for extraneous variables that are believed to affect the relationship between the independent variables and the composite dependent variable.

2. Unlike MANOVA, MANCOVA examines the variations in the composite dependent variable due to extraneous variables, which reduces the sampling error, within-subjects variance. This reduction in sampling error, in turn, increases the statistical power of the test.

Sources of Variance

As with ordinary ANOVA, the variance (SS) in MANOVA is partitioned into two sources of variability: *between-subjects* variability (SS_B) and *within-subjects* variability (SS_W). In MANCOVA, however, there is a third source of variability due to the control variables (SS_{COV}).

The *between-subjects* variability, as said, is the variation in the dependent variable which is accounted for by each independent variable (IV) and their interactions (first IV by second IV, etc.). The dependent variable is the composite variable in MANOVA and adjusted composite variable in MANCOVA.

Total Between Sum of Squares

$$SS_B = SS_{BIV1} + SS_{BIV2} \cdots + SS_{BIVK} + SS_{BIV1 * IV2 * \ldots * IVK}$$

SS_B = between-subjects sum of square variance

$IV_1, IV_2, \ldots IV_K$ = first, second, ... and K independent variable

---

The *within-subjects* variability is the error variance (residuals). It is the variation in the dependent variable (DV) (the composite variable in MANOVA and adjusted composite variable in MANCOVA) which is due to the differences between subjects within each group within each independent variable.

A *composite variable* in MANOVA/MANCOVA, however, consists of multiple dependent variables. In other words, each subject has multiple scores, one for each dependent variable. Thus the *within-subjects* variation is also partitioned into variations in each dependent variable due to differences between subjects within each group within each independent variable.

Total Within Sum of Squares

$$SS_W = SS_{WDV1} + SS_{WDV2} + \ldots + SS_{WDVK}$$

SS_W = within-subjects sum of square variance

$DV_1, DV_2, \ldots DV_K$ = first, second, ... and K dependent variable

---

In MANOVA, the sum of both variances equals the *total variance* (SS_T).

Total Sum of Squares

$$SS_T = SS_W + SS_B$$

On the other hand, in MANCOVA, the *total variance* (SS_T) equals the sum of between-subjects variance, within-subjects variance, and covariate variance.

Total Sum of Squares

$$SS_T = SS_W + SS_B + SS_{COV}$$

Mathematically, MANOVA computes the variance due to each source by calculating a series of algebra matrices: one column matrix for the scores of each dependent variable, one column matrix for each group in each independent variable, one column matrix for each cell consisting of the cell's mean, and a single matrix consisting of the grand mean for each dependent variable. Next, matrices of difference scores are computed by subtracting each matrix from another matrix. These matrices are then used to compute the between-subjects variance matrix and the error variance (within-subjects variance) matrix. The sum of both matrices equals the matrix of the total variance.

MANOVA Total Sum of Squares

$$T = B + W$$

T = sum-of-square and cross-product matrix (SSCP)
B = between sum-of-square and cross-product matrix
W = within sum-of-square and cross-product matrix

MANCOVA also follows the same mathematical procedures; however, all matrices are first adjusted to accommodate the effects of each control variable on the composite dependent variable.

MANCOVA Total Sum of Squares

$$T^* = B^* + W^*$$

T^* = adjusted sum-of-square and cross-product matrix (SSCP)
B^* = adjusted between sum-of-square and cross-product matrix
W^* = adjusted within sum-of-square and cross-product matrix

Multivariate Tests

Multivariate analysis of variance and covariance use a number of multivariate tests to examine group differences and their interactions on the composite dependent variable. These tests include *Pillai-Bartlett trace, Wilks' lambda, Hotelling-Lawley trace,* and *Roy's largest root.* The differences between these tests relate to their robustness to violations of the test's assumptions and their mathematical computations.

Pillai-Bartlett trace.   Simply known as Pillai's trace, it is, perhaps, the most reported multivariate test when the assumptions of homogeneity of variance-covariance matrices and homogeneity of variances are violated. Pillai's trace is also more robust to violation of the assumption of univariate and multivariate normality. Moreover, Pillai's trace has greater reliability over other multivariate tests and provides greater protection against the inflation of type I error when small sample sizes are used (Foster, Barkus, & Yavorsky, 2006; Tabachnick & Fidell, 2007).

Mathematically, Pillai's trace is the ratio of the between-subjects variance-covariance matrix and the total variance-covariance matrix (adjusted matrices in MANCOVA). It ranges between 0 and 1, where the closer it is to 1, the stronger the relationships between the independent and dependent variables. In a sense, Pillai's trace value is the same as the partial eta squared value: proportion of variance in the dependent variable accounted for by the independent variable.

$$PT = \frac{SS_{B1}}{SS_{T1}} * \frac{SS_{B2}}{SS_{T2}} * \ldots * \frac{SS_{Bk}}{SS_{Tk}} = \frac{B}{T}$$

PT = Pillai's trace
SS_B = within sum of squares of variance for first, second, . . . and K
      dependent variable
SS_T = total sum of squares of variance for first, second, . . . and K dependent variable

Note: MANCOVA uses the adjusted matrices.

Wilks' lambda.   Counter to Pillai's trace, Wilks' lambda is the most reported multivariate test when the assumptions of homogeneity of variance-covariance matrices and homogeneity of variances are fulfilled. It is the multivariate *F* ratio, which is analogous to the univariate *F* ratio in ordinary ANOVA and ANCOVA. It examines the overall group differences on the linear combination of all dependent variables. It signifies the proportion of variance in the composite dependent variable that is *not* accounted for by the main and interaction effects of the independent variables. In other words, "1 – *Wilks' lambda*" equals the proportion of variance in the composite dependent variable that is accounted for by the main and interaction effects of the independent variables.

Mathematically, Wilks' lambda is the ratio of the error variance-covariance matrix and the effect variance-covariance matrix. It ranges between 0 and 1, where the closer it is to 0, the stronger the relationships between the independent and dependent variables are. In other words, the closer Wilks' lambda is to 1, the greater the proportion of the variance accounted for by the main and interaction effects.

$$\Lambda = \frac{SS_{W1}}{SS_{T1}} * \frac{SS_{W2}}{SS_{T2}} * \ldots * \frac{SS_{Wk}}{SS_{Tk}} = \frac{W}{T}$$

Λ = Wilks' lambda

SS_W = within sum of squares of variance for first, second, . . . and K dependent variable

SS_T = total sum of squares of variance for first, second, . . . and K dependent variable

Note: MANCOVA uses the adjusted matrices.

Hotelling-Lawley trace. Also known as Hotelling's trace or Hotelling's T^2, it is equivalent to the *t* value of the independent *t*-test. It examines the mean difference among *only* two groups on the composite variable of the linear combination of all dependent variables. In other words, it is appropriate for reporting only when the independent variable(s) are dichotomous (two groups).

$$HT = \frac{SS_{B1}}{SS_{W1}} * \frac{SS_{B2}}{SS_{W2}} * \ldots * \frac{SS_{Bk}}{SS_{Wk}} = \frac{B}{W}$$

HT = Hotelling's trace

SS_B = between sum of squares of variance for first, second, . . . and K dependent variable

SS_W = within sum of squares of variance for first, second, . . . and K dependent variable

Note: MANCOVA uses the adjusted matrices.

Roy's largest root. It is similar to Pillai's trace test. However, it first evaluates the loading (eigenvalues or correlation) of each dependent variable on the linear combination of all dependent variables (composite variable) and then computes the ratio of the between-subjects variance-covariance matrix and the total variance-covariance matrix using only the matrices of the dependent variable with the highest loading (see chapter 10 for a discussion of variable loading). It is less reported than Pillai's trace or Wilks' lambda.

$$Roy's = \frac{SS_{B1}}{SS_{T1}}$$

SS_B = between sum of squares of variance for the dependent variable with highest loading on the linear combination
SS_T = total sum of squares of variance for the dependent variable with highest loading on the linear combination

In general, it is worth mentioning that the results of Pillai's trace, Hotelling's trace, and Roy's largest root are similar with large sample sizes (Foster et al., 2006). Also, when the independent variable(s) have *only* two levels (groups), the *F* values for Pillai's trace, Wilks' lambda, and Hotelling's trace are identical (Tabachnick & Fidell, 2007).

Post Hoc Tests

As said earlier, one of the advantages of MANOVA and MANCOVA is that they examine group differences on a composite variable of several dependent variables simultaneously. However, as a disadvantage, when significant results are detected by Wilks' lambda or any other multivariate test, neither MANOVA nor MANCOVA pinpoints which dependent variable(s) are responsible for the group differences. In addition, like ANOVA and ANCOVA, neither MANOVA nor MANCOVA pinpoints which pair(s) of groups are significantly different on the composite variable.

Therefore, a series of multiple comparison tests should be undertaken to examine (1) what dependent variable(s) are responsible for the significant results and (2) what groups are significantly different and on what dependent variable(s).

Luckily, most of the statistical packages, including SPSS, compute a number of *between-subjects effects* tests simultaneously with MANOVA and MANCOVA. These tests examine group differences on each dependent variable. In addition, these programs compute a number of post hoc tests that examine each pair of groups on each dependent variable. As noted in chapters 6, 7, and 8, SPSS has fourteen post hoc tests that are appropriate when groups have equal variances (e.g., LSD, Bonferroni, and Sidak) and four tests that are appropriate when groups have unequal variances (e.g., Tamhane's T2).

In other words, when significant results are detected by multivariate tests, the researcher needs to follow up by inspecting the results of the between-subjects effects. Also, when the independent variable(s) have more than two groups, the researcher needs to inspect the results of the post hoc tests.

Assumptions

As said earlier, MANOVA and MANCOVA are the same as ANOVA and ANCOVA, respectively, with multiple dependent variables. Therefore,

MANOVA and MANCOVA require the same set of assumptions as ordinary ANOVA and ANCOVA. They are the following:

1. SAMPLE REPRESENTATIVENESS: The sample must be representative of the population from which it is drawn and to which findings will be generalized. This assumption is sometimes known as *independence of observations.* In other words, each participant's score is independent from all other participants' scores.

    This assumption, perhaps, is one of the most important assumptions and cannot be violated. It is usually fulfilled when samples are selected based on the probability theory, such as random samples.

2. LEVELS OF MEASUREMENT:

    a. All dependent variables must be continuous data and measured at the interval level of measurement or higher.

    b. In *MANCOVA,* all covariates must be continuous data and are measured at the interval level of measurement or higher.

    c. All independent variables must be categorical variables with two or more mutually exclusive and exhaustive groups.

    Levels of measurement can be evaluated by referring to the research methodology and by inspecting the specific data file. Also, if independent variables are not categorical variables, they must be recoded into groups. This recoding can be done in SPSS through the *Transform* and *Recode into Different Variables* commands (see chapter 2).

3. SAMPLE SIZE: Multivariate analysis of variance and covariance are sensitive to small sample sizes, especially when there are extreme outlier cases (see chapter 2), which will affect the normality of the distribution of the dependent variables. While the *central limit theorem* has shown normal distribution with sample sizes as low as 30 cases, the number of cases per cell in MANOVA and MANCOVA *must* be greater than the number of dependent variables in the analysis. For example, with a 3x4 MANOVA (that is, two independent variables with three and four levels each; twelve cells) and three dependent variables, each cell must have more than three cases, at least four cases. That is, $N = 12 \times 4 = 48$ cases or more. However, researchers have recommended a sample size of at least 10 cases per cell as adequate for multivariate analysis, especially when the assumption of normality is violated.

    Sample size can be evaluated simply by inspecting the number of levels of each independent variable in the analysis and the number of valid cases in the specific data file.

4. NORMAL DISTRIBUTION:

    a. UNIVARIATE NORMALITY: The shape of the distribution of each dependent variable must approach the shape of a normal curve.

b. In *MANCOVA,* the shape of the distribution of each covariate also must approach the shape of a normal curve.

c. MULTIVARIATE NORMALITY: The distributions of the linear combination of all dependent variables (composite scores) must approach the shape of a normal distribution for each level of the independent variable(s).

The first two parts, as discussed in previous chapters, can be evaluated by inspecting measures of skewness and kurtosis, histograms, and normal probability plots for each dependent variable. If non-normality exists in one or more dependent variable, consider data transformation as discussed in chapter 2.

On the other hand, evaluation of the assumption of multivariate normality is not an easy task. Also, there are no statistical tests yet available in most statistical software to examine this assumption. Traditionally, however, researchers assume multivariate normality when the assumption of univariate normality is satisfied.

Fortunately, MANOVA can be robust to violation of univariate and multivariate normality with sample sizes of at least 20 cases in the smallest cells or even with sample sizes as low as 40 cases (10 per cell in a 2x2 MANOVA) (Tabachnick & Fidell, 2007).

Thus with a sample size of at least 40 cases, if the smallest cell has more cases than the number of dependent variables and univariate normality is satisfied, it is safe to assume multivariate normality.

5. HOMOGENEITY OF VARIANCES: As with ANOVA and ANCOVA, the variances on all dependent variables must have equal variances across all groups of the independent variable(s).

Homogeneity of variances can be assessed by inspecting the results of Levene's test of equality of variances in MANOVA and MANCOVA. As a reminder, a $p > .001$ indicates that the variances for all dependent variables across all groups are equal.

In addition to these assumptions, MANOVA and MANCOVA require three additional assumptions:

6. LINEAR RELATIONSHIP:

a. The relationship between all pairs of dependent variables must be linear. In other words, all dependent variables must be related to each other.

b. Also, in *MANCOVA,* the relationship between the covariate(s) and the dependent variables must be linear.

The first part can be evaluated by plotting and inspecting the scatterplots for all possible pairs of dependent variables. In addition, it can be statistically evaluated by *Bartlett's test of sphericity.* This test examines whether the dependent variables are significantly correlated. It is computed along with MANOVA and MANCOVA. In this case, a $p \leq .05$ is desired, thus indicating significant relationships between the dependent variables.

If either no relationship or a curvilinear relationship exists between one or more pairs of the dependent variables, re-evaluate to determine whether any multivariate outlier cases exist. Also re-evaluate normality of those variables, and consider data transformation. Remember: always inspect data for univariate and multivariate outlier cases prior to any analysis (see chapter 2). If no relationship continues to exist, *stop!* MANOVA and MANCOVA are probably not the right tests; consider ordinary ANOVA or ANCOVA.

The second part, the relationship between covariates and dependent variables, can be examined by simply inspecting the Pearson correlation coefficients and the scatterplots of all possible pairs of covariates and dependent variables.

7. HOMOGENEITY OF VARIANCE-COVARIANCE MATRICES: Also known as the assumption of *homoscedasticity* or *multivariate variances* (Tabachnick & Fidell, 2007), it implies that the covariances of all dependent variables across all levels of the independent variable(s) are equal.

When cells have an equal number of cases, MANOVA and MANCOVA are robust to violation of the assumption. However, when cells have an unequal number of cases, violation of the assumption is severe. The assumption can be evaluated by inspecting the results of Box's M test of equality of covariance matrices, produced simultaneously with the results of MANOVA and MAN-COVA. As a general rule, a $p > .001$ indicates that the assumption is fulfilled.

As a general guideline, when the assumption of homogeneity of variance-covariance matrices is met (Box's M is not significant; $p > .001$), researchers report the results of the multivariate Wilks' lambda test to infer the results of MANOVA or MANCOVA on main and interaction effects. On the other hand, when the assumption is violated (Box's M is significant; $p < .001$), researchers report the results of Pillai's trace to infer the results of MANOVA or MAN-COVA on both effects.

8. MULTICOLLINEARITY: As with regression analysis, multicollinearity occurs when the relationship between any pair of the dependent variables is too high ($r > .80$).

Multicollinearity can be evaluated in MANOVA and MANCOVA by inspecting the results of the *residuals SSCP matrix* (sums-of-squares and cross-products), produced along with *Bartlett's test of sphericity.* You can also examine multicollinearity by inspecting both *VIF* and *tolerance* values of all dependent variables. (See chapter 4 for more on multicollinearity and how to deal with the problem.)

Furthermore, as does ANCOVA, MANCOVA requires two additional assumptions:

1. RELIABILITY OF COVARIATE(S): All covariates should have no measurement errors.

As said in chapter 7, this assumption is almost impossible to achieve. However, as a general rule, this assumption can be ignored when all covariates have reliability coefficients of .80 or above.

2. HOMOGENEITY OF REGRESSION: The relationship between the composite dependent variable and the covariates should be the same for each level of the independent variables. In other words, there should be no relationship between the independent variables and covariates (no interaction between the independent and control variables on the composite variable).

Homogeneity of regression is evaluated by inspecting the interaction effect between the independent variables and the covariates on the composite dependent variable. A nonsignificant p value ($p > .05$) indicates that the assumption is fulfilled. This assumption can be tested in SPSS in the MANCOVA custom model. If homogeneity of regression is violated, *stop*! MANCOVA is not appropriate; consider MANOVA.

Research Questions and Hypotheses

Research questions and hypotheses answered by MANOVA and MANCOVA are similar to those answered by ANOVA and ANCOVA, respectively. The number of questions and hypotheses depends on the number of effects (factors), one factor, two factors, or multiple factors.

With only one independent variable (factor), there is only one main effect or group. With two independent variables, as discussed in chapters 6 and 7, there are two main effects and one interaction effect. With multiple independent variables (factorial MANOVA and MANCOVA), there are multiple main effects and multiple interaction effects.

The discussion in this chapter is limited to the two-way MANOVA and two-way MANCOVA. One-way and factorial MANOVA and MANCOVA follow the same path. The only difference is with one-way MANOVA and MANCOVA; each has only one main effect and thus no interaction effect.

Main and interaction effects of MANOVA.   As with two-way ANOVA, two-way MANOVA examines three effects: two main effects and one interaction effect.

Main effect 1 is the effect of the first independent variable on the composite dependent variable of the linear combination of all dependent variables.

Main effect 2 is the effect of the second independent variable on the composite dependent variable of the linear combination of all dependent variables.

Interaction effect is the effect of the levels of the first independent variable across the second independent variable (joint cells of first independent variable by second independent variable) on the composite dependent variable of the linear combination of all dependent variables.

Main and interaction effects of MANCOVA.   These effects are similar to those of MANOVA, however adjusting for the effects of the control variables.

Main effect 1 is the effect of the first independent variable on the composite dependent variable of the linear combination of all dependent variables while adjusting for the effects of the covariates.

Main effect 2 is the effect of the second independent variable on the composite dependent variable of the linear combination of all dependent variables while adjusting for the effects of the covariates.

Interaction effect is the effect of the levels of the first independent variable across the second independent variable (joint cells of first independent variable by second independent variable) on the composite dependent variable of the linear combination of all dependent variables while adjusting for the effects of the covariates.

Research questions and hypotheses in MANOVA.

The example of well-being among immigrants mentioned earlier will be used to illustrate the research questions and hypotheses.

RESEARCH QUESTION 1: Are there significant differences between the levels of the first independent variable on the composite dependent variable (variable 1, variable 2, . . . , and variable K)?

EXAMPLE: Are there significant differences between male and female immigrants with regard to their overall well-being (life satisfaction, self-esteem, and depression)?

RESEARCH HYPOTHESIS 1: There are significant differences between the levels of the first independent variable on the composite dependent variable (variable 1, variable 2, . . . , and variable K).

EXAMPLE: There are significant differences between male and female immigrants with regard to their overall well-being (life satisfaction, self-esteem, and depression).

RESEARCH QUESTION 2: Are there significant differences between the levels of the second independent variable on the composite dependent variable (variable 1, variable 2, . . . , and variable K)?

EXAMPLE: Are there significant differences between immigrants who have high school or less education, college education, and graduate education with regard to their overall well-being (life satisfaction, self-esteem, and depression)?

RESEARCH HYPOTHESIS 2: There are significant differences between the levels of the second independent variable on the composite dependent variable (variable 1, variable 2, . . . , and variable K).

EXAMPLE: There are significant differences between immigrants who have high school or less education, college education, and graduate education with regard to their overall well-being (life satisfaction, self-esteem, and depression).

RESEARCH QUESTION 3: Are there significant differences between the levels of the first independent variable across the levels of the second independent variable on the composite dependent variable (variable 1, variable 2, . . . , and variable K)?

EXAMPLE: Are there significant differences between male immigrants with high school or less education, male immigrants with college education, male immigrants with graduate education, female immigrants with high school or less education, female immigrants with college education, and female immigrants with graduate education with regard to their overall well-being (life satisfaction, self-esteem, and depression)?

Or simply: Is there a significant gender by levels of education interaction effect on immigrants' overall well-being (life satisfaction, self-esteem, and depression)?

RESEARCH HYPOTHESIS 3: There are significant differences between the levels of the first independent variable across the levels of the second independent variable on the composite dependent variable (variable 1, variable 2, . . . , and variable K).

EXAMPLE: There are significant differences between male immigrants with high school or less education, male immigrants with college education, male immigrants with graduate education, female immigrants with high school or less education, female immigrants with college education, and female immigrants with graduate education with regard to their overall well-being (life satisfaction, self-esteem, and depression).

Or simply: There is a significant gender by levels of education interaction effect on immigrants' overall well-being (life satisfaction, self-esteem, and depression).

Research questions and hypotheses in MANCOVA. The same example will be used to show the similarity and differences between research questions and hypotheses of MANOVA and MANCOVA.

RESEARCH QUESTION 1: Controlling for the effect of the first covariate (second, . . . K covariate), are there significant differences between the levels of the first independent variable on the composite dependent variable (variable 1, variable 2, . . . , and variable K)?

EXAMPLE: Controlling for the effect of age and socioeconomic status, are there significant differences between male and female immigrants with regard to their overall well-being (life satisfaction, self-esteem, and depression)?

RESEARCH HYPOTHESIS 1: Controlling for the effect of the first covariate (second, . . . K covariate), there are significant differences between the levels of the first independent variable on the composite dependent variable (variable 1, variable 2, . . . , and variable K).

EXAMPLE: Controlling for the effect of age and socioeconomic status, there are significant differences between male and female immigrants with regard to their overall well-being (life satisfaction, self-esteem, and depression).

RESEARCH QUESTION 2: Controlling for the effect of the first covariate (second, . . . K covariate), are there significant differences between the levels of the second independent variable on the composite dependent variable (variable 1, variable 2, . . . , and variable K)?

EXAMPLE: Controlling for the effect of age and socioeconomic status, are there significant differences between immigrants who have high school or less education, college education, and graduate education with regard to their overall well-being (life satisfaction, self-esteem, and depression)?

RESEARCH HYPOTHESIS 2: Controlling for the effect of the first covariate (second, . . . K covariate), there are significant differences between the levels of the second independent variable on the composite dependent variable (variable 1, variable 2, . . . , and variable K).

EXAMPLE: Controlling for the effect of age and socioeconomic status, there are significant differences between immigrants who have high school or less education, college education, and graduate education with regard to their overall well-being (life satisfaction, self-esteem, and depression).

RESEARCH QUESTION 3: Controlling for the effect of the first covariate (second, . . . K covariate), are there significant differences between the levels of the first independent variable across the levels of the second independent variable on the composite dependent variable (variable 1, variable 2, . . . , and variable K)?

EXAMPLE: Controlling for the effect of age and socioeconomic status, are there significant differences between male immigrants with high school or less education, male immigrants with college education, male immigrants with graduate education, female immigrants with high school or less education, female immigrants with college education, and female immigrants with graduate education with regard to their overall well-being (life satisfaction, self-esteem, and depression)?

Or simply: Controlling for the effect of age and socioeconomic status, is there a significant gender by levels of education interaction effect on immigrants' overall well-being (life satisfaction, self-esteem, and depression)?

RESEARCH HYPOTHESIS 3: Controlling for the effect of the first covariate (second, . . . K covariate), there are significant differences between the levels of the first independent variable across the levels of the second independent variable on the composite dependent variable (variable 1, variable 2, . . . , and variable K).

EXAMPLE: Controlling for the effect of age and socioeconomic status, there are significant differences between male immigrants with high school or less education, male immigrants with college education, male immigrants with graduate education, female immigrants with high school or less education, female immigrants with college education, and female immigrants with graduate education with regard to their overall well-being (life satisfaction, self-esteem, and depression).

Or simply: Controlling for the effect of age and socioeconomic status, there is a significant gender by levels of education interaction effect on immigrants' overall well-being (life satisfaction, self-esteem, and depression).

The practical examples will focus on a two-way MANOVA and a two-way MANCOVA. Analyses of one-way and factorial MANOVA and MANCOVA follow the same steps of the two-way MANOVA and MANCOVA, including statement of hypotheses, evaluation of assumptions, SPSS commands, SPSS outputs, interpreting the SPSS tables, and writing the results. The only difference, as said, is in the number of independent variables entered in the analysis.

The first detailed example will demonstrate the utilization of a two-way MANOVA to examine the effect of gender and owning a home on overall mental health status (emotional balance and depression) among older people. Next, we will examine the effect of gender and owning a home on overall mental health status among older people when controlling for the effect of immigrants' levels of cognitive status.

FIRST PRACTICAL EXAMPLE: MULTIVARIATE ANALYSIS OF VARIANCE

We will use the SPSS Mental Health data file to examine immigrants' overall mental health based on their gender and home ownership. In this file, gender and home ownership are dichotomous variables; each consists of two groups (Gender: 0 = male, 1 = female; Home: 0 = no home, 1 = yes home). The dependent variables emotional balance (EB) and levels of depression (CESD) are continuous data and measured at the interval level of measurement. In other words, this is a two-way, or a 2x2, MANOVA design.

Hypothesis Testing

Step 1: State the Research Hypotheses.

MAIN EFFECT 1:

H_{o1}: There are no statistically significant differences between male (M) and female (F) older people with regard to their overall mental health status (emotional balance and depression).

$$\mu_M = \mu_F$$

H_{a1}: There are statistically significant differences between male and female older people with regard to their overall mental health status (emotional balance and depression).

$$\mu_M \neq \mu_F$$

MAIN EFFECT 2:

H_{o2}: There are no statistically significant differences between older people who own their home (Y) and older people who do not own their home

(N) with regard to their overall mental health status (emotional balance and depression).

$$\mu_Y = \mu_N$$

H_{a2}: There are statistically significant differences between older people who own their home (Y) and older people who do not own their home (N) with regard to their overall mental health status (emotional balance and depression).

$$\mu_Y \neq \mu_N$$

INTERACTION EFFECT:

H_{o3}: There is no statistically significant gender by home interaction effect on older people's overall mental health status (emotional balance and depression).

$$\mu_{MY} = \mu_{MN} = \mu_{FY} = \mu_{FN}$$

H_{a3}: There is a statistically significant gender by home interaction effect on older people's overall mental health status (emotional balance and depression).

$$\mu_{MY} \neq \mu_{MN} \neq \mu_{FY} \neq \mu_{FN}; \text{ for at least two groups}$$

Step 2: Set the Criteria for Rejecting the Null Hypotheses.
We will set alpha at .05 ($\alpha = .05$). That is, reject H_o only if $p \leq .05$.

Step 3: Select the Appropriate Statistical Test.
As mentioned previously, our research question consists of two independent variables measured at the nominal level of measurement (categorical variables) and a composite dependent variable of two measures of mental health status (two dependent variables).

We could conduct four independent *t*-tests to examine the differences between gender and home ownership on each dependent variable (Emotional Balance by Gender, Emotional Balance by Home, Depression by Gender, and Depression by Home). We also could conduct two two-way ANOVA tests to examine these differences and their interactions (Gender by Home on Emotional Balance and Gender by Home on Depression).

Yet, as said earlier, conducting multiple tests has a number of disadvantages, such as the inflation of type I error. Therefore, to avoid these disadvantages, we will consider the multivariate version of the two-way ANOVA, that is, the two-way MANOVA. However, before we do so, we must first evaluate the test's assumptions and examine whether they are met. They are as follows:

1. SAMPLE REPRESENTATIVENESS (INDEPENDENCE OF OBSERVATIONS): The sample must be representative of the population.

In this study, a representative sample of 155 older people ages fifty to ninety-five years old completed the Mental Health surveys. They were randomly selected from Islamic community centers and mosques in the northeastern

United States and two Middle Eastern countries (see appendix), thus satisfying the assumption of independence of observations.

2.   LEVELS OF MEASUREMENT: The independent variable(s) must be categorical data, and the dependent variables must be measured at the interval level or higher.

   In the current study, there are two independent variables and two dependent variables. Both independent variables (Gender and Home) are categorical variables, and the dependent variables are continuous data and measured at the interval level of measurement.

3.   SAMPLE SIZE: A minimum of 30 subjects should be sufficient for MANOVA. However, there should be more cases in each cell than the number of dependent variables. Also, MANOVA is robust to violations of univariate and multivariate normality when the smallest cell has as few as 10 cases.

   One hundred and fifty five subjects participated in the current study. Of them, 74 were males and 78 were females (three cases were missing). Also, 75 owned their home and 77 did not own their home (three cases were missing). Moreover, a gender by home cross-tabulation shows that the smallest cell has 29 subjects, thus exceeding the minimum requirement for MANOVA ($n = 10$). *Note:* to produce this table, use SPSS *Analyze, Descriptive Statistics,* and *Crosstabs* commands, enter the first independent variable in the *Row* box and the second independent variable in the *Column* box, and click on *OK.*

4.   NORMAL DISTRIBUTION: The dependent variables must have univariate and multivariate normal distributions for each level of the independent variables.

   This assumption is one of the most critical, especially with small sample sizes and unequal cells. As said earlier, MANOVA is robust to violation of normality with sample sizes as low as 10 cases per cell. Thus distribution should not be a major problem in our study, because, as we said under assumption 3, we have a minimum of 29 cases per cell.

   However, we will examine the univariate distributions for each variable for each level of the independent variables. First, we will evaluate the overall shape of depression and emotional balance.

   To do so, we will examine both measures of skewness and kurtosis and will inspect the histogram and normal probability plot for each variable.

   Table 9.2 displays the results of skewness and kurtosis for levels of depression and emotional balance. The table shows that the skewness coefficient for depression is greater than twice its standard error (.703/.199 = 3.53), thus indicating severe positive skewness. On the other hand, kurtosis for depression falls within the normal range (.363/.396 = .92). Skewness and kurtosis for emotional balance fall within the normal range, thus indicating a normal distribution.

   Next, we will visually inspect the histograms and normal probability plots for levels of depression. They are displayed in figures 9.1.A and 9.1.B, respectively.

Table 9.2:   Measures of Skewness and Kurtosis for Dependent Variables

Statistics

		CESD Depression	EB Emotional balance
N	Valid	148	153
	Missing	7	2
	Skewness	.703	-.196
	Std. Error of Skewness	.199	.196
	Kurtosis	.363	.091
	Std. Error of Kurtosis	.396	.390

Figure 9.1:   Histogram and Normal Probability Plot for Depression

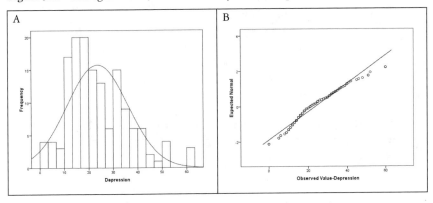

Figure 9.1.A shows that the distribution of depression has a positive skewness. The Q-Q plot (figure 9.1.B) also shows departure from normality (a number of cases depart from the horizontal line). Thus, based on measure of skewness and eyeballing the histogram and the Q-Q plot, it appears that depression has a severe positive skewness. Therefore, we will conduct a data transformation on depression.

As discussed in chapter 2, we will transform depression to the square root. A simple frequency table for depression, however, shows that the minimum score for depression is 0. Thus, as discussed in chapter 2, we must add 1 to each raw score in depression to avoid the square root of 0. We will use the following SPSS syntax to conduct the transformation:

Transformation Syntax

```
COMPUTE SQRT_CESD=SQRT(CESD+1).
EXECUTE.
```

After transformation is completed, we will evaluate the distribution of the transformed depression (SQRT_CESD) by inspecting its skewness, kurtosis, histogram, and Q-Q plot. Table 9.3 and figure 9.2 display these measures and plots.

Table 9.3:   Measures of Skewness and Kurtosis for Square Root of Depression

Statistics

SQRT CESD

N	Valid	148.000
	Missing	7.000
	Skewness	**-.238**
	Std. Error of Skewness	**.199**
	Kurtosis	.639
	Std. Error of Kurtosis	.396

Notice that both skewness and kurtosis for the newly transformed depression fall within the normal range (skewness = −.238/.199 = −1.20; kurtosis = .639/.396 = 1.61; within ±1.96).

Furthermore, eyeballing both the histogram and the normal probability plot for the transformed depression shows a normal distribution with minor deviation (see figure 9.2). Thus we will use the square root of depression hereafter to represent participants' levels of depression.

Next, we will examine the distribution of the overall emotional balance by eyeballing its histogram and normal probability plot (figure 9.3).

Figure 9.2:   Histogram and Normal Probability Plot for Square Root of Depression

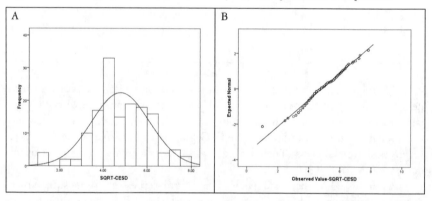

Figure 9.3:   Histogram and Normal Probability Plot for Emotional Balance

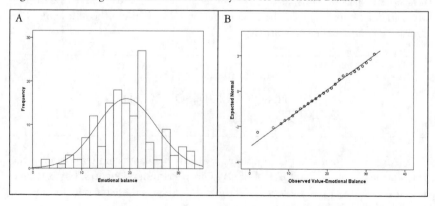

As it appears, both the histogram (figure 9.3.A) and the Q-Q plot (figure 9.3.B) show a normal distribution. This finding is consistent with measures of skewness and kurtosis, thus indicating that emotional balance is normally distributed.

Now that we have examined the overall shape of each dependent variable and have done the proper measure (transformation) to *fix* the violation of normality, we will examine the shape of each distribution for each level of each independent variable.

We will begin by evaluating measures of skewness and kurtosis of the transformed depression and emotional balance for both genders. Table 9.4 displays these measures.

Table 9.4 reveals that each skewness coefficient is smaller than twice its standard error (skewness/std. error of skewness). In addition, all kurtosis coefficients are within the normal range (Female SQRT_CESD = 1.084/.535 = 2.03). Thus both skewness and kurtosis show normal distributions for both dependent variables for each group of the independent variables.

Eyeballing the histograms and the normal probability plots of the transformed depression and emotional balance for male participants (figures 9.4 and 9.6, respectively) and the transformed depression and emotional balance for female participants (figures 9.5 and 9.7, respectively) also shows normal distributions with *minor,* but not severe, deviations in the histogram of transformed depression for females and of emotional balance for males (figures 9.5.A and 9.6.A, respectively).

Now we will look at the histograms of both depression and emotional balance by home. Table 9.5 reports measures of skewness and kurtosis for both variables on both groups of home ownership (yes vs. no).

Table 9.5 shows that three of the four distributions have skewness and kurtosis coefficients within the normal range (± 1.96). They are depression for both yes and no home and emotional balance for yes home. However, the table shows that the skewness coefficient of emotional balance for participants with no home

Table 9.4: Measures of Skewness and Kurtosis for Square Root of Depression and Emotional Balance by Gender

Statistics				SQRT_CESD	EB Emotional balance
GENDER					
0 Male	N	Valid		69	74
		Missing		6	1
		Skewness		**.020**	**-.553**
		Std. Error of Skewness		**.289**	**.279**
		Kurtosis		.599	.649
		Std. Error of Kurtosis		.570	.552
1 Female	N	Valid		79	79
		Missing		1	1
		Skewness		**-.473**	**-.076**
		Std. Error of Skewness		**.271**	**.271**
		Kurtosis		1.084	.153
		Std. Error of Kurtosis		.535	.535

Figure 9.4:   Histogram and Normal Probability Plot for Transformed Depression—Male

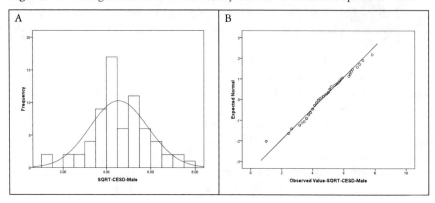

Figure 9.5:   Histogram and Normal Probability Plot for Transformed Depression—Female

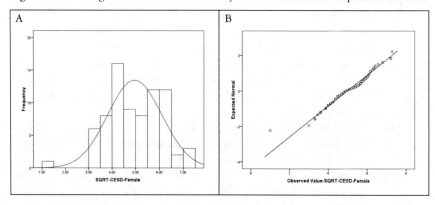

Figure 9.6:   Histogram and Normal Probability Plot for Emotional Balance—Male

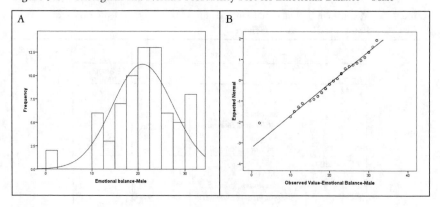

Figure 9.7: Histogram and Normal Probability Plot for Emotional Balance—Female

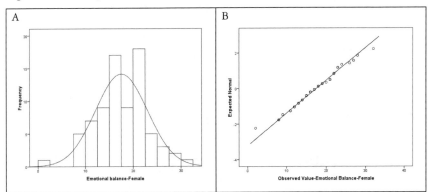

Table 9.5: Measures of Skewness and Kurtosis for Square Root of Depression and Emotional Balance by Home

Statistics

HOME Own Home			SQRT_CESD	EB Emotional balance
0 No	N	Valid	70	73
		Missing	5	2
		Skewness	**-.010**	**-.736**
		Std. Error of Skewness	**.287**	**.281**
		Kurtosis	.457	.921
		Std. Error of Kurtosis	.566	.555
1 Yes	N	Valid	75	77
		Missing	2	0
		Skewness	**-.401**	**.122**
		Std. Error of Skewness	**.277**	**.274**
		Kurtosis	1.513	-.455
		Std. Error of Kurtosis	.548	.541

(skewness = −.736) falls outside the normal range (−.736/.281 = −2.62), thus indicating severe negative skewness. On the other hand, the kurtosis coefficient of this distribution (kurtosis = .921) falls within the normal range (.921/.555 = 1.66).

Next we will eyeball the distributions of transformed depression and emotional balance for both home ownership groups. They are displayed in figures 9.8 through 9.11.

Eyeballing the histograms and normal probability plots of the transformed depression and emotional balance for participants with yes home (figures 9.8 and 9.10, respectively) and the depression and emotional balance for participants with no home (figures 9.9 and 9.11, respectively) shows results consistent with both skewness and kurtosis. These figures and normal probability plots show that the distributions of depression and emotional balance for both groups, except one, appear to approach the shape of a normal curve.

Figure 9.8:   Histogram and Normal Probability Plot for Depression—Yes Home

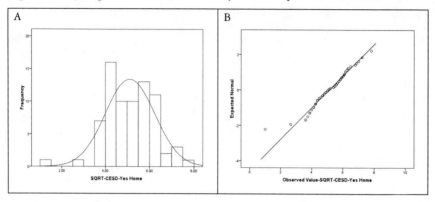

Figure 9.9:   Histogram and Normal Probability Plot for Depression—No Home

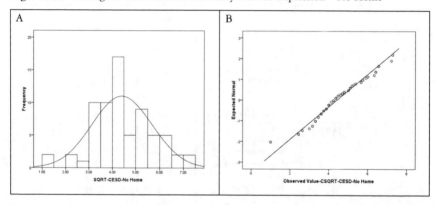

Figure 9.10:   Histogram and Normal Probability Plot for Emotional Balance—Yes Home

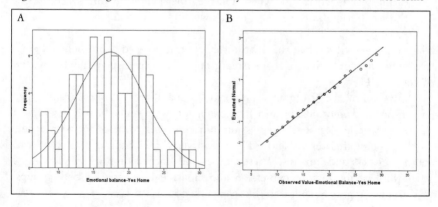

Figure 9.11:   Histogram and Normal Probability Plot for Emotional Balance—No Home

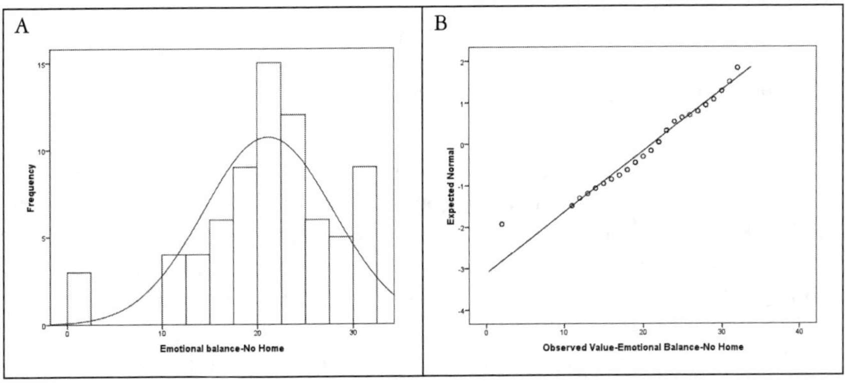

On the other hand, the histogram of emotional balance for no home (figure 9.11.A) is skewed to the left. However, the normal probability plot (figure 9.11.B) shows only minor deviations from normality.

To conclude, although there are a few minor, but not severe, deviations on some distributions, we could conclude that the shape of the distributions of both dependent variables as a whole and for each level of the independent variables approach the shape of a normal curve. Furthermore, based on the univariate measures of skewness, kurtosis, histogram, and normal probability plot, we could assume that both variables meet the assumption of multivariate normality. In addition, given that we have a large sample size with the smallest cell having 29 cases, we should not worry about violation of the assumptions of normality.

5.   HOMOGENEITY OF VARIANCES: The variances of the dependent variables, Depression and Emotional Balance, across all levels of the independent variables, Gender and Home, must be equal.

We will examine homogeneity of variances by inspecting the results of Levene's test of equality of error variances. These results are presented in table 9.6 (this table is produced simultaneously with MANOVA).

The results of Levene's test of equality of error variances for emotional balance ($p = .539$) and the square root of depression ($p = .750$) show no significant

Table 9.6:   Results of Levene's Test of Equality of Error Variances

Levene's Test of Equality of Error Variances[a]

	F	df1	df2	Sig.
EB Emotional balance	.724	3	141	**.539**
SQRT_CESD	.405	3	141	**.750**

Tests the null hypothesis that the error variance of the dependent variable is equal across groups.

a. Design: Intercept + GENDER + HOME + GENDER * HOME

differences in the variances of both variables across all groups, thus indicating that the assumption is fulfilled.

6.   LINEAR RELATIONSHIP: The relationship between the dependent variables should be linear. When a nonlinear or curvilinear relationship exists, MANOVA should not be used.

We will evaluate this assumption by inspecting the results of Bartlett's test of sphericity and the scatterplots of all possible pairs of dependent variables (here we have two dependent variables, and thus there is only one pair).

Table 9.7 presents the results of Bartlett's test of sphericity (this table also is produced simultaneously with the results of MANOVA). As said earlier, here we look for significant results ($p < .05$).

The results of Bartlett's test of sphericity show a significant correlation between the dependent variables (chi-square$_{(df = 2)}$ = 266.21, $p < .05$).

Note: If no significant correlation exists between the dependent variables ($p > .05$), *stop.* MANOVA is not appropriate to examine the research hypotheses. Consider ordinary ANOVA tests.

Next, although not necessary, we will examine the scatterplot for the square root of depression and emotional balance. Figure 9.12 is a scatterplot of depression and emotional balance.

Figure 9.12 shows a linear negative relationship between depression and emotional balance. Notice that the dots are fairly clustered around the fit line with few deviations. Thus both the results of Bartlett's test of sphericity and the scatterplot indicate that linearity is satisfied.

7.   HOMOGENEITY OF VARIANCE-COVARIANCE MATRICES: The covariance matrices of all groups on both dependent variables must be equal.

As in chapter 8, we will evaluate this assumption by inspecting the results of Box's test of equality of covariance matrices (also produced simultaneously with the results of MANOVA). These results are presented in table 9.8.

The results of Box's M test are not statistically significant ($F = 1.86$, $p > .001$). In other words, the covariance matrices of emotional balance and depression across all groups of the independent variables are equal, thus showing that the assumption is met.

Table 9.7:   Results of Bartlett's Test of Sphericity

Bartlett's Test of Sphericity[a]	
Likelihood Ratio	.000
Approx. Chi-Square	**266.207**
df	**2.000**
Sig.	**.000**

Tests the null hypothesis that the residual covariance matrix is proportional to an identity matrix.

a. Design: Intercept + GENDER + HOME + GENDER * HOME

Figure 9.12:   Scatterplot for Depression and Emotional Balance

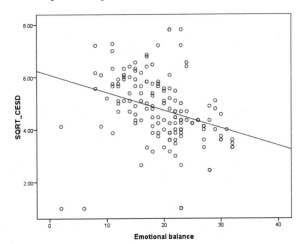

Table 9.8:   Results of Box's Test of Equality of Covariance Matrices

Box's Test of Equality of Covariance Matrices[a]

Box's M	17.249
F	1.864
df1	9.000
df2	114918.009
Sig.	**.052**

Tests the null hypothesis that the observed covariance matrices of the dependent variables are equal across groups.

a. Design: Intercept + GENDER + HOME + GENDER * HOME

Note: if Box's *M* is significant ($p < .001$), consider reporting the results of other multivariate tests, as discussed earlier.

8.   MULTICOLLINEARITY: The correlations between all pairs of dependent variables must not be larger than .80.

We will evaluate multicollinearity by inspecting the correlation coefficients between all pairs of dependent variables. They can be found in the residual SSCP matrix produced along with MANOVA. Table 9.9 displays the residual SSCP matrix. In this example, there is only one pair of dependent variables (Emotional Balance with Depression). As it appears in table 9.9, the correlation coefficient between emotional balance and depression is –.32, indicating a moderate negative correlation. In other words, multicollinearity is not a problem.

To conclude, the results of Box's *M* test, Levene's test of equality of variances, and Bartlett's test of sphericity show that our data have met the assumptions of

Table 9.9:   Residual SSCP Matrix

Residual SSCP Matrix

		EB Emotional balance	SQRT_CESD
Sum-of-Squares and Cross-Products	EB Emotional balance	4428.460	-303.266
	SQRT_CESD	-303.266	201.502
Covariance	EB Emotional balance	31.408	-2.151
	SQRT_CESD	-2.151	1.429
Correlation	EB Emotional balance	1.000	-.321
	SQRT_CESD	**-.321**	1.000

Based on Type III Sum of Squares

homogeneity of variance-covariance matrices, homogeneity of variances, and linearity. Also, measures of skewness and kurtosis, histograms, and probability plots all show that the assumptions of univariate and multivariate normality have been met. In addition, the sample size and the number of cases per cell are fairly large. Thus we will proceed and utilize the two-way MANOVA to examine the main and interaction effects gender and home on older people's overall mental health status.

How to Use SPSS to Run MANOVA

Step 4: Compute the MANOVA Test Statistic.
To run the MANOVA in SPSS, follow these steps:

1.   Open the Mental Health SPSS data file.

2.   Click on *Analyze,* scroll down to and click on *General Linear Model,* and click on *Multivariate* to open the "Multivariate" main dialog box.

3.   Scroll down in the variables list, click on *EB* (first dependent variable), and click on the upper arrow button to move *Emotional Balance* into the *Dependent Variables* box.

4.   Repeat step 3 to move *SQRT_CESD* (second dependent variable) into the *Dependent Variables* box. *Note:* repeat this step if you have more dependent variables.

5.   Scroll down in the variables list, click on *Gender* (first independent variable), and click on the second arrow button to move *Gender* into the *Fixed Factor(s)* box.

6.   Repeat step 5 to move *Home* (second independent variable) into the *Fixed Factor(s)* box (see screen 9.1). *Note:* repeat this step if you have more independent variables.

7.   Click on *Options* in the right-side menu to open the "Multivariate: Options" dialog box (see screen 9.2).

Screen 9.1:   SPSS Multivariate Tests Dialog Box

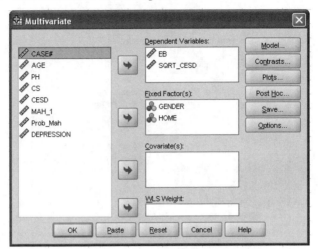

8. This dialog box is the same as in two-way ANOVA (see screen 6.3). Click on *Overall,* and click on the middle arrow button to move it into the *Display Means For* box.

9. Repeat step 8 to move *Gender, Home,* and *Gender * Home* into the *Display Means For* box.

10. Check the *Compare Main Effects* box.

11. Click on the drop-down arrow for *Confidence Interval Adjustment,* and click on *Bonferroni.*

12. As in ANOVA, check the *Descriptive Statistics, Estimates of Effect Size,* and *Homogeneity Tests* boxes. Unlike ANOVA, check the *Residual SSCP Matrix* box. This command, as the name implies, produces the residuals SSCP matrix and Bartlett's test of sphericity (see screen 9.2).

13. Click on *Continue* to return to the "Multivariate" main dialog box.

14. Click on *Plots* in the right-side menu to open the "Multivariate: Profile Plots" dialog box.

15. Click on *Gender,* and click on the upper arrow to move *Gender* into the *Horizontal Axis* box.

16. Click on *Home,* and click on the middle arrow to move *Home* into the *Separate Lines* box.

17. Click on *Add* to move *Gender * Home* into the *Plots* box. This command will generate plots for the main effect and interaction effect for each dependent variable (see screen 9.3).

Screen 9.2:   SPSS Multivariate Options Dialog Box

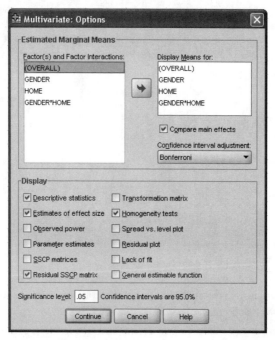

Screen 9.3:   SPSS Multivariate Profile Plots Dialog Box

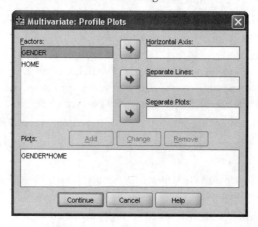

18. Click on *Continue* to return to the "Multivariate" main dialog box. *Note:* Ideally, you should click on *Post Hoc* to request group comparisons (e.g., LSD, Bonferroni) for all possible pairs of the independent variables. However, as you already know, this command is needed only when independent variables have more than two groups. In our case, Gender and Home each has only two groups and thus post hoc is not necessary.

19. Click on *OK* in the "Multivariate" main dialog box to execute these commands.

SPSS Syntax for MANOVA

GLM EB SQRT_CESD BY GENDER HOME
/METHOD=SSTYPE(3)
/INTERCEPT=INCLUDE
/PLOT=PROFILE(GENDER*HOME)
/EMMEANS=TABLES(OVERALL)
/EMMEANS=TABLES(GENDER) COMPARE ADJ(BONFERRONI)
/EMMEANS=TABLES(HOME) COMPARE ADJ(BONFERRONI)
/EMMEANS=TABLES(GENDER*HOME)
/PRINT=DESCRIPTIVE ETASQ RSSCP HOMOGENEITY
/CRITERIA=ALPHA(.05)
/DESIGN= GENDER HOME GENDER*HOME.

Reading the SPSS Output of MANOVA

The execution of these SPSS commands or syntax will produce eighteen tables and two graphs. (The number of tables and graphs depends on the number of variables in the analysis; the greater the number of variables, the more tables and graphs produced.) Four of these tables were discussed under step 3. They are Box's M test (table 9.8), Levene's test (table 9.6), Bartlett's test (table 9.7), and residual SSCP matrix (table 9.9).

In addition, another four tables are not necessary for our purposes and thus will be omitted from this discussion. The remaining ten tables (9.10–9.19) are discussed in the following. As you will see, many of these tables are similar to the tables of a two-way ANOVA (see chapter 6).

Table 9.10 describes the between-subjects factors: frequency for each group for each independent variable. As it appears in the table, 68 participants were males and 77 were females. Of both genders, 75 had their own home and 70 did not.

Table 9.11 conveys the observed means, standard deviation, and frequency for each dependent variable for each group for each independent variable and their interactions.

Table 9.10: Between-Subjects Factors

Between-Subjects Factors

		Value Label	N
GENDER	0	Male	68
	1	Female	77
HOME	0	No	70
	1	Yes	75

Table 9.11 is divided into two parts: one for each dependent variable. Each part has three rows, one for each level of the first independent variable (Gender, two groups) and one for the total. Each row has three lines, one for each level of the second independent variable (Home, two groups) and one for the total.

Emotional balance.   The first part shows that male participants who have their own home have greater emotional balance (first part, first row, second line: mean = 19.11, SD = 4.956, n = 27) than females who have their own home (first part, second row, second line: mean = 16.5, SD = 4.802, n = 48).

Table 9.11 also shows that males in general have greater emotional balance (first part, first row, third line: mean = 21.46, SD = 6.190, n = 68) than females (first part, second row, third line: mean = 17.55, SD = 5.438, n = 77).

Overall, table 9.11 shows that participants in the study have a mean of 19.38 on the emotional balance scale (first part, third row, third line: mean = 19.38, SD = 6.104, N = 145).

Depression.   The second part shows that female participants who do not have their own home have slightly more depression (second part, second row, first line: mean = 4.5557, SD = 1.136, n = 29) than males who do not have their own home (second part, first row, first line: mean = 4.300, SD = 1.358, n = 41).

Table 9.11 shows that males in general have slightly lower depression (second part, first row, third line: mean = 4.559, SD = 1.321, n = 68) than females (second part, second row, third line: mean = 4.961, SD = 1.142, n = 77).

Overall, table 9.11 shows that participants in the study have a mean of 4.77 on the CES-D scale (second part, third row, third line: mean = 4.772, SD = 1.241, N = 145).

Table 9.11:   Descriptive Statistics for Dependent Variables by Gender and Home

Descriptive Statistics

	GENDER	HOME	Mean	Std. Deviation	N
Emotional balance	0 Male	0 No	23.00	6.485	41
		1 Yes	19.11	4.956	27
		Total	21.46	6.190	68
	1 Female	0 No	19.28	6.047	29
		1 Yes	16.50	4.802	48
		Total	17.55	5.438	77
	Total	0 No	21.46	6.529	70
		1 Yes	17.44	4.987	75
		Total	19.38	6.104	145
SQRT_CESD	0 Male	0 No	4.3003	1.35849	41
		1 Yes	4.9510	1.17954	27
		Total	4.5586	1.32082	68
	1 Female	0 No	4.5557	1.13602	29
		1 Yes	5.2054	1.08543	48
		Total	4.9607	1.14214	77
	Total	0 No	4.4061	1.26870	70
		1 Yes	5.1138	1.11904	75
		Total	4.7721	1.24126	145

Table 9.12:   Results of Multivariate Tests

Multivariate Tests[b]

Effect		Value	F	Hypothesis df	Error df	Sig.	Partial Eta Squared
Intercept	Pillai's Trace	.976	2.788E3	2.000	140.000	.000	.976
	Wilks' Lambda	.024	2.788E3	2.000	140.000	.000	.976
	Hotelling's Trace	39.826	2.788E3	2.000	140.000	.000	.976
	Roy's Largest Root	39.826	2.788E3	2.000	140.000	.000	.976
GENDER	Pillai's Trace	.072	5.453[a]	2.000	140.000	.005	.072
	Wilks' Lambda	.928	5.453[a]	2.000	140.000	.005	.072
	Hotelling's Trace	.078	5.453[a]	2.000	140.000	.005	.072
	Roy's Largest Root	.078	5.453[a]	2.000	140.000	.005	.072
HOME	Pillai's Trace	.107	8.378[a]	2.000	140.000	.000	.107
	Wilks' Lambda	.893	8.378[a]	2.000	140.000	.000	.107
	Hotelling's Trace	.120	8.378[a]	2.000	140.000	.000	.107
	Roy's Largest Root	.120	8.378[a]	2.000	140.000	.000	.107
GENDER * HOME	Pillai's Trace	.003	.187[a]	2.000	140.000	.830	.003
	Wilks' Lambda	.997	.187[a]	2.000	140.000	.830	.003
	Hotelling's Trace	.003	.187[a]	2.000	140.000	.830	.003
	Roy's Largest Root	.003	.187[a]	2.000	140.000	.830	.003

a. Exact statistic

b. Design: Intercept + GENDER + HOME + GENDER * HOME

Table 9.12 reports the results of the multivariate tests for the intercept effect, main effects (each independent variable), and interaction effect.

Generally, the number of rows of this MANOVA table depends on the number of independent variables and their interaction(s). For example, with one-way MANOVA, there will be only two rows, one for the intercept and one for the independent variable (there is no interaction). With three independent variables, there will be eight rows: one intercept, three main effects (one for each independent variable), and four interactions (there are four-way interactions).

Table 9.12 has four rows, and each row has four lines corresponding with the four multivariate tests discussed earlier: Pillai's trace, Wilks' lambda, Hotelling's trace, and Roy's largest root. We are interested in only the main effects and their interactions. They are as follows:

FIRST ROW (INTERCEPT): This is a default, or hypothetical, effect. It examines whether the overall mean of the composite variable (linear combination of the mental health variables, Depression and Emotional Balance) differs from zero. This effect is not of interest and thus will not be discussed.

SECOND ROW (GENDER): This row examines the first research hypothesis (main effect 1). Recall that Box's M test was not significant ($p > .001$), and therefore, we should report the results of Wilks' lambda.

The results of Wilks' lambda show a significant difference between the two genders on their overall mental health status (Wilks' lambda = .928, $F = 5.453$, $df = 2$ and 140, $Sig. = .005$, partial eta squared = .072).

The Wilks' lambda value indicates that 92.8 percent (Wilks' lambda = .928) of the variance in the overall mental health status is *not* accounted for by gender. Thus only $1 - 92.8\% = 7.2\%$ of the variance in the overall mental health status is accounted for by gender. Notice that this percentage is the same as the partial eta squared (.072). In other words, $1 -$ Wilks' lambda = partial eta squared.

> *Note:* if Box's *M* test is significant or if the assumptions of univariate and multivariate normality are not met, report the results of Pillai's trace (or Hotelling's trace since the gender has only two groups).

The results of Pillai's trace also show a significant difference between males and females on their overall mental health status (Pillai's trace = .072, F = 5.453, *df* = 2 and 140, *Sig.* = .005, partial eta squared = .072). Notice that the *F, df, Sig.*, and *partial eta squared* values of Hotelling's trace are identical to those of Pillai's trace.

> *Note:* These significant results do not, however, mean that gender is significantly different on all dependent variables (Depression and Emotional Balance). They mean only that gender is significantly different on at least one dependent variable. Which one? The answer will be found in table 9.13, "Results of Between-Subjects Effects."

THIRD ROW (HOME): This row examines the second research hypothesis (main effect 2). The results of Wilks' lambda also show a significant difference between participants who own their home and participants who do not on the overall mental health status (Wilks' lambda = .893, F = 8.378, *df* = 2 and 140, *Sig.* = .000, partial eta squared = .107).

Wilks' lambda shows that 89.3 percent of the variance in overall mental health status, however, is *not* accounted for by home. Only 10.7 percent (partial eta squared = $1 - 89.3\% = 10.7\%$) of the variance in overall mental health is accounted for by home.

> *Note:* if Box's *M* test is significant, report the results of Pillai's trace (or Hotelling's trace since Home also has only two groups).

The results of Pillai's trace also show significant difference between the two home ownership groups on the overall mental health status (Pillai's trace = .107, F = 8.378, *df* = 2 and 140, *Sig.* = .000, partial eta squared = .107).

FOURTH ROW (GENDER * HOME): This row examines the third research hypothesis (interaction effect). The results of Wilks' lambda show *no* significant gender by home interaction effect on participants' overall mental health status (Wilks' lambda = .997, F = .187, *df* = 2 and 140, *Sig.* = .830, partial eta squared = .003).

Wilks' lambda shows that 99.7 percent of the variance in overall mental health status is *not* accounted for by gender and home interaction. In other words, only .3 percent of the variance in the overall mental health status is accounted for by the interaction between gender and home (partial eta squared = .003).

Note: if Box's *M* test is significant, report the results of Pillai's trace.

The results of Pillai's trace also show no significant gender by home interaction effect on the overall mental health status (Pillai's trace = .003, *F* = .187, *df* = 2 and 140, *Sig.* = .830, partial eta squared = .003).

Now that we have found significant gender and home effect on overall mental health (but no interaction effect), we need to find out which dependent variable(s) are responsible for these significant results. The answer for this question is in the *post hoc* between-subjects effects tests presented in table 9.13.

Table 9.13 reports the same information as table 6.6. It reports the sum of squares deviations (SS), the degrees of freedom (*df*), mean square deviations (MS), *F* ratio, level of significance (*Sig.*), and partial eta squared for each main effect and their interaction effect.

Table 9.13 has eight rows, of which only five are of interest. They include the two main effects, Gender and Home; the interaction effect, Gender * Home; the error; and the corrected total. Unlike table 6.6, each row has two lines corresponding with the two dependent variables (generally, there is one line for each dependent variable).

Table 9.13:   Results of Between-Subjects Effects

Tests of Between-Subjects Effects

Source	Dependent Variable	Type III Sum of Squares	df	Mean Square	F	Sig.	Partial Eta Squared
Corrected Model	Emotional balance	937.678[a]	3	312.559	9.952	.000	.175
	SQRT_CESD	20.363[b]	3	6.788	4.750	.003	.092
Intercept	Emotional balance	51963.383	1	51963.383	1654.489	.000	.921
	SQRT_CESD	3096.256	1	3096.256	2166.586	.000	.939
GENDER	Emotional balance	343.792	1	343.792	10.946	.001	.072
	SQRT_CESD	2.227	1	2.227	1.558	.214	.011
HOME	Emotional balance	380.483	1	380.483	12.114	.001	.079
	SQRT_CESD	14.487	1	14.487	10.137	.002	.067
GENDER * HOME	Emotional balance	10.612	1	10.612	.338	.562	.002
	SQRT_CESD	7.623E-6	1	7.623E-6	.000	.998	.000
Error	Emotional balance	4428.460	141	31.408			
	SQRT_CESD	201.502	141	1.429			
Total	Emotional balance	59822.000	145				
	SQRT_CESD	3524.000	145				
Corrected Total	Emotional balance	5366.138	144				
	SQRT_CESD	221.866	144				

a. R Squared = .175 (Adjusted R Squared = .157)

b. R Squared = .092 (Adjusted R Squared = .072)

Main effect 1—Gender (third row). In the first line (Emotional Balance), table 9.13 shows a significant difference between male and female participants on their levels of emotional balance ($F = 10.946$, $df = 1$, $Sig. = .001$). Gender accounted for 7.2 percent of the variance in emotional balance (partial eta squared $= .072$).

In the second line (Depression), table 9.13, on the other hand, shows no significant difference between male and female participants on their levels of depression ($F = 1.558$, $df = 1$, $Sig. = .214$). In this study, gender accounted for only 1.1 percent of the variance in depression (partial eta squared $= .011$).

Main effect 2—Home (fourth row). In the first line (Emotional Balance), table 9.13 shows a significant difference between participants who own their home and participants who do not on their levels of emotional balance ($F = 12.114$, $df = 1$, $Sig. = .001$). In this case, home accounted for 7.9 percent of the variance in emotional balance (partial eta squared $= .079$).

In the second line (Depression), table 9.13 also shows a significant difference between participants who own their home and participants who do not on their levels of depression ($F = 10.137$, $df = 1$, $Sig. = .002$). Home accounted for 6.7 percent of the variance in depression (partial eta squared $= .067$).

Interaction effect—Gender * Home (fifth row). In the first line (Emotional Balance), table 9.13 shows no significant gender by home interaction effect on participants' levels of emotional balance ($F = .338$, $df = 1$, $Sig. = .562$). In this study, gender by home interaction accounted for less than half a percent of the variance in emotional balance (partial eta squared $= .002$).

In the second line (Depression), table 9.13 also shows no significant gender by home interaction effect on participants' levels of depression ($F = .000$, $df = 1$, $Sig. = .998$). Gender by home interaction accounted for no variance in depression (partial eta squared $= .000$).

Next, we should look at the group means to find out their levels of emotional balance and levels of depression. As said earlier, when significant results occur between the groups, we should examine the results of the post hoc Bonferroni test. In this case, however, Bonferroni is not needed because each independent variable has only two groups. Thus we should simply look at their means to find what gender reported greater levels of emotional balance and what group of home ownership experienced greater depression and/or greater emotional balance. These means are reported in the following tables.

Table 9.14 simply reports the estimated grand mean (overall mean) for each dependent variable regardless of group membership, their standard error, and the 95th confidence interval.

Table 9.14 shows that the mean of emotional balance is 19.47 (SE $= .479$, 95th CI $= 18.53–20.42$) and the mean of depression is 4.75 (SE $= .102$, 95th CI $= 4.55–4.96$). Recall that we used the square root of depression and not the actual raw scores.

Table 9.14:   Estimated Grand Mean for Dependent Variables

Grand Mean

Dependent Variable	Mean	Std. Error	95% Confidence Interval	
			Lower Bound	Upper Bound
Emotional balance	19.472	.479	18.525	20.418
SQRT_CESD	4.753	.102	4.551	4.955

Table 9.15 reports the estimated descriptive statistics on both dependent variables for each gender.

Table 9.15 shows that male participants reported greater levels of emotional balance (mean = 21.06, SE = .69) than their female counterparts (mean = 17.89, SE = .66). Recall that there was a significant difference between males and females on emotional balance. Thus we conclude that males reported significantly greater levels of emotional balance than females.

Table 9.15 shows that males reported slightly lower levels of depression (mean = 4.63, SE = .15) than females (mean = 4.88, SE = .14). This mean difference, as we saw earlier, is not statistically significant.

Table 9.16 conveys the results of the post hoc Bonferroni on gender. As said, because there are only two groups, this table is unnecessary. It is presented here only for clarification. It shows a significant difference between males and females with regard to emotional balance (first row, first line: *Sig.* = .001) but no significant difference between males and females on depression (second row, first line: *Sig.* = .214).

Table 9.15:   Estimated Means for Dependent Variables by Gender

Estimates

Dependent Variable	GENDER	Mean	Std. Error	95% Confidence Interval	
				Lower Bound	Upper Bound
Emotional balance	0 Male	21.056	.694	19.683	22.429
	1 Female	17.888	.659	16.585	19.191
SQRT_CESD	0 Male	4.626	.148	4.333	4.918
	1 Female	4.881	.141	4.603	5.158

Table 9.16:   Bonferroni Pairwise Comparison for Dependent Variables by Gender

Pairwise Comparisons

Dependent Variable	(I) GENDER	(J) GENDER	Mean Difference (I-J)	Std. Error	Sig.[a]	95% Confidence Interval for Difference[a]	
						Lower Bound	Upper Bound
Emotional balance	0 Male	1 Female	3.168*	.957	.001	1.275	5.060
	1 Female	0 Male	-3.168*	.957	.001	-5.060	-1.275
SQRT_CESD	0 Male	1 Female	-.255	.204	.214	-.659	.149
	1 Female	0 Male	.255	.204	.214	-.149	.659

Based on estimated marginal means

*. The mean difference is significant at the .05 level.

a. Adjustment for multiple comparisons: Bonferroni.

Table 9.17 reports the estimated descriptive statistics on both dependent variables for each home ownership group (yes and no).

Table 9.17 shows that participants who do not have their own home reported greater levels of emotional balance (mean = 21.14, SE = .68) than participants who do own their home (mean = 17.81, SE = .67). The between-subjects effects test shows that this difference was significant. Thus we conclude that participants who do not own their home reported significantly greater levels of emotional balance than participants who do own their home.

Table 9.17 also shows that participants who do not have their own home reported lower levels of depression (mean = 4.43, SE = .15) than participants who do own their home (mean = 5.08, SE = .14). The between-subjects effects test also shows that this difference was significant. Thus we conclude that participants who do not own their home experienced significantly lower levels of depression than participants who do own their home.

Table 9.18 is similar to table 9.16. It conveys the results of the post hoc Bonferroni on home. This table confirms what we just reported. It shows a significant difference between participants who do not have their own home and participants who do have their own home on levels of emotional balance (first row, first line: *Sig.* = .001) and on depression (second row, first line: *Sig.* = .002).

Participants who do not have their own home reported 3.33 points, on average, more than those who do have their own home on the emotional balance scale (first row, first line: mean difference = 3.33) and .65 points, on average, less on the depression scale (second row, first line: mean difference = −.65) than those who do have their own home.

Table 9.17:   Estimated Means for Dependent Variables by Home

Estimates

Dependent Variable	Home	Mean	Std. Error	95% Confidence Interval	
				Lower Bound	Upper Bound
Emotional balance	0 No	21.138	.680	19.794	22.482
	1 Yes	17.806	.674	16.473	19.138
SQRT_CESD	0 No	4.428	.145	4.141	4.715
	1 Yes	5.078	.144	4.794	5.362

Table 9.18:   Bonferroni Pairwise Comparison for Dependent Variables by Home

Pairwise Comparisons

Dependent Variable	(I) Home	(J) Home	Mean Difference (I-J)	Std. Error	Sig.[a]	95% Confidence Interval for Difference[a]	
						Lower Bound	Upper Bound
Emotional balance	0 No	1 Yes	3.332*	.957	.001	1.440	5.225
	1 Yes	0 No	-3.332*	.957	.001	-5.225	-1.440
SQRT_CESD	0 No	1 Yes	-.650*	.204	.002	-1.054	-.246
	1 Yes	0 No	.650*	.204	.002	.246	1.054

Based on estimated marginal means

*. The mean difference is significant at the .05 level.

a. Adjustment for multiple comparisons: Bonferroni.

Table 9.19 conveys the estimated mean, standard error, and 95th confidence interval for each group of the first independent variable across each group of the second independent variable on each dependent variable. In other words, these are the interaction means.

Table 9.19 shows that males who do not have their own home reported greater emotional balance (first part, first row, first line: mean = 23, SE = .88) than males who do have their own home (first part, first row, second line: mean = 19.11, SE = 1.08) and than females who do have their own home (first part, second row, second line: mean = 16.50, SE = .81). However, these cell differences are not statistically significant, as shown by Wilks' lambda and by the between-subjects effects tests of interaction.

Inspection of the second part (SQRT_CESD) also shows slight differences among the four joint cells on their levels of depression; however, these differences are not statistically significant as shown by both Wilks' lambda and between-subjects effects tests.

Figure 9.13 displays two means plots. Figure 9.13.A compares males with females on home ownership group on their levels of depression. The graph shows that males and females who do not have their own home have lower levels of depression than those who do have their own home. However, as we said, this

Table 9.19:   Estimated Means for Dependent Variables by Gender by Home Interaction

GENDER * Own Home

Dependent Variable	GENDER	Home	Mean	Std. Error	95% Confidence Interval	
					Lower Bound	Upper Bound
Emotional balance	0 Male	0 No	23.000	.875	21.270	24.730
		1 Yes	19.111	1.079	16.979	21.243
	1 Female	0 No	19.276	1.041	17.219	21.333
		1 Yes	16.500	.809	14.901	18.099
SQRT_CESD	0 Male	0 No	4.300	.187	3.931	4.669
		1 Yes	4.951	.230	4.496	5.406
	1 Female	0 No	4.556	.222	4.117	4.995
		1 Yes	5.205	.173	4.864	5.547

Figure 9.13:   Means Plot for Depression and Emotional Balance by Gender by Home

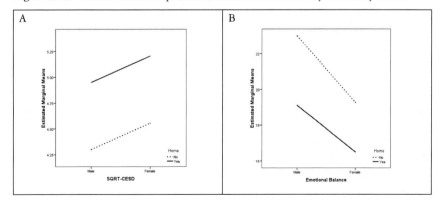

difference is not statistically significant. Notice that the segments of the two lines are parallel to each other, indicating no interaction effect.

Finally, figure 9.13.B compares males with females on each home ownership group on their emotional balance. The graph shows that males and females who do not have their own home have higher levels of emotional balance than those who do have their own home. These differences, as we said, are statistically significant. On the other hand, the segments of the two lines are parallel to each other, therefore indicating no interaction effect between gender and home on emotional balance.

Step 5: Write the Results of MANOVA.

Writing the results of MANOVA is the same as ordinary ANOVA. First, you should address the test assumptions, including sample size, univariate and multivariate normality, homogeneity of variances, homogeneity of variance-covariance matrices, linearity, and multicollinearity.

After you address these issues, you need to present the results of the overall multivariate tests (e.g., Wilks' lambda and Pillai's trace), their F ratio, degrees of freedom (df), p value, and partial eta squared for main and interaction effects.

Next, you need to report the results of the between-subjects effects for each effect on each dependent variable, their F, df, and p values. If significant results were found between groups, you need to report the results of the post hoc test(s) you used for pairwise comparisons. Moreover, you need to report the estimated means and standard errors for each group on each dependent variable. Finally, you may present the means plots to visually display the results.

Writing the Results of MANOVA

The following sections present the results of the two-way MANOVA for gender and home ownership on overall mental health status.

Evaluation of assumptions.   Prior to the analysis, data were evaluated to ensure that the assumptions for multivariate tests were fulfilled. First, a cross-tabulation of the two independent variables shows that all cells have a minimum of 29 cases per cell, thus showing a large sample size for MANOVA.

Second, measures of skewness and kurtosis, histograms, and normal Q-Q plots were examined for overall levels of emotional balance and depression. Inspection of these measures and plots shows a normal distribution on levels of emotional balance. On the other hand, depression was severely skewed to the right, and thus it was transformed to the square root. Evaluation of the skewness, kurtosis, and plots of the transformed depression revealed a normal distribution. Next, measures of skewness and kurtosis and plots were evaluated for each dependent variable for each level of the independent variables. No major departure from normality was found, and thus both assumptions of univariate and multivariate normality were presumed fulfilled.

Third, the results of Levene's test of equality of variances and Box's test of variance-covariance matrices were inspected and indicated that homogeneity of variances and homogeneity of variance-covariance matrices were satisfied ($p > .05$), respectively.

Finally, eyeballing the scatterplot of the dependent variables and inspecting the results of Bartlett's test and the residuals SSCP matrix show that both emotional balance and depression met the assumptions of linearity and multicollinearity.

Results of MANOVA.   A two-way MANOVA (or a 2x2 MANOVA) was utilized to examine the effects of gender and home ownership on the overall mental health status among a sample of 155 older people ages fifty and above. For this purpose, mental health was conceptualized as a composite of individuals' levels of emotional balance and depression.

MAIN EFFECT 1—GENDER: The results of the two-way MANOVA show an overall significant difference between male and female older people on their overall mental health status (Wilks' lambda = .93, $F_{(2, 140)} = 5.45, p < .05$). Gender, however, accounted for only 7.2 percent of the variance in overall mental health status ($\eta^2 = .072$).

The results of the post hoc between-subjects effects, however, indicate that males and females were significantly different on their emotional balance ($F_{(df = 1, 141)} = 10.95, p < .01, \eta^2 = .072$) but not on their levels of depression ($F_{(df = 1, 141)} = 1.56, p > .05, \eta^2 = .011$).

In this study, male older people experienced significantly greater levels of emotional balance (mean = 21.06, SE = .69) than their female counterparts (mean = 17.89, SE = .66). On the other hand, both males and females experienced similar levels of depression (Male: mean = 4.63, SE = .15; Female: mean = 4.88, SE = .14).

MAIN EFFECT 2—HOME: The results of the two-way MANOVA also show an overall significant difference between older people who have their own home and those who do not have their own home on their overall mental health status (Wilks' lambda = .89, $F_{(2, 140)} = 8.38, p < .001$). In this study, home ownership accounted for 10.7 percent of the variance in overall mental health status ($\eta^2 = .107$).

The results of the post hoc between-subjects effects show that older people who do have their own home were significantly different than those who do not have their own home on both measures of mental health: emotional balance ($F_{(df = 1, 141)} = 12.11, p < .010, \eta^2 = .079$) and levels of depression ($F_{(df = 1, 141)} = 10.14, p < .010, \eta^2 = .069$).

In this study, older people who have their own home experienced significantly lower levels of emotional balance (mean = 17.81, SE = .67) than older people who do not have their own home (mean = 21.14, SE = .68). Also, older people who have their own home experienced significantly greater depression (mean = 5.08, SE = .14) than older people who do not have their own home (mean = 4.43, SE = .15).

INTERACTION EFFECT—GENDER BY HOME: The results of the two-way MANOVA, on the other hand, show no significant gender by home ownership interaction effect on older people's overall mental health status (Wilks' lambda = .99, $F_{(2, 140)}$ = .19, p > .05). In this study, gender by home interaction accounted for less than half a percent of the variance in overall mental health status (η^2 = .003).

The results of the post hoc between-subjects effects confirm the results of Wilks' lambda of no gender by home interaction effect on either measure of mental health status: emotional balance ($F_{(df = 1, 141)}$ = .34, p > .05, η^2 = .002) or levels of depression ($F_{(df = 1, 141)}$ = .00, p > .05, η^2 = .000).

Presentation of the results of MANOVA in summary tables. The presentation of the results of MANOVA in summary tables is similar to the tables of two-way ANOVA. In MANOVA, however, the first table should display the descriptive statistics (mean, standard error, and number of cases) for all dependent variables for each level of the independent variable(s). The second table should also report the sum of squares, degrees of freedom, and mean squares for all sources of variation. It should also report the F ratio and level of significance for each effect. Unlike two-way ANOVA, the table should also report the overall results of the multivariate tests (e.g., Wilks' lambda).

As an example, tables 9.20.A and 9.20.B and figure 9.13 display the results of both the MANOVA and the between-subjects effects tests.

Table 9.20.A: Estimated Means of Gender, Home, and Gender by Home on Emotional Balance and Depression

Variables		Mean	SE	N
Emotional Balance	Home			
Male	No	23.00	.86	41
	Yes	19.11	1.08	27
	Total	21.06	.69	68
Female	No	19.28	1.04	29
	Yes	16.50	.81	48
	Total	17.89	.66	77
Total	No	21.14	.68	70
	Yes	17.81	.67	75
	Total	19.47	.47	145
Depression	Home			
Male	No	4.30	.19	41
	Yes	4.95	.23	27
	Total	4.63	.15	68
Female	No	4.56	.22	29
	Yes	5.21	.17	48
	Total	4.88	.14	77
Total	No	4.43	.15	70
	Yes	5.08	.14	75
	Total	4.75	.10	145

Table 9.20.B: MANOVA Summary Table

Source	Dependent Variable	SS	df	MS	F	p
Gender[a]	Emotional Balance	343.80	1	343.79	10.95	.001
	Depression	2.23	1	2.23	1.56	.214
Home[b]	Emotional Balance	380.48	1	380.48	12.11	.001
	Depression	14.49	1	14.49	10.14	.002
Gender* Home[c]	Emotional Balance	10.62	1	10.61	.34	.562
	Depression	.00	1	.00	.00	.998
Error	Emotional Balance	4428.46	141	31.41		
	Depression	201.50	141	1.43		
Corrected Total	Emotional Balance	5366.14	144			
	Depression	221.87	144			

[a]Wilks' lambda = .93, $F_{(df = 2, 140)}$ = 5.45, $p < .05$, η^2 = .072
[b]Wilks' lambda = .89, $F_{(df = 2, 140)}$ = 8.38, $p < .05$, η^2 = .107
[c]Wilks' lambda = .99, $F_{(df = 2, 140)}$ = 0.19, $p > .05$, η^2 = .003

SECOND PRACTICAL EXAMPLE: MULTIVARIATE ANALYSIS OF COVARIANCE

We will now use a two-way MANCOVA to examine the effect of gender and home ownership on older people's mental health while controlling for their cognitive status (CS). Bear in mind that the results of the two-way MANCOVA may be different than those of a two-way MANOVA. Also, you may have more than one covariate as long as they follow the test assumptions concerning covariates.

Hypothesis Testing

Step 1: State the Research Hypotheses.

MAIN EFFECT 1:

H_{o1}: Controlling for the effect of cognitive status, there are no statistically significant differences between male (M) and female (F) older people with regard to their overall mental health status (emotional balance and depression).

$\mu^*_M = \mu^*_F$; adjusted means are equal

H_{a1}: Controlling for the effect of cognitive status, there are statistically significant differences between male and female older people with regard to their overall mental health status (emotional balance and depression).

$\mu^*_M \neq \mu^*_F$; adjusted means are not equal

MAIN EFFECT 2:

H_{o2}: Controlling for the effect of cognitive status, there are no statistically significant differences between older people who own their home (Y) and older people who do not own their home (N) with regard to their over-all mental health status (emotional balance and depression).

$\mu^*{}_Y = \mu^*{}_N$; adjusted means are equal

H_{a2}: Controlling for the effect of cognitive status, there are statistically sig-nificant differences between older people who own their home (Y) and older people who do not own their home (N) with regard to their over-all mental health status (emotional balance and depression).

$\mu^*{}_Y \neq \mu^*{}_N$; adjusted means are not equal

INTERACTION EFFECT:

H_{o3}: Controlling for the effect of cognitive status, there is no statistically significant gender by home interaction effect on older people's overall mental health status (emotional balance and depression).

$\mu^*{}_{MY} = \mu^*{}_{MN} = \mu^*{}_{FY} = \mu^*{}_{FN}$; adjusted means are equal

H_{a3}: Controlling for the effect of cognitive status, there is a statistically sig-nificant gender by home interaction effect on older people's overall men-tal health status (emotional balance and depression).

$\mu^*{}_{MY} \neq \mu^*{}_{MN} \neq \mu^*{}_{FY} \neq \mu^*{}_{FN}$; at least two adjusted means are not equal

Step 2: Set the Criteria for Rejecting the Null Hypotheses.
We will set alpha at .05 ($\alpha = .05$). That is, reject H_o only if $p \leq .05$.

Step 3: Select the Appropriate Statistical Test.
Recall that this example is an extension of the previous example. Thus we do not need to evaluate the assumptions we already evaluated in the previous example. However, keep in mind that the values of Box's M and Levene's test of equality of variances may change due to the addition of the covariate(s). In this case, although not discussed here, they still show their corresponding assump-tions are fulfilled. We will evaluate the assumptions concerning MANCOVA. They include the following:

1. LEVELS OF MEASUREMENT: The covariate(s) must be continuous data and mea-sured at the interval level of measurement.

    In this study, Cognitive Status, the covariate, consists of continuous data and is measured at the interval level of measurement.

2. NORMAL DISTRIBUTION: The shape of the covariate must approximate the shape of a normal distribution.

    To evaluate this assumption, we will examine the measures of skewness and kurtosis of cognitive status and will inspect its histogram and normal probabil-ity plot.

Table 9.21 displays the results of skewness and kurtosis for cognitive status. The table shows that the skewness coefficient for cognitive status is greater than twice its standard error ($-.607/.197 = -3.08$), thus indicating severe negative skewness. On the other hand, kurtosis for cognitive status falls within the normal range ($.413/.391 = 1.06$), thus indicating normal distribution.

Eyeballing the histogram for cognitive status (figure 9.14.A) shows a negative skewness on the distribution of cognitive status. The normal probability plot (figure 9.14.B) also shows a departure from normality, however not severe. Also, as discussed earlier, MANCOVA is robust to violation of normality with large sample sizes. Thus normality of the covariate in this case is not an issue.

3. LINEAR RELATIONSHIP: The relationship between the covariate and the dependent variables should be linear.

To examine this assumption, we will compute the correlation between Cognitive Status (covariate) and both dependent variables (Emotional Balance and Depression). We will also generate two scatterplots for the covariate, one with each dependent variable.

Table 9.22 displays the correlation coefficients between the covariate and the dependent variables. As it appears, cognitive status has a significant correlation with emotional balance ($r = .57, p < .001$) and depression ($r = -.35, p < .001$).

Table 9.21:   Measures of Skewness and Kurtosis for Covariate

Statistics

CS Cognitive status

N	Valid	152.000
	Missing	3.000
	Skewness	**-.607**
	Std. Error of Skewness	.197
	Kurtosis	**.413**
	Std. Error of Kurtosis	.391

Figure 9.14:   Histogram and Normal Probability Plot for Cognitive Status

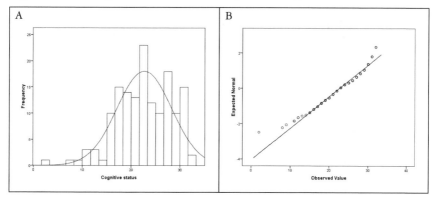

Table 9.22:   Pearson's Correlation between Covariate and Dependent Variables

Correlations

		Cognitive status	SQRT_CESD
Cognitive status	Pearson Correlation	1.000	
	Sig. (2-tailed)		
Emotional balance	Pearson Correlation	.565[**]	
	Sig. (2-tailed)	.000	
SQRT_CESD	Pearson Correlation	-.350[**]	1.000
	Sig. (2-tailed)	.000	

[**]. Correlation is significant at the 0.01 level (2-tailed).

Also, the scatterplots for cognitive status and emotional balance (figure 9.15.A) and cognitive status and depression (figure 9.15.B) show linear relationships between the covariate and each dependent variable.

4.   RELIABILITY OF COVARIATE: The covariate should be error free. This can be assumed only when the reliability coefficient of the covariate is .80 and above.

The covariate, Cognitive Status, was measured using a subscale of the standardized Iowa Self-Assessment Inventory, which has seven subscales. The internal consistency reliability coefficients for these subscales range from .74 to .86 (see appendix).

5.   HOMOGENEITY OF REGRESSION: The relationship between the covariate (Cognitive Status) and the linear combination of the dependent variables (Emotional Balance and Depression) should be the same for each level of the independent variables. In other words, there should be no gender by home by cognitive status interaction effect on overall mental health.

We will evaluate homogeneity of regression by inspecting the results of the MANOVA custom table (see step 4 in the following).

Table 9.23 presents the results of MANCOVA custom table. We are interested in only the last row, Gender * Home * CS. This row represents the interaction effect of the covariate and the independent variables on the composite

Figure 9.15:   Scatterplots for Covariate with Dependent Variables

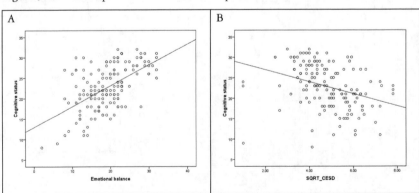

Table 9.23:   MANCOVA Custom Table—Homogeneity of Regression

Multivariate Tests[c]

Effect		Value	F	Hypothesis df	Error df	Sig.
Intercept	Pillai's Trace	.692	1.529E2	2.000	136.000	.000
	Wilks' Lambda	.308	1.529E2	2.000	136.000	.000
	Hotelling's Trace	2.249	1.529E2	2.000	136.000	.000
	Roy's Largest Root	2.249	1.529E2	2.000	136.000	.000
GENDER	Pillai's Trace	.011	.765[a]	2.000	136.000	.467
	Wilks' Lambda	.989	.765[a]	2.000	136.000	.467
	Hotelling's Trace	.011	.765[a]	2.000	136.000	.467
	Roy's Largest Root	.011	.765[a]	2.000	136.000	.467
HOME	Pillai's Trace	.026	1.788[a]	2.000	136.000	.171
	Wilks' Lambda	.974	1.788[a]	2.000	136.000	.171
	Hotelling's Trace	.026	1.788[a]	2.000	136.000	.171
	Roy's Largest Root	.026	1.788[a]	2.000	136.000	.171
CS	Pillai's Trace	.271	25.283[a]	2.000	136.000	.000
	Wilks' Lambda	.729	25.283[a]	2.000	136.000	.000
	Hotelling's Trace	.372	25.283[a]	2.000	136.000	.000
	Roy's Largest Root	.372	25.283[a]	2.000	136.000	.000
GENDER * HOME * CS	Pillai's Trace	.057	1.349	6.000	274.000	.236
	Wilks' Lambda	.943	1.358[a]	6.000	272.000	.232
	Hotelling's Trace	.061	1.368	6.000	270.000	.228
	Roy's Largest Root	.060	2.754[b]	3.000	137.000	.045

a. Exact statistic

b. The statistic is an upper bound on F that yields a lower bound on the significance level.

c. Design: Intercept + GENDER + HOME + CS + GENDER * HOME * CS

variable. A p value greater than .05 (*Sig.* > .05) indicates that the assumption of homogeneity of regression is fulfilled.

Table 9.23 shows no significant interaction effect between gender, home, and cognitive status on older people's mental health ($F_{(df = 6, 272)} = 1.358$, $p = .232$), thus indicating that the assumption of homogeneity of regression is met.

Note: If the assumption is violated ($p < .05$), *stop*! MANCOVA is not the right test. Consider conducting multiple regression analysis by treating the covariate(s) as independent variables. Another alternative is to recode the covariate(s) into categorical variables and then conduct factorial MANOVA.

To conclude, our data and variables appear to satisfy all the assumptions of a two-way MANCOVA.

How to Use SPSS to Test the Assumptions of MANCOVA and Run the Analysis

Step 4: Compute the MANCOVA Test Statistic.

First, we will use SPSS to examine the assumption of homogeneity of regression. To do so, follow these SPSS steps:

1. Open the Mental Health SPSS data file.

2. Click on *Analyze,* scroll down to *General Linear Model,* and click on *Multivariate.* This command will open the "Multivariate" dialog box.

3. Follow step 3 from the first example to move *EB* and *SQRT_CESD* into the *Dependent Variables* box.

4. Also, move *Gender* and *Home* into the *Fixed Factor(s)* box.

5. Move *CS* (covariate) into the *Covariate(s)* box (see screen 9.4).

6. Click on *Model* in the upper right corner to open the "Multivariate: Model" dialog box.

7. Check *Custom* under "Specify Model."

8. Click on *Gender* in the *Factors & Covariates* box, and click on the arrow under "Build Term(s)" to move *Gender* into the *Model* box.

9. Repeat step 8 to move *Home* and *CS* into the *Model* box.

10. While holding down the *Ctrl* button on the keyboard, click on *Gender, Home,* and *CS* and click on the arrow to move them into the *Model* box (see screen 9.5).

11. Make sure that *Type III* appears next to *Sum of Squares.* This is the SPSS default. If not, click on the drop-down arrow for *Sum of Squares* and click on *Type III.* This type adjusts for unequal cell frequencies.

12. Click on *Continue* to return to the "Multivariate" main dialog box.

13. Click on *Options* on the right menu to open the "Multivariate: Options" dialog box.

14. Check the *Residual SSCP Matrix* and *Homogeneity Tests* boxes to request Box's test, Levene's test, Bartlett's test of sphericity, and the residual SSCP matrix (see screen 9.6).

15. Click on *Continue* and then *OK.*

Screen 9.4: SPSS GLM Multivariate Dialog Box

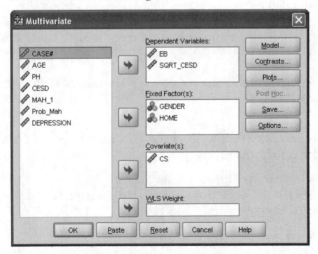

Screen 9.5:   SPSS Multivariate Custom Model Dialog Box

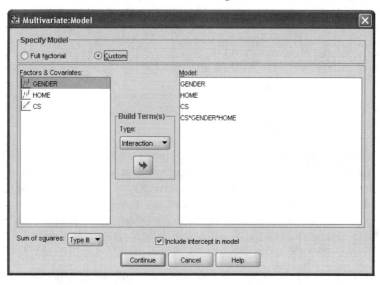

Screen 9.6:   SPSS Multivariate Options Dialog Box

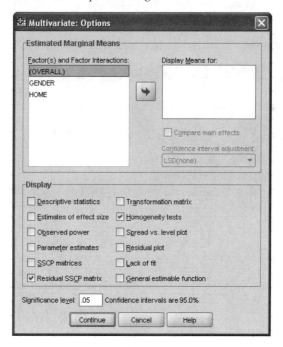

Homogeneity of Regression, Covariance-Variance Matrices, Variances, and
Bartlett's Test of Sphericity SPSS Syntax Commands

GLM EB SQRT_CESD BY GENDER HOME WITH CS
/METHOD=SSTYPE(3)
/INTERCEPT=INCLUDE
/PRINT=RSSCP HOMOGENEITY
/CRITERIA=ALPHA(.05)
/DESIGN=GENDER HOME CS CS*GENDER*HOME.

The execution of these commands will produce a number of tables, including Box's test, Bartlett's test of sphericity, multivariate tests, Levene's test of equality of variances, and residual SSCP matrix. These tables are used for evaluation of test assumptions and were discussed earlier.

Now that we have satisfied all test assumptions, we will use the SPSS to conduct a full MANCOVA analysis to examine our research hypotheses.

To run MANCOVA in SPSS, follow these steps:

1. Follow steps 1 through 6 for examining the assumption of homogeneity of regression to open the "Multivariate: Model" dialog box (see screen 9.7).

2. Click on *Full Factorial* under "Specify Model" (this command will dim all variables), and click on *Continue* to return to the "Multivariate" main dialog box.

Screen 9.7: SPSS Multivariate Full Factorial Model Dialog Box

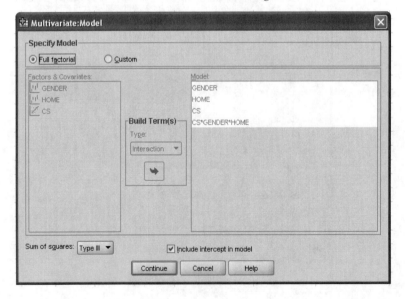

Screen 9.8:   SPSS Multivariate Options Dialog Box

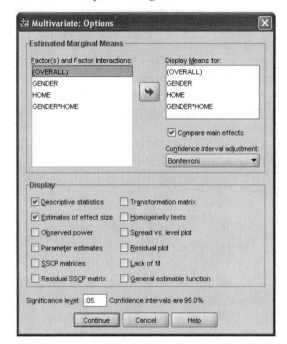

3. Click on *Options* in the right menu to open the "Multivariate: Options" dialog box.

4. Move *Overall, Gender, Home,* and *Gender * Home* into the *Display Means For* box.

5. Check the *Compare Main Effects* box.

6. Click on the drop-down arrow for *Confidence Interval Adjustment,* and click on *Bonferroni.*

7. Check the *Descriptive Statistics* and *Estimates of Effect Size* boxes. Uncheck the *Residual SSCP Matrix* and *Homogeneity Tests* boxes (which we checked previously) (see screen 9.8).

8. Click on *Continue* to return to the "Multivariate" main dialog box.

9. Click on *Plots* on the right menu to open the "Multivariate: Profile Plots" dialog box.

10. Follow steps 15 through 18 for running MANOVA from the first example to generate plots for all effects (see screen 9.3).

11. Click on *Continue,* and click on *OK* in the "Multivariate" main dialog box.

SPSS Syntax for MANCOVA

GLM EB SQRT_CESD BY GENDER HOME WITH CS
/METHOD=SSTYPE(3)
/INTERCEPT=INCLUDE
/PLOT=PROFILE(GENDER*HOME)
/EMMEANS=TABLES(OVERALL) WITH(CS=MEAN)
/EMMEANS=TABLES(GENDER) WITH(CS=MEAN) COMPARE
  ADJ(BONFERRONI)
/EMMEANS=TABLES(HOME) WITH(CS=MEAN) COMPARE
  ADJ(BONFERRONI)
/EMMEANS=TABLES(GENDER*HOME) WITH(CS=MEAN)
/PRINT=DESCRIPTIVE ETASQ
/CRITERIA=ALPHA(.05)
/DESIGN=CS GENDER HOME GENDER*HOME.

Reading the SPSS Output of MANCOVA

Reading the output of MANCOVA is the same as in MANOVA. The only difference here is that there is one more source of variability due to the addition of the covariate(s). Thus the results of MANCOVA are based on the adjusted means and therefore may be different than those obtained by MANOVA. In reality, as discussed earlier, the results of MANCOVA have greater statistical power than those of MANOVA because MANCOVA reduces the error variances.

This section will present only the results of the multivariate tests and the between-subjects effects test to illustrate how the covariance might impact the overall relationship between the independent variables and the dependent variables. The rest of the tables are the same as those presented in the first example, however, based on the adjusted means. Their results will be discussed later under "Writing the Results" and "Presentation of the Results of MANCOVA in Summary Tables."

Table 9.24 presents the results of the full factorial multivariate tests. Remember, because Box's M test was not significant, we will report only the results of the Wilks' lambda test. (*Note:* if Box's M test is significant, report the results of Pillai's trace test.)

Table 9.24 is similar to table 9.12 in the first example. It examines the effect of each independent variable (Gender and Home) and their interaction overall on the composite dependent variable (Mental Health). Unlike table 9.12, table 9.24 has an extra row, CS, which examines the effect of the covariate on the composite dependent variable.

In the second row (CS), the results of Wilks' lambda show a significant relationship between cognitive status (covariate) and overall mental health (Wilks' lambda = .72, $F_{(df = 2, 138)} = 26.87, p = .000$). Remember, one of the assumptions of MANCOVA is that the covariate and composite variable must have a linear

Table 9.24:   Results of the Full Factorial Multivariate Tests (MANCOVA)

Multivariate Tests[b]

Effect		Value	F	Hypothesis df	Error df	Sig.	Partial Eta Squared
Intercept	Pillai's Trace	.696	157.919[a]	2.000	138.000	.000	.696
	Wilks' Lambda	.304	157.919[a]	2.000	138.000	.000	.696
	Hotelling's Trace	2.289	157.919[a]	2.000	138.000	.000	.696
	Roy's Largest Root	2.289	157.919[a]	2.000	138.000	.000	.696
CS	Pillai's Trace	.280	26.872[a]	2.000	138.000	.000	.280
	Wilks' Lambda	.720	26.872[a]	2.000	138.000	.000	.280
	Hotelling's Trace	.389	26.872[a]	2.000	138.000	.000	.280
	Roy's Largest Root	.389	26.872[a]	2.000	138.000	.000	.280
GENDER	Pillai's Trace	.099	7.607[a]	2.000	138.000	.001	.099
	Wilks' Lambda	.901	7.607[a]	2.000	138.000	.001	.099
	Hotelling's Trace	.110	7.607[a]	2.000	138.000	.001	.099
	Roy's Largest Root	.110	7.607[a]	2.000	138.000	.001	.099
HOME	Pillai's Trace	.032	2.254[a]	2.000	138.000	.109	.032
	Wilks' Lambda	.968	2.254[a]	2.000	138.000	.109	.032
	Hotelling's Trace	.033	2.254[a]	2.000	138.000	.109	.032
	Roy's Largest Root	.033	2.254[a]	2.000	138.000	.109	.032
GENDER * HOME	Pillai's Trace	.026	1.837[a]	2.000	138.000	.163	.026
	Wilks' Lambda	.974	1.837[a]	2.000	138.000	.163	.026
	Hotelling's Trace	.027	1.837[a]	2.000	138.000	.163	.026
	Roy's Largest Root	.027	1.837[a]	2.000	138.000	.163	.026

a. Exact statistic

b. Design: Intercept + CS + GENDER + HOME + GENDER * HOME

relationship. Wilks' lambda shows that 72 percent of the variance in mental health is not accounted for by cognitive status. In other words, 28 percent of the variance in mental health is accounted for by the covariate, Cognitive Status (partial eta squared = .28).

In the third row (Gender), the results of Wilks' lambda show a significant difference between males and females on their overall mental health (Wilks' lambda = .90, $F_{(df = 2, 138)}$ = 7.61, p = .001). Wilks' lambda, however, shows that 90 percent of the variance in mental health is not accounted for by gender. That is, only 10 percent of the variance in mental health is accounted for by gender (partial eta squared = .099).

Recall that gender accounted for only 7.2 percent of the variance in mental health in the first example. Thus the relationship between gender and mental health was improved when controlling for cognitive status.

In the fourth row (Home), the results of Wilks' lambda, on the other hand, show no significant difference between participants who have their own home and those who do not on their overall mental health (Wilks' lambda = .97, $F_{(df = 2, 138)}$ = 2.25, p > .05). Wilks' lambda shows that 96.8 percent of the variance in mental health is not accounted for by home. That is, only 3.2 percent of the variance in mental health is accounted for by home (partial eta squared = .032).

As you may remember, the results of Wilks' lambda in the first example show a significant difference between the two home ownership groups on their overall mental health. In fact, home accounted for 10.7 percent of the variance in mental health. However, when controlling for the effect of cognitive status, the difference between the two groups is no longer significant. Notice the significant drop in the amount of variance in mental health before and after controlling for cognitive status: from 10.7 percent to 3.2 percent.

In the fifth row (Gender * Home), the results of Wilks' lambda also show no significant interaction between gender and home ownership effect on participants' overall mental health (Wilks' lambda = .97, $F_{(df = 2, 138)}$ = 1.84, $p > .05$). Wilks' lambda shows that 97.4 percent of the variance in mental health is not accounted for by the interaction between gender and home. In other words, only 2.6 percent of the variance in mental health is accounted for by the gender and home interaction (partial eta squared = .026).

While still consistent with the results of MANOVA, the results of MANCOVA show a slight increase in the overall mental health variance that is accounted for by gender and home interaction when controlling for cognitive status, from .03 percent to 2.6 percent, but it is still not significant.

Now that MANCOVA shows significant gender differences on their overall mental health, the question is what dependent variable(s) are responsible for the differences. As with MANOVA, the answer for this question is found in the tests of between-subjects effects table (table 9.25).

Table 9.25 is similar to table 9.13 in the first example. It presents the post hoc univariate test of between-subjects effects. Unlike table 9.13, table 9.25 has an additional row for the covariate, Cognitive Status.

Covariate effect—CS (third row).   In the first line, Emotional Balance, the between-subjects effects tests show a significant relationship between cognitive status and emotional balance ($F = 46.522$, $df = 1$, $Sig. = .000$). The table shows that cognitive status accounted for 25.1 percent of the variance in emotional balance (partial eta squared = .251).

Table 9.25:   Results of the Between-Subjects Effects Tests

Tests of Between-Subjects Effects

Source	Dependent Variable	Type III Sum of Squares	df	Mean Square	F	Sig.	Partial Eta Squared
Corrected Model	Emotional balance	2082.712[a]	4	520.678	24.292	.000	.411
	SQRT_CESD	43.336[b]	4	10.834	9.171	.000	.209
Intercept	Emotional balance	308.404	1	308.404	14.389	.000	.094
	SQRT_CESD	281.867	1	281.867	238.605	.000	.632
CS	Emotional balance	997.147	1	997.147	46.522	.000	.251
	SQRT_CESD	26.136	1	26.136	22.125	.000	.137
GENDER	Emotional balance	325.910	1	325.910	15.205	.000	.099
	SQRT_CESD	.868	1	.868	.735	.393	.005
HOME	Emotional balance	79.158	1	79.158	3.693	.057	.026
	SQRT_CESD	2.523	1	2.523	2.136	.146	.015
GENDER * HOME	Emotional balance	78.482	1	78.482	3.662	.058	.026
	SQRT_CESD	.185	1	.185	.157	.693	.001
Error	Emotional balance	2979.288	139	21.434			
	SQRT_CESD	164.202	139	1.181			
Total	Emotional balance	59818.000	144				
	SQRT_CESD	3523.000	144				
Corrected Total	Emotional balance	5062.000	143				
	SQRT_CESD	207.538	143				

a. R Squared = .411 (Adjusted R Squared = .395)

b. R Squared = .209 (Adjusted R Squared = .186)

In the second line, Depression, table 9.25 also shows a significant correlation between cognitive status and depression ($F = 22.125$, $df = 1$, $Sig.$ = .000). Cognitive status accounted for 13.7 percent of the variance in depression (partial eta squared = .137).

Main effect 1—Gender (fourth row).   In the first line, Emotional Balance, table 9.25 shows a significant difference between male and female participants in their levels of emotional balance ($F = 15.205$, $df = 1$, $Sig.$ = .000). Gender accounted for 9.9 percent of the variance in emotional balance (partial eta squared = .099).

On the other hand, in the second line, Depression, table 9.25 shows no significant difference between male and female participants in their levels of depression ($F = .735$, $df = 1$, $Sig.$ = .393). In this study, gender accounted for only .5 percent of the variance in depression (partial eta squared = .005).

Main effect 2—Home (fifth row).   In the first line, Emotional Balance, table 9.25 (unlike table 9.13 in the first example) shows no significant difference between participants who own their home and participants who do not on their levels of emotional balance when controlling for their cognitive status ($F = 3.693$, $df = 1$, $Sig.$ = .057). In this case, home accounted for only 2.6 percent of the variance in emotional balance (partial eta squared = .026).

In the second line, Depression, table 9.25 also shows no significant difference between participants who own their home and participants who do not on their levels of depression when controlling for their cognitive status ($F = 2.136$, $df = 1$, $Sig.$ = .146). Home accounted for only 1.5 percent of the variance in depression (partial eta squared = .015).

Interaction effect—Gender * Home (sixth row).   In the first line, Emotional Balance, table 9.25 (as in table 9.13 in the first example) shows no significant gender by home interaction effect on participants' levels of emotional balance ($F = 3.662$, $df = 1$, $Sig.$ = .058). In this study, gender by home interaction accounted for 2.6 percent of the variance in emotional balance when controlling for cognitive status (partial eta squared = .026).

In the second line, Depression, table 9.25 also shows no significant gender by home interaction effect on participants' levels of depression ($F = .157$, $df = 1$, $Sig.$ = .693). Gender by home interaction accounted for only .1 percent of the variance in depression (partial eta squared = .001).

Step 5: Write the Results of MANCOVA.
Writing the results of MANCOVA is the same as writing the results of MANOVA. However, when addressing the test assumptions, also address the assumptions of linear relationship between covariates and dependent variables, reliability of covariates, and homogeneity of regression.

Also, when presenting the results of the multivariate and between-subjects effects tests, present the results of these tests on the covariates.

Writing the Results

The following presents the results of the two-way MANCOVA for gender and home ownership on overall mental health status controlling for the effect of cognitive status.

Evaluation of assumptions.   Prior to utilizing the two-way MAN-COVA, data were evaluated to ensure that the assumptions for multivariate tests were fulfilled. First, a cross-tabulation of the two independent variables shows that all cells have a minimum of 29 cases per cell, thus showing a large sample size for MANCOVA.

Second, measures of skewness and kurtosis, histograms, and normal Q-Q plots were examined for both dependent variables (Emotional Balance and Depression) and the covariate (Cognitive Status). Inspection of these measures and plots shows a normal distribution on levels of emotional balance and cognitive status. On the other hand, depression was severely skewed, and thus it was transformed to the square root. Evaluation of the distribution of the transformed depression revealed a normal distribution. Also, the distributions for each dependent variable for each level of the independent variables approached the normal curve.

Third, the results of Levene's test of equality of variances and Box's test of variance-covariance matrices indicated that homogeneity of variances and homogeneity of variance-covariance matrices were satisfied ($p > .05$), respectively. In addition, both the scatterplot of the dependent variables and the results of Bartlett's test and the residuals SSCP matrix show that both emotional balance and depression met the assumptions of linearity and multicollinearity.

Fourth, the results of Pearson's correlation and scatterplots showed a linear relationship between the covariate and the dependent variables.

Finally, the results of MANCOVA show no significant interaction between gender, home ownership, and cognitive status on older people's mental health ($F_{(df = 6, 272)} = 1.358, p = .232$), thus indicating homogeneity of regression.

Results of MANCOVA.   A two-way MANCOVA was utilized to examine the effects of gender and home ownership on the overall mental health status among a sample of 155 older people ages fifty and above while controlling for their cognitive status. In this study, mental health was conceptualized as a composite of levels of emotional balance and depression.

COVARIATE EFFECT—COGNITIVE STATUS: The results of the two-way MAN-COVA show a significant covariate effect on older people's overall mental health status (Wilks' lambda = .72, $F_{(2, 138)} = 26.87, p < .001$). In this study, cognitive status accounted for 28 percent of the variance in overall mental health status ($\eta^2 = .28$).

The results of the post hoc between-subjects effects show a significant cognitive status effect on emotional balance ($F_{(df = 1, 139)} = 46.52, p < .001, \eta^2 = .25$) and on levels of depression ($F_{(df = 1, 139)} = 22.13, p < .001, \eta^2 = .14$).

MAIN EFFECT 1—GENDER: The results of the two-way MANCOVA show an overall significant difference between male and female older people on their overall mental health status controlling for cognitive status (Wilks' lambda = .90, $F_{(2, 138)} = 7.61, p < .010$). Gender accounted for almost 10 percent of the variance in overall mental health status ($\eta^2 = .099$).

The results of the post hoc between-subjects effects, however, indicate that males and females were significantly different on their emotional balance ($F_{(df = 1, 139)} = 15.21, p < .001, \eta^2 = .099$) but not on their levels of depression ($F_{(df = 1, 139)} = .74, p > .05, \eta^2 = .005$).

In this study, when controlling for their levels of cognitive status, male older people experienced significantly greater levels of emotional balance (mean = 21.02, SE = .58) than their female counterparts (mean = 17.92, SE = .54). On the other hand, both males (mean = 4.723, SE = .14) and females (mean = 4.88, SE = .13) experienced similar levels of depression.

MAIN EFFECT 2—HOME: The results of the two-way MANCOVA show no significant difference between older people who have their own home and those who do not have their own home on their overall mental health status (Wilks' lambda = .97, $F_{(2, 138)} = 2.25, p > .05$). In this study, home ownership accounted for only 3.2 percent of the variance in overall mental health status ($\eta^2 = .032$).

The results of the post hoc between-subjects effects show significant difference between the two home ownership groups neither on their emotional balance ($F_{(df = 1, 138)} = 3.69, p > .05, \eta^2 = .026$) nor on their levels of depression ($F_{(df = 1, 138)} = 2.14, p > .05, \eta^2 = .015$).

In this study, older people who have their own home and those who do not have their own home experienced similar levels of emotional balance when controlling for their cognitive status (mean = 18.66, SE = .57 and mean = 20.28, SE = .59, respectively). Also, both groups experienced similar levels of depression (Yes Home: mean = 4.94, SE = .13; No Home: mean = 4.65, SE = .14).

INTERACTION EFFECT—GENDER BY HOME: The results of the two-way MANCOVA also show no significant gender by home ownership interaction effect on older people's overall mental health status (Wilks' lambda = .97, $F_{(2, 138)} = 1.84$, $p > .05$). In this study, gender by home interaction accounted for less than 3 percent of the variance in overall mental health status ($\eta^2 = .026$).

The results of the post hoc between-subjects effects show no gender by home interaction effect on either measure of mental health status: emotional balance ($F_{(df = 1, 139)} = 3.66, p > .05, \eta^2 = .026$) or levels of depression ($F_{(df = 1, 139)} = .16, p > .05, \eta^2 = .001$).

Presentation of the results of MANCOVA in summary tables. Presentation of the results of MANCOVA in summary tables is exactly the same as in MANOVA with the exception that the adjusted means should be reported in MANCOVA. For this example, the results are presented in tables 9.26.A and 9.26.B and figure 9.16.

Table 9.26.A: Adjusted Means of Gender, Home, and Gender by Home on
Emotional Balance and Depression

Variables		Mean	SE	N
Emotional Balance	Home			
Male	No	22.60	.75	41
	Yes	19.44	.89	27
	Total	21.02	.58	68
Female	No	17.97	.88	29
	Yes	17.88	.70	48
	Total	17.92	.54	77
Total	No	20.28	.59	70
	Yes	18.66	.57	75
	Total	19.47	.40	145
Depression	Home			
Male	No	4.53	.18	41
	Yes	4.90	.21	27
	Total	4.72	.14	68
Female	No	4.77	.21	29
	Yes	4.98	.16	48
	Total	4.88	.13	77
Total	No	4.65	.14	70
	Yes	4.94	.13	75
	Total	4.80	.09	145

Table 9.26.B: MANCOVA Summary Table

Source	Dependent Variable	SS	df	MS	F	p
Covariate[a]	Emotional Balance	997.15	1	997.15	46.52	.000
	Depression	26.14	1	26.14	22.13	.000
Gender[b]	Emotional Balance	325.91	1	325.91	15.21	.000
	Depression	.87	1	.87	.74	.393
Home[c]	Emotional Balance	79.16	1	79.16	3.69	.057
	Depression	2.52	1	2.52	2.14	.146
Gender* Home[d]	Emotional Balance	78.48	1	78.48	3.66	.058
	Depression	.19	1	.19	.16	.693
Error	Emotional Balance	2979.29	139	21.43		
	Depression	164.20	139	1.18		
Corrected Total	Emotional Balance	5062.00	143			
	Depression	207.54	143			

[a]Wilks' lambda = .72, $F_{(df = 2, 138)}$ = 26.87, $p < .001$, η^2 = .280
[b]Wilks' lambda = .90, $F_{(df = 2, 138)}$ = 7.61, $p < .010$, η^2 = .099
[c]Wilks' lambda = .97, $F_{(df = 2, 138)}$ = 2.25, $p > .05$, η^2 = .032
[d]Wilks' lambda = .97, $F_{(df = 2, 138)}$ = 1.84, $p > .05$, η^2 = .026

Figure 9.16: Means Plots for Gender and Home

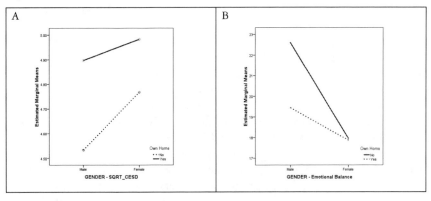

Notice how the emotional balance means plot (figure 9.16.B) is different than in the first example (9.13.B). Whereas figure 9.16.B (MANCOVA) shows that females on both groups of home ownership have similar means on emotional balance after controlling for the effect of their cognitive status, figure 9.13.B (MANOVA) shows significant difference between the two female groups on their emotional balance.

SUMMARY

Chapter 9 presented two complex statistical techniques. It introduced two of the three multivariate techniques that are discussed in this book. Multivariate techniques, unlike univariate techniques, analyze multiple dependent variables simultaneously by creating a composite variable of the centroid of all dependent variables and then examining the relationship between this composite variable and the independent variable(s).

Chapter 9 focused on multivariate analysis of variance and covariance, simply known as MANOVA and MANCOVA, respectively. The chapter discussed the primary purpose of both tests. As said, MANOVA is used to examine the effect of one or more categorical independent variables on multiple dependent variables simultaneously. MANCOVA examines the effect of one or more categorical variables on multiple dependent variables, as does MANOVA. It differs from MANOVA in that this examination occurs after adjusting for extraneous effects, known as covariates.

The chapter then discussed the advantages of MANOVA and MANCOVA. Unlike ordinary ANOVA and ANCOVA, multivariate tests have the advantages of examining group effects and their interactions on multiple measures simultaneously. By creating a single linear combination of multiple measures, researchers increase the probability of finding significant group differences that otherwise may not be found with ordinary ANOVA or ANCOVA. Furthermore, by conducting analysis on the composite variable, multivariate ANOVA and ANCOVA protect against the inflation of type I error, which occurs when multiple tests are utilized on the same data.

Next, chapter 9 discussed the sources of variance in MANOVA and MANCOVA. As said, the variance in MANOVA is partitioned in two sources: between-subjects variance and error variance. In addition to these two sources, a third source can be examined in MANCOVA due to the covariate(s).

Chapter 9 then discussed four different multivariate techniques, all of which examine the overall group differences on the composite variables. They are Pillai's trace, Wilks' lambda, Hotelling's trace, and Roy's largest root. The differences among these tests relate to their robustness to violation of the test assumptions and to their mathematical computation. Following these tests, the chapter also discussed the post hoc tests required for MANOVA and MANCOVA. Unlike ANOVA and ANCOVA, multivariate tests require two additional analyses (post hoc tests). The first examines what dependent variable(s), if any, are responsible for the group and/or interaction differences, and the second examines what groups, if any, are significantly different.

The chapter then discussed the research questions and hypotheses examined by both MANOVA and MANCOVA. The number of questions and hypotheses depends on the number of independent variables. With a two-way MANOVA and MANCOVA, they include two main effects (one for each independent variable) and one interaction effect.

Chapter 9 also discussed the tests' assumptions. In addition to the univariate assumptions, MANOVA and MANCOVA require a sufficient number of cases per cell, multivariate normality, a linear relationship between all pairs of dependent variables, homogeneity of variance-covariance matrices, and multicollinearity among all dependent variables. Furthermore, MANCOVA requires that the covariates are error free and have reliability coefficients of .80 and above and that there is a linear relationship between covariates and the dependent variables. It also requires no interaction between the independent variables and covariates on the composite dependent variable, that is, homogeneity of regression.

Finally, chapter 9 presented two detailed examples illustrating the use of a two-way MANOVA and a two-way MANCOVA. These examples illustrated how to write both null and alternative hypotheses, evaluate the tests' assumptions, use the SPSS main menu and syntax commands, write the results of a two-way MANOVA and MANCOVA, and present the results in summary tables.

Chapter 10 will examine canonical correlation analysis. As in this chapter, chapter 10 will discuss the purpose and advantages of canonical correlation and the research questions and hypotheses answered by it. An example illustrating the utilization of canonical correlation and demonstrating how to use SPSS to run the statistics will also be presented.

PRACTICAL EXERCISES

A social work researcher was interested in the differences in levels of job satisfaction (Satisfaction) and burnout (Burnout) based on ethnicity (Ethnicity) and marital status (MStatus) among social and human services employees. For this purpose, the researcher collected data from 218 social services employees who completed the *Job Satisfaction* survey (see appendix, Data File 3).

Part 1

1. State the null and alternative hypotheses.
2. What statistical test(s) will you utilize to examine the null hypotheses? Why? Discuss your answer in detail.
3. Write the SPSS syntax file for the test statistic.
4. Run the statistical test you chose in question 2.
5. What is your decision with regard to the null hypotheses? Discuss your answer in detail.
6. Present the results in summary table(s) and graph(s).

Part 2

Now control for the effect of working with colleagues (Colleague) and answer the following questions:

1. Restate the null and alternative hypotheses.
2. What statistical test will you utilize to examine the null hypotheses? Why? Discuss your answer in detail.
3. Write the SPSS syntax file for this test statistic.
4. Run this test statistic.
5. What is your decision with regard to the null hypotheses? Discuss your answer in detail.
6. Present the results in summary table(s) and graph(s).
7. Are there any differences between the results of the two tests you utilized in parts 1 and 2? If yes, discuss these differences.

CHAPTER 10

Canonical Correlation Analysis

LEARNING OBJECTIVES

1. Understand the purpose of canonical correlation
2. Understand the concepts of canonical correlation
3. Understand the statistical tests used in canonical correlation
4. Understand the advantages of canonical correlation
5. Understand the research questions and hypotheses of canonical correlation
6. Understand the assumptions underlying canonical correlation
7. Understand how to use SPSS to compute canonical correlation
8. Understand how to interpret and present the results of canonical correlation

DATA SET (APPENDIX)

Job Satisfaction

INTRODUCTION

Chapter 4 presented multiple regression analysis. As said, the purpose of multiple regression analysis is to predict a single outcome variable based on several factors, independent variables. In a sense, multiple regression analysis first creates a composite factor based on a linear combination of all factors and then examines the correlation coefficient (R) between the "composite factor" and the outcome variable.

Suppose that you are interested in predicting several outcome variables that, conceptually, formulate one overall score. For example, suppose a mental health researcher is interested in predicting immigrants' overall well-being (life satisfaction, self-esteem, and depression) based on several personal characteristics, such as age, education, income, and language proficiency. Or suppose that a university admissions officer is interested in predicting prospective graduate students' GRE scores (quantitative, analytical, and verbal test scores) based on their undergraduate GPA, parents' education, and socioeconomic status.

As you may notice, the outcome variables in both examples consist of multiple variables: life satisfaction, self-esteem, and depression in the first example and quantitative, analytical, and verbal in the second example.

Given these three outcome variables, ordinary researchers may conduct three multiple regression analyses, one for each outcome variable. The problem with this approach is twofold: first, conducting multiple tests on the same data set, as has been discussed, is likely to increase the probability of making type I error; second, conducting three separate multiple regression analyses will predict only a single outcome, and it will not predict the overall outcome. The question is then, what statistical test will be suitable to predict multiple outcome variables while avoiding these problems?

This chapter will introduce and discuss a new multivariate statistical technique that, unlike the previous techniques, allows researchers to predict several outcome variables based on several factors. This technique is *canonical correlation analysis.*

CANONICAL CORRELATION ANALYSIS

Purpose

Canonical correlation analysis is an advanced technique of multiple regression analysis. It is frequently referred to as multivariate multiple regression (MMR). It is perhaps the least utilized multivariate technique in social sciences research due to its mathematical complexity and interpretation.

The purpose of canonical correlation is to predict multiple outcomes based on multiple factors. In other words, it examines the relationships between two sets of variables. One set includes multiple independent variables $(X_1, X_2, \ldots, X_p)$, and the other set includes multiple dependent variables $(Y_1, Y_2, \ldots, Y_q)$.

However, like Pearson's correlation coefficient and multiple regression analysis, canonical correlation analysis does not test for causality. It examines only the strengths and directions of the relationships between the two sets of variables.

Concepts of Canonical Correlation

Canonical variate.   Canonical variate, also known as *canonical variable,* is a *latent,* a *composite,* or an *overall* variable representing all variables within each set. It is a linear combination of all variables in a particular set. Canonical correlation analysis consists of at least two canonical variates, one for each set: (1) *dependent canonical variate* (Y canonical variate) and (2) *independent,* or *covariate, canonical variate* (X canonical variate).

In the first example, *overall well-being* represents the dependent canonical variate. It is a latent variable, or a composite variable, of life satisfaction, self-esteem, and depression. *Personal characteristics* represent the independent, or covariate, canonical variate. It is a latent, or a composite, variable of age, education, income, and language proficiency. In the second example, *GRE score* represents the dependent canonical variate. It is a latent, or a composite, variable of quantitative, analytical, and verbal test scores. *Student background* is the independent, or covariate, canonical variate. It is a latent, or a composite, variable of undergraduate GPA, parents' education, and socioeconomic status.

Canonical variates pair.   Each two canonical variates form one pair of variates. The number of possible canonical variates pairs equals the number of variables in the smaller set. In the first example, there are three variables in the dependent canonical variate (Life Satisfaction, Self-Esteem, and Depression) and four variables in the independent canonical variate (Age, Education, Income, and Language Proficiency). Therefore, the number of possible variates pairs is three, one for each dependent variable.

Canonical correlation coefficient.   It represents the correlation coefficient between both variates within each pair (dependent and independent canonical variates); it is denoted by R_{XY}. The number of canonical correlation coefficients equals the number of canonical variate pairs. Usually, the first canonical correlation coefficient is the most significant one. It maximizes the correlation between the first two canonical variates (first canonical variates pair).

Variance.   It represents the proportion of variance in each dependent canonical variate that is accounted for by the corresponding independent canonical variate. It is equivalent to the coefficient of determination in Pearson's correlation and R squared coefficient in multiple regression analysis. Variance is simply the square of the canonical correlation coefficient and is symbolized by R^2_{XY}.

Redundancy variance.   It represents the proportion of variance in the variables in one canonical variables pair accounted for by the canonical variate of the other set. Typically, there are two redundancy variance values for each canonical correlation, one for the independent canonical variate and the dependent variables and another for the dependent canonical variate and the independent variables. They are denoted by R^2_{YqX} and R^2_{XpY}, respectively. The first represents the proportion of variance in the dependent variables (Y_q) accounted for by the independent (X) canonical variate, and the second represents the proportion of variance in the independent (X) variables accounted for by the dependent (Y) canonical variate.

Researchers, however, are most interested in the first redundancy variance, R^2_{YqX}, that is, the variance in the dependent variables accounted for by the independent canonical variate. In general, the greater the redundancy variance is, the more likely the independent canonical variate predicts the dependent variables.

Loadings.   They represent the correlation coefficient between each variable and the corresponding canonical variate (e.g., the correlation between X variables and X canonical variate). They are denoted as R_{X1X}, R_{X2X}, R_{XpX}, R_{Y1Y}, R_{Y2Y}, and R_{YqY}.

As a general rule, variables with loadings (correlation coefficients) of .30 and above are considered significant contributors to their corresponding variate.

Figure 10.1 displays a canonical correlation path diagram. It illustrates the relationship between these concepts.

Figure 10.1:   Canonical Correlation Path Diagram

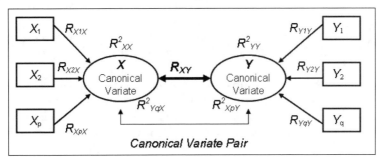

X = independent variable (factor)
X *canonical variate* = independent canonical variate
R_{XX} = loading of each factor on the independent canonical variate
R^2_{XX} = variance in the X canonical variate accounted for by all X variables
R^2_{YqX} = first redundancy variance
Y = dependent variable (outcome)
Y *canonical variate* = dependent canonical variate
R_{YY} = loading of each dependent variable on the dependent canonical variate
R_{XY} = canonical correlation coefficient = correlation between canonical variate pair
R^2_{YY} = variance in the Y canonical variate accounted for by all Y variables
R^2_{XpY} = second redundancy variance

Statistical Tests

Canonical correlation analysis uses several statistical tests to examine various relationships between the independent and dependent variables. These tests include *multivariate tests of significance, dimension reduction analysis,* and *multiple regression analysis.*

Multivariate tests of significance.   As with multivariate analysis of variance and covariance, canonical correlation analysis uses four multivariate tests to examine whether the independent and dependent canonical variates are significantly correlated. These tests are Pillai-Bartlett trace, Hotelling's trace, Wilks' lambda, and Roy's largest root.

These tests, however, examine only whether the *first* variate pair is significantly correlated with each other. A $p \leq .05$ shows an overall significant correlation between the first independent canonical variate and the first dependent canonical variate (first pair).

As with MANOVA and MANCOVA, Wilks' lambda is the most reported test. It represents the variance in the first dependent canonical variate that is *not* accounted for by the first independent canonical variate. Thus the smaller the Wilks' lambda, the stronger the relationship between the two variates. In other words, "1 − Wilks' lambda" equals the shared variance between the two variates.

Dimension reduction analysis.   Recall that the number of canonical variate pairs equals the number of variables in the smaller set of variables. The correlations between all possible pairs will not necessarily be significant. The dimension reduction analysis uses the Wilks' lambda test to examine the level of significance for each canonical variate pair. There should be one test for each variate pair. The results of the first tests are the same as the results of Wilks' lambda under the multivariate tests of significance.

Multiple regression analysis.   In addition to the overall multivariate tests and reduction analysis, canonical correlation analysis also uses univariate multiple regression analysis to examine the effect of all factors on each dependent variable, separately. In a sense, they are post hoc tests similar to the between-subjects ANOVA tests on MANOVA and MANCOVA (see chapter 4 for more on multiple regression analysis).

Advantages of Canonical Correlation

Canonical correlation analysis has several advantages over multiple regression analysis and other multivariate tests. These advantages include the following.

One of the most considerable advantages of canonical correlation analysis is that it allows researchers to examine linear relationships between two sets of multiple variables, simultaneously, without the need to conduct multiple analyses.

Second, as with multivariate analysis of variance and covariance, canonical correlation analysis increases the probability of detecting significant relationships between two composite variables as opposed to utilizing multiple univariate analyses.

Third, by conducting a single test to examine multiple correlations, canonical correlation analysis protects against the inflation of type I error, which occurs due to the utilization of a number of multiple regression analyses.

Fourth, unlike multiple regression analysis, the utilization of canonical correlation analysis allows researchers to test various relationships between the independent variables and dependent variables, concurrently. They include the relationship between the independent and dependent canonical variates (canonical variates pair), the relationship between variables within each set (e.g., relationship between first and second dependent variables, etc.), the relationship between the dependent canonical variate and the independent variables, and the relationship between the independent canonical variate and the dependent variables.

Research Questions and Hypotheses

The research questions and hypotheses examined by canonical correlation analysis are similar to those examined by Pearson's product-moment correlation coefficient (Abu-Bader, 2006). However, the questions in canonical correlation analysis examine multiple dependent variables simultaneously. In particular, these questions and hypotheses examine the relationship between the two canonical variates.

RESEARCH QUESTION: Are there significant correlations between the independent canonical variate (X_1, X_2, . . . , and X_p) and the dependent canonical variate (Y_1, Y_2, . . . , and Y_q)?

EXAMPLE: Are there significant correlations between personal characteristics (age, education, income, and language proficiency) and overall well-being (life satisfaction, self-esteem, and depression) among immigrants?

HYPOTHESES:

H_o: There are no significant correlations between the independent canonical variate (X_1, X_2, . . . , and X_p) and the dependent canonical variate (Y_1, Y_2, . . . , and Y_q).

H_a: There are significant correlations between the independent canonical variate (X_1, X_2, . . . , and X_p) and the dependent canonical variate (Y_1, Y_2, . . . , and Y_q).

EXAMPLES:

H_o: There are no significant correlations between personal characteristics (age, education, income, and language proficiency) and overall well-being (life satisfaction, self-esteem, and depression) among immigrants.

H_a: There are significant correlations between personal characteristics (age, education, income, and language proficiency) and overall well-being (life satisfaction, self-esteem, and depression) among immigrants.

In addition, because canonical correlation analysis is a multivariate multiple regression analysis, it examines research questions similar to those examined by multiple regression analysis.

RESEARCH QUESTION: What set of the independent canonical variate (X_1, X_2, . . . , and X_p) best predicts the dependent canonical variate (Y_1, Y_2, . . . , and Y_q)?

EXAMPLE: What set of personal characteristics (age, education, income, and language proficiency) best predicts immigrants' well-being (life satisfaction, self-esteem, and depression)?

Assumptions

As said, canonical correlation analysis is the multivariate version of multiple regression analysis (MMR). In other words, canonical correlation requires assumptions of both multiple regression analysis and multivariate tests. These assumptions are listed in the following.

1. SAMPLE REPRESENTATIVENESS: The sample must be representative of the population to which prediction will be made.

2. LEVELS OF MEASUREMENT:

    a. The dependent variables (outcomes) must be continuous data and measured at the interval level of measurement or higher.

    b. The independent variables (factors) must be continuous data and measured at the interval level of measurement or higher. In addition, as with multiple regression analysis, independent variables can also be categorical data (Thompson, 1984). However, they must be coded into "0" and "1" (see chapters 2 and 4).

These assumptions are methodological issues and can be examined by referring to the research methodology section of a study. Also, if categorical variables are used in the analysis, they need to be recoded into dummy variables.

3. SAMPLE SIZE: As with multiple regression analysis, canonical correlation analysis requires a sufficient sample size to examine the relationship between the two variable's sets. Sample size depends on two factors: number of variables in the analysis and reliability of each variable.

As a general rule, with reliability coefficients of .80 and above, a sample size of 10 cases per variable in the analysis is considered sufficient for conducting canonical correlation analysis. With higher reliability coefficients, the ratio can be even smaller (Tabachnick & Fidell, 2007). On the other hand, the ratio should be greater with reliability coefficients less than .80.

This assumption is also a methodological one and can be examined by referring to the research methodology section of a study. It also can be examined by considering the ratio of the number of cases by the number of variables in the analysis.

4.   NORMALITY: Unlike multiple regression analysis, canonical correlation analysis does not require univariate normality of distributions. However, the results of canonical correlation are enhanced when the distributions are normal (Tabachnick & Fidell, 2007).

On the other hand, canonical correlation analysis requires that variables in each set meet the assumption of *multivariate normality*. In other words, the shape of the distributions of all linear combinations of all factors (composite factor) and dependent variables (composite outcome) must approach the shape of a normal curve.

Multivariate normality, however, is hard to assess. On the other hand, the assumption is more likely to be fulfilled if all univariate distributions of continuous variables are normally distributed. Univariate normality can be evaluated by inspecting measures of skewness and kurtosis and by eyeballing histograms and normal probability plots for all continuous variables in both sets (see chapter 2).

5.   LINEAR RELATIONSHIP: The relationship between all pairs of dependent variables and independent variables must be linear.

As with multiple regression analysis, linearity can be examined by inspecting the correlation coefficient between the dependent and independent variables and by inspecting the scatterplots of all possible pairs of dependent and independent variables.

If nonlinearity exists, re-examine data for extreme outlier cases and/or conduct data transformation, as outlined in chapter 2. If the problem continues to exist, *stop*! Canonical correlation is not the appropriate test. Consider multiple regression analysis on each dependent variable separately.

6.   HOMOSCEDASTICITY: For each value of the independent variables (X's), the dependent variables (Y's) should be normally distributed. In other words, they should have equal variances.

As with regression analysis, homoscedasticity can be evaluated by inspecting the plots for the residual scores against the predicted scores. These plots can be produced in the SPSS multiple regression commands (see chapter 4). There should be one plot for each dependent variable. Homoscedasticity, as with linearity, can also be evaluated by inspecting the scatterplot for all possible pairs of dependent and independent variables.

7.   MULTICOLLINEARITY: Multicollinearity occurs when the correlation between any pair of independent variables or any pair of dependent variables is too high ($r > .80$).

Multicollinearity can be evaluated by inspecting the correlation coefficients within each set separately, that is, within the dependent variables as well as within the independent variables. It can also be evaluated by inspecting both tolerance and VIF values (see chapter 4).

PRACTICAL EXAMPLE

We will use the Job Satisfaction SPSS data file (see appendix) to predict job behaviors based on a number of demographic and job facets among social workers. In particular, we will examine the following research question: Are there significant correlations between job behaviors (job satisfaction, burnout, and turnover) and demographic and job facets (ethnicity, working with colleagues, quality of supervision, opportunities for promotion, autonomy at work, comfort, and role conflict) among social workers?

Hypothesis Testing

Step 1: State the Null and Alternative Hypotheses.

H_0: There are no significant correlations between job behaviors (satisfaction, burnout, and turnover) and demographic and job facets (ethnicity, working with colleagues, quality of supervision, opportunities for promotion, autonomy at work, comfort, and role conflict) among social workers.

H_a: There are significant correlations between job behaviors (satisfaction, burnout, and turnover) and demographic and job facets (ethnicity, working with colleagues, quality of supervision, opportunities for promotion, autonomy at work, comfort, and role conflict) among social workers.

You can also simply state a research question as follows: What set of demographic and job facets (ethnicity, working with colleagues, quality of supervision, opportunities for promotion, autonomy at work, comfort, and role conflict) best predicts job behaviors (satisfaction, burnout, and turnover) among social workers?

Step 2: Set the Criteria for Rejecting H_0.
We will set alpha at .05 ($\alpha = .05$). That is, reject the null hypothesis only if $p \leq .05$.

Step 3: Select the Appropriate Statistical Test.
In this research question we have two sets of variables. The first set includes three dependent variables labeled as job behaviors. They include job satisfaction, burnout, and turnover. The second set is labeled as demographic and job facets and includes seven job-related factors: ethnicity, working with colleagues, qual-

ity of supervision, opportunities for promotion, autonomy at work, role conflict, and comfort. All variables, except Ethnicity, consist of continuous data and are measured at the interval level of measurement. Ethnicity, on the other hand, is a dichotomous variable and coded as "0" and "1."

Therefore, we will consider utilizing the canonical correlation analysis to examine the correlations between the two sets. First, however, we must evaluate the test assumptions to make sure that canonical correlation analysis is the most reliable test to examine the null hypothesis. These assumptions include the following:

1. SAMPLE REPRESENTATIVENESS: The sample should be representative of the population.

In this study a random sample of 218 social workers completed the survey (see appendix). Thus the sample is presumed to be representative of the population.

2. LEVELS OF MEASUREMENT: All dependent variables must be measured at the interval level or higher. The independent variables can be measured at the interval level or dummy variables.

The dependent variables include Job Satisfaction, Burnout, and Turnover, all of which consist of continuous data and are measured at the interval level of measurement. The independent variables include Ethnicity, Working with Colleagues, Quality of Supervision, Opportunities for Promotion, Autonomy at Work, Role Conflict, and Comfort. Ethnicity is coded as "0" and "1," and all other variables are continuous data and measured at the interval level of measurement.

3. SAMPLE SIZE: The sample must be large enough to conduct canonical correlation. With a reliability coefficient of .80, there should be a minimum of 10 cases per variable. With higher reliability coefficients, the ratio can be even smaller. On the other hand, the ratio should be greater with reliability coefficients less than .80.

In this study, there are ten variables (three dependent and seven independent). The reliability coefficients for all variables, except three, range between .82 and .94. Autonomy and Role Conflict, however, have reliability coefficients of .78 and .62, respectively (Abu-Bader, 2005). Ethnicity, on the other hand, is a demographic variable consisting of qualitative data, and thus reliability is not an issue.

In this study, however, 214 subjects completed the survey, indicating a ratio of 21.4 cases per variable. Thus the ratio is more than twice the minimum requirement, which overcomes the problem of reliability in the Role Conflict variable.

4. MULTIVARIATE NORMALITY: The distributions of the linear combinations of all independent variables and all dependent variables must be normal.

As said, this assumption is hard to assess. However, multivariate normality can be assumed if all univariate distributions are normally distributed.

Therefore, we will examine the shape of the distribution for each dependent and independent variable separately.

In chapter 2, we examined the distribution of quality of supervision. As said, supervision was severely skewed to the left, and therefore it was first reflected and then transformed into the square root.[1] Thus the square root of supervision will be used in the canonical correlation analysis. In chapter 6, we examined the distribution of job satisfaction and concluded that it was normally distributed. Furthermore, the distributions of both burnout and promotion were evaluated in chapter 7 and found to be normally distributed.

Therefore, in this chapter we will evaluate the distributions of the remaining five variables: Turnover, Working with Colleagues, Autonomy at Work, Comfort, and Role Conflict. First, we will look at measures of skewness and kurtosis for the five variables, and then we will inspect their histograms and normal probability plots.

Table 10.1 displays measures of skewness and kurtosis for turnover, colleague, autonomy, comfort, and role conflict.

Table 10.1 shows that the skewness and kurtosis coefficients for autonomy, comfort, and role conflict fall within the normal range of ± 1.96 (skewness/std. error of skewness; kurtosis/std. error of kurtosis), thus indicating that the distributions of these variables are normal.

Furthermore, the skewness coefficient for turnover also falls within the normal range of ± 1.96, indicating normal distribution. However, turnover's kurtosis coefficient falls outside the normal range of ± 1.96 (.882/.328 = 2.69). In addition, coefficients of both skewness and kurtosis for colleague indicate that the distribution of colleague is severely skewed.

Next, we will visually inspect the histograms and normal probability plots for all variables (see figures 10.2–10.6).

Eyeballing both histograms and normal probability plots for turnover (figure 10.2), autonomy (figure 10.3), comfort (figure 10.4), and role conflict (figure 10.5) shows that the shape of these distributions approaches the shape of a normal curve. These results are consistent with the results of measures of skewness and kurtosis coefficients, except kurtosis for turnover.

Table 10.1:   Measures of Skewness and Kurtosis for Turnover, Colleague, Autonomy, Comfort, and Role Conflict

				Statistics		
		Turnover	Colleague	Autonomy	Comfort	RoleConflict
N	Valid	218	218	218	218	218
	Missing	0	0	0	0	0
Skewness		-.007	-.744	.053	.308	-.060
	Std. Error of Skewness	.165	.165	.165	.165	.165
Kurtosis		.882	**1.307**	.255	.470	.091
	Std. Error of Kurtosis	.328	.328	.328	.328	.328

---

[1] Remember, the lower the score of square root of supervision is, the higher the quality of supervision.

Figure 10.2:   Histogram and Normal Probability Plot for Turnover

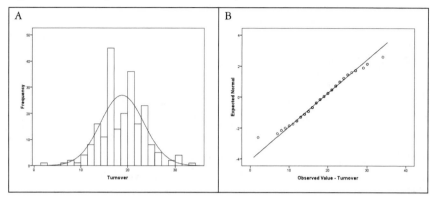

Figure 10.3:   Histogram and Normal Probability Plot for Autonomy

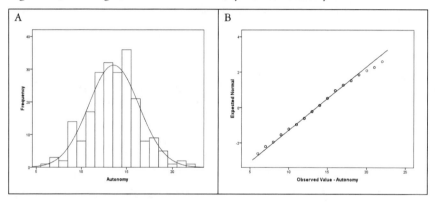

Figure 10.4:   Histogram and Normal Probability Plot for Comfort

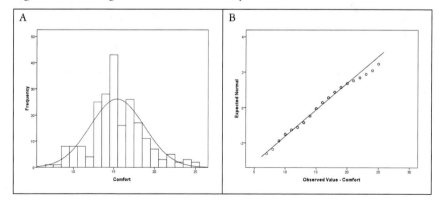

On the other hand, eyeballing both the histogram and the normal probability plot for colleague (figure 10.6) shows that colleague is severely skewed to the left, as suggested by measures of skewness and kurtosis. Therefore, we must conduct data transformation on colleague.

Figure 10.5:   Histogram and Normal Probability Plot for Role Conflict

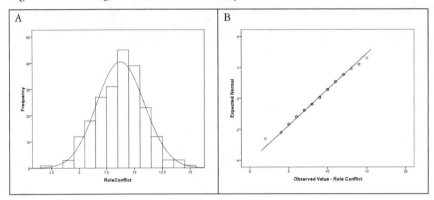

Figure 10.6:   Histogram and Normal Probability Plot for Colleague

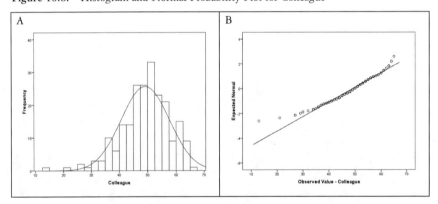

To conduct data transformation on colleague, we must first reflect the distribution of colleague and then conduct data transformation on the reflected variable to the square root (see chapter 2 for data transformation).

SPSS Syntax for Data Reflection and Transformation

COMPUTE Reflect_Colleague=66-Colleague.
EXECUTE.
COMPUTE SQRT_Colleague=SQRT(Reflect_Colleague).
EXECUTE.

Next, we will inspect measures of skewness and kurtosis and look at both the histogram and the normal probability plot for the square root of colleague.

Table 10.2 displays measures of skewness and kurtosis, and figure 10.7 displays the histogram and the normal probability plot for the square root of col-

Table 10.2:   Measures of Skewness and Kurtosis for Square Root of Colleague

Statistics

SQRT_Colleague

N	Valid	218.000
	Missing	.000
	Skewness	-.173
	Std. Error of Skewness	.165
	Kurtosis	.237
	Std. Error of Kurtosis	.328

Figure 10.7:   Histogram and Normal Probability Plot for Square Root of Colleague

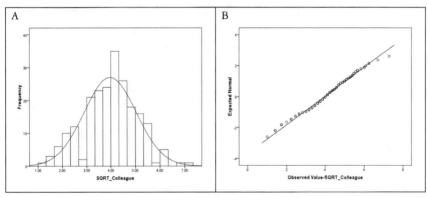

league. Both methods indicate that the distribution of the square root of colleague approaches the shape of a normal curve. *Remember,* due to the reflection, high scores on the square root of colleague indicate lower collegial relationships and lower scores indicate greater collegial relationships.

To conclude, univariate normality can be assumed for job satisfaction, burnout, turnover, autonomy, comfort, and role conflict. Also, it can be assumed for both transformed variables of supervision and colleagues.

5.   LINEAR RELATIONSHIP: The relationship between all pairs of dependent variables and independent variables must be linear.

First, we will inspect the Pearson's correlation coefficients between all pairs of independent and dependent variables (see table 10.3). (*Note:* Ethnicity will not be included because it is a dummy variable.)

Table 10.3 shows significant correlations between all pairs of dependent variables (table 10.3.A); all pairs of independent and dependent variables (table 10.3.B), except between Satisfaction and Role Conflict ($r = .064, p > .05$); and all pairs of independent variables (table 10.3.C), except between Role Conflict and Colleague ($r = .002, p > .05$) and Role Conflict and Supervision ($r = -.053$, $p > .05$). In other words, role conflict has significant correlation with five of the eight variables in the analysis.

Table 10.3:   Correlation Matrix

Correlations

		Satisfaction	Burnout	Turnover	SQRT_Colleague	SQRT_Super	Promotion	Autonomy	Comfort
Satisfaction	Pearson Correlation								
	Sig. (1-tailed)			**A**					
Burnout	Pearson Correlation	-.405			**B**				
	Sig. (1-tailed)	.000							
Turnover	Pearson Correlation	-.446	.584						
	Sig. (1-tailed)	.000	.000						
SQRT_Colleague	Pearson Correlation	-.321	.514	.472					
	Sig. (1-tailed)	.000	.000	.000					
SQRT_Super	Pearson Correlation	-.356	.407	.392	.479			**C**	
	Sig. (1-tailed)	.000	.000	.000	.000				
Promotion	Pearson Correlation	.213	-.311	-.334	-.456	-.321			
	Sig. (1-tailed)	.001	.000	.000	.000	.000			
Autonomy	Pearson Correlation	-.317	.153	.216	.246	.218	-.196		
	Sig. (1-tailed)	.000	.012	.001	.000	.001	.002		
Comfort	Pearson Correlation	-.224	.292	.303	.171	.196	-.232	.245	
	Sig. (1-tailed)	.000	.000	.000	.006	.002	.000	.000	
RoleConflict	Pearson Correlation	.064	-.170	-.135	.002	-.053	.148	-.120	-.285
	Sig. (1-tailed)	.174	.006	.023	.487	.221	.015	.039	.000

Next, we will examine the scatterplots of all pairs of variables. However, due to the large number of pairs, we will use SPSS to generate three scatterplot matrices, one for dependent variables, a second for independent variables, and a third for each dependent variable with independent variables. As with correlation matrix, you can request a scatterplot matrix through the *Graph* menu. To request these matrices, follow these steps:

1. Open the SPSS Job Satisfaction data file.

2. Click on *Graph, Legacy Dialogs,* and *Scatter/Dot.*

3. Click on *Matrix Scatter.* Click on *Define.* This command will open the "Scatterplot Matrix" dialog box (see screen 10.1).

4. Scroll down in the variables list, click on *Satisfaction,* and click on the upper arrow to move it into the *Matrix Variables* box.

5. Repeat step 4 to move *Burnout* and *Turnover* into the *Matrix Variables* box (see screen 10.1).

6. Click on *OK.*

7. Use the same steps to generate a scatterplot matrix for the independent variables as well as for each dependent variable with the independent variables. You can move all nine variables to generate scatterplots for all possible pairs.

You may also use the SPSS syntax commands to generate these matrices:

SPSS Scatterplot Matrix Syntax

GRAPH
/SCATTERPLOT(MATRIX)=V_1 V_2 V_3 . . . V_k
/MISSING=LISTWISE.

For the above syntax, V = variable.

Screen 10.1:   SPSS Scatterplot Matrix Main Dialog Box

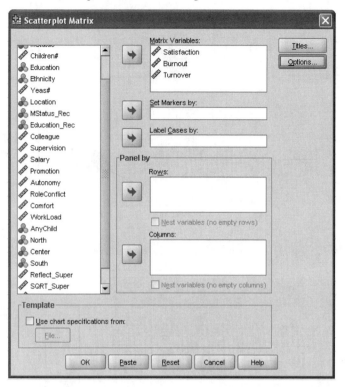

Once the scatterplot matrix is generated, you should insert a fit line on each cell. To insert fit lines, follow these steps:

1. Double-click anywhere on the scatterplot matrix to open the "Chart Editor" menu.

2. Click on *Elements* in the main menu, and click on *Fit Line at Total.* This command will insert a horizontal line on the graph.

3. Click on X to close the "Chart Editor" dialog box and return to SPSS output.

Figures 10.8, 10.9, and 10.10 display these scatterplot matrices. Figure 10.8 displays a scatterplot matrix for all dependent variables. As it appears, there is a linear relationship between all pairs of the dependent variables, perhaps with minor deviations from the fit line, especially in the satisfaction and burnout scatterplot.

Figure 10.9 displays a scatterplot matrix for all independent variables. Again, figure 10.9 shows a linear relationship between most pairs of the independent variables. The fit lines of the scatterplots for role conflict with square

Figure 10.8:   Scatterplot Matrix for the Dependent Variables

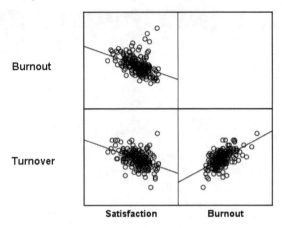

Figure 10.9:   Scatterplot Matrix for the Independent Variables

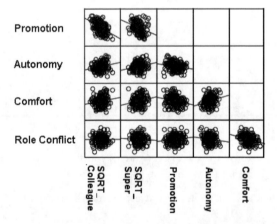

Figure 10.10:   Scatterplot Matrix for Dependent and Independent Variables

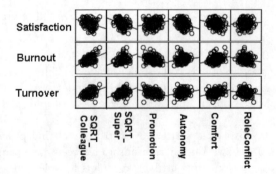

root of supervision and square root of colleague appear to be parallel to the X axis, thus indicating no significant relationship between role conflict and either variable.

Figure 10.10 displays scatterplots for all pairs of dependent variables and independent variables. Figure 10.10 also shows a linear relationship between all dependent and independent variables, except for Role Conflict and Satisfaction, which shows no significant relationship between the two variables.

To conclude, both the correlation and scatterplot matrices show linear relationships between all thirty-five possible pairs except three: role conflict with satisfaction, supervision, and colleague. Role conflict, however, has a linear relationship with all other six variables. Therefore, we will include role conflict in the canonical correlation analysis.

6.   HOMOSCEDASTICITY: For each value of the independent variables (X's), the dependent variables (Y's) should be normally distributed. In other words, they should have equal variances.

To evaluate homoscedasticity, we will use the SPSS regression commands to plot the residual scores on the predicted scores for each dependent variable. To do so, follow the steps outlined in chapter 3 or, simply, use the following SPSS syntax:

First Dependent Variable—Job Satisfaction

REGRESSION
/DEPENDENT Satisfaction
/METHOD=ENTER Ethnicity SQRT_Colleague SQRT_Super Promotion
   Autonomy RoleConflict Comfort
/SCATTERPLOT=(*ZRESID, *ZPRED).

Second Dependent Variable—Burnout

REGRESSION
/DEPENDENT Burnout
/METHOD=ENTER Ethnicity SQRT_Colleague SQRT_Super Promotion
   Autonomy RoleConflict Comfort
/SCATTERPLOT=(*ZRESID, *ZPRED).

Third Dependent Variable—Turnover

REGRESSION
/DEPENDENT Turnover
/METHOD=ENTER Ethnicity SQRT_Colleague SQRT_Super Promotion
   Autonomy RoleConflict Comfort
/SCATTERPLOT=(*ZRESID, *ZPRED).

Figures 10.11.A, 10.11.B, and 10.11.C display scatterplots for the residuals and predicted scores for job satisfaction, burnout, and turnover, respectively. Eye-balling these scatterplots shows that the data appear to be homoscedastic. As it appears in the three figures, the horizontal line is almost parallel to the X axis, thus indicating equal distributions around the line, with, however, minor departure.

Furthermore, inspecting the scatterplots for all pairs of dependent and independent variables (figure 10.10) also shows that the scores of each dependent variable are homoscedastic, equally distributed around the fit lines. In other words, the assumption of homoscedasticity is fulfilled.

7. MULTICOLLINEARITY: The correlation between any pair of independent vari-ables or any pair of dependent variables should be .80 or less.

As can be seen in table 10.3, the correlation coefficients between all pairs of dependent variables range between .405 and .584 and between all pairs of independent variables range between .002 and .479. Thus the assumption of multicollinearity is fulfilled.

Figure 10.11:   Scatterplot for the Residuals and Predicted Scores

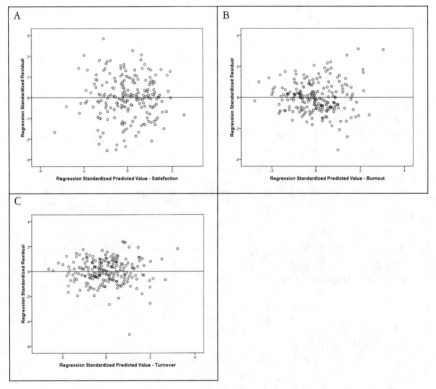

You can also examine multicollinearity by inspecting the VIF (variance inflation factor) and tolerance values for each set. They can be generated in the SPSS regression commands. In this case, two regression analyses will be required, one for each set. In the first regression analysis, all variables in the first set will be entered as independent variables and any variable from the second set (e.g., Autonomy) can serve as a dependent variable. In the second regression analysis, all variables in the second set will be entered as independent variables and any variable from the first set (e.g., Turnover) will be entered as a dependent variable.

To request *collinearity diagnosis* (VIF and tolerance values), follow the steps discussed in chapter 4 or simply use the following SPSS syntax commands:

For the First (Dependent Variables) Set

REGRESSION
/STATISTICS COEFF OUTS R ANOVA COLLIN TOL
/DEPENDENT Promotion
/METHOD=ENTER Satisfaction Burnout Turnover.

For the Second (Independent Variables) Set

REGRESSION
/STATISTICS COEFF OUTS R ANOVA COLLIN TOL
/DEPENDENT Satisfaction
/METHOD=ENTER Ethnicity SQRT_Colleague SQRT_Super Promotion
   Autonomy RoleConflict Comfort.

Tables 10.4 and 10.5 present the tolerance and VIF values for the dependent and independent variables sets, respectively. As it appears in both tables, all VIF values are smaller than 10 and all tolerance values are greater than .10. Thus no multicollinearity problem exists in either set.

Table 10.4:   Collinearity Diagnosis for the Dependent Variables Set

Coefficients

Model		Collinearity Statistics	
		Tolerance	VIF
1	Satisfaction	.770	1.299
	Burnout	.633	1.581
	Turnover	.606	1.649

Table 10.5:   Collinearity Diagnosis for the Independent Variables Set

Coefficients

Model		Collinearity Statistics	
		Tolerance	VIF
1	Ethnicity	.814	1.229
	SQRT_Colleague	.628	1.592
	SQRT_Super	.739	1.353
	Promotion	.730	1.369
	Autonomy	.880	1.137
	RoleConflict	.866	1.155
	Comfort	.762	1.313

How to Use SPSS to Run Canonical Correlation

Step 4: Run Canonical Correlation Analysis.

Up to this point, data were evaluated for canonical correlation's assumptions. We ensured that all assumptions were satisfied, especially after two variables were transformed to the square root. Now we will conduct a canonical correlation analysis on the two canonical variates. We will utilize SPSS to run the analysis.

Unfortunately, canonical correlation analysis can be computed only through the SPSS MANOVA syntax commands.[2] The SPSS syntax file for canonical correlation analysis is as follows:

Canonical Correlation SPSS Syntax

MANOVA
$Y_1 Y_2 \ldots Y_q$ WITH $X_1 X_2 \ldots X_p$
/DISCRIM RAW STAN ESTIM CORR
/PRINT SIGNIF (MULT UNIV EIGN DIMENR)
/DESIGN.

Y_q represents the dependent variables (Y_1, Y_2, Y_3, etc.), and X_p represents the independent variables (X_1, X_2, X_3, etc.). Make sure that the variable names are exactly the same as they appear in the SPSS "Variable View" screen. Also, there should be a single space between the Y_q variables as well as between the X_p variables with no commas.

---

[2]*Note:* SPSS Student's Version does not support syntax.

As a reminder, to open the SPSS syntax file, follow these steps:

1. Open the SPSS Job Satisfaction data file.

2. Click on *File, New,* and *Syntax.* A new SPSS Syntax Editor file will open.

3. Type the canonical correlation syntax from above in screen 10.2.A if you have SPSS Version 17 or earlier and in screen 10.2.B if you have SPSS Version 18.

4. Point the mouse anywhere on the syntax.

5. Right-click on the mouse, and click on *Run Current.* Or, simply click on the *Run Current* arrow on the main toolbar as shown in screens 10.2.A and 10.2.B.

Reading the SPSS Output

Running this SPSS syntax will produce the SPSS outputs for canonical correlation analysis. Unfortunately, these outputs are not displayed in tables with borders and cells and are not as neat as those tables we have witnessed in the previous chapters and in SPSS in general. Therefore, some editing may be required

Screen 10.2.A: SPSS Syntax Editor for SPSS 17 or Earlier

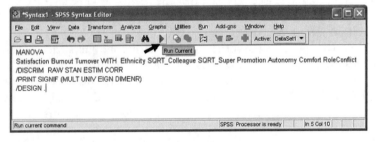

Screen 10.2.B: PASW (SPSS) Syntax Editor for SPSS Version 18

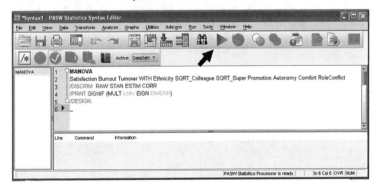

Table 10.6:   Multivariate Tests of Significance

```
EFFECT .. WITHIN CELLS Regression
Multivariate Tests of Significance (S = 3, M = 1 1/2, N = 100 1/2)
Test Name        Value       Approx. F      Hypoth. DF      Error DF      Sig. of F

Pillais          .52848      6.26214          21.00         615.00         .000
Hotellings       .87363      8.38962          21.00         605.00         .000
Wilks            .51228      7.28784          21.00         583.46         .000
Roys             .43693
```

for the purpose of presentations. These outputs include many parts, some of which are not necessary and thus will not be discussed. We will focus on only those tables that will address our research question and hypotheses: tables 10.6 through 10.15.

Table 10.6 presents the results of the multivariate tests of significance: Pillai-Bartlett trace, Hotelling's trace, Wilks' lambda, and Roy's largest root. As discussed earlier, these tests only examine if the first *canonical variates pair* is statistically significant.

The results of Wilks' lambda show a significant correlation between the first canonical variates pair (Wilks' = .51228, F = 7.287, df = 21 and 583.46, p = .000). In other words, there is a significant correlation between the first dependent canonical variate (job behaviors) and the first independent canonical variate (demographic and job facets). Notice that the results of both the Pillai-Bartlett trace and Hotelling's trace also show significant correlations between the first canonical variates pair.

Table 10.7 presents the correlation coefficients and proportion of variance between all possible canonical variates pairs. Remember, there are as many possible pairs as the number of variables in the smaller set. This, however, does not mean that the correlations between all possible pairs need to be significant.

The *Root No.* indicates the order and number of possible pairs. Recall that in our example there are three variables in the first set and seven in the second set. Thus the number of possible pairs is three, corresponding to Root No. 1, 2, and 3 in table 10.7.

In table 10.7, we are interested in only the last two columns, Canon Cor. and Sq. Cor. The first is the correlation coefficient (R_{XY}) between each canonical variates pair, and the second is the proportion of variance shared between the corresponding pairs (R^2_{XY}).

Table 10.7:   Overall Canonical Correlations

```
Eigenvalues and Canonical Correlations
Root No.    Eigenvalue    Pct.        Cum. Pct.     Canon Cor.     Sq. Cor

  1          .77597       88.82173     88.82173      .66101         .43693
  2          .07878        9.01726     97.83899      .27023         .07302
  3          .01888        2.16101    100.00000      .13612         .01853
```

Table 10.7 shows that the correlation coefficient between the first canonical variates pair is .66. The table also shows that the two pairs share 43.69 percent of the variance. In other words, 43.69 percent of the variance in the first dependent canonical variate is accounted for by the first independent canonical variate. Recall that table 10.6 shows a significant correlation between the first pair.

Table 10.7 also shows that the correlation coefficient between the second canonical variates pair is .27. The two variates, however, share only 7.30 percent of the variance (Root No. 2, Canon Cor. = .27023, Sq. Cor. = .07302).

In addition, table 10.7 shows that the correlation coefficient between the third canonical variates pair is .14. The two variates share only 1.85 percent of the variance (Root No. 3, Canon Cor. = .13612, Sq. Cor. = .01853).

The question then is whether the second and third canonical variates pairs are statistically significant. The answer is found in table 10.8.

Table 10.8 displays the results of the dimension reduction analysis test. It uses the Wilks' lambda test to examine the level of significance for each possible canonical variates pair. The number of rows (Roots) corresponds to the number of possible pairs. In this case, there are three possible pairs.

The first row (Roots 1 to 3) shows a significant correlation between the first canonical variates pair. This row is always identical (redundant) to the results of Wilks' lambda in the multivariate tests of significance (table 10.6).

The second row (Roots 2 to 3), on the other hand, shows no significant correlation between the second canonical variates pair (Wilks' lambda = .9098, F = 1.646, df = 12 and 408, p = .077). Recall from table 10.7 that the correlation between the second canonical variates pair is .27. *Note:* if this pair is not significant, the next pair will definitely not be significant.

The third row (Roots 3 to 3) also shows no significant correlation between the third canonical variates pair (Wilks' lambda = .981, F = .774, df = 5 and 205, p = .569).

Thus only the first canonical variates pair is statistically significant, and therefore it will be further investigated and reported. The other two pairs will not be reported.

Table 10.9 conveys the correlation coefficients between each dependent variable and the corresponding dependent canonical variate. As said, only the first canonical variate (Function No. 1) will be discussed.

Table 10.8:   Results of the Dimension Reduction Analysis Tests

Dimension Reduction Analysis					
Roots	Wilks L.	F	Hypoth. DF	Error DF	Sig. of F
1 TO 3	.51228	7.28784	21.00	583.46	.000
2 TO 3	.90980	1.64562	12.00	408.00	.077
3 TO 3	.98147	.77405	5.00	205.00	.569

Table 10.9: Loadings of Dependent Variables on Dependent Canonical Variates

```
Correlations between DEPENDENT and canonical variables
                    Function No.
        Variable            1          2
        Satisfac         .64429     .75353
        Burnout         -.89888     .29967
        Turnover        -.82822     .04260
```

These correlation coefficients represent the loadings each variable has on the dependent canonical variate (job behaviors). *Remember,* only variables with loadings of *.30* and above should be interpreted.

Table 10.9 shows that the correlation between job behaviors (dependent canonical variate) and job satisfaction is .644, between job behaviors and burnout is −.899, and between job behaviors and turnover is −.828. The "±" signs represent the direction of the relationships between these variables and the variables in the second set.

Note: Canonical correlation outputs also report two sets of correlations (not discussed here) labeled as *raw canonical coefficients for dependent variables* and *standardized canonical coefficients for dependent variables.* The first is similar to the unstandardized correlation coefficients (B's) in multiple regression analysis, and the second is similar to the standardized regression coefficients (Beta's).

Table 10.10 presents the proportion of variances between the dependent variables and their canonical variate (Pct Var DEP) and between the dependent canonical variate and the variables in the other set (Pct Var COV). The second represents a *redundancy variance* (R^2_{XpY}). The table also presents the cumulative variances accounted for by all canonical variates pairs. *Note:* report only the variances of significant pairs, in this case the first pair.

Table 10.10 shows that the first dependent canonical variate, job behaviors, accounted for 63.63 percent of the variance in the dependent variables, Job Satisfaction, Burnout, and Turnover (CAN. VAR. 1, Pct Var DEP = 63.63475). On the other hand, the first dependent canonical variate accounted for 27.80 percent of the variance in the variables in the second set, the independent variables (CAN. VAR. 1, Pct Var COV = 27.80383).

Furthermore, if, *and only if,* the second canonical variates pair was significant, we would report the results of the second row as follows.

Table 10.10 shows that the second dependent variate accounted for 21.98 percent of the variance in the dependent variables, Job Satisfaction, Burnout, and

Table 10.10: Variance and Redundancy Variance of Dependent Canonical Variates

```
Variance in dependent variables explained by canonical variables
CAN. VAR.   Pct Var DEP   Cum Pct DEP   Pct Var COV   Cum Pct COV

    1         63.63475      63.63475      27.80383      27.80383
    2         21.98084      85.61559       1.60515      29.40898
```

Turnover (CAN. VAR. 2, Pct Var DEP = 21.98084). In all, the two canonical variates pairs accounted for 85.62 percent of the variance in the dependent variables (CAN. VAR. 2, Cum Pct DEP = 85.61559).

The second dependent canonical variate, however, accounted for 1.61 percent of the variance in the variables in the second set (CAN. VAR. 2, Pct Var COV = 1.60515). The two dependent canonical variates together accounted for 29.41 percent of the variance in the independent variables (CAN. VAR. 2, Cum Pct COV = 29.40898).

Tables 10.11 and 10.12 examine the canonical variates of the independent variables set. Table 10.11 is similar to table 10.9, and table 10.12 is similar to table 10.10.

Table 10.11 presents the correlation coefficients between each independent variable and each independent canonical variate. Again, only the first canonical variate (Function No. 1) will be presented.

Table 10.11 shows that all independent variables have correlation coefficients (loadings) of (±) .30 and above, except Role Conflict, with the first independent canonical variate. Role Conflict, on the other hand, has a correlation of .25 with the first independent canonical variate. *Remember,* only variables with loadings of *.30* and above will be reported. Therefore, Role Conflict will not be reported.

The "±" signs indicate the directions of the relationship between these variables and variables in the first dependent canonical variate.

Table 10.12 presents the proportion of variances between the independent variables and their canonical variate (Pct Var COV) and the redundancy variance (Pct Var DEP), that is, the variance in the dependent variables accounted for by the independent canonical variate.

Table 10.11: Loadings of Independent Variables on Independent Canonical Variates

Correlations between COVARIATES and canonical variables
CAN. VAR.

Covariate	1	2
Ethnicit	-.46318	-.19549
SQRT_Col	-.82870	.19854
SQRT_Sup	-.71941	-.24335
Promotio	.54588	-.08931
Autonomy	-.35183	-.79497
Comfort	-.51263	-.03538
RoleConf	.25331	-.22953

Table 10.12: Variance and Redundancy Variance of Independent Canonical Variates

Variance in covariates explained by canonical variables

CAN. VAR.	Pct Var DEP	Cum Pct DEP	Pct Var COV	Cum Pct COV
1	13.52941	13.52941	30.96481	30.96481
2	.86664	14.39605	11.86773	42.83255

Table 10.12 shows that the first independent canonical variate, demographic and job facets, accounted for 30.96 percent of the variance in the independent variables, Ethnicity, Colleague, Supervision, Promotion, Autonomy, Comfort, and Role Conflict (CAN. VAR. 1, Pct Var COV = 30.96). On the other hand, the first independent canonical variate accounted for 13.53 percent of the variance in the dependent variables (CAN. VAR. 1, Pct Var DEP = 13.52941).

Remember, this redundancy variance is the most important variance because it shows the strength of the relationship between the independent variables and the dependent canonical variate.

Again, if the second canonical variates pair was significant, we would report the second row as follows.

Table 10.12 shows that the second independent canonical variate, demographic and job facets, accounted for 11.87 percent of the variance in the independent variables (CAN. VAR. 2, Pct Var COV = 11.86773). In all, the two independent canonical variates accounted for 42.83 percent of the variance in the independent variables (CAN. VAR. 2, Cum Pct COV = 42.83255).

The second independent canonical variate accounted for .87 percent of the variance in the dependent variables (CAN. VAR. 2, Pct Var DEP = .86664). The two independent canonical variates accounted for 14.40 percent of the variance in the dependent variables (CAN. VAR. 2, Cum Pct DEP = 14.39605).

Next, canonical correlation analysis produces multiple regression post hoc analyses examining the impact of all factors (independent variables) entered in the canonical correlation analysis on each dependent variable separately. They are the same as multiple regression analysis (see chapter 4). They are labeled as *Regression analysis WITHIN CELLS error term—Individual univariate .9500 confidence intervals.* They include tables 10.13, 10.14, and 10.15.

Each table displays the unstandardized regression coefficient (*B*), standardized regression coefficient (*Beta*), standard error (Std. Err.), *t*-test (*t* value), level of significance (*Sig.* of *t*), and the lower and upper 95th confidence interval (Lower—95% and CL—Upper) for each covariate (factor) on each dependent variable. We are interested in only the *Beta, t* value, and *Sig.* of *t* columns.

Table 10.13 displays the results of the regression analysis for the first dependent variable. Inspection of the table shows that only two factors emerged as significant predictors of job satisfaction. They are SQRT_Sup ($t = -3.02, p = .003$) and autonomy ($t = -2.91, p = .004$). In other words, greater quality of supervision (*Beta* = −.216) and more autonomy (*Beta* = −.191) are associated with greater job satisfaction. Remember, the lower the score in the transformed supervision is, the higher the quality of supervision. Also, the lower the score in autonomy is, the greater autonomy (see appendix).

Table 10.13:   Regression Analysis for Job Satisfaction

Dependent variable .. Satisfaction

COVARIATE	B	Beta	Std. Err.	t-Value	Sig. of t	Lower -95% CL- Upper	
Ethnicit	-2.465	-.132	1.266	-1.946	.053	-4.961	.031
SQRT_Col	-.908	-.110	.639	-1.421	.157	-2.169	.351
SQRT_Sup →	-1.338	-.216	.442	-3.023	→ .003	-2.210	-.465
Promotio	.029	.025	.084	.350	.726	-.136	.195
Autonomy →	-.606	-.191	.208	-2.912	→ .004	-1.016	-.195
Comfort	-.157	-.059	.185	-.848	.397	-.522	.207
RoleConf	.086	.021	.268	.322	.747	-.442	.616

Table 10.14 displays the results of the regression analysis for the second dependent variable, Burnout. Table 10.14 shows four significant predictors of burnout, unlike job satisfaction. These predictors are ethnicity (t = 2.64, p = .009), SQRT_Col (t = 5.02, p = .000), SQRT_Sup (t = 2.72, p = .007), and role conflict (t = −2.52, p = .012). That is, being an Arab social worker (*Beta* = .163) with lower collegial relationships (*Beta* = .353), poorer quality of supervision (*Beta* = .176), and lower role conflict (*Beta* = −.151) is associated with higher burnout. *Recall* that role conflict was excluded from reporting due to low loading on the independent canonical variate.

Table 10.15 displays the results of the regression analysis for the third and last dependent variable, Turnover. The table shows three significant predictors of turnover. These predictors include SQRT_Col (t = 3.95, p = .000), SQRT_Sup

Table 10.14:   Regression Analysis for Burnout

Dependent variable .. Burnout

COVARIATE	B	Beta	Std. Err.	t-Value	Sig. of t	Lower -95% CL- Upper	
Ethnicit →	2.174	.163	.824	2.638	→ .009	.549	3.800
SQRT_Col →	2.089	.353	.416	5.019	→ .000	1.268	2.909
SQRT_Sup →	.784	.176	.288	2.723	→ .007	.216	1.352
Promotio	-.043	-.051	.054	-.788	.432	-.151	.064
Autonomy	-.143	-.063	.135	-1.059	.290	-.410	.123
Comfort	.199	.105	.120	1.653	.100	-.038	.437
RoleConf →	-.441	-.151	.174	-2.523	→ .012	-.785	-.096

Table 10.15:   Regression Analysis for Turnover

Dependent variable .. Turnover

COVARIATE	B	Beta	Std. Err.	t-Value	Sig. of t	Lower -95% CL- Upper	
Ethnicit	.497	.051	.620	.801	.424	-.725	1.720
SQRT_Col →	1.236	.290	.313	3.949	→ .000	.619	1.854
SQRT_Sup →	.569	.177	.216	2.626	→ .009	.141	.996
Promotio	-.054	-.089	.041	-1.319	.189	-.135	.026
Autonomy	.025	.015	.101	.251	.802	-.175	.226
Comfort →	.216	.159	.090	2.388	→ .018	.037	.395
RoleConf	-.158	-.075	.131	-1.205	.229	-.417	.100

($t = 2.63, p = .009$), and comfort ($t = 2.39, p = .018$). In other words, lower collegial relationships (*Beta* = .29), poorer quality of supervision (*Beta* = .18), and lower comfort at work (*Beta* = .16) are associated with higher turnover.

> *Note:* Notice that not all independent variables emerged as significant predictors of each dependent variable in the regression analyses. However, when the linear combinations of both independent and dependent variables were examined, all factors, except role conflict, emerged as significant predictors of the composite dependent variables in canonical correlation. This indicates the superiority of canonical correlation over multiple regression analysis.

Step 5: Write the Results of Canonical Correlation.

As discussed in the previous chapters, when presenting the results of any statistical test, first discuss the test assumptions and whether they are fulfilled. Next, you should report the results of canonical correlation analysis. However, writing the results of canonical correlation analysis is somewhat more complex than previous tests because it involves many concepts and different tests. In general, to report the results of canonical correlation analysis follow these guidelines:

First, you should report the results of the overall multivariate tests of significance (Wilks' lambda) followed by the results of the dimension reduction analysis tests and the number of significant canonical variates pairs. For each significant pair, report the values of Wilks' lambda, *F, df,* and level of significance. Next, report the overall canonical correlation coefficient for each canonical variates pair (R_{XY}) and the proportion of variance each pair shares (R^2_{XY}).

In the next part, you need to report the results for each canonical variates pair. You should start by reporting the correlation coefficient (loading) between each variable and its canonical variate. Next, report the variance and the redundancy variance for each canonical variate. We also recommend that you report the results of the univariate regression analysis for each dependent variable.

Finally, you need to present these results in a readable table and a path diagram. The diagram should illustrate the relationships between the variables and their variates and between the two variates. Remember, variables with loadings of .30 and above should be reported.

Writing the Results of Canonical Correlation

The following text presents the results of the canonical correlation analysis in the practical example.

Evaluation of assumptions. Canonical correlation analysis was conducted to examine what demographic and job facets (ethnicity, colleagues, supervision, promotion, autonomy, comfort, and role conflict) predict job behaviors (job satisfaction, burnout, and turnover) among a representative sample of 214 social workers. However, prior to hypothesis testing, data were screened to ensure that the assumptions for canonical correlation analysis were met.

First, measures of skewness and kurtosis, histograms, and normal Q-Q plots were examined for all variables in both sets, except for Ethnicity. Inspections of these measures and plots indicated that all variables were normally distributed, except Supervision and Colleague. Therefore, both variables were first reflected and then transformed to the square root. Evaluations of the transformed variables revealed that both were normally distributed.

Second, the results of Pearson's correlation coefficients and scatterplots revealed a linear relationship between all pairs of dependent variables, independent variables, and dependent and independent variables.

Third, eyeballing the scatterplots of the dependent and independent variables and of the residual scores against the predicted scores indicated that data met the assumption of homoscedasticity.

Finally, the results of Pearson's correlation coefficients, VIF, and tolerance values were examined and indicated no evidence of a multicollinearity problem.

Results of canonical correlation.   Canonical correlation analysis was conducted to examine the impact of demographic and job facets (ethnicity, collegial relationship, quality of supervision, opportunities for promotion, autonomy, comfort at work, and role conflict) on social workers' job behaviors (job satisfaction, burnout, and turnover).

The results of the overall Wilks' lambda multivariate tests of significance show a significant correlation between the job behaviors variate and the demographic and job facets variate (Wilks' lambda = .51, $F_{(21, 583)}$ = 7.29, $p < .001$).

The results of the Wilks' lambda dimension reduction analysis test revealed that only the first canonical variates pair was significant (Wilks' lambda = .51, $F_{(21, 583)}$ = 7.29, $p < .001$).

Overall, the correlation between the job behaviors and the demographic and job facets was .66. Ethnicity and the job facets canonical variate accounted for 44 percent of the variance in the job behaviors canonical variate (R^2 = .44).

FIRST CANONICAL VARIATES PAIR: With a cutoff correlation of .30, the job behaviors canonical variate had a high loading on job satisfaction (R = .64), burnout (R = −.90), and turnover (R = −.83). In addition, the demographic and job facets canonical variate had a high loading on ethnicity (R = −.46), working with colleagues (R = −.83), quality of supervision (R = −.72), promotion (R = .55), autonomy (R = −.35), and comfort (R = −.51). In other words, being a Jewish social worker with better collegial relationships, greater quality of supervision, more opportunities for promotion, greater autonomy, and a feeling of comfort at work were associated with higher job satisfaction, lower burnout, and lower turnover.

The results of canonical correlation show that the first dependent canonical variates pair accounted for 63.64 percent of the variance in job satisfaction, burnout, and turnover. On the other hand, the demographic and job facets canonical variate accounted for 30.96 percent of the variance in the independent variables (Ethnicity, Colleague, Supervision, Promotion, Autonomy, Comfort, and Role Conflict).

Furthermore, the first demographic and job facets canonical variate accounted for 13.53 percent of the variance in the dependent variables. On the other hand, the first job behaviors canonical variate accounted for 27.80 percent of the variance in the independent variables.

REGRESSION ANALYSIS: While the results of canonical correlation show that the linear combination of the three job behaviors variables was a function of six of the seven independent variables, the results of the regression analysis show that job satisfaction, burnout, and turnover are not necessarily driven by the same set of factors.

The results of the univariate regression analysis show that job satisfaction was a function of quality of supervision ($\beta = -.22$, $t = -3.02$, $p < .05$) and autonomy ($\beta = -.19$, $t = -2.91$, $p < .05$). On the other hand, burnout was a function of ethnicity ($\beta = .16$, $t = 2.64$, $p < .05$), working with colleagues ($\beta = .35$, $t = 5.02$, $p < .05$), quality of supervision ($\beta = .18$, $t = 2.72$, $p < .05$), and role conflict ($\beta = -.15$, $t = -2.52$, $p < .05$). Turnover was a function of working with colleagues ($\beta = .29$, $t = 3.95$, $p < .05$), quality of supervision ($\beta = .18$, $t = 2.63$, $p < .05$), and comfort at work ($\beta = .16$, $t = 2.39$, $p < .05$).

Presentation of the results in a summary table.   Presentation of the results of canonical correlation is different than in the previous tests. In canonical correlation, the table should be divided into two sets, one for the factors (independent variables) and the second for the dependent variables. The table should report the loading of each variable on its corresponding variate for each significant canonical variate pair. The table should also report the variance and redundancy variance for each set of variables for each significant canonical variate pair. In addition, the table should display the overall correlation coefficient and proportion of variance accounted for by each canonical variate pair. Moreover, the table should report the overall results of the multivariate tests of significance and the dimension reduction analysis tests. Finally, the results of canonical correlation should be displayed in a diagram.

The results of canonical correlation analysis for the practical example are presented in table 10.16 and figure 10.12.

Note: If the second canonical variates pair is significant, report the results of Wilks' lambda dimension reduction analysis test for the second pair and report the loadings, variance, and redundancy variance of the second canonical variates pair in the same way as the results of the first canonical variates pair. Also, add another column for Pair 2 in table 10.16.

Table 10.16:   Results of Canonical Correlation Analysis between Job Behavior and Demographic and Job Facets

Set	Canonical Variates Pair[a] Pair 1[b]
Job Behavior	
Job Satisfaction	.64
Burnout	−.90
Turnover	−.83
Variance	63.64
Redundancy	27.80
Demographic and Job Facets	
Ethnicity	−.46
Colleagues	−.83
Supervision	−.72
Promotion	.55
Autonomy	−.35
Comfort	−.51
Role Conflict	——
Variance	30.96
Redundancy	13.53
Coefficients	
R	.66
Variance (R^2)	.44

[a]Wilks' lambda = .51, $F_{(21, 583.46)}$ = 7.29, $p < .001$
[b]Wilks' lambda = .51, $F_{(21, 583.46)}$ = 7.29, $p < .001$

Figure 10.12:   Canonical Correlation Path Diagram

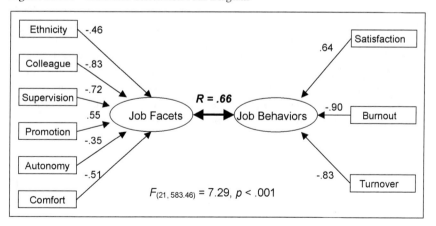

SUMMARY

This chapter discussed canonical correlation analysis, the multivariate version of multiple regression analysis. Although canonical correlation has superior advantages over multiple regression analysis, it is perhaps the least used multivariate statistical technique in social sciences research due to its mathematical complexity and interpretation.

Chapter 10 first introduced and discussed the purpose of canonical correlation analysis. As said, canonical correlation analysis is utilized to examine the linear relationship between two sets of variables in which one set includes multiple independent variables and the other includes multiple dependent variables.

The chapter then defined key concepts used in canonical correlation analysis: canonical variate, canonical variates pair, canonical correlation coefficient, variance, redundancy variance, and loadings. As discussed, canonical variate is a linear combination of all variables in a particular set. There are two variates: independent canonical variate and dependent canonical variate, in which they form one canonical variates pair. The number of possible pairs, not necessarily significant pairs, equals the number of variables in the smaller set. Canonical correlation coefficient, variance, and redundancy variance examine the relationship within and between each pair. Canonical correlation coefficient is the correlation between the independent and dependent canonical variates. The variance represents the proportion of variance in one canonical variate that is accounted for by the variables in its corresponding set. The redundancy variance, on the other hand, is the proportion of variance in one variate that is accounted for by all variables in the other set.

Chapter 10 then discussed the main tests of canonical correlation. They include the multivariate tests of significance and the Wilks' lambda dimension reduction analysis. The first examines whether the first canonical variates pair is statistically significant, and the second examines whether each canonical variates pair is statistically significant.

Next, chapter 10 discussed the advantages of canonical correlation analysis over multiple regression analysis. As an advantage, canonical correlation analysis allows researchers to examine linear relationships between multiple dependent variables and multiple independent variables simultaneously, which increases the probability of detecting significant results otherwise not found by multiple regression analysis. Furthermore, canonical correlation analysis allows researchers to test for various relationships between variables within each set and between sets while protecting against the inflation of type I error due to the utilization of a number of multiple regression analyses.

The chapter also discussed the assumptions underlying canonical correlation analysis. These assumptions are related to the level of measurement of the dependent and independent variables, ratio of cases per variable, multivariate normality, linearity of the relationship between all pairs of dependent and independent variables, homoscedasticity, and multicollinearity. The chapter also discussed various methods for evaluating each assumption.

Finally, the chapter presented a detailed example to illustrate the use of canonical correlation analysis in social sciences research. The example illustrated how to evaluate each assumption, use SPSS syntax to execute canonical correlation analysis, interpret the output, write and present the results of canonical correlation analysis, and present the findings in a table and a graph.

PRACTICAL EXERCISES

A mental health researcher was interested in predicting levels of well-being, life satisfaction (Satisfaction) and self-esteem (SelfEsteem), among older immigrants based on the seven IOWA self-assessment factors: physical health (PH), mobility (MOB), emotional balance (EB), cognitive status (CS), economic resources (ER), trusting others (TRO), and social support (SS). For this purpose, the researcher collected data from a sample of 155 immigrants ages fifty and older who completed the *Mental Health* survey (see appendix, Data File 4).

Access the Mental Health data file, use the above variables, and answer the following questions:

1. What are the research question and hypotheses under study?

2. What statistical test(s) will you utilize to examine the null hypothesis? Why? Discuss your answer in detail.

3. Write the SPSS syntax file for the test statistic.

4. Run the test statistic using the SPSS syntax in question 3.

5. What is your decision with regard to the null hypotheses? Discuss your answer in detail.

6. Discuss the results of the post hoc regression analysis.

7. Present the results of the test statistic and its post hoc tests in summary tables.

8. Present the results in graph(s).

Appendix: SPSS Data Files

DATA FILE 1: ANXIETY (*N* = 50)

This file contains data collected from 50 women who were exposed to interpersonal violence. All women participated in a ten-session group therapy to reduce their levels of anxiety. Prior to administering the therapy, all women completed a twenty-item self-administered survey measuring levels of anxiety on a five-point Likert scale (Anxiety_Pre). They also completed the anxiety survey after they completed the therapy (Anxiety_Post). Total scores range from 20 to 100, with higher scores indicating greater levels of anxiety.

DATA FILE 2: HEALTH CONTROL (*N* = 60)

This file contains data collected from a random sample of 60 Muslim American immigrants ages sixty and above in the Washington, D.C., metropolitan area. Participants in the study completed the Multidimensional Health Locus of Control Scale (MHLC) (Wallston et al., 1978). This eighteen-item instrument rates respondents according to internal health locus of control (IHLC), powerful others health locus of control (PHLC), and chance health locus of control (CHLC). Respondents answer questions on a four-point Likert-type scale (1 = strongly disagree to 4 = strongly agree). Total scores for each scale range between 6 and 24, with higher scores indicating more external beliefs about locus of control. Participants in the study also indicated their age and gender. Table A.1 describes the Health Control variables list.

Table A.1: Health Control SPSS Variables List

Variable Name	Variable Label	Range	Value Labels
Age		60+	Actual age
Gender		0–1	0 = Male
			1 = Female
IHLC	Internal health locus of control	6–32	Scale (from low to high)
PHLC	Powerful others health locus of control	6–32	Scale (from low to high)
CHLC	Chance health locus of control	6–32	Scale (from low to high)

DATA FILE 3: JOB SATISFACTION (*N* = 218)

This file contains data collected from a random sample of 218 Arab and Jewish social services employees in Israel. Participants answered questions related to their gender, age, marital status, number of children, education, ethnicity, time at current job, and region of employment. They also completed the Index of Job Satisfaction (Brayfield & Rothe, 1951) and the Correlates of Work Satisfaction (Abu-Bader, 1998). In addition, participants completed a number of items related to autonomy and role conflict (Quinn & Staines, 1979), comfort (Quinn & Shepard, 1974), and workload (Caplan, Cobb, French, Harrison, & Pinneau, 1975). Table A.2 describes the Job Satisfaction variables list.

Table A.2: Job Satisfaction SPSS Variables List

Variable Name	Variable Label	Range	Value Labels
Gender		0–1	0 = Male
			1 = Female
Age		22–62	Actual age
MStatus	Marital status	1–3	1 = Married
			2 = Single
			3 = Divorced
Children#	Number of children	0–8	Actual number
Education	Levels of education	1–3	1 = B.S.W./B.A.
			2 = M.S.W.
			3 = Other
Ethnicity		0–1	0 = Jews
			1 = Arabs
Years#	Years at job	1–35	Number of years
Location	Region	1–3	1 = North
			2 = Center
			3 = South
MStatus_Rec	Marital status (recoded)	0–1	0 = Married
			1 = Never married
Education_Rec	Levels of education (recoded)	0–1	0 = Undergraduate
			1 = Graduate
Satisfaction	Levels of job satisfaction	39–85	Scale (from low to high)
Burnout	Levels of burnout	8–49	Scale (from low to high)
Turnover	Levels of turnover	2–34	Scale (from low to high)
Colleague	Satisfaction with colleagues	13–65	Scale (from low to high)
Supervision	Satisfaction with supervisor	2–79	Scale (from low to high)
Salary	Satisfaction with salary	4–35	Scale (from low to high)
Promotion	Satisfaction with promotion	12–48	Scale (from low to high)
Autonomy	Autonomy at work	6–22	Scale (from high to low)[a]
RoleConflict	Role conflict	2–15	Scale (from low to high)
Comfort	Comfort at work	7–25	Scale (from high to low)[b]
WorkLoad	Load at work	6–20	Scale (from low to high)

[a]Higher scores in autonomy indicate lower levels of autonomy at work.
[b]Higher scores in comfort indicate lower levels of comfort at work.

DATA FILE 4: MENTAL HEALTH (*N* = 155)

This file contains data collected from a sample of 155 immigrant Muslims ages fifty and above. Participants in the study were recruited from the Washington, D.C., metropolitan area using various recruitment methods. Participants were asked to indicate their gender, age, and whether they owned their home. They were also asked to complete the Center for Epidemiologic Studies Depression Scale (CES-D) (Radloff, 1977). Total scores for CES-D range between 0 and 60, with higher scores indicating greater depression. Participants were also asked to complete the Iowa Self-Assessment Inventory (IOWA) (Morris & Buckwalter, 1988). The IOWA contains seven subscales measuring participants' emotional balance (EB), physical health (PH), cognitive status (CS), economic resources (ER), trusting others (TRO), mobility (MOB), and social support (SS). Total scores for each subscale range between 8 and 32, with higher scores indicating greater value with respect to each subscale. Finally, participants were asked to complete the Rosenberg Self-Esteem Scale (Royse, 1999) and the Life Satisfaction Index (Wood, Wylie, & Sheafor, 1969). Table A.3 describes the Mental Health variables list.

Table A.3:   Mental Health SPSS Variables List

Variable Name	Variable Label	Range	Value Labels
Gender		0–1	0 = Male
			1 = Female
Home	Own home?	0–1	0 = No
			1 = Yes
Age		50+	Actual age
EB	Emotional balance	8–32	Scale (from low to high)[a]
PH	Physical health	8–32	Scale (from low to high)
CS	Cognitive status	8–32	Scale (from low to high)
ER	Economic resources	8–32	Scale (from low to high)
TRO	Trusting others	8–32	Scale (from low to high)
MOB	Mobility	8–32	Scale (from low to high)
SS	Social support	8–32	Scale (from low to high)
CESD	Levels of depression	0–47	Scale (from low to high)
SelfEsteem	Levels of self-esteem	18–40	Scale (from low to high)
Satisfaction	Life satisfaction	3–14	Scale (from low to high)

[a]Low scores indicate lower value of the corresponding scale (i.e., the lower the scores in emotional balance are, the less the emotional balance; the lower the scores in depression, the lower the levels of depression, etc.).

DATA FILE 5: PTSD (*N* = 230)

This file contains data collected from a sample of 230 newly arrived refugees from Africa and Asia in the Washington, D.C., metropolitan area. Participants answered questions about their gender, age, marital status, level of education, and country of origin. They also completed self-report measures on physical health and post-traumatic stress disorder. In addition, they completed the Multidimensional Health Locus of Control Scale (MHLC) (Wallston et al., 1978).

Higher scores on physical health, PTSD, and health locus of control indicate better physical health, greater PTSD, and more belief on internal, chance, and powerful others health locus of control, respectively. Table A.4 describes the PTSD variables list.

Table A.4:   PTSD SPSS Variables List

Variable Name	Variable Label	Range	Value Labels
Gender		0–1	0 = Male
			1 = Female
Age		18–76	Actual age
Country	Country of origin	0–1	0 = Asia
			1 = Africa
MStatus	Marital status	1–3	1 = Married
			2 = Widowed/divorced
			3 = Never married
Education	Level of education	1–3	1 = >3 years college
			2 = Undergraduate degree
			3 = Graduate degree
Health	Overall physical health	10–50	Scale (from low to high)
PTSD	Post-traumatic stress disorder	0–60	Scale (from low to high)
IHLC	Internal health locus of control	6–32	Scale (from low to high)
CHLC	Chance health locus of control	6–32	Scale (from low to high)
PHLC	Powerful others health locus of control	6–32	Scale (from low to high)

DATA FILE 6: WELL-BEING (N = 182)

This file contains data collected from a random sample of 182 college students selected from two universities in the Washington, D.C., area. Participants in the study were asked to indicate their gender, age, race, marital status, financial status, weight, and height. Students were also asked to rate their physical health on a single five-point Likert scale and complete the Satisfaction with Life Scale (Diener, Emmons, Larsen, & Griffin, 1985), the Rosenberg Self-Esteem Scale (Royse, 1999), and the CES-D (Radloff, 1977). In addition, they were asked to complete a self-perception scale developed for this purpose. Total scores for life satisfaction range between 7 and 35, for self-esteem between 10 and 50, for depression between 0 and 60, and for self-perception between 12 and 60. Greater scores indicated greater satisfaction with life, higher self-esteem, greater depression, and greater self-perception. Finally, for this study, weight and height were used to compute students' body mass index (BMI). Table A.5 describes the Well-Being variables list.

Table A.5:   Well-Being SPSS Variables List

Variable Name	Variable Label	Range	Value Labels
Gender		0–1	0 = Male
			1 = Female
Age		18–45	Actual age
Race		1–3	1 = African American
			2 = White
			3 = Other
MaritalStatus	Marital status	1–3	1 = Single
			2 = Married
			3 = Other
FinancialStatus	Financial status	1–3	1 = Overextended
			2 = Making ends meet
			3 = Comfortable
PhysicalHealth	Overall physical health	1–5	1 = Poor
			2 = Fair
			3 = Good
			4 = Very good
			5 = Excellent
LifeSatisfaction	Life satisfaction	7–35	Scale (from low to high)
SelfEsteem	Levels of self-esteem	10–50	Scale (from low to high)
Depression	Levels of depression (CESD)	0–60	Scale (from low to high)
SelfPerception	Levels of self-perception	12–60	Scale (from low to high)
Weight	Body mass index (BMI)	1–4	1 = Underweight
			2 = Normal weight
			3 = Overweight
			4 = Obese
Overweight	Are you overweight?	0–1	0 = No
			1 = Yes

References

Abu-Bader, S. H. (1998). *Predictors of work satisfaction between Arab and Jewish social workers in Israel.* Unpublished doctoral dissertation, University of Utah, Salt Lake City.

Abu-Bader, S. H. (2005). Gender, ethnicity, and job satisfaction among social workers in Israel. *Administration in Social Work, 29*(3), 7–21.

Abu-Bader, S. H. (2006). *Using statistical analysis in social work practice: A complete SPSS guide.* Chicago: Lyceum Books.

Brayfield, A. H., & Rothe, H. F. (1951). An index of job satisfaction. *Journal of Applied Psychology, 35*(5), 307–311.

Caplan, R., Cobb, S., French, J. R. P., Harrison, R. V., & Pinneau, S. R. (1975). *Job demands and workers' health.* Washington, DC: U.S. Department of Health, Education, and Welfare.

Diener, E., Emmons, R. A., Larsen, R. J., & Griffin, S. (1985). The Satisfaction with Life Scale. *Journal of Personality Assessment, 49,* 71–75.

Foster, J. J., Barkus, E., & Yavorsky, C. (2006). *Understanding and using advanced statistics: A practical guide for students.* Newbury Park, CA: Sage.

Hair, J. F., Black, B., Babin, B., Anderson, R. E., & Tatham, R. L. (2006). *Multivariate data analysis* (6th ed.). Upper Saddle River, NJ: Prentice-Hall.

Hinkle, D. E., Wiersma, W., & Jurs, S. G. (2003). *Applied statistics for the behavioral sciences* (5th ed.). Boston: Houghton Mifflin.

Landauer, T. (1997). Behavior research methods in HCI. In M. Helander, et al. (Eds.), *Handbook of human-computer interaction* (2nd ed., pp. 203–228). Amsterdam: Elsevier.

Mertler, C. A., & Vannatta, R. A. (2005). *Advanced and multivariate statistical methods: Practical application and interpretation* (3rd ed.). Glendale, CA: Pyrczak.

Morris, W. W., & Buckwalter, K. C. (1988). Functional assessment of the elderly: The Iowa Self-Assessment Inventory. In C. F. Waltz & O. L. Stricklan (Eds.), *Measurement of nursing outcomes: Vol. 1. Measuring client outcomes* (pp. 328–351). New York: Springer.

Munro, B. H. (2005). *Statistical methods for health care research* (5th ed.). Philadelphia: Lippincott Williams & Wilkins.

Quinn, R. P., & Shepard, L. J. (1974). *The 1972–73 quality of employment survey.* Ann Arbor, MI: Institute for Social Research.

Quinn, R. P., & Staines, G. L. (1979). *The 1977 quality of employment survey.* Ann Arbor, MI: Institute for Social Research.

Radloff, L. S. (1977). The CES-D Scale: A self-report depression scale for research in the general population. *Applied Psychological Measurement, 1*(3), 385–401.

Royse, D. (1999). *Research methods in social work* (3rd ed.). Chicago: Nelson-Hall.

SPSS Inc. (1999). Intermediate Topics: SPSS for Windows 10.0. Chicago: Author.

SPSS Inc. (2001). Advanced Techniques: ANOVA. Chicago: Author.

SPSS Inc. (2001). Advanced Techniques: Regression. Chicago: Author.

SPSS Inc. (2002). Syntax I: Introduction to Syntax. Chicago: Author.

SPSS Inc. (2002). Syntax II: Programming with SPSS Syntax and Macros. Chicago: Author.

SPSS Inc. (2003). Survey Methodology. Chicago: Author.

Tabachnick, B. G., & Fidell, L. S. (2007). *Using Multivariate Statistics* (5th ed.). Boston: Pearson.

Thompson, B. (1984). *Canonical correlation analysis: Uses and interpretation.* Newbury Park, CA: Sage.

Wallston, K. A., Wallston, B. S., & DeVellis, R. (1978). Development of the multidimensional health locus of control (MHLC) scales. *Health Education Monographs, 6*(2), 160–170.

Wood, V., Wylie, M. L., & Sheafor, B. (1969). An analysis of a short self-report measure of life satisfaction: Correlation with rater judgments. *Journal of Gerontology, 24,* 465–469.

Index

About the Author

Soleman H. Abu-Bader (PhD, University of Utah; MSW, Augsburg College) is associate professor in the School of Social Work at Howard University. He has worked as a social work practitioner, researcher, and teacher. He is the author of *Using Statistical Methods in Social Work Practice* (2006) as well as several articles that focus on the elderly, mental health, gerontology, and organizational behavior. He also serves on the editorial boards of a number of peer-reviewed journals, including *Best Practices in Mental Health: An International Journal*.